Winter Tales and Trails

Skiing, Snowshoeing and Snowboarding in Idaho, the Grand Tetons and Yellowstone National Park

WINTER TALES AND TRAILS

Skiing, Snowshoeing and Snowboarding in Idaho, the Grand Tetons and Yellowstone National Park

Ron Watters

GR The Great Rift Press

WINTER TALES AND TRAILS
Skiing, Snowshoeing and Snowboarding in Idaho, the Grand Tetons and Yellowstone National Park

Printed in the United States of America

Published by:
The Great Rift Press
1135 East Bonneville Avenue
Pocatello, ID 83201

ISBN: 1-877625-05-1 (paperbound)
        1-877625-06-X (hardbound)

Library of Congress Catalog Card Number: 97-73838

The author wishes to express his sincere thanks to the following for permission to use selected materials:

North of the Narrows: Men and Women of the Upper Priest Lake Country, Idaho, by Claude & Catherine Simpson. Published by Keokee Co., Sandpoint, Idaho.

Land of the Yankee Fork, by Esther Yarber and Edna and Arthur McGown. Published by Sage Books. Copyright 1963.

The Lochsa Story: Land Ethics in the Bitterroot Mountains, by Bud Moore. Published by Mountain Press Publishing Company. Copyright 1996.

Additionally, a special thanks is due to the following photographers: Mike Beiser, Katherine Daly, Dann and Ross Hall, Leo Hennessy, Phil Schofield, Robert Wuthrich. Additional photos came from the collections of the Idaho Historical Society, Margret McMahon, Al Taylor, Frank Daniels, University of Idaho Outdoor Program, Idaho State University Outdoor Program and the U.S. Forest Service. All other uncredited photographs are by the author.

Pen and ink renditions of aerial photographs: Mark Sibley.

Back cover photo: Katherine Daly.

Warning

The activities described within this book are dangerous. It is the reader's responsibility to ensure that they have sufficient skill and fitness to participate in these activities safely. The author or publisher does not assume liability or responsibility to any person or entity for injuries, death, loss or damages which is caused, directly or indirectly, by the information contained within this book.

TABLE OF CONTENTS

PREFACE

*W*ORK ON THIS BOOK began during one of the most memorable winters in recent Idaho history. During the Christmas
holidays a series of storms swept across the state, pounding it with
one wet snow fall after another. Snow packs in the high country
went from a few feet to 15 feet deep within a few days. Hundreds
of trees snapped and large areas were left without power. When I
traveled to Priest Lake nearly two months later, some areas on the
east side of the lake were still without phone service.

So many trees and limbs were downed by the heavy snow that
the Forest Service gave up on one popular cross-country skiing area
north of Coeur d'Alene, and instead decided to wait until summer
to remove all the debris. Two yurts partially collapsed in the
Pocatello area, and work crews went up daily to try to keep snow
off. In McCall, a wall tent placed below Jughandle Mountain was
flattened like a pop can.

In short, it was a great winter. In North Idaho, skiers and
boarders were calling it "the winter of legendary snow." Everything about it was eventful. By the time storm patterns returned to
normal, the Hale-Bopp comet made a sudden appearance and the
remainder of the winter season was marked by its beauty and
brilliance in the night sky. Indeed, it was a most unusual and
propitious year in which to work on a book about the winter.

This book is the revised edition of a work originally titled *Ski
Trails and Old-timers' Tales* published in 1978. *Ski Trails* took
four years of driving throughout Idaho in a Volkswagen Bug,
searching for trails, interviewing old-timers and wading through
reels of microfilm of old newspapers. Perhaps Hale-Bopp provided
a little extra cosmic energy to nudge me along quicker on the
second version. I was relieved to finish the research and writing
within a year's time. If you compare the first version with this new
version, you'll see that it has been totally rewritten. I've incorpo-

rated new historical information that I've come upon over the intervening 20 years and completely updated the trail chapters.

The most delightful task of the whole process has been selecting and writing the stories which appear throughout the book. In each chapter I've tried to include at least one story from years past to add dimension and texture to the respective region. In some regions, I've also included a closing story of more recent vintage. One example is the story of Sandpoint's Baldy Mountain Jim, who has stayed true to the faith, steadfastly holding to skiing's traditions and who has not been seduced by the glamour of such things as fiberglass skis and synthetic clothing. He does his skiing on wood and wears all wool—except for a Harley Davidson T-shirt.

The stories, particularly those of the old days, are more than just colorful fillers; they remind us that men and women have come before us and traveled the same mountain trails that we now travel. Many generations have preceded us and many more generations will follow. It is a long and never ending continuum and celebration of winter life.

The orientation of the book has changed from the first version and is now more encompassing. Included along with cross-country ski trails are places to go snowshoeing, snowboarding and Alpine skiing. To reflect this change in content, the name was changed from *Ski Trails and Old-timers' Tales* to *Winter Trails and Tales*. This new approach goes hand in hand with natural evolutionary changes occurring in the sports and the blurring of boundaries. Cross-country skiers find that snowshoeing is a great alternate to skiing when snow conditions aren't so good. Alpine skiers are learning about the joys of cross-country skiing and dabbling in more backcountry skiing, including spring ski descents. Nordic skiers are spending more time at Alpine ski areas practicing telemark turns. And snowboarders often do it all: snowboard, ski and snowshoe.

There's also a difference in the broad area covered by the book. *Ski Trails* included trails in the states of Idaho and Montana. In this version, I've concentrated on Idaho and bordering Teton and Yellowstone National Parks. Both the parks are exquisite snow regions, have a fascinating winter history, and I'd be remiss not to include them.

Trail descriptions within this book are succinct. It's not my purpose to describe every bend in the trail, every uphill and downhill pitch. I think that takes a lot of the fun out of it. Instead, I try to give a clear explanation of how to get there and a rough idea of difficulty, and then it's all up to you to explore and enjoy.

My reason for bringing the book back to print is the same as the first. Healthy outdoor activities like cross-country skiing and snowshoeing need nurturing and support. Mechanized users and manufacturers aren't holding back when it comes to promoting their sports. Yet, the activities that really ought to be promoted are those in which people can escape momentarily from a machine dominated world and return to their natural roots, to breathe fresh air and to experience in an intimate way this wonderful land of ours. Herein is the key to a truly rich lifestyle and a sane and peaceful world.

Any author whose work has the potential to attract people to specific outdoor locations must consider the potential environmental consequences. In that regard, I've tried to structure the book in a way that minimizes such impact. The great majority of trails included within this book are in roaded areas and follow snow-bound roads. A large number of trails have purposely been included to help disperse use. And many of the trails are near population centers so people can take advantage of resources located close to their community.

I hope that you'll also find within these pages a reason to support the preservation of our wild lands. As users of the land, we know more than anyone why it is so important to leave the outdoor environment in the best possible shape for our children. That means setting aside lands protected from development in which streams run clear and pure, wildlife find refuge and in which we can find inspiration and freedom. One of the best ways in which you can help is to join a conservation group of your choosing. Some suggested groups are included in the General Information chapter, but there are many other deserving organizations out there that need your help and financial support.

Finally, a note of caution. The winter is a beautiful time of year, but it is also a deceptive and dangerous time too. Before you go on outings, prepare carefully. Carry the proper clothing and equipment. Turn back if conditions deteriorate. Never lose your respect for the power of the natural world.

"I feel sorry for people that have to live where they cannot snowshoe. Life must indeed be a burden where there are no amusements but dancing." —W. Petit. Atlanta, Idaho 1883

Part I

Winter Tales:
History of Skiing in Idaho

Idaho Historical Society

CHAPTER 1
THE LONG SNOWSHOE

THE WINTER SNOWS still lay deep in the Clearwater Country. But I.C. Smith was eager to leave his party and return to the nearest settlement at Walla Walla. His party of 33 men, led by an adventurous soldier of fortune, Captain Elias Davidson Pierce, had spent the winter on Orofino Creek, south of the present town of Pierce.

Earlier in the fall of 1860, Pierce had led a smaller party to Orofino and found a small amount of gold in what was to become the state of Idaho. With Pierce were seasoned California prospectors. Accustomed to the coarse-grained gold of the Sierras, the Californians ridiculed the fine, dust-like particles of the yellow metal and gave the creek the name Oro Fino, Spanish for fine gold. Even so, Pierce was confident that the small find might lead to something much larger, and was successful in convincing Smith and the others to accompany him back to the Orofino camp for the winter.

All winter long Smith had worked along with Pierce's men, whip sawing lumber for cabins and sluice boxes, panning other streams for likely places and washing out gravels for gold. It became obvious that Pierce's find was significant. Fine or not, it was gold and there was plenty of it.

Restless with the coming of spring and a poke full of $800 of *oro fino* dust, Smith was ready to make the long trip. The snow, however, was deep and the trip would have been arduous, perhaps nearly impossible for a person traveling alone, had Smith not utilized a method of travel known to him as snowshoeing. Now, well over a hundred years later, it is known as skiing. Smith strapped his skis on and glided easily across the drifts of snow toward Walla Walla.

In doing so, he glided his way into history. Smith, on a pair of skis, carried the first substantial amount of gold out of Idaho triggering a stampede of dreamers and fortune seekers which has continued to the present day. As best as I can determine from 20 years of off and on research of Idaho historical works, his trip is the first written mention of skiing in Idaho, and I.C. Smith is Idaho's first known skier.

❄   ❄

IN AUGUST OF 1861 more gold was discovered in Idaho. This time south of the Clearwater on a drainage of the Salmon River. The mining town of Florence sprang to life as quickly as Pierce and Orofino. More hopeful miners poured into Idaho, and what they found in Idaho was no picnic. The trails were rough, the country was up and down, and by the time the next winter mercilessly came to a close, many had learned that this vast wilderness of mountains and river valleys was not exactly a promised land.

For years afterwards, around the glow of fires in pole cabins or when the drinks flowed in sawdust floored saloons in towns with names like Elk City, Idaho City, Leesburg, Atlanta and Galena, old prospectors would tell stories of that second winter in the Idaho gold fields. The winter had approached full of potential, yet measured and quiet as in the soft steps of a lynx. Long periods of warm sunny fall weather were interrupted occasionally with light snowfalls dressing the mountains in white. "November and December," Sister Elsenholn, a noted northern Idaho historian, wrote "continued mild and pleasant, but the day before Christmas, the weather turned colder, and the winter of 1861-62 ultimately proved to be one of the coldest in the history of Idaho."

For William Armistead Goulder, tucked away in his cabin among the Orofino diggings, the beginning of the winter was one of beauty. "December comes," he wrote, "and the snow is falling, gently and steadily, and almost constantly day after day and night after night. Down and down it comes in the tiniest-sized flakes and particles, while the atmosphere, white with the thickly falling mass, is still as death."

As the snow pack became deeper and deeper, mining work in Orofino came to a halt, and miners turned their attentions to whip sawing lumber for the following season and keeping fire wood supplies well stocked. To keep entertained during the long winter nights, Goulder, who had a talent for oration, read from Sir Walter Scott. His cabin mates had purchased for him a nearly complete set of novels by Scott with the understanding that he would read aloud in the evening while they rested in their bunks. "To this I very willingly agreed," wrote Goulder, "with the condition that they should keep duly awake and attentive."

Goulder had something up his sleeve.

"I would begin to read, throwing into my voice all the mellifluous tones and soporific effects that I could muster. Very soon they would be both sound asleep and snoring in perfect rhythm and harmony with the voice of the reader."

Upon putting his friends to sleep, he would then settle back "for an hour or two of intense delight and profitable reading." Now and then one would wake and Goulder would continue reading in a soothing voice and put him back to sleep so he could continue his own private reading.

"I thus read for the first time all of Scott's stories," Goulder wrote, "except 'The Fair Maid of Perth,' whose delicate constitution and refined superstructure has thus far kept her away from the rude scenes of a wild mining camp."

Goulder also kept entertained by playing chess with a Mr. Schwatka, who was looking after a cache of supplies in the town and was in his 40s as was Goulder. Though Goulder became "fast friends" with Schwatka, he found him a poor loser, and to avoid unpleasantries and not lose a chess partner—which was hard to find in Orofino—Goulder would let him win most of the games. I mention Schwatka's name because he is a connection to later ski history. His son, Lieutenant Schwatka, gained considerable fame because of his Arctic explorations and a winter expedition to Yellowstone. The expedition, which is described in a later chapter, was more hype than substance, and, for Lieutenant Schwatka, it was ill-fated.

The unbroken series of storms combined with cold temperatures allowed snow to accumulate throughout the Clearwater country, including the normally dry valleys. The use of horses became impossible and travel between gold camps and the supply centers in eastern Washington took place on foot. Surprisingly under the conditions, there was considerable movement from place to place—and those that used skis had a considerable advantage.

Goulder describes one party of two Canadian guides and two merchants traveling from Lewiston to Orofino. The trail along the Clearwater was packed, but upon climbing up out of the Clearwater, they reached fresh snow which had covered up the packed trail. One of the merchants, Harrison, became exhausted wading in the deep snow and was left behind to fend for himself while the other three struggled in darkness to a ranch ten miles away. The next day, Goulder who was visiting the ranch at the time, accompanied the ranch owner back to where Harrison had been left. They found him floundering in the snow, dazed and heading in the wrong direction. They managed to get him back to the ranch, but both legs were frozen. Gangrene set in and Harrison died about 10 days later.

For getting around and surviving in the winter of 1861-62, skis, undoubtedly, were the best and safest mode of transportation. Unlike the inexperienced Harrison, many used them. "All winter long," wrote Goulder, "men were daily leaving Oro Fino on snow-shoes with heavy packs on their backs for the distant mining camp, Florence in the Salmon River country being the principal point that attracted them. The whole country above Lewiston lay buried under a thick mantle of snow."

A considerable storehouse of supplies had been built up at Orofino, but the new town of Florence was lacking, and the need for food and essentials became more acute due to the increasing severity of the winter and the swelling population. Since horses were out of the question, supplies were moved the next best way: on men's backs. Goulder said that "it seemed like a fit of madness for men to undertake to battle with all the difficulties and dangers that attended this transit on foot across snowfields for a distance of one hundred miles, and with heavy loads on their backs, but there were hundreds who did not hesitate to confront the task."

In his book, *Reminiscences of a Pioneer*, Goulder writes that the combination of both reward and suffering was an attraction to men traveling the trail to Florence: "The account which all brought of the wonderful richness of the Florence mines and the lack of provisions and supplies in the distant camp served to increase the excitement and keep the tide of travel moving." Goulder's observations have a universality about them. It is the promise of reward, whatever form it may take, combined with risk, and sometimes danger that motivates and drives people forward.

Idaho Historical Society

However, there was another less lofty motivation for getting supplies to Florence. Florence was running dry. Goulder explains: "One of the great needs felt at Florence at this time was that of a well-appointed and well supplied first-class saloon. To meet this crying want, several kegs of alcohol were carried over the snowy trail, accompanied by the enterprising proprietor of the contemplated liquor emporium, traveling on snowshoes and carrying in a satchel the little vials of chemical that should convert this alcohol into mildly-exhilarating fluids of various names and flavors to suit the whims and tastes of his future customers."

Such liquor salesmen could do wonders. Goulder reported that Bourbon and Cognac could be made in five minutes by mixing alcohol, water, burned sugar and some other ingredients. It equaled the taste of the best imported beverages and produced the desired effect to boot.

Also hitting the trail to Florence were about a dozen gamblers, led by Dick Pucket. They had remained in Orofino most of the winter, starting with $1,000 amongst them. With that princely sum, they played poker during all waking hours. "Nothing but extreme illness," said Goulder "or its equivalent disability, too much hastily concocted whiskey, was accepted as an excuse for any one's absence." When one of the gamblers lost everything, he was immediately restaked by the most recent winner.

Other residents couldn't be enticed into the games. They either didn't have the money, or the inclination to take part. Consequently, the gamblers original $1,000 dwindled, going to pay their considerable lodging and food expenses. A change of location was needed if they were to find others with similar recreational tastes and bring in fresh capital.

"One bright February morning," Goulder observed, "they all left in a body, taking up the line of march on snowshoes, and in single file, for the more promising field of Florence. I had the pleasure of witnessing the gay procession as it skimmed over the frozen snow surface with the irrepressible Pucket leading and cheering, as he had done on so many occasions."

❄   ❄

*T*HE LONG SNOWSHOES used by Dick Pucket and his merry band of gamblers were simply constructed out of one solid piece of wood. Many skis were just a whipsawed piece of lumber four to six inches in width with an upturned tip. That was it, but it worked well enough to get the wearer where he wanted to go.

Tamarack was the preferable wood in the north, but in the central and southern parts of the state, pine or fir was used as well. The length varied from 5 feet to as long as 12, but averaged around 6 to 8 feet. Stories of 15 foot skis are probably apocryphal. For Idaho and adjacent mountain areas, I've found only one written reference to a 12 foot ski which was in Yellowstone. Moreover, the use of skis as long as twelve feet borders on the fantastic. I've tried, rather unsuccessfully, to maneuver around on a pair of 75 year old skis that were 8 feet long, and I can't imagine the difficulties of handling longer skis.

Elwood Hofer, in an article in *Forest and Stream*, provided exact measurements of the skis he used in Yellowstone. His description is one of the best surviving treatises on how skis of the late 1800s were made in our part of the west: "I used long snowshoes—'skeys' or Norwegians—made of red fir, nine feet long, one inch thick, four inches wide in the middle, tapering to three and three-quarter inches at the back end. Fourteen inches of the front was thinned down to one half inch, steamed and bent up so that the end was eight inches off the ground. The tops of the shoes were beveled to allow the snow to slide off readily."

In many winter mountain communities, there were certain men who were the town's ski craftsmen. Alta Grete Chadwick in her book, *Tales of Silver City*, explains that her father made most of the skis used in that town. In Atlanta, it was the town carpenter, Jimmy Davis. Nick Nichols, a long time skier from Ashton, talks highly of the skis made by a Mr. Caton: "He made many, many skis, and many people around here skied on his skis."

In the Ketchum area, Roy McCoy was a noted ski craftsman who sold his skis to those traveling the winter trails during the Thunder Mountain gold rush around the turn of the century. George Castle, Roy McCoy's nephew, learned as a boy some of the basics of ski craftsmanship from his uncle. According to George, his uncle would obtain a 1" x 4" piece of straight-grained fir. Using a draw knife, the skis would be thinned in the curvature of the tip and in the area near the tail. This helped the ski to flex more evenly while skiing.

The tip was boiled in a brass kettle for part of the day. A template to form the tip was made from a log. Fastening the tips of both skis to the log template, they were pulled down by their tails until the desired bend in the tips was achieved. They were then held in place with a weight for a couple of days until dry. The dry skis were sanded, coated with linseed oil, and sanded again. Camber, or the arch of the ski, was steamed into some, and others were even side-cut with wider tips and tails, helping the ski turn and track better.

The upturn of the tip was important. It allowed the ski to ride on top of the snow, and without it, the ski would plunge into the snow. With time, however, a ski tip would begin to lose its curve and sag, especially when the skis were used in wet, sloppy snow. To help keep it up, some skiers attached a wire to the tip and stretched it taut, nailing it down to a point lower on the ski.

Frank Daniels, who at one time trapped in the Bone area east of Blackfoot, had a secret for maintaining the bend of his skis. When I interviewed him in the mid seventies, he told me that he had used a chair for a form. "The chair had to be turned on its back and weighted down," he told me, "I tucked the skis in the chair rounds and let the skis hang by their own weight out in the air. Then I took paraffin, keeping it real hot with an iron, and put it on the bottom of the ski in the tip area. I'd keep working the paraffin in with the hot iron until it came clear through on the other side."

When the skis were dry, they were ready for use. "Boy," he said, his face lighting with memories from his carefree trapping days, "we'd take that hot wax and put that bend in them, and they'd stay pretty good. In fact, mine still are staying pretty good—for 40 years now!"

To attach the wearer's boot to the ski, the usual method was a simple leather strap binding that was cinched snug against the boot. Some skiers, such as those in the Island Park area, preferred moose hide for the binding material. These ski "harnesses" as they were called were a wide strip of tanned hide, tapered in the front to keep the boot from slipping forward. Laces were employed to bind the boot more securely than a single strap.

I found in my own experimentations with old skis that because of the way the boots are secured, they're a formidable piece of equipment. The simple leather strap over the foot provides absolutely no turning power. On a gentle slope, when I tried turning the tip of the ski, the boot would twist completely off the ski and the ski would continue running straight. It is rather akin to driving an automobile, turning the steering wheel and having nothing happen. A simple task such as making a turn to the right while on flat ground is a major effort requiring many small steps until the desired angle is reached. A kick turn is almost out of the question.

As I made my ungainly attempts to control the skis on flat and low angled hills, I often found myself spread-eagle on the snow. As I struggled to get back up, I was reminded of a description of a fellow in similar straights which appeared in the *Owyhee Avalanche* in 1865: "One shoe stuck perpendicular in the road, while the other went through the wood pile . . . while his legs sticking out the snow, gave him the appearance of having made a dive for China. Such maneuvers on tolerably level ground only show what the man could do on a mountain side." I was glad that no reporters were on hand to describe my attempts at the long snowshoe.

※   ※

*E*LWOOD HOFER, who skied in Yellowstone in the late 1800s, explains how he handled the maneuverability problem on his 9 foot red fir skis: "Measuring from the front end of the shoe back 4 ft., I put on a hard wood cross piece or cleat, 4 in. long 5/8 in. wide, 1 1/2 in. thick, thinned down to 1/2 in. the middle to allow the foot to fit in well." The "cleat" provided a pocket in which he placed his boot. When he turned his foot, his foot pressed against high edges of the "cleat" and wouldn't slip off the ski, thus affording him some control.

On some skis, a one to two foot long cylinder of canvas was nailed around the binding. The top of the canvas had a drawstring. Skiers could slip their entire boot into the canvas, buckle into the binding, and by pulling the drawstring tight against their pant leg, they had something that looked and worked like a gaiter. The built-in gaiter not only kept their feet warmer and the snow out of their boots, but it also kept sticky snow from wetting the leather of their binding strap and clumps of snow from forming under the boot.

The use of two poles did not begin appearing in Idaho until sometime after the turn of the century. Before that time, a single pole, often referred to as the ski "balancing pole," was used. The balancing pole did just as the name implies; it helped the skier keep his balance, but it was also used effectively for descending hills. Placed between the legs with the skier in a half-sitting position, the pole acted as a brake with which a skier could easily control his speed and at the same time, with some skill, make turns. Elwood Hofer used a seven foot long pole. Besides its use in walking and steering, he used the pole for measuring snow depth, that is "until," he said, "the snow was too deep for the pole to touch bottom."

Most poles were simply a straight branch of a tree, shaved smooth for handling, but sometimes broom handles served the purpose quite well. Al Taylor, who skied in the Kilgore area, said that the little tuft left on an old broom had just enough resistance to support itself on the snow surface. Then, there were other skiers who used no poles at all. "I remember Clarence Neihart used no poles," said Frank Daniels. "To this day, I still don't know how he got up hills!"

For clothing, wool was the preferred choice. Writer, Emerson Hough, described what he and his guide wore on an 1880s ski trip in Yellowstone: "heavy wool underwear, wool trousers, canvas overalls and canvas leggings. The underwear was supplemented by a lighter wool undershirt, over which a blue flannel shirt was worn."

A felt hat with a brim was the most common form of head wear. Hough said that such hats were good because they kept snow from getting down the neck. And in very cold weather, they would tie up their ears with a large silk handkerchief.

Women, as dictated by the rigid styles of 1880s, always wore long woolen dresses, and for the head, either used scarves or felt hats. By the 1920s, however, women's dress standards had relaxed considerably and slacks or wool knickers and woolen stocking hats were common on ski outings.

Waxes were applied to the bottom of the ski primarily to keep the ski from sticking to the snow, but some of the more proficient skiers used wax combinations for climbing and gliding. Paraffin was the most commonly used wax, but pine pitch, beeswax, bacon rinds, and other concoctions were also used.

Waxes were called dope. In a letter to the *Idaho World*, Idaho City's newspaper, a correspondent wrote from Banner, a nearby mining town, announcing that the residents of Banner would be skiing the 30 mile distance between the towns to attend the Christmas festivities in Idaho City. The last part of the trip from Banner to Idaho City is a long downhill stretch starting at Mores Creek Summit. "Look out for us," he warned. "Our snowshoes are doped, and will go flying."

Young lad skiing in Atlanta, Idaho. Skiing in the 1880s
was done with one pole—and sometimes without a pole.

✳   ✳

*I*N IDAHO'S NASCENT DAYS, skis, as the letter from Banner
attests, were called snowshoes, Norwegian snowshoes or long
snowshoes. Alta Grete Chadwick in her book, *Tales of Silver City*,
describes her first skiing experiences and refers to them as "skis,"
but she adds, "to us they were not skis, however, they all went by
the name of snowshoes and to distinguish between them, snowshoes
were termed webs." Webs were also sometimes called Canadian
webs or simply Canadians. Webs were more common in the
heavily timbered country north of the Clearwater, while skis or
long snowshoes were more prevalent in the more open forests of
central and southern Idaho. The change in names: webs to snowshoes, and snowshoes to skis, occurred gradually in the early
decades of the twentieth century. In some areas of Idaho the names
stuck longer. George Castle remembers referring to skis as snowshoes even into the 1930s.

Whatever appellation they took, skis were used extensively for
travel through the snow country of the west. In the early years of
Idaho, their use was so universal that one author, Thomas Donald,
in *Idaho of Yesterday*, in his reminiscence of Idaho from 1869 to
1875, wrote: "All through the Idaho mountains one could see, lying
on the ground near the roads or trails, rough snowshoes made of
split tamarack or pine logs. These shoes were about six feet long,
half an inch thick, five or six inches wide and bent at one end and
were split and tied on the end with strings or thongs. A man could
make a pair in a very short time and invariably dropped them at the
spot on the road where he had no further need of them. The next
man who came along was entitled to their use as well. When I saw
these made and used I recalled the pictures in books of beautiful
bent-wood and skin-crossed snowshoes [websl. Experience is a sad
teacher! I never saw anything in the snowshoe line in Idaho fancier
than those."

Skis were used because they were an important means of
transportation. "They had to use them," one old-timer told me, but
even though they were a necessity, skis were also a means of
recreation, a fun way by which those living in lonely snowbound
towns could enjoy the beauty of the winter.

In another letter to the *Idaho World* in 1880 from Atlanta, a
mining town located deep in the rugged snow-covered mountains of
central Idaho, the writer reports, "We are at the present time

snowed in, the roads all being blocked. We are deprived of the many sleigh rides you are probably enjoying, but then we don't care, as there is plenty of good snow-shoe timber in this country. Our people, old and young, are good snow-shoers."

Skiing was so enjoyed by W. Pettit, superintendent of the Monack Mine and mill at Atlanta that he was moved to write in 1883: "I feel sorry for people that have to live where they cannot snowshoe. Life must indeed be a burden where there are no amusements but dancing."

There was, however, one newcomer to Atlanta who probably would have preferred dancing. The newcomer was one of the "Idaho City Boys" who was wintering in Atlanta. Not wanting to miss out on any of the fun, he undertook some ski instruction from an experienced Atlanta skier. They climbed to the top of one of the highest hills they could find. At the top, they pointed their skis downhill and pushed off. "Before going fifty feet," described the newcomer, "I found I wasn't running that craft, simply because it was running me."

About half way down the hill, a stump appeared in front of his path. By now his speed was uncontrollable, and losing what balance was left, he collided into the stump and plummeted into the snow "I have a dim recollection of seeing one shoe sticking out of the snow and the other going in the direction of Oregon." Fortunately, our friend only suffered a few stiff and bruised muscles, but laying spread-eagle in the snow, his original enthusiasm for the sport had taken a turn. Referring to his skis as "narrow-gauged stump extractors," the newcomer told his skiing partner that if he had any use for them, he could have them.

The Atlanta women, as well as the men, loved to ski. One of their favorite outings was to fasten on their skis and climb to the Atlanta hot springs nearby.* Even though their garb of long skirts did not allow them the necessary freedom of movement, they got along well.

---

*In an article for the *Idaho Yesterdays*, a publication of the Idaho Historical Society, I had said that the Atlanta women would fasten their skis and glide *down* to the Atlanta hot springs. Betty Penson, a historical writer for the *Idaho Statesman*, caught me. "It is a small point, perhaps," she wrote in 1979 poking a little fun at me, "but for the record: The Atlanta hot springs was and still is uphill above the town. It was a low-gear pull in Uncle Bill's old open touring car in the summer when I was a kid, and certainly must have been a steep jaunt in winter on 'the shoes' when he was a kid; but what a great gleeful gliding back down." Of course, she is right. Uncle Bill's touring car grinding uphill says it all.

In Atlanta, ready for a spin on skis. "Look out for us. Our skis are doped and we'll come flying."

Women had been strapping on skis since the early days of the Idaho gold fields. The first historical mention that I have found of a female skier is seven-year-old Minnie Brown skiing near Florence. According to her father Alonzo Brown in his memoirs, it snowed nearly 113 days in a row during the winter of 1862-63. "The snow fell so deep that I had nine steps made in solid snow to go down to our front door," he wrote. The snow covered the cabin, and Brown watched Minnie playfully ski over the top of it.

Early women skiers relished the same thrills that attract modern day skiers. Betty Penson, a historical writer, has pointed out the lack of automobiles and air planes in nineteenth century life meant that skiing probably "was the fastest physical speed their bodies would ever know." Mrs. Robbins, a teacher at Banner, loved to strap on her long snowshoes for a tour in the surrounding deep snow country. Her favorite was the trip to the top of Lightning Point and its exhilarating descent. "She sticks 'em like a California rider does a mustang," exclaimed one of the admirers of her skiing prowess.

Ann Sullivan, a waitress at the boarding house in Vienna, on a trip to Ketchum made a remarkable descent of Galena Summit without using poles. She took a spill and sprained an ankle, but hobbled on to Hailey.

Women didn't settle for second place to men. Some became known for their expertise on the long snowshoes, passing gaily by many a fallen male skier floundering in the snow. One group of women in Bellevue in the 1880s was so well known for their fine technique and dazzling speed that the Silver City newspaper a couple hundred miles away reported that they "were the most expert snowshoers and races among them are of daily occurrence."

Ski racing was also a pastime of the Owyhee boys in Silver City. These racers felt so confident about their ability that they offered a sum of $1,000 to $2,000 to the winner of a ski race. Challenging all comers in the territory, the race was to take place from the top of Florida Mountain down to Ruby City, one mile northwest of Silver City. Unfortunately, we'll never know the outcome of the race, if held, since the *Owyhee Avalanche*, Silver City's newspaper, did not carry any further news items about the race.

For the confident ski racers of Silver City, for the well-dressed ladies of Atlanta, and for the many other skiers of the yesteryears of Idaho, skiing was fun, an enjoyable form of recreation for exercise, competition, and appreciation of the beautiful winter world. But for some, skiing was a serious business. In particular, it was deadly serious business for a military scout stationed in Yellowstone National Park. In March of 1894 while on skis, the scout was hot on the trail of Edgar Howell, a notorious and dangerous poacher.

Idaho Historical Society

CHAPTER 2
POACHERS, LAWMAKERS AND THE GLORY DAYS

*F*ELIX BURGESS STOOD on his skis surveying the macabre scene. Six bison heads were wrapped in gunny sacks and hung in trees high enough to keep the wolves from them. As Burgess and fellow scout Sergeant Troike picked around the camp for more evidence, six shots rang out in the distance.

The shots were from Edgar Howell's rifle. He had just downed five more buffalo.

Howell was a poacher, a furtive and effective one. He was described by one reporter as dirty and ragged with a beard that had been scissored off. He was 5' 10" with large sloping shoulders and greasy, unkempt hair that curled up the back of his neck. Earlier that winter, the winter of 1893-94, Howell had established a camp on a tributary of Pelican Creek to the east of Yellowstone Lake in the middle of the park. His purpose was to kill as many bison as he could.

Amazingly, Howell was doing his sordid winter work with no shoes. He wore just a ragged pair of thin socks. He managed adequately, though, by wrapping his feet in meal sacks which were nailed to his 12 foot long skis and lashed in place with leather thongs. Sometime during the winter, he had broken one of his skis and had fixed it by cutting a triangular piece of fir five feet long and then nailing it to the bottom of the ski. The fir splice and his skis were waterproofed by a coating of pine resin.

Burgess and Troike, both military scouts stationed in Yellowstone, were alerted to Howell's illegal business and had been sent out to find and apprehend him.

The two scouts skied in the direction of the shots. Coming to the edge of an opening, they caught sight of the poacher in the distance. Since Troike had no weapon, Burgess sent him into the trees while he moved in closer.

29

"Howell made his killing out in a little valley," said Burgess later, "and when I saw him he was about 400 yards away from the cover of timber."

Burgess was apprehensive. He had only a .38 caliber army revolver, while Howell's rifle was leaning up against a dead buffalo a mere 15 feet away from him. Poachers were always regarded as dangerous and Howell was no exception. One winter, a soldier on patrol in the Yellowstone backcountry had disappeared, and it was suspected at the time that he was the victim of a poacher.

"His hat was sort of flapped down over his eyes, and his head was toward me," Burgess continued, "He was leaning over, skinning on the head of one of the buffalo."

Howell, with the rifle, had the distinct advantage. Having only a revolver with limited range, Burgess had to move as close as possible to Howell. The wind was blowing, and Burgess hoped that noise from the wind might be enough to keep Howell from hearing him. Nevertheless, he would have to move quickly on his skis— and hope that Howell didn't look up.

"I started out from cover, going as fast as I could travel. Right square across the way I found a ditch about 10 feet wide, and you know how hard it is to make a jump with snowshoes on level ground. I had to try it anyhow, and some way I got over."

Burgess skied up to within 15 feet of Howell, getting between him and his rifle. "I called to him to throw up his hands, and that was the first he knew of anyone but him being anywhere in that country. He kind of stopped and stood stupid like, and I told him to drop his knife."

Howell did as instructed and Troike came from the trees to help Burgess with the job of transporting the prisoner out of the area.

The irony of Burgess's gutsy capture was that once Howell was apprehended there wasn't much officials could do. Howell, himself, was unfazed by the whole affair, chatting away and enjoying his captivity by wolfing down 24 pancakes one morning at the Canyon Hotel for breakfast. Howell bragged that he stood to make $2,000 from poaching and could lose only $26.75. By the pitiful condition of his patched skis and greasy clothes he wore, his estimate of $26.75 might have been a bit high. Yet the sad truth is that Howell was right. He had little to be concerned about. Laws at the time only allowed park authorities to confiscate his equipment and throw him out of the park.

❊   ❊

POACHING WAS a perennial problem in Yellowstone. Paul Schullery in his book, *Yellowstone Ski Pioneers*, notes that when the park was created in 1872, hunting *was* permitted. Commercial killing was not; however, there was no enforcement. In the 1870s and early 1880s thousands of elk and buffalo were killed by a contemptible kind of commercial hunter that left the meat to rot and took only the hides which were later sold to fur dealers.

General W. E. Strong was on hand to witness the slaughter. "When the snow falls and the fierce winter storms begin in November and December," he wrote in 1875, "the elk, deer and sheep leave the summits of the snowy ranges and come in great bands to the foothills and valleys, where they are met and shot down shamefully by the merciless human vultures."

The way these unsavory hunters moved around was by skis. They can "glide up to bands of elk on snowshoes and shoot them when too poor and weak to run," Strong wrote.

Partly because of Strong's descriptions and other reports coming from the Park, the Secretary of Interior changed the rules and made most hunting within the park illegal. The slaughter of great numbers of animals was finally stopped, but poaching by men like Howell continued unabated.

In 1886, the U.S. Cavalry arrived in Yellowstone to help bring order to the park and to try to do something about the rampant poaching. For their winter work, soldiers were trained how to use skis and would conduct patrols in the park's backcountry, staying nights in small, rough patrol cabins in an attempt to discourage poachers.

The same winter that the cavalry began operations in the park, the explorer Lieutenant Frederick Schwatka who had recently resigned from a career in the military, organized a winter expedition through the park. You may remember that Schwatka's father was mentioned in the first chapter. He was William Goulder's chess playing partner during Orofino's first winter. Goulder was the Orofino pioneer whose memoirs provide us with an eloquent and intimate portrait of winter in Idaho's first gold camp.

Lieutenant Schwatka's expedition in Yellowstone really wasn't much of an adventure since he planned to stay in lodges and cabins each night. It was also poorly planned. He originally proposed that his party would walk and use dog sleds assisted by mounted Crow

Indians. When Yellowstone veterans convinced him that the consistency and the depth of the snow required skis, he changed his plans but grossly overloaded his men with heavy camping supplies.

Nevertheless, his expedition was significant in that the first winter photographs were taken of Yellowstone. It was a stroke of luck, at least for the edification of the public at large, that he invited F. J. Haynes to be the expedition photographer. Haynes was no ordinary photographer. He was an adventurer. As Schwatka's expedition began unraveling, and Schwatka, himself, became disabled because of an illness, Haynes went on. Haynes gleaned a small group from Schwatka's original party, and using skis and carrying lighter loads, he traveled throughout the park, taking photographs. Ultimately, his photographs gave the outside world a glimpse of the sublime beauty of Yellowstone during the winter.

Although Haynes's photographs certainly must have whet the appetite of at least some of the public to visit Yellowstone in the winter, it would still be another 90 years before the Park would be visited by winter tourists to any degree—and those tourists mostly came by machine, a new kind of machine which allowed over-the-snow travel.

For a while, even after the cavalry arrived, wintertime visitors continued to be the unlawful kind. Poachers were seasoned backcountry woodsmen, and many of the troops assigned to the park were green and were little match for the poachers. With near impunity poachers would move in and out of the park. In the late 1880s, they could sell elk and bison heads to unscrupulous taxidermists who would pay anywhere from $10 to $124 each. The taxidermist could then sell them to New York buyers for $275 or more.

In 1894 Burgess changed all that. His adept use of skis and apprehension of Howell caught the interest of reporter Emerson Hough who was in Yellowstone at the time. Hough's story was picked up by Eastern newspapers, and the resulting outcry over Howell's slap-on-the-wrist punishment finally exerted enough pressure on governmental officials to put considerably more teeth in Yellowstone poaching laws.

❋   ❋

*F*OR YELLOWSTONE'S SOLDIERS and poachers, skis were an integral part of the job—legal or illegal. They also were useful for the occasional odd job that came along in the winter. A Swede by the name of Whistling Anderson was always looking for such jobs, and one that came his way really was an *odd* job: transporting the corpse of a Chinese cook. Members of Silver City's Chinese community had contracted him to retrieve the cook's body for a proper Chinese burial in the graveyard outside of town.

As his name suggests, Anderson liked to whistle. Wherever he went and however he went—walking, riding or skiing—the air would be filled with melodies escaping his pursed lips. The body he had been contracted to pick up was located along Reynolds Creek to the north of Silver City. So off to Reynolds Creek he went, whistling and skiing his way through the Owhyee Mountains of southern Idaho.

The trail he followed to Reynolds Creek was the first of the established freighting routes to the Boise valley from the Owhyees. Later, another route farther to the south would become more popular for Boise travel and remains so to this day, but not before tons of supplies had moved across the first route and the Owhyee gold fields had been firmly established as among the richest in Idaho.

The story of Anderson's trip is told in the book *Idaho Lore* which was edited by an Idaho native and one of the west's great writers, Vardis Fisher. *Idaho Lore* was prepared as part of one of Roosevelt's New Deal programs, the Federal Writer's Project, which provided jobs for artists and writers who had been left

Posing for a picture in De Lamar, Idaho, one of the mining towns in the Owyhee Mountains. Until fashion standards relaxed in the 1920s, women always wore long woolen dresses while skiing.

unemployed during the Depression years. While not pretending to be historically accurate, the book's primary purpose was to preserve a part of Idaho's early story-telling traditions before they were lost.

Whistling Anderson probably existed, though the details of his story may have gone through some revisions with each retelling. The version that Fisher's researchers brought to print tells that Anderson reached the corpse and found the cook wrapped in canvas and frozen solid.

It is likely that Anderson had thought it over in advance how he would bring the body back. Finding the cook frozen stiff as a board made it all the easier. Anderson fashioned a sled out of his skis and lashed the corpse on top with leather thongs.

After a night's rest, the Swede took off dragging the sled and body behind him with a tow rope. It must have been quite a chore getting the sled up and out of the Reynolds Creek drainage, and certainly by the time Anderson reached the summit outside of Booneville, he was ready for some easier traveling. He found respite by climbing atop the corpse, pushing off and riding it down the hill like a child riding a toboggan—only in this case the toboggan happened to be a frozen cadaver.

"All went well," according to *Idaho Lore*, "until he struck a curve in the trail; the Swede, corpse and all took to the air and went down the mountain like something out of a cannon. At the bottom, the Swede dug himself out and seized his rope and set off again."

At Booneville, tired of dragging the load, he propped the corpse up against the outside wall of a saloon and went in for a few drinks. He staggered out sometime later and skied into Silver City dragging his load off to the graveyard.

Having arrived, Anderson found that it wasn't easy collecting from his Chinese employers. The principals gathered at the graveyard with Anderson demanding payment for his services and the Chinese prevaricating. Word spread fast and eventually all of Silver City's Chinese population were at the graveyard listening to the Swede's heavily accented protestations, eyeing nervously the corpse strapped to Anderson's skis.

"To hell with you all!" Anderson finally said in frustration. "Ay tank Ay tak him home and feed him to my pet fox!"

He started dragging the sled back home. That finally brought a response from the Chinese, who promptly dug up $50 amongst them and took possession of the corpse.

Untying the dead cook from the skis and removing the canvas covering, they leaned him against a tombstone and cleaned off the snow and ice which had accumulated on the body from Anderson's rather rough handling. They also put a clean shirt on him.

All of this, however, was of no concern to Anderson. He was hungry—and thirsty, again—and was off, whistling his way back to Silver City.

❊ ❊

*T*HE USE OF SKIS by Silver City's Anderson, and by Yellowstone's explorers, military scouts and poachers illustrate how popular they were. It illustrates something else too. When skiing is viewed in its purest, most original form, as a means of travel, the last three decades of the 1800s in the west were the Glory Years. In the history of western skiing there would never be another time like it.

Skis these days are used for recreation and very rarely are they used for work or transportation between mountain towns. In the 1800s, however, they were winter wheels. They were as important as the horse was at other times of the year.

Travelers who didn't mind a little cold weather and snow could throw a pack over their shoulders, strap on long snowshoes and head out across the wilderness. It wasn't necessarily unpleasant. Skiers of this period often timed their travels so that they spent nights in existing shelters protected from the cold. Anderson stayed overnight at the Jordan place when he picked up the frozen Chinese cook. In Yellowstone Park, authorities encouraged the building of cabins and lodges at popular sites such as Old Faithful, Canyon, Mammoth and other locations which were about a day apart on skis. Early park travelers could ski through the park and be able to stay in relative comfort beside a warm fire each night.

Throughout the Idaho mountains, travelers heading to and from mining towns in the winter preferred having a roof over their heads rather than sleeping in the snow. Shelters that they used included ranches, way stations or small cramped cabins often referred to as smoke houses, which had been built specifically for the winter stops. Most of the smoke houses are gone now, but the remains of one can still be seen and is marked by the Forest Service along the road between Warren and Big Creek.

Of course, there were many who eschewed winter travel and waited until spring or until the trails were sufficiently broken to

Family gathering in Ivers, Idaho on the southern edge of what is now the River of No Return Wilderness.

allow sleigh or horse travel. Others simply moved to the lower elevations and waited for spring before returning to the mountains. Yet, those well versed in winter nuances—and there were lots from all walks of life—thought nothing of getting around in the snow. All across Idaho skis and webs were used: from Orofino to Florence, from Florence to Warrens, from Custer to Loon Creek, from Atlanta to Rocky Bar, from Sawtooth City to Galena, from the Buffalo Hump Mines to Thunder Mountain, and on and on the list goes.

Often it was a combination of traveling methods that were utilized. When the deep snow of the higher elevations prevented stages from getting in to Silver City in the Owyhee Mountains south of Boise, passengers were transferred to sleighs. If the snow was deep and the trail hadn't been broken out for sleighs, passengers who were prepared for it would strap on snowshoes or webs and foot it the rest of the way.

It was the same for the trip out to Boise from Idaho City. In 1881, the *Idaho World* reported that "travelers are still compelled to foot it or go on snowshoes between here and Boise." Once the skiers would reach the lower elevations close to Boise where the snow thinned, they would remove their skis and walk the rest of the way.

❊   ❊

*S*OME OF THE MOST FASCINATING STORIES of travel in the late 1800s are the long trips, during which energetic travelers would cover hundreds of miles of mountain terrain. Unfortunately, the accounts that are left to us are only bits and pieces, but they are tantalizing bits and pieces. Take, for instance, Bill Richardson of Florence. He learned from a letter written by his brother about promising possibilities in Leesburg. "When Bill finally received the letter," wrote historian G. E. Shoup, "winter had set in, snow lay deep over the mountains, miners on high altitudes holed up for the winter, and travel curtailed to adventurous snowshoers." This didn't stop Richardson, nor did a lack of precise information on where Leesburg was located. He knew that the new diggings were to the east of Florence and that was good enough.

Shoup continued: "A few pounds of flour mixed with yeast powder and salt was put in a serviceable sack, with tobacco and matches stowed away in warm clothes suitable for his require-ments. A single wool blanket slung over his shoulder, Bill put on his snowshoes and, alone, turned his face eastward." A few days later he arrived at his brother's cabin in Leesburg, having traversed some 140 miles of the Salmon River Mountains.

The Idaho City newspaper carried this news item in March 1880: "Messrs J. C. Fox and George Perody arrived here from Bonanza City last Tuesday evening. They came over on snowshoes by way of Cape Horn and Banner, and made the trip in six days." There's no doubt they used skis in their 150 mile journey. J. C. Fox said that they had little problem finding fresh meat, using his snowshoe [ski] pole to kill several fool chickens. The men reported snow depths of 4 1/2 feet of snow at Bonanza, 7 feet at Cape Horn, 12 at the lakes at the head of Deadman Canyon and 2 1/2 feet on the hills on the north side of the Payette River. They also saw several snow slides which had slid into the River and their wildlife counts included 1 goat, 3 elk and 20 deer. "Although the thermom-eter was very low," said the *Idaho World*, "these gentlemen say they did not suffer any from the cold."

Of all the professions, it would seem that lawmakers would be the least likely to ski. Yet, at least two early Idaho legislators got to Boise doing just that. George Shearer used skis to travel from the Shearer's Ferry, 14 miles up river from Riggins, to Boise for the Idaho Territorial Legislatures. Even though made of wood, skis were pretty hardy in those day. He used the same pair of skis for the 150 mile trip to and fro.

Thomas Elder has the distance record. When elected to the Idaho legislature, he used skis to travel from Leesburg to Boise, a distance of nearly 275 miles. He said he used skis because he dreaded the long, jarring stage coach ride there.

❄   ❄

*I*T *IS UNFORTUNATE* that there is not more information available on the long ski journeys. If George Shearer and Thomas Elder were still with us, I'd have a hundred questions for them. How far could they travel in a day? What did they carry? (Law books and legislative papers?) How much did their packs weigh? What was their exact route and where did they stay? And so on.

The reason little information is available is that they probably didn't think what they were doing was out of the ordinary. Others did it. Why write or make a big deal of it? Certainly eager would-be miners in Hailey thought there was nothing unusual about using skiers to stake claims. In the winter of 1882, about 100 claims in the Wood River area on the books had been abandoned and officials had decided to open them to new owners. The process involved remarking the boundaries of the claim and re-filing new ownership papers.

It was quite a scene according to the *Wood River Times*: "Hailey lost about one-half of her male population, last week, nearly all the men who knew of claims open to relocation having gone out to locate them. All day Friday and Saturday men could have been seen starting out on snowshoes, in every direction, some with and others without blankets." The claimants encountered soft and unconsolidated snow and they found their skis sinking deep into the snow.

"Several returned to town exhausted, having been unable to reach their destination. Most of the re-locators slept on their claims Sunday night. Monday when they returned, the snow had somewhat thawed and packed, and snowshoeing became more profitable."

Two lovers living in Vienna in the Sawtooth Mountains thought nothing of using skis to get to their wedding. After a blossoming romance, D.W. Kelly and Miss Birdie Smith decided that they would wed in Pocatello. It was February of 1887, however, and there were no plowed or broken trails between the Sawtooths and the railroad station at Ketchum.

The *Ketchum Keystone* described the first part of their "ante-bridal" trip: "Snow shoes were brought into requisition, and the morning sun next day shone out upon the path of the two venture-some spirits as they gaily skirted along the unbroken field of glittering snow, dragging behind them a toboggan on which were securely lashed their trucks and bundles of other little indispensable effects necessary to the trip."

Once over the Pass, they skied down to Boulder Station north of Ketchum, where they took a horse drawn sleigh to Ketchum. They spent the night in Baxter Hotel and the next day took the train to Pocatello where they would be united.

If skiing was common, there were certainly among the early skiers those who were uncommon. Of all the long snowshoers of the 1800s, one group, because of uncommon deeds, has come best to symbolize the spirit of early western skiing and has earned a secure place in western mythology. They are the heroes of the western winter, the mail carriers.

William Borden, the Thunder Mountain mail carrier. In Warren, Idaho 1897.

CHAPTER 3
THE MAIL CARRIERS . . .
HEROES OF THE LONG SNOWSHOE

The Banner mail carrier, (Moses Kempner is his name, and he "snowshoes" for scads and fame), stops for no barrier, great or small—skims over 'em all—and is known farther and wider—this handsome snow-shoe glider—than any other slider round about "these here diggins." Right through drifts of snow heaped hugely high, he'd go, in times gone by, and come gracefully flying in on time.

*T*HIS LIGHT HEARTED, poetic quotation in the *Idaho World* on December 7, 1883, tells much about the reputation of early mail carriers. Carriers who had demanding mail routes, those impossible wintertime trails which climbed over mountain summits and passed through miles of deep snow, were looked upon with a combination of respect, awe—and fondness. To the people of isolated, winter-locked towns, the expressman arriving on skis with a pack full of mail was their link to the outside world. The carrier brought them newspapers, letters from friends and loved ones, and sometimes small needed items such as medicines. They were heroes and rightfully so.

William Goulder wrote that Orofino's expressmen carried "treasures richer than any the mines can yield." He described the scene in town upon the arrival of the mail carrier: "[He] delivers his precious charge into the hands of W. A. Atlee, Wells-Fargo's express agent. The head of a long procession of all the various elements of the population, now begins to enter the door of the office. Atlee is behind the counter, busily engaged in opening and classifying packages. As soon as he can get ready, he begins to call the roll, beginning with John Smith and proceeding upward or downward, to the right or to the left as the case demands, and delivering letters, papers, and packages to each one as the names are responded to."

There were many winter mail routes that were skied between towns across Idaho. Most of these were located in the central part of the state, where the mail route lay across many miles of high elevations and deep, boggling snow.

Moses Kempner's mail route was between Idaho City and Banner, a 30-mile trip. From Idaho City, Kempner skied through thickly timbered country and climbed continuously along the side of Mores Creek to the top of Mores Creek Summit, a vertical rise of over 2,000 feet. Once on the top, he passed through the rolling, deeply snow-covered country until reaching Banner.

At times during the winter when the snow would consolidate enough, Kempner would switch from skis to a mule-drawn sled. The same year that the *Idaho World* waxed poetically about his skiing feats, he had a sled specially constructed for his mail work at Cowan's Blacksmith shop in Idaho City. The sled was painted red, but before he had picked it up at the blacksmith's some unknown prankster had painted the side with black letters: "Banner or Bust, by the gods of war."

No doubt when using the "gods of war," Kempner kept his skis handy. Once in the high, unpredictable country above Idaho City, mules or horses could bog down in the snow, entrapping both the carrier and his animal. Indeed, that's exactly what happened to Charley Magee two years earlier.

Magee, one of Kempner's mail carrying predecessors, rode out from Banner in late December, and only three miles from the mining camp, he ran into trouble. The snow had drifted so badly that it was impossible to get through. Magee tied the horse to a tree and "slid off" toward Idaho City on his skis. Meanwhile, when Magee didn't arrive on time, Idaho City residents began to get nervous.

"A crowd left here on Tuesday, a little after noon, in one of McClintock's sleighs to bring him, fearing that he had 'pegged out' " reported the *Idaho World*. The rescuers took along skis which they expected to use after traveling six or eight miles by sleigh. But they weren't necessary. Magee hadn't pegged out. He was quite well and nearly back to Idaho City when he was found. Afterwards, the *World* noted, friends helped retrieve his horse: "Four or five of the boys left here about ten o'clock Wednesday night to bring in the horse. They have a big job on their hands, as a track will have to be beaten most of the way to the summit."

Magee was taking no chances with horses the next year, carrying the mail most of the winter of 1881-82 on skis. "Charley Magee, the indefatigable mail carrier has made his regular trips this winter on snowshoes, between this place and Banner. His last trip was storming all the time, and many were of the opinion that he could not make it. Tuesday evening, however, at 8 o'clock Charley hove into the post office with his mail, apparently not the least weary," bragged the *World*."

It was also reliance upon horses which led to Timothy Carroll's survival epic in the snow. In December of 1879, Carroll, the Foreman of the Elmira Company's mines at Banner, and J.D. Emery left Idaho City for Banner on horseback. Near Mores Creek Summit, the snow became too deep to take their mounts any further. Anxious to get to the mine, Carroll elected to go on using skis while Emery returned to Idaho City with the horses.

Carroll's troubles began shortly after leaving Emery and the horses. Nearing the summit, he found it difficult to maneuver his skis through the heavy trees and brush, and upon reaching the top, a fierce snowstorm hit. Lost, and with night drawing in around him, he took shelter in a dense grove of firs. If there is one mistake which cemented his plight, it became evident here: he could not make a fire. All night he exercised and walked around within the shelter of the trees to keep warm.

The next morning, he attempted to go farther, but by now he was exhausted. He hollowed a snow cave, and as the cold seeped into his body, he clung to the hope that someone might find him.

That someone was the mail carrier, but it wasn't until four days later that Ben Miller, another one of Moses Kempner predecessors, was skiing his mail route over the summit when he found Carroll dazed and huddled in his damp cave. Miller could see that Carroll was suffering from severe exposure and that his feet were frozen. He would need help to get him back to Idaho City where a doctor could treat him. Wrapping Carroll in his own jacket, Miller skied off towards Banner. Even though Miller raced through the snow, it was a cold day, and without his jacket, he became chilled. He got the word through, and several men went to Carroll's rescue.

"When the men arrived," the *Idaho World* reported, "a sled was made, snowshoes being used for runners. Carroll drank some coffee, and then the men started for this place with him." They were met by the sheriff who transferred Carroll to a large horse drawn sleigh and got him back to Idaho City.

Miller, who had alerted Carroll's rescue party and who had given up his jacket, suffered frost bite, but later in January, the *Idaho World* announced that Miller had recovered and was carrying the mail again. Carroll, on the other hand, went through three surgical operations which removed both of his feet. In April, The *Idaho World* carried information on his progress: "Mr. Tim Carroll now goes down and up the stairs at the Luna House, to and from his meals, without assistance. He gets around on his knees. His many friends will be pleased to learn that he is now getting along so well."

❄　　　　❄

ONE OF THE MORE BIZARRE TALES of mail carrying occurred on the ski route to Bullion, a mining town seven miles west of Hailey. George Henninghouse was a short, stout German who was contracted to carry the mail to Bullion. During the winter, the mail route between the two towns was up and over the mountains. In March of 1883 on a Thursday afternoon, he left with a 70 pound mail sack over his shoulder.

As he skied down Bullion Street, he could see that a storm was approaching, and approximately two miles out of town, Henninghouse was caught in it. The *Wood River Miner* which recounted his trip said that "all signs of the road and trail were soon obliterated and as the outline of the mountains were not distinguishable through the descending snow and sleet, Henninghouse was forced to go considerably by guess."

Unfortunately, Henninghouse's instincts failed and led him in the wrong direction into the "bleak wild mountains" to the north. Struggling his way to the highest elevation, he was unable to locate anything that looked familiar. He roamed aimlessly in the same area where another man on a similar trip had perished several weeks earlier.

The light faded, and Henninghouse resigned himself to being lost. Just as he was about to lie down for a rest, he heard the "dismal howl" of a wolf. "Roused by this ominous sound, fear leant strength to his weary muscles and he started along the ridge—he knew not where." Madly, he dashed into the darkening night, away from the ghostly cry of the wolves. He heard more of their howls and barks as he skied wildly, floundering and searching vainly for the sanctuary of a cabin.

"Soon he could hear their loud breathing and the pat, pat, pat of their many feet as they came swiftly over the frozen snow." With the wolves almost upon him, he dropped his mail sack, and taking a match to some papers in his pocket, he lit them, trying to scare the creatures. "This gave him time to mount his shoes, and turning them down the steep mountain side, he flew forward with the speed of the wind, knowing nothing of the course before him." With all his remaining energy, he skied towards a shimmering light in the distance.

Mr. and Mrs. Virgil Lamb were inside their cozy cabin, when outside they heard a scream. Opening the door, they found the exhausted and frightened skier. Henninghouse promptly fainted at their door step, the paper reported, and had to be carried into the cabin.

The editor of the *Wood River Miner* to whom Henninghouse had told his story must have had some fun embellishing it for the

Idaho Historical Society

Mail carrier for the Blue Jacket Mine in western Idaho. He cuts a fine figure in his ski version of the Postal Service uniform. With U.S. insignia on his sweater and mail sack on his back, there's no doubt about who he is.

benefit of his readership. "Henninghouse is all right again," the editor announced, "except a little soreness of the muscles from over exertion. He affirms, however, if he packs any more mail for Uncle Sam, in these parts, it will be done during sunshine."

If it would increase circulation, newspapers, like the *Wood River Miner*, weren't adverse to taking liberties with the news. Indeed, mining town editors had a rich tradition to uphold and would be failing in their duty to readers if they didn't do a little embellishing. In the 1880s, Hailey area newspapers weren't letting their readers down. Considerable column space was being devoted to reports of a wild man who was terrorizing travelers and prospectors in the Camas Plains to the south of Hailey and Fairfield. Newspapers from as far away as Chicago and New York picked up the stories. It was exciting stuff, the Idaho version of big foot, and readers throughout the country were fascinated with the accounts.

Then it all came to a glorious end when the *Bellevue Sun* in February of 1883, ran an article which reported in detail how the Wild Man of Camas Prairie was killed by a duck hunter in self-defense. The editor of *Hailey Times*, a competing paper, cried foul on the *Bellevue* report. He had invented the Wild Man, he said, and it was patently unfair and downright underhanded of the *Bellevue Sun* to come along and invent the Wild Man's death.

❊   ❊

*W*ILD MEN AND WOLVES were not normally a threat to the early mail carriers, but dangers of avalanches were. One of the most dangerous mail routes in all of Idaho lay between the towns of Rocky Bar and Atlanta, deep in the central Idaho mountains.

In 1870, *The Idaho Statesmen* printed news of the death of an Atlanta mail carrier. On the morning of December 8th Brisco Hicks and his brother, James, left Rocky Bar. Their journey was ominous from its beginning. "It was one of the most stormy days known in these mountains," wrote the *Statesman's* Rocky Bar corespondent.

Approximately nine to ten miles northeast of Rocky Bar, the brothers were skiing beneath a steep snow-covered slope on Bald Mountain. Suddenly, the slope gave way above them, and began to slide, descending upon them "with the velocity of lightening."

James Hicks pointed his skis downhill and attempted to outrun the avalanche.

"Oh God! Oh Bris," he yelled to his brother.

The attempt to outrun the slide was futile; the white torrent overtook both men and engulfed them in a churning mass of snow.

Brisco, his skis ripped from his feet, was carried a quarter of a mile down the slope by the avalanche and up the other side of a ravine. As it is with avalanches sometimes, Brisco was lucky. Still alive, he was able to extract himself. James was not so lucky. He was carried to his death over a steep incline of rocks. "A deep gloom pervades the whole community," wrote the correspondent.

Several years later, the residents of Rocky Bar and Atlanta were once again confronted with tragedy. In March of 1882, 27-year-old Rufus Lester was the mail carrier between Rocky Bar and Atlanta. Carrying the Atlanta mail, he was only five miles out of town at the Bailer Grade when he was caught and buried in an avalanche. Hearing of the news, a large number of men strapped on skis and, carrying shovels, went to search for Lester. A storm was raging, but the men, upon arriving at the scene, kept up the search all night. Finally, the next day, his body was located under six feet of snow.

Eulogizing the man who had brought the residents of the remote town letters and news from the outside, *The Idaho Tri-weekly Statesman* dedicated a poem to his memory on April 4, 1882. It was in a small section of the paper entitled "In Memory of Rufus Lester." In part, it read:

> *Our brother has fallen*
> *We have laid him to rest*
> *His arms we laid peacefully*
> *Across his strong breast.*
> *A true man has fallen,*
> *He fell at his post.*
> *While doing his duty*
> *In a snow storm he was lost.*
>
> *Our mail carrier has fallen*
> *He was buried in snow.*
> *The heart that beat lovingly,*
> *No more sorrow will know.*
> *He has passed away before us,*
> *While we are left to toil here;*
> *He has gone to meet his Maker*
> *And one day we will meet him there.*

The dangerous winter route between Rocky Bar and Atlanta continued to take its toll. Three years after Lester's tragic death, Otto Mayer, the new mail carrier, had stopped to take a drink from a creek when he was surprised and fatally buried by an avalanche. Later another mail carrier, George McKinney, froze to death with the Christmas season's mail in his pack. Another, Charley Heath, disappeared on the way to Rocky Bar and his body was never found. It would seem that postal officials would have difficulties attracting someone to carry the mail between the towns of Rocky Bar and Atlanta, but if they did, there appears to be no record of it.

In 1888, Foley Abbott almost joined the list of those lost along this dangerous stretch. He and a number of companions were traveling to Rocky Bar from Atlanta. An avalanche swept down from above and caught the men. Most of them managed to stay on top of the slide, avoiding burial, but Abbott was not so fortunate. Trapped in the slide, he was carried downward and deposited with his face down, under two feet of hardened snow. Still conscious, he yelled for help, but none of his companions on top of the snow could hear his cries. "Seconds seemed to him like hours during his helpless condition," reported the *Idaho Daily Statesman*.

Though shaken, the other men began probing the snow with their balancing poles in search of Abbott. Bill Mackey, one of the party, struck something, and uncovering it, discovered the en-trapped—and very grateful—Abbott.

The *Idaho Statesmen* article doesn't say who the source of the story is, but if it came from Foley Abbott, there is cause to have suspicions about some of the details. Foley is the same person who had been out on skis near Beaver Gulch in the Sawtooths and discovered a room in a cave presumably used by a prehistoric race of people. Abbott reported his find to the *Ketchum Keystone*, telling the *Keystone* that the room was "brilliantly lighted by a flame in the center." The flame came from gas escaping from a vent hole which probably led to an immense body of coal under the Sawtooths, the paper theorized. In the room, Foley reported that he found a large human skeleton nine feet high, a stone tomahawk, and a crossbow which fell into pieces when he picked it up.

After Foley's article appeared in the *Keystone*, a party was organized to accompany him and to further explore the cave. But upon reaching the location, the party found—surprise of sur-prises—no cave. Where the cave entrance had been was now a slope of broken rock. Foley shrugged. He really wanted to show the party the cave, but a landslide must have come down, he said, and covered up the entrance.

✷   ✷

AMONG THE LETTERS in a mail carrier's pack were small packages. The packages might contain medicines, a pair of spectacles, catalogs, newspapers, a book, or a gift from a loved one. In Jack Anderson's pack were a number of tins of tobacco addressed to Chinese miners. Anderson was the mail carrier between Mount Idaho, near Grangeville, to Elk City. As he was traveling to Elk City, the tobacco tins that protruded from the back of the pack were rubbing against his shoulders. What made it particularly bothersome was that the mail pack he carried had a lock on top and he couldn't get into it to rearrange the load.

That night while nursing his bruised shoulders at the Ten Mile Cabin, part way to Elk City, Anderson came up with a solution. After eating supper, he took a club to the pack, beating it until the offending lumps were flattened. It did the trick. His pack was much more comfortable the next day and for the rest of journey to Elk City.

It wasn't long after Anderson arrived that his reputation in town quickly went from mail carrying hero to *persona non grata*. Lumped in with Anderson, were Elk City's Chinese mining population to whom the tobacco tins were addressed. The uproar had to do with the tobacco tins. They were carrying opium.

The main problem concerning Elk City residents was not the fact that opium was being smuggled into town. It was what it had done to their mail. In its raw form, opium is a sticky substance resembling molasses in consistency. When Anderson had beaten the pack, the tins had broken open and opium had run out, saturating everything in the mail sack. Town residents, eagerly awaiting their mail, learned that what was left of it was at the post office, glued together in one great sticky mass. The rumblings finally settled down, but it became quite clear to Elk City's Chinese that future supplies of opium would have to come by means other than the U.S. Mail.

Another unusual story involving the contents of a mail sack involves a letter written by the infamous Cowboy Joe of the Sawtooths. Adele McGown, in her reminiscences, *The Far Side of*

49

Dan McRae and George Short leave from the hotel in Warren on their way to Big Creek. Until the early 1900s, snowshoes such as those used by McRae and Short were called webs.

the Mountain, tells of a mail carrier who in 1894 made the trip each month on snowshoes between Bonanza and Loon Creek, northeast of the Sawtooths. It is unclear from her description whether the mail carrier wore webs or skis. It was probably skis. In the Sawtooths and wilderness country north of Stanley, skis were the most common means of transportation prior to the turn of the century, particularly for the long mail routes between mining towns. Webs picked up in popularity after the turn of the century and were used for shorter mail routes, trapping excursions and ranch work.

Whatever the carrier had strapped to his boots, on one of his trips, he failed to show up at his appointed time. Volunteers from Bonanza, who started a search when he was overdue by a week, finally found him dead, buried in a snowslide.

While the incident is more evidence of the danger of winter mail carrying, it's not the carrier that is the focal point of Adele McGown's story. It's about Cowboy Joe's letter.

The dead mail carrier's sack of mail was retrieved and the mail forwarded on. When Adele McGown finally received the letter from Cowboy Joe it was still moist from being buried in the snow-slide and upon opening it, the envelope fell apart. Inside, however, Cowboy Joe's writing was still legible.

Cowboy Joe was described by McGown as a large framed woman with hair the color of dogwood which she wore in two long braids wrapped around her head. She had gone into Loon Creek with prospector Pete Albert, her husband. Before the long winter set in, she had made 25 gallons of gooseberry wine to help pass the snowy season.

"Cap Varney came to their place every evening," said McGown describing the contents of the letter, "and they would play poker. One night Pete asked her to get out a gallon of wine and it was stronger than they thought it would be." As the card game went on into the night, all three of them got very drunk.

"Pete got so drunk," McGown continued, "that he gambled off everything they had but the house and cookstove." Cowboy Joe was famous for her prodigious appetite for alcohol. The smallest whiff could draw her halfway across the country. Her nose was twitching now that the remaining wine was going with Cap.

For Cowboy Joe, there was no thinking about what to do next. "Cap had won all the wine," said McGown matter of factly, "so she went with him to his cabin and left Pete to finish out the winter." No doubt, Pete was sore about losing everything in his cabin, and his wife, too, to Cap. McGown never reported how Pete actually felt about the whole thing, but Cowboy Joe seemed satisfied with the new arrangement and signed off her newsy letter telling McGown she'd see her in the spring.

❄   ❄

*L*OON CREEK, where Cowboy Joe had wintered, continued to produce ore for a number of years, and in the early 1900s, it still had a mail route between it and Custer. The mail route was still as dangerous as it was when the Cowboy's mail carrier had been killed a decade earlier. In 1904, the mail was carried by Silas Romer, a strapping young Norwegian. Romer's mail route led from Custer, located northeast of Stanley along Jordan Creek, to Sunbeam Mine and then over Loon Creek Summit to the mines in the Loon Creek area.

Silas Romer's story is told in Esther Yarber's book *Land of the Yankee Fork*. Yarber writes that in February, Romer was on his way back after delivering mail in the Loon Creek area. It had been cold up to that point, but it suddenly turned warm, and within a short time, the snowpack was wet and loose.

Wet snowpacks are dangerous snowpacks. Idaho snow is never very predictable as far as avalanches are concerned, but when cold snow warms due to rain or higher midwinter temperatures, it becomes terribly unstable. In researching newspapers from backcountry mining towns around Idaho, I found that the majority of avalanches and associated deaths to winter travelers could be attributed to one or two causes: a major storm laying down lots of new snow or a sudden warming trend after a period of cold weather.

Romer, experienced with the ways of the mountains, knew that. He would accept the risks of winter travel during much of the winter but not during the first several days of a warming trend. Quickly, he skied to the Sunbeam Mine. There he would wait until the warm spell ended before continuing on to Custer.

He arrived at Sunbeam Mine, but before he settled in he was told of a child in the camp that was very ill and in need of medicine. The medicine, available in Custer, might mean the difference between life or death.

C. E. Gable, the superintendent of the Sunbeam Mine, aware of Romer's reluctance to travel under the conditions, had asked another to make the trip. That was enough to rouse Romer. The trip was dangerous, but if anyone should go, it should be he.

He went to Gable and told him that he would go.

"But—you Romer, if you think it is that dangerous—what about you?" said Gable.

"Me . . . I'm young and strong,'" Romer replied, "and I know these mountains like the back of my hand. I'll leave at once and I'll be back here tomorrow evening."

Immediately, Romer gathered his things, and buckling into his skis, he journeyed into the mountains. He made his way along the ridge above Jordan Creek, trying to stay on the ridge top to stay above potential slide areas. He had ample reason to be cautious. Below him avalanches broke loose and crashed into the Jordan Creek drainage.

He arrived in Custer, picked up the medicine for the child and set out on the return trip into the mountains. The balmy weather continued to keep the snow wet and mushy. He made progress, keeping to his high route, but every so often, he was forced to cross exposed slopes. Within two miles of his destination, he was crossing the head of a steep slope when it broke, unleashing an avalanche which swept him downward.

The avalanche threw his hat high in the air, and it caught in a pine tree. Five days later, below the hat, a search party found the lifeless body of Romer.

True life and death is accompanied by a full complement of irony. As it was with Romer, the sick child recovered without ever needing the medicine for which Romer had risked—and lost—his life.

Romer is symbolic among Idaho mail carriers not only for his heroism, but as a sign, too, that their time in Idaho was drawing to a close. During the same period that Romer was skiing through the mountains of the Yankee Fork and Loon Creek country, other mail carriers were carrying the mail to Thunder Mountain, which was the scene of the last of Idaho's great gold rushes. The mail route to Thunder Mountain was one of the longest ski mail routes in Idaho. It was 90 miles long, starting at the Garden Valley Post Office and ending at Roosevelt in the Thunder Mountain area.

Ole M. Olsen was the youngest skier of the Thunder Mountain mail carriers. Born in Larvik, Norway, in 1884, he emigrated to America when he was 19. On one of his return trips from Thunder Mountain, he met an old man making his way out with a sled and team of horses. Olsen knew what could happen if the horses ran into too deep of snow—or if the weather took an abrupt turn and triggered snow slides along the steep slopes along the trail. Changing his schedule, Olsen accompanied the old man assisting him with the sleigh.

While making their way to Garden Valley, they were caught in a snowstorm. The snow deepened on the trail slowing their progress to crawl. Olsen skied in front breaking a trail through the snow for the man mounted on his horse. Olsen was exhausted and nearly pegged out, but with his charge in tow, he arrived safely in Garden Valley. Without Olsen, the man surely would have perished.

The list of deeds of these hardy, generous skiers of old goes on and on. Romer and Olsen in the early 1900s were among the last.

In a letter to the editor of the *Idaho Statesman* that appeared inconspicuously in 1967, a quiet, but generous man wrote telling briefly of his pride in being one of those mail carriers who skied the long route to Thunder Mountain. He concluded his short letter by adding, "I was the youngest of the ski troops in the winter of 1904 that carried mail over Thunder Mountain to Roosevelt. I am the last survivor of the mail carriers," signed O. M. Olsen.

Olsen, "the last of the mail carriers," died April 8, 1971 at the age of 87. With him ended an era, an era of heroes, who, on skis, traveled the remote and rugged Idaho mountains, bringing messages and happiness to the residents of towns cut off from the outside. Their passing has left a void that will never be filled. No more do we see the sight of mail carriers with packs bulging with letters, gliding across the snow. No more are the scenes of a small town turning out to cheer their arrival. Their time has passed, but for those who are inspired by their generous deeds, Ole Olsen, the last of the mail carriers, and those who preceded him, will always be remembered.

CHAPTER 4
ONE LAST LOOK BACK

THE END OF THE GLORY YEARS of western skiing—and along with it the end of the skiing mail carriers—can be traced to an event which occurred in the Midwest. It was an event that would have repercussions going far beyond skiing and would in a few years change the face of the US: in 1908, in a factory along Mack Avenue in Detroit, Michigan, Henry Ford unveiled the Model T automobile. It was the first automobile with a price that could be afforded by America's growing middle class. With 4 cylinders and a 20 horsepower engine, the Model T was capable of going 45 miles per hour and traveling 25 miles on a gallon of gas. By the second decade of the twentieth century, Americans were snapping up Model T's as fast as they came off Ford's assembly lines. When the Model T was retired, 15,000,000 had been sold.

With Ford's Model T, and new competing automobiles, came better roads and trucks with plows to keep roads open in the winter. Gradually routes between Idaho mountain towns were plowed on a regular basis. Where it was too remote and too expensive to plow, winter supplies and mail came by another new form of transportation, the airplane. Men such as Ole Olsen, who carried mail on skis across mountain trails, slowly and quietly disappeared into history.

Despite the improving transportation system in Idaho, there were times now and then when nature disrupted things, and some of the old ways again were called upon by some for emergency travel. A. C. "Nick" Nichols was one of those who in his work relied on his trusty skis when other more modern methods had failed.

Nichols, to the residents of Ashton and Island Park, is best known as "Nick the Mailman," where for 25 years he carried the mail in his Volkswagens from Ashton to West Yellowstone. Before

Once the roads between mountain communities were plowed, the use of skis and webs diminished.

Nick was a mailman, he was a truck driver carrying freight over the roads of eastern Idaho in the 1930s.

First learning how to ski when he and his father would make frequent winter trips between their ranch and Ashton, 12 miles to the west, Nick found use for his skis many times when the snow-plows were unable to clear the roads because of heavy and drifting snow. When it became impossible to drive any further in those conditions, Nick would slip his boards on and ski to the nearest ranch to wait until the plows could again open the roads.

In March of 1936 on one of his regular trips from Pocatello and Idaho Falls to Victor, which followed a route by way of Sugar City, Newdale, and Driggs, Nick was slowly making his way to Tetonia. A furious blizzard had been raging for several days, and the roads were now so bad that he had been forced to stop frequently and shovel a path for the truck through the drifts which blocked his path. Coming out of the worst of the storm near Tetonia, he was shocked to meet a Mr. Davis and his wife driving their 1934 Plymouth towards the severe stretch of road beyond Tetonia that he had just battled his way across.

"I pulled over," Nick said, retelling me the events of that day. "I cautioned them from attempting to go any further. They informed me that they had been prevented by the blizzard from reaching their home in St. Anthony where they had a number of children waiting."

"They were anxious to get back to their children, but after my warnings Mr. Davis promised me that he wouldn't attempt to go any further. 'I'll just drive to the top of this hill,' he said, 'and show Ethel how bad it is and turn around.'" Assured that the Davises would return, Nick went on to Driggs where he got a room in the hotel.

The blizzard continued to rage all night and into the next day. The stretch of road between Tetonia and Newdale was so deeply drifted and covered with snow that the snowplows had completely given up trying to clear the road.

The next evening, Nick was still in Driggs waiting for the storm to blow over and the roads to open again. In the lobby of the hotel, on his way to supper, he was stopped by the Sheriff.

The Sheriff told him that the Davises had not been seen since Nick had talked with them the previous day. Alarmed, Nick realized that the Davises had gone on and were most likely stranded somewhere on that exposed windy stretch of road between Tetonia and Newdale. He feared for their lives.

A party of searchers was hastily assembled: Nick, Deputy Sheriff Ardon Stevens and Rosco Reese, who had a sled dog team. The snowplow driver broke a path for them from Driggs to the railroad crossing just west of Tetonia. Here they left the vehicles.

"We harnessed up the dogs and took off into that vicious black night," Nick said. "We couldn't see anything. The snow was driving and hitting us in the face and it was getting colder." Nick and the Deputy Sheriff were on skis while Reese mushed the dogs.

"The blizzard began to slacken a bit, but the wind was whipping and coming from the north, which it can do in this country. Then we knew that the temperature would drop. That, more than anything, caused us fear that these people would most certainly freeze to death—if they were still alive."

The three men grappled in the darkness with drifts that the winds had heaped as high as buildings. Regularly, the dog sled would flip over, and the men would have to untangle the dogs. At one point the Deputy Sheriff slipped on his skis and fell against Nick. As the men toppled over, Nick felt a sharp pain, and after untangling their skis and standing up again, he realized that his ankle had been sprained. He rose slowly and tried to put the discomfort out of his mind and skied on.

The storm was over now and stars were appearing. Along with it, the temperature plunged and the skiers groped in the darkness. "The thermometer, while it was only 3 to 4 degrees below zero when we started at midnight, by 8:00 A.M., had dropped to 45 degrees below," Nick said.

Just as daylight began to break, they had reached a point seven to eight miles west of Tetonia at what is called Casper Hill. There they spotted the car, or what was the shape of the car. It had been entirely covered by a drift of snow.

"We found the people, and they were in very bad shape. Fortunately, they were not frost bitten, but they did have what we now call hypothermia. They were incoherent and had hallucinations. You might say that they had lost their minds."

The men coaxed the Davises from their car, wrapped them in blankets and tied them securely to the dog sled. As he skied behind the sled heading back to Tetonia, Nick's ankle and leg became worse. "My leg had swollen, cutting off the circulation, and causing my feet to freeze," he remembered. The sled pulled ahead. Nick tried yelling to the others, but because of the exertion and the long night of drawing cold, dry air in and out of his lungs, he found that he had lost his voice. Slowly, Reese and Stevens disappeared in the distance as they hurried ahead with the Davises. Nick's condition worsened, falling frequently and eventually losing most of his coordination.

Nick managed to stumble on, finally struggling to within sight of a snowplow driver who was waiting for him. The driver, seeing Nick floundering in the snow realized something was terribly wrong and ran to him. Finding Nick barely conscious, the driver helped him back to the waiting plow and sped off to the nearest ranch house.

Once in the warmth of the ranch house, Nick began to recover. As he regained his senses, he started worrying about his feet and asked for Unguentine, a salve which was and is used for a variety of ailments. Thinking back over the incident after a span of several decades, Nick believed that the Unguentine rubbed on his feet is what saved them.

Nick the mailman and one of his buddies.

It had been some rescue. It had taxed all Nick's reserves and had nearly left him with frostbitten feet, but he had survived the "vicious black night" and fully recovered to ski many more miles. The news about the Davises was equally as good. After being rushed to the doctor in Driggs, they also recovered.

❋   ❋

NOT VERY FAR from Nick Nichol's home of Ashton, to the north, is the Island Park area. This high, lodge pole, forested country adjoining Yellowstone National Park is covered with a deep snow pack and regularly receives spells of cold temperatures. Robert Wuthrich, a short, sparkly eyed Swiss, spent his first winter in Island Park in 1923. Fresh from Switzerland, Robert learned quickly how cold an Island Park winter could get. "The thermometer on the wall froze," he remembered. "For over a week the temperature stayed around 55 below zero."

"During this time I invented freeze-dried coffee. I'd set a pot of coffee by the stove at night, and even if the stove was burning, by morning everything would be frozen, coffee and all."

In the winter, Robert used skis to travel through Island Park and the surrounding country. When Robert was caretaking at

Robert Wuthrich at Big Springs in Island Park.

Silvertip Lodge in the upper Yellowstone country, his skis came in handy once for an unpleasant chore. A miner had skied out to the lodge and told Robert that his partner had died of pneumonia. The miner requested Robert's help to carry out the body.

Unlike Whistling Anderson of Silver City, Robert had plenty of help transporting the corpse out of the mountains. Along with him were the miner, a Yellowstone ranger and the other caretaker of the lodge. They used skis and hauled a sled the 10 mile distance to Horse Shoe Basin where the miner's prospect was located.

Arriving in the basin, the miner gestured to a steep slope rising upward for nearly a half mile. At the top was a small black dot, the miner's deceased partner.

They had no choice but to leave their sled, remove their skis and kick steps up the slope. Breathing heavily upon reaching the top, they started making preparations to carry the frozen body down the hill. "We wrapped him up in a tarpaulin like a mummy," Robert said.

Robert looked down the steep slope and at the body. He didn't relish the trip back down the slope.

"Why don't we take it to the edge and push it off, and let it make its own way down," Robert suggested to the others.

Robert didn't have to do much arguing. The men, still tired with the climb, readily agreed that it was a fine idea. Moving the body to the edge, they gave it a push and watched it tumble and roll all the way to the base of the slope.

"It was a good thing that the slope leveled off at the bottom," Robert said. "I was a little worried that it might have kept tumbling and become lost out there somewhere."

Retrieving the tarpaulin-covered corpse, they lashed it to the sled and skied back to the lodge. Eventually, Yellowstone rangers carried it out for more gentle treatment and a decent burial in a nearby town.

Frank Daniels never had to carry a corpse out of the mountains on his skis, but his skis were essential to earning a living in the winter. Frank was a trapper in his younger days in Bone, Idaho, located east of Blackfoot. He started trapping in 1925 and continued until 1935.

"In the country around Bone, the snow was deep and hard," he said. "Some used snowshoes in that country, but I preferred skis.

You could cover a lot more country by ski, moving along as much as six miles per hour."

Frank's trap lines were placed so that he could travel between cabins that were scattered around the area. He covered the large area around Gray's Lake, Paradise Valley, Sheep Mountain and other points. His lines varied in distance, anywhere between 5 to 20 miles in length.

"When we were carrying provisions to our cabins or furs to the Post Office, we'd ski more or less at night. In the day time the snow became soft and sticky and skiing was a chore, but at night the snowpack was frozen and traveling was relatively easy."

❋   ❋

*L*IKE FRANK DANIELS, Lum Turner also used skis for winter work, but not for trapping. I first met Lum Turner in a Riggins bar in the mid 1970s. For me it was propitious. He had lived in Idaho since 1908, most of it in the Salmon River Country. He was tall and lean with huge hands weathered by years of work in the outdoors. Lum was known as one of the most colorful and well-known old timers on the lower Salmon River, and in my experiences with him, I found nothing to the contrary.

He still lived alone in a cabin that he built 40 years before our meeting near the end of a road leading east along the Salmon River out of Riggins. He was in town to pick up his social security check when I had met him, and after a few drinks he invited me to his cabin.

I followed him as he weaved back and forth on the narrow one lane track along the Salmon. He pulled off here and there, stopping to relieve himself and to tell me a story. At a narrow bridge which crosses the river, 14 miles east of Riggins, he pointed to where a trail climbed up and back down to pass around a cliff. He explained that one night in the 1930s while the bridge was being built, several workers were walking back on the trail. One of the workers in the front had a flashlight and had just gone up and around the small stretch above the cliff. Manning, another of the workers, lagged behind, and as he walked towards the light, he must not have seen that the trail climbed upwards. With the light shining in the dark in front of him it probably appeared to him that the trail went straight. Walking towards the light, he stepped off the cliff and was killed. Since then, the bridge has always been known as the Manning Bridge.

Lum also bragged how he was the first to cross Manning's bridge. One night when the steel framework was in place and before the workers had begun to cover the top of the bridge with timbers, he drove his automobile to the edge. Hopping from beam to beam, he placed a couple of boards just wide enough for his automobile tires. He drove to the edge of the first set of boards and then placed two more boards down and drove to the edge of those. Then, balancing on the beams, he walked back and got the first set of boards and set those in front and continued to drive and set boards down until he had driven all the way across.

After the Manning Bridge, the road narrows even more and has no shoulder, dropping straight into the river. Several times on that last portion of the trip, I watched horrified as Lum drifted towards the edge of the road, but he always corrected, steering his truck back on track.

At his cabin as he puttered around making dinner for me, he talked of his skiing job. In the 1930s each weekend, he would ski 10 miles south of his cabin up the Carey Creek drainage to the Kimberly Mine where he would pick up, of all things, parachutes. Because winter closed off transportation routes to the mine, the parachutes were used for the air dropping of supplies. Parachutes were a valuable item, and no further supplies could be dropped to the miners unless someone carried the parachutes back out. That was Lum's job.

Lum would load approximately 80 pounds of chutes in his pack and then take off down the steep trail leading back to the Salmon River. "I didn't follow any trails, I just took off down the drainage," Lum said.

Lum used a single pole between his legs to slow himself down as he made the descent. "Hell," he said, getting exited and waving his arms, "when you get going 40 miles per hour, you need that pole. You got to stop!"

All the time he was telling me stories of skiing, he had been preparing something on the stove. When he finally put the plate down in front of me, I lost my appetite. It was the worst looking concoction I'd ever seen: black, brown and white lumps. He called it "maiden heads," but when I had a close look at the jar in his waste basket sometime later, I found that he fried up pickled cauliflower.

Lum had been draining a whiskey bottle all this time and as the night went on, he began to mumble and become incoherent. Eventually, he fell asleep on the coach. I went around and turned off most of the lights in the house and slipped into my sleeping bag. All of a sudden, Lum was yelling.

"My lights! My lights!" he cried. "Who turned off my lights? Who turned off my lights?"

I jumped out of my bag and quickly turned on some lights. "It's all right," I reassured Lum, thinking that the whiskey had been giving him bad dreams.

He stared at me with an unnerving wild look. I tried to step back, but he grabbed my arm, startling me by the power that he still possessed in his old body.

"Never, never, never turn off Lum's lights," he shouted. "Never, never turn off Lum's lights." Then he let go and fell back to sleep on the coach.

Hoping that Lum would stay asleep this time, I left all of his lights on. Unfortunately, he was a fitful sleeper. Every so often he would wake and mumble or shout something unintelligible. Unable to sleep and uneasy with his drunken dreams, I eventually went outside where it was quiet, and I finally went to sleep on his porch.

In the morning, I learned what the ruckus had been about. The power for his cabin came from a generator on a stream, and without the electric load that the lights in his cabin provided, the generator would burn out. By turning out all his lights, I risked destroying his whole electrical system. Fortunately, everything was working fine that next morning, and I was spared the great embarrassment of being known along the Salmon River as that damn fool that burned out Lum's generator.

Before I left later in the day, he showed me his skis. He had made them, and the beautiful reddish hue of the wood of the skis, he told me, came from alder. Many years prior he had used them with leather bindings, but more recently he had mounted a set of metal bindings providing him better control. Just in front of the bindings, he had attached a wooden thread spool which was used to tie on climbers or skins for going up steep hills. When I asked him what sort of climbers he used, thinking that a sleek pair of seal skin climbers used by arctic explorers would look nice against the red

Lum Turner on the porch of his cabin near French Creek: "Never, never turn off Lum's lights."

wood of his skis, he told me that the material from the leg of a worn out pair of Levi's did the job just fine.

He seemed perplexed why anyone would be interested in his skiing stories or skis, and before I drove off, he offered me his skis. "I can't possibly take them," I said. But he wouldn't hear any arguments to the contrary and insisted I take them. To this day, Lum's skis, another old pair of skis and a canoe paddle that was hand made by my friend, Walt Blackadar, are my most prized possessions.

I visited Lum on a couple of other occasions. Then one year, I heard the news of his death. Knowing Lum, it didn't come as a surprise. Lum had been in Riggins, perhaps picking up his monthly Social Security check as he had when I first met him. Returning home, he drove off the narrow road and his pickup plunged into the Salmon River.

❋   ❋

*W*HEN LUM HAD TAKEN UP SKIING, the numbers of those using long snowshoes had diminished greatly since the late 1800s. Besides the few people like Lum who used skis for work, others used them for quite another purpose, a purpose that portended the future: sport and recreation. As early as 1911, miners in Dixie were organizing a ski club just for the fun of skiing. "It is said that there is plenty of snow in the mountains and the prospects for the sport are unlimited," said the *Idaho Country Free Press*.

What finally put Idaho on the map for this new, recreational form of skiing was Averell Harriman's decision to build a world class ski resort in a sheep pasture near Ketchum, Idaho. Shortly after Union Pacific opened Sun Valley in 1936, McCall's Payette Lakes Ski Area came into existence with the help of the local logging baron, Carl Brown. Brown, incidentally, had occasionally used skis for a mail carrying contract that he had prior to his involvement in the logging business. Other areas sprung up all across the state. While Sun Valley was using the world's first chairlift to carry skiers to the top of Proctor and Dollar Mountains, other Idaho ski areas used rope tows powered by automobile engines. Skiing, after a brief lull, was back again.

The early rope tows used at Idaho's budding ski areas bore little resemblance to today's lifts. Blaine Gasser, who was a member of Pocatello's first ski club, said "it was more exciting riding it up than it was skiing down. The cable was moving so fast that there was no way you could grab it from a standing start. So we built a ramp to give us a running start."

"The cable was greasy, and we got carpenter aprons from several of the lumber yards. You would wear the apron sideways to keep your clothes from getting dirty. No one had heard of safety switches, and we sent gloves and scarves to the top through the pulley, but no one got hurt. We worked hard for the skiing, and we all had a great time."

While historically Sun Valley has always been connected with Alpine Skiing, recreational backcountry skiing has important roots there as well. The father of Idaho backcountry skiing as we know it today is Andy Hennig, a small-framed, energetic Austrian who was a ski instructor at Sun Valley. In the 1930s and 1940s, there was no difference between Alpine and backcountry ski equipment. Skiers would use the same equipment to take a run down Galena Pass as they did down the lift-served Dollar Mountain.

Hennig explored the untracked mountain wilderness around Sun Valley and pioneered backcountry ski routes in the Pioneer, Boulder and Smokey Mountain ranges. Armed with this knowledge, Hennig organized spring ski tours for Sun Valley guests and established two ski touring cabins. All of his popular backcountry ski routes remain today as Idaho classics. Ski mountaineering historian, Louis Dawson writes in *Wild Snow* that other than Otto Steiner who explored California's Mineral King area, Hennig was North America's most active backcountry skier of the period.

Under Andy Hennig's guidance, Sun Valley continued to run ski touring trips for its guests through the 1940s. The Union Pacific published Hennig's book *Sun Valley Ski Tours*, in which both the Alpine and backcountry touring routes were described making it the first backcountry ski book ever published in the U.S. or Canada. Moreover, it was a beautifully done book, and even today, there are few guidebooks illustrated so beautifully.

In the mid 1940s, Hennig's Idaho backcountry excursions were put on hold when the Unites States entered World War II. He, along with Willie Helming, Sigi Enl and Sep Frolick of the Sun Valley Ski School, and other Idaho skiers, joined the U.S. Army and become a part of the famous 10th Mountain Division. During the war little happened in Idaho skiing, nor did it matter much. The war was all consuming.

When the war was all over, veterans of the 10th Mountain Division had a tremendous impact on skiing and mountaineering in the years that followed. Hundreds of them worked in the growing Alpine ski industry in the U.S. helping to develop new ski areas and working as mountain managers and instructors. A few became mountain guides and still others found work in the outdoor equipment industry.

The emphasis in the post war years was on Alpine skiing. Equipment in the 1950s and 1960s went through rapid changes, but all of it was designed to enhance lift-serviced skiing. While wonderful improvements had been made for downhill skiing, new ski equipment with stiff, inflexible boots and bindings which locked down the heel, could no longer be used in the backcountry. Those rare individuals that still did backcountry trips had to settle for old Alpine boots and cable bindings picked up at garage sales—or they used cross-country racing equipment.

In the 1970s things changed. The baby boom generation reached maturity and skiing experienced explosive growth. Many of the new comers to skiing experimented with new skiing styles: cross-country touring, Nordic downhill and backcountry skiing. Cross-country and backcountry skiing, of course, weren't new, but to the boomers it was, and it fit in well with the back-to-the-land ethic that many of them embraced. The result was that once again glistening snow fields in the back country areas of Idaho were seeing the tracks of passing skiers.

The generation following the boomers has made a new contribution. Snowboarding, a completely new form of winter recreation, has made and will continue to make its mark on Alpine slopes and in the backcountry. During the quickly evolving latter third of the twentieth century, many individuals played important roles in the development of Idaho skiing. I have had the great fortune to meet and interview many of them, and much of the remainder of the book could be spent singling out their contributions. The scope of this narrative, however, is limited to those older pioneers who are mostly gone. The historical reach back to the events of their lives is farther, and like a painting which is viewed from a distance we have perspective and greater understanding of their contributions.

Of these historical figures of skiing, there is one last person that I want to introduce. His name is Russ Keene. He is the only one of all of the Idaho old-timers that I interviewed in the mid and late 1970s that was still alive when I traveled around the state some 20 years later working on the revision to this book. He lives near Sandpoint, Idaho, and he is North Idaho's Grand Dean of backcountry skiing.

❊   ❊

THE WIND WHIPPED SNOW up and around the towers of Schweitzer Basin and wildly swung the chairs. The decision had already been made to shut down the ski area when one of the lift operators looked out through the blowing snow and spotted a skier trudging uphill.

"It's old man Keene and his dog," the lift operator reported over the phone to the mountain manager. The manager was annoyed. He knew Keene, knew him all too well. He had warned Keene about cross-country skiing to the top of the mountain in high winds a couple of times in the past and here he was at it again.

There was another reason why the manager was annoyed. Keene held the record for climbing from the parking lot to the top of Schweitzer. He had done the 1800 feet ascent in 50 minutes, not bad for someone in their mid 60s. The manager had tried it and come close at 55 minutes but had nearly killed himself in the process.

"Well, I hope the wind blows that crazy son of a bitch off the mountain," the manager shouted back on the phone.

As Keene neared the top, alternating blasts of wind forced him to flatten face first against the snow. He had planned to find shelter in a forested area, but the wind was tearing off chunks of rime ice and the projectiles shot by him "like cannon balls."

His dog, Sam, ran ahead to where Keene had built and was maintaining a couple of snow caves that winter. The entrance was drifted over and the dog scratched away trying to find the portal of the cave and get out of the terrific winds.

Suddenly, Sam was airborne. "A gust just picked up Sam," Keene remembered, "and like an old sock, he sailed by me. He had this weird look on his face. I never saw him again until I got back down to the bottom." Wearing an imperious expression, Sam was found by Keene huddled up against the side of a condominium at the base of the ski area.

Life was never boring for Sam, or anyone, for that matter, who accompanied Russ Keene on his frequent winter trips into the mountains. If there ever was a person who truly lived, seizing each day as in the fullest meaning of the Epicurean maxim *carpe diem*, it was Russ.

Russ Keene's family first moved to the Sandpoint area in 1912. He got his first taste of skiing when he and his school mates would strap barrel stays to their feet and ski down a logging chute behind the school house. Mostly, like everyone in the Panhandle area, he would use snowshoes to get around in the winter.

When World War II broke out, Russ joined the Tenth Mountain Division. He had asked to be a medic because "I wanted to save lives, not take them." But the army had other plans, and he was assigned to infantry.

During the two winters of training at Camp Hale in Colorado his snowshoeing skills came in handy. Keene knew that skiers could always out run a snowshoer—unless, the terrain for the race was carefully chosen. He came up with an idea to pick up a little pocket change: "All the guys would be out skiing, and I'd pick one out of them and I'd say, 'I can beat you.' And he'd look at me with my snowshoes and say 'Oh, yeah you clodhopper.' " It wasn't long before a small crowd had formed. Several others joined the race and bets were placed.

Russ chose just the right spot: a hill descending into a gully with lots of aspens and then a steep climb back up the other side. Russ had developed a method where he'd take a leaping stride on his snowshoe, slide 10 feet or so, then stride again and slide another 10 feet. Even though the skiers could out ski him going downhill, the method kept them within range. It was at the bottom where he could catch the skiers, as they would invariably get tangled in the trees and then be forced to put on skins to climb up the steep slope on the other side. By that time, Russ was already up and at the finish line with a broad smile on his face.

"We'd only get $30 a month at first, and one time I made $25," said Russ of his fortunes from the snowshoe-ski competitions.

Watching one of Russ's races was a Colonel in the Medical Corps. An admirer of Russ's cleverness, he and Keene became friends, and when the Tenth was shipped to Italy, Russ went there as a medic.

Not long after he arrived in Italy, he and a buddy were called to help a soldier injured by a mine. While inspecting the soldier, part of the embankment above them collapsed and in the ensuing commotion another mine went off. Russ was injured badly by shrapnel, but his buddy who had been between Keene and the exploding mine, absorbed most of the shock and was killed along with several others.

Russ was confined to the hospital for a number of weeks. When released, he immediately joined the advancing front, reassuming his medical duties. At one point, the American forces drew back from a German counteroffensive. Russ had been manning a make shift forward hospital with several injured soldiers on IV's. There was no way to move the critically injured, and he made a risky decision to stay behind with the wounded.

The Germans barged into his make shift hospital, but when the German commander arrived, he told Russ that he was a man of honor, a member of the old Weimar, not a member of the Hitler Youth and that he and his patients would be safe. The German commander posted guards outside the hospital. Eventually, the

Ross Hall

Russ Keene and Hazel Hall enjoy a hot drink in
one of Russ's snow caves on top of Schweitzer.

Allies retook the town, and Russ and his patients were found
unharmed.

After the war, Russ went to work for Pacific Gas and Electric
in California. He was involved in several jobs, but it was his snow
surveying work on the King's River Drainage that he clearly
enjoyed the most. The surveys had always been done on snowshoes, but he suggested trying skis. "We had to buy our own skis
the first year," Russ said, "But from then on they bought them for

us." That was because PG&E could see that Russ's method could save them money. Using skis, the snow surveyors could run the 145 mile survey course two days faster than they could using snowhoes.

"By the time they took over snow surveying work with helicopters, we had covered 4,200 miles . . . . well, that is the official number of miles we were supposed to have covered. But, you see, on skis we covered more distance. On a good day we couldn't resist climbing and screaming down some nearby mountain!"

He returned to Sandpoint in the 1960s, going into a semi-retirement, running a family tree farm and exploring mountains of his boyhood. In those carefree years, he figured that he spent just as many days out in the winter as he did in the summer.

The winter before I interviewed him, in 1977, he had climbed the South Ridge to the top of Schweitzer Basin 31 times. Adept at both skiing and snowshoeing, he felt that a combination of the two was the perfect way to travel in the Panhandle country. Snowshoes were useful in the brushy, heavily timbered areas and skis were great above timberline and made the descents more interesting and fun.

He commonly skied to the top of Blue Mountain, four miles north of Schweitzer. He did winter ascents of Scotchman and Snowshoe Peak in the Cabinet Mountains. And he was the first to make an attempt at a ski traverse of the Selkirks, being stormed off in the Sundance Burn area.

In the years after our 1977 interview, Russ kept up his activity level. When his balance began to falter, and he became concerned about keeping up with others on winter and summer trips in the mountains, he shifted his interest to canoeing and later to rowing a canoe rigged with a special frame for oars. Russ Keene became as familiar as Lake Pend Oreille's ospreys. Residents along the lake could look out on nearly any calm day and see the lone form of Russ Keene quietly and rhythmically stroking across the lake. For several years, Russ racked up impressive mileage tallies, oaring hundreds of miles a year—until a series of small strokes robbed him of his muscular command and tenacious spirit. When I talked to him in the late 1990s, Russ Keene could no longer oar his boat and his once sharp mind had dimmed considerably.

It is, however, a small blip on a life well lived. What impressed me most about Russ's vitality is that early on, likely in his twenties, he had unknowingly injured his heart. When he was 40 years old, a doctor saw the telltale signs of it on an EKG. The heart had healed, the doctor told him, but he advised caution and warned him not to compete with younger men. This revelation is significant in Russ's life, and his full and active lifestyle in his later years may have been a rebellion against the limitations that doctors' pronouncements implied.

Did he do as the doctor advised, did he exercise caution or did he throw caution to errant winds blowing off the Selkirk crest? Perhaps the answer might found be found in the last of his stories.

During a backpack trip to the Sierras, Russ found himself stacked up behind a group of young hikers heading to a lake campsite much further and higher in elevation. They were slowing down his pace, and he asked politely to be let around.

They let him around, but Russ saw on their faces concealed amusement that they would no doubt be passing the old man winded along the trail someplace. It was not to be. Russ bounded up the trail and arrived at the campsite long before the tired hikers arrived.

"By God," one of the hikers said to Russ, "you weren't kidding. You can hike. How did you do that?"

Russ told the hiker that actually he'd slowed down a little and that in his younger days he used to "dog trot" all over the Sierras. Enjoying where the conversation was leading, Russ continued, explaining that the reason that he had slowed down was because of doctors' orders. "This doctor told me when I was 40 years old that I shouldn't compete with young men," Russ said just barely setting the hook. "But, so far young men are no competition."

❄   ❄

EVEN THOUGH I MET RUSS late in his life and even though age clouded my last conversation with him, I still think of him as a person fully in possession of the spirit of youth. It was a common denominator in all of the old timers that I interviewed. From Lum Turner, laughing as he fried up pickeled cauliflower to Robert Wuthrich telling me about how he discovered freeze-dried coffee as we skied together to Big Springs. What they did and what those before them did, was to pass a gift on to all of us. In that gift is the secret of their youthfulness. It is the gift of skiing, a gift which enables us to travel through and enjoy Idaho's mountains in the most glorious of all seasons. It is a gift that has become increasingly more important as we step into the early years of the new millennium, to help keep our sanity in a crazy, fast-paced world and to tread lightly in this wonderful place we call Idaho.

Nick Nichols, the beloved mailman for many years in the Island Park area, summarized it simply and beautifully: "I've been a cross-country skier all my life, and I love it! On skis I see everything and am able to enjoy the beauty of the outdoors without doing any harm. I don't chase the game away. I don't pollute the ground or snow. My mode of recreation is compatible with everything in the mountains."

Part II

Winter Trails:
Skiing, Snowshoeing and Snowboarding

CHAPTER 5
GENERAL INFORMATION &
KEY TO TRAILS AND SYMBOLS

Timothy Carroll, shivering in his damp snow cave on top of Mores Creek Summit in 1879, had plenty of time to think. If he had looked at his predicament objectively, he would have known that he had made a small but crucial error. Had he been prepared, he would have been able to build a fire and save himself. As we know from his story, which is told in the *Mail Carriers* chapter, he could not, and he ended up losing his limbs to frostbite.

What might have been an inconvenience, or an uncomfortable night out, turned into a nightmare for him. Indeed, Carroll's ordeal shows that winter is indifferent and capricious. Yet, his experience also shows that what happened to him need not happen to you. The key to avoiding a similar situation lies in two very simple concepts: preparation and respect for the winter environment.

If you are skiing at an Alpine ski area or on a groomed Nordic trail system, it obviously isn't necessary to carry a pack full of survival gear. However, if you go off on a snowshoeing trip, take general ski tours or head into the backcountry for downhill skiing or snowboarding, you'll want to carry enough equipment to enable you to survive in the event something goes wrong. Many books and videos are available that will provide more details on how to prepare, but let me pass on some suggestions on what equipment has worked well for me.

I have two versions of an emergency kit. One is a close-to-the-vehicle version which I use for trips where I am not going very far from the road. It is lightweight and will fit in a hip pack, but I carry enough with me to keep me and my loved ones alive in the case of an emergency.

Close-to-the-vehicle emergency kit:

- ☐ Extra clothing. In the lightweight version I carry at least a lightweight nylon or Gortex wind shell with a hood to provide wind protection, and if, for some reason, I'm not wearing it, I make sure I also carry a good warm hat.

- ☐ Matches, fire starter and knife. All carried on your person. Don't put them in your pack. If you get separated from your pack, you'll have no way to get a fire going.

- ☐ Lightweight space blanket. The kind that is compressed the size of a bar of soap.

- ☐ Map and compass.

- ☐ Sunglasses. You'll probably be wearing them.

- ☐ Small first aid kit. It's in a stuff sack smaller than the space blanket.

- ☐ Power Bar. Or your choice of something which packs a lot of energy.

- ☐ Water or a sport drink.

- ☐ You may also want to bring a little duct tape which can be used to make all sorts of temporary repairs including torn clothing, split shoes, broken poles and bindings. The tape can be wrapped around your ski pole and you'll never have to worry about it again.

All this easily fits in a hip pack, and even though it's not a lot of gear, it's a realistic load for trips which don't take me far from my vehicle—and with it I can survive a night out.

If I go farther, then I'll beef up the above list and carry it in a rucksack. For the **far-from-the-vehicle** or backcountry emergency kit, I take all of the above items with *more clothing* and *food, a better first aid kit, and the following additional items:*

- ☐ Metal cup. For melting snow in an emergency.

- ☐ Headlight. It gets dark early in the winter. Every year I end up using one because I couldn't resist one last run.

☐ Repair kit. Epoxy, bailing wire, duct tape, small vice grips, nylon cord, or other repair items.

☐ Portable shovel. Even if you don't go into avalanche country, you can construct an emergency snow shelter quickly with one.

☐ Avalanche Transceiver. For trips into avalanche terrain.

Think of the equipment outlined above as being an insurance policy. The premium is ridiculously cheap. Yet, if something goes wrong, you have the means to survive.

Avalanche Hazard

Everyone who recreates in the winter, needs to have at least a rudimentary understanding of avalanches. Granted, such knowledge is not necessary at Alpine or Nordic ski areas, but my guess is that sooner or later if you like to spend time outdoors in the winter you will find yourself in avalanche terrain. Knowing how to recognize avalanche danger and how to protect yourself can save lives. For winter recreationalists, it is as important as knowing basic first aid and CPR.

Several good avalanche books and videos are on the market, but the best way of gaining knowledge and skills is to take an avalanche course. Avalanche courses are available from university outdoor programs, commercial backcountry ski guides and the National Ski Patrol.

If you are a backcountry skier or snowboarder, taking a course is not only desirable, it's essential. It's not enough to carry a transceiver and a shovel. You need to know how to use the transceiver, and you need to know when are the safest times to travel and what are the safest routes.

One of the most important developments in winter safety over the last few years has been the availability of avalanche forecasting information. In the chapters that follow, I've included information on where you can obtain forecasts, either via recorded phone message or off the Internet. Unfortunately, this service is not available in all areas, but I have also included the phone numbers of

A close call with a slab avalanche. Backcountry skiers and snowboarders can minimize their risk in places like that shown above by taking an avalanche course, carrying shovels and transceivers, checking forecasts provided by the Forest Service—and always maintaining a healthy respect for the power of the natural world.

local Forest Service offices which may be able to provide general information on local conditions.

What is so good about professional avalanche forecasts is that the person preparing the report will also describe the current skiing and boarding conditions and let you know where the best powder is found. It's like a ski area snow report but far better. Since forecasters are in the field on a daily basis, they know when the conditions are bad and will issue appropriate warnings. This is lifesaving information. Make time to check it out before going on a backcountry trip.

Environmental Concerns

Every outdoorsperson needs to be concerned with the outdoor environment. Here in the interior west, we live in a blessed land. We can still enjoy wide open spaces, unroaded wild areas, and clean rivers and streams. The last thing we want is for this country to become another east or west coast. We have an opportunity to protect this wonderful environment, to preserve the natural qualities which drew us here, and to rein in rampant development which threatens our western lifestyle.

The only way that we can achieve these goals is by supporting organizations which are willing to wade through the political process and make our points be heard. You may not be interested in getting in the fray of political fights, but you can help by donating to the conservation group of your choice. They are out there on the front lines, fighting to keep our corner of the west the special place that it is. They need your help *and* dollars. Some suggestions are: Idaho Conservation League (PO Box 844, Boise, Idaho 83701), Greater Yellowstone Coalition (13 South Wilson, Bozeman, Montana 59715), Northern Rockies Chapter of the Sierra Club (PO Box 552, Boise, ID 83701) and the Boulder-White Clouds Council (PO Box 3719, Ketchum, ID 83340).

Please don't sit back and let others do the work while you reap the benefits. Join now. You'll feel much better knowing that you have played a part in protecting our magnificent outdoors.

Minimizing Impact

The winter covering of snow negates almost any impact that skiing, snowboarding or snowshoeing might have on the environment. However, snow also makes it easy to hide small pieces of litter. Be careful, even at Alpine Ski areas, to pick up litter. One thing to be aware of is that some food items, particularly orange peels, take a long time to degrade. If you carry them in, carry them out.

If you stop to build a fire or if you do any winter camping, remember that aluminum foil (found in soup, cocoa and tea packages) doesn't burn. In the spring when the snow melts, little pieces get scattered about in the wind. If it's foil, carry it out. You probably know all the other ways of minimizing impact such as keeping soap out of streams, going to the toilet away from water sources. In the winter, you can burn toilet paper, but please don't burn it in the summer. A number of forest fires have been started in that manner. If burning is impossible, mix the paper in with the feces to help in the degradation process.

Snowshoeing

The nice thing about snowshoeing is that it doesn't matter what kind of snow there is—powder, crust, wet snow, icy trails—you can always snowshoe. Unlike skiing, you'll never find yourself with legs wobbling, screaming out of control down an icy slope. You can take your time, and no matter what the snow conditions, falling is not a concern. Many northern Idaho skiers have long known that snowshoeing is a good supplement to cross-country touring. When the snow is cold and powdery, they use cross-country skis and when snow conditions aren't so good, they slip on webs and still have a wonderful weekend.

The other advantage of snowshoes is that the range of trail difficulty expands. With snowshoes, a beginner can go up and down steep trails that he or she wouldn't even begin to think about doing on skis. Throughout the book, those trails which are good for snowshoeing are noted and marked with a snowshoe symbol.

When you use trails which are commonly used by skiers, as a matter of courtesy, you should snowshoe off to the side to keep from obliterating the ski tracks. I don't think it's such a big deal to follow this procedure if only one skier has been through, but if you come upon the ski tracks of several which have been nicely imprinted in the snow, then stay to one side.

We are just starting to see more trails established for snowshoeing and more are likely to be established in the future. At the same time, many of the groomed cross-country ski trail systems are also starting to designate certain trails for snowshoeing. Some groomed systems like those around the Idaho City area welcome snowshoers on all trails, but they ask that snowshoers use the skating lane.

Generally, however, most snowshoers like getting away from groomed trails and going into the backcountry. To assist you, every chapter lists a number of different trails, usually old snowbound roads where you can strike off on your own.

Cross-country Skiing

Since the first version of this book, great improvements have been made in cross-country ski trails throughout the state. There's still room for much more improvement, but we are in better shape now than 20 years ago. In almost every case, it has been an organized group of skiers behind the improvements. Quite often, it's just two or three dedicated people within a community that do all the work, but they have accomplished much because of the backing of an organization, no matter how small or humble that organization might be. If you have needs for trails or access in your area, start a club. Land management agencies are more apt to listen and help you.

On the following pages, I've included a variety of general touring options. Some of the trails are groomed, some are marked

trails and others are snowbound roads or hiking trails. I've tried to
stay away from trails used by snowmobilers, but that isn't always
possible. In some areas a snowmobiling road is the only access
into an area, and in other areas, plowed pullouts are rare and have
to be shared with mechanized users. I have noted where snowmobile use is likely to occur and where it is prohibited.

When you are the first one out after a new snowfall and are
breaking a new trail, try to keep your skis even and shoulder width
apart to begin the process of creating a nice track. If those behind
you stay in the same track and round out the corners, the track will
continue to improve. You can't expect nice ski tracks on steep
sections of trail where skiers have to herringbone or snowplow, but
a great set of ski tracks can be created on rolling and flat areas. Of
course, if you primarily ski at an area which is machine groomed
then you don't have to worry about all this. The grooming machine
does it for you.

One last note for cross-country skiers. Be sure to support the
Idaho Park N' Ski program. This program has done so much for
cross-country skiing in the state. It has made it possible to plow
pullouts where none were being plowed before. It has helped
establish and mark trails and has provided seed money for grooming programs. Even if you don't use Park N' Ski Areas very much,
buy a sticker anyway. They are inexpensive, and they do so much
good in Idaho. Consider it a donation to a healthy Idaho. The more
people we can get on snowshoes and skis the better.

Backcountry Skiing & Snowboarding

While great strides have been made with cross-country touring
trails, backcountry skiers and snowboarders still have a long way to

go. The needs are simple, but hard to attain: plowed pullouts and access to high country. Those who don't understand backcountry skiing or snowboarding, often ask why it is necessary to provide any special facilities. Backcountry users, they say, can go anywhere.

The problem is that backcountry skiers and snowboarders can't start anywhere. They have to start from a parking area and parking is a problem. Often backcountry users are crammed into one parking area at the top of a pass. If more parking pullouts were created in key locations on the way to the top of a pass and on the way back down, use could be dispersed and a greater range of options would be available than presently exists.

The other problem is the fallacy of the they-can-go-anyplace argument. Realistically, backcountry skiers and boarders are pretty much limited to slopes that are within a range of three or four miles

Backcountry snowboarding on Blizzard Mountain near Craters of the Moon National Monument.

from the parking area. It's not possible to go any farther back and still have time to catch a downhill run.

Backcountry users are at the same point cross-country skiers were 20 years ago. Use is increasing greatly, but not much is happening in the way of accessibility. It's possible to get more pullouts plowed—and it may even be possible to gain new access to high country, but it's not going happen unless backcountry users get organized in some manner. The easiest route is to work through existing ski, Nordic or outdoor clubs. Once organized, public agencies like the Forest Service and county officials will start listening.

Lastly, one note about the use of snowmobiles by backcountry skiers and snowboarders. Most snowmobilers don't realize it but they regularly pass by slopes that skiers or boarders would die for. The slopes, however, are so far removed from the nearest road that there's no way a backcountry skier could possibly get there.

A number of skiers and boarders across the state have dabbled with using snowmobiles to access some of those places with mixed success. Snowmobiles bring on a whole new set of problems. Almost everyone who has used snowmobiles for skiing or boarding has horror stories to tell about machines breaking down. Snowmobilers travel in large groups for good reason. They have plenty of help to make repairs and haul out disabled machines. Before you rush out to buy a snowmobile, think it over carefully. You have to love tinkering with them and one isn't enough. You'll need at least two machines in the event that one of them sputters to a stop miles from your vehicle.

Snowboarding

The popularity of snowboards in the backcountry has mushroomed. Granted getting to the top of a slope isn't as easy as skiing, but once there, boarders can handle a far greater range of snow conditions than their skiing brethren. Slope steepness has little bearing either. In the Tetons and elsewhere, boarders have shown they can make cutting edge descents just as handily as skiers.

But there is one aspect which many boarders lag behind skiers and that is a respect and understanding of the nuances of the backcountry. Backcountry boarding comes with the same risks as skiing, and it is important to carry basic survival equipment and know how to use it. It's also important to become trained in avalanche awareness. Don't depend solely on Karma. Check the most recent avalanche forecast and carry transceivers and shovels.

Alpine Skiing

In the following chapters all of Idaho's ski areas are listed. Descriptions of the areas include the type of services available, number of chairlifts, amount of vertical and number of runs. Also included are anecdotes or historical information to help you get a feel for the area. There are some real gems out there. Every so often you should pack up the vehicle and try out a new ski area. No matter where the area is or how far off the beaten trail, you'll find something new and surprising which will make your visit worth it.

Dogs

One of the side benefits of winter recreation is that you can take your dog along. There are, however, places where dogs are not welcome. Generally they are not acceptable on groomed trail systems since they can destroy the grooming. Groomed trails also have greater concentrations of people, and dogs, as you know, can be a nuisance. Lately there has been some loosening of the no dogs policy at some areas and special trails have been established where you can take pets, but be sure to check it out before leaving home.

Ideal places to take your dog are on the many trails listed in this book which are not official ski or snowshoe trails. Most follow snowbound roads or trails, but they are great locations to explore and let the dog run without the worry of bothering others. Dogs also can be taken in all the backcountry skiing and snowboarding areas listed in the book.

Trail Difficulty

This book uses a simple system of classifying trails. For general cross-country skiing and snowshoeing, the scale is: *easy, moderately difficult* and *difficult.*

The same sort of scale is used for backcountry skiing and snowboarding: *easy backcountry, moderately difficult backcountry* and *difficult backcountry.*

The difficulty scale for Alpine skiing (*easiest, more difficult* and *most difficult*) is well known and often reprinted on ski area maps, and I won't elaborate on it here.

It's important to note that trail classifications are always relative. Stormy weather, fog, icy snow packs or heavy wet snow falls can change a trail rating from easy to difficult. Always use trail rating as an approximate assessment of trial difficulty.

Here's a summary of difficulty and how it compares with other rating systems:

General Touring Difficulty Scale (For *cross-country skiing* and *snowshoeing*)

 Easy (Beginner level, or the "easiest" designation used at groomed ski areas.)

Ideal for families or seniors. Generally the trail is flat, and what hills it has are gentle. No sharp turns are found at the bottom of hills.

Occasionally, I also use the rating of *moderately easy.* This means there are a few more hills with a bit more grade. In good snow conditions such as powder or spring corn, these trails are not any more difficult than the easy trails. In icy or crusty snow, however, the hills may be a bit hard for a basic beginning skier to negotiate.

For snowshoeing, the easy and moderately easy trails are a breeze. Even if you're not in the best of shape, you should be able to handle them. Deep snow conditions, of course, can slow you down, but should not cause any problems if you take your time.

 Moderately Difficult (Intermediate level or the "More Difficult" rating used at groomed areas.)

Many of these trails have steep sections on them which require that skiers have the ability to turn and to be able to slow down. Some sharp turns at the bottom of hills may be involved. In icy conditions, the steep sections on moderately difficult trails can be very challenging.

For snowshoers, a moderately difficult rating means that climbing is involved. But, if you don't mind going up and down hills, these are ideal for snowshoeing.

 Difficult (Advanced or the "Most Difficult" rating used at groomed areas.)

From a general ski touring standpoint, these trails are the most difficult. They have very steep hills and skiers must be able to turn reliably in a variety of snow conditions. When the trail is icy, downhill skiing is hair-raising.

Snowshoers who go on these trails need to be in good shape and accustomed to vigorous activity in the outdoors. The climbing can be steep and sustained.

Backcountry Difficulty Scale (For *backcountry skiing* or *snowboarding*):

 Easy Backcountry (Beginning telemark skills, intermediate Alpine skiing skills or intermediate snowboarding skills.)

Since backcountry areas are not groomed and there's no ski patrol out there, Alpine skiers and snowboarders should first hone their skills at an Alpine area. Telemark skiers should gain experience on practice slopes close to the road first before venturing into the backcountry. Avalanche potential on easy backcountry slopes is generally low, but you should have an awareness of what constitutes avalanche terrain and should carry basic winter survival equipment.

Moderately Difficult Backcountry (Intermediate telemark or Alpine skiing skills. Intermediate snowboarding skills.)

This is avalanche terrain. In addition to having solid and practiced intermediate skills, you should have taken a course in avalanche safety. Backcountry survival equipment, avalanche transceivers and a shovel are mandatory for every member of the party. You should know how to use a topographic map and compass and be able to navigate in adverse weather conditions. Remember there's no ski patrol in the backcountry. You are on your own and need to be able to take care of yourself in an emergency.

Difficult Backcountry (Advanced to very advanced telemarking, Alpine skiing or snowboarding)

These are the steepest slopes. Some slopes may require basic mountaineering skills and the ability to stop oneself with an ice axe. In some snow conditions, a fall may be fatal. Excellent knowledge of avalanches is required. Survival gear and avalanche transceiver and shovels are a given. Generally these slopes are best skied or snowboarded in spring when avalanche activity can be better judged

Trail Symbols

In the chapters which follow, symbols are placed off to the side of the text for quick identification of the main features of a particular trail. Where there is not enough room to place all the appropriate symbols, one or two of the most important are included while all other trail features are identified in the accompanying description. The symbols are:

 Snowshoeing trails

 Backcountry snowboarding area

 Alpine ski area

 Marked cross-country ski trail

 Groomed trails for cross-country skiing

 Idaho Park N' Ski stickers required for these trails

 Dogs are OK on this trail

 Yurts, backcountry cabins or huts available in this area

Map Symbols

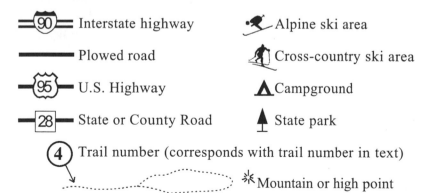

Dotted lines indicate cross-country ski trails, snowshoe trails or backcountry ski and snowboard routes. (Note that since the maps cover a sizeable area, the scale used for trails is enlarged slightly relative to the map's overall scale. This helps to more clearly show general trail direction and the overall layout of the trail.)

Overview Map

The map on the facing page shows the locations of all 14 regional areas covered in this book. One of the regional areas, the High Desert Mosaic, is a grouping of four separate areas (Fairfield, Twin Falls-Burley, Arco-Craters of the Moon and Spencer-Kilgore) which are widely dispersed in the southern half of Idaho. The rest of the regions shown on the map cover major cross-country skiing, snowshoeing and backcountry areas in Idaho, the Grand Tetons, Yellowstone and important bordering areas with Montana, Wyoming, Washington and Oregon.

Long poles, wood skis and fresh powder: West Slope of the Tetons, circa 1975.

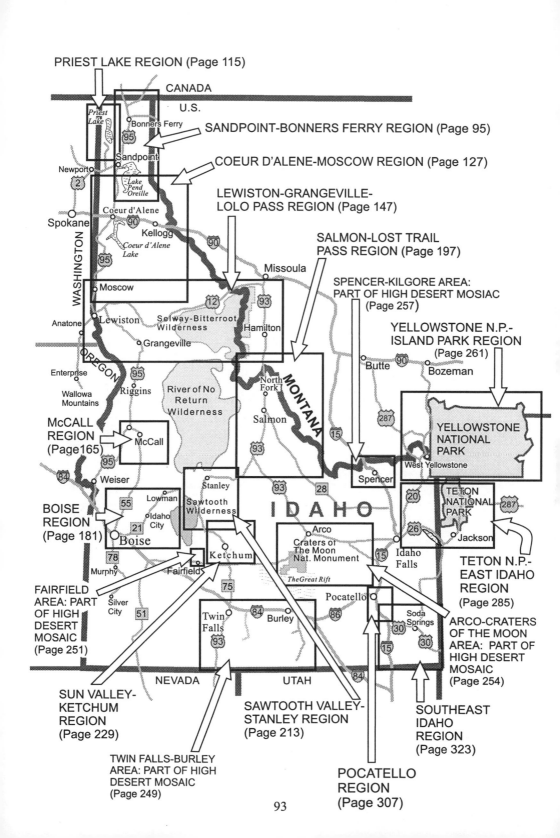

PRIEST LAKE REGION (Page 115)

CANADA

U.S.

SANDPOINT-BONNERS FERRY REGION (Page 95)

COEUR D'ALENE-MOSCOW REGION (Page 127)

LEWISTON-GRANGEVILLE-
LOLO PASS REGION (Page 147)

SALMON-LOST TRAIL
PASS REGION (Page 197)

SPENCER-KILGORE AREA:
PART OF HIGH DESERT MOSIAC
(Page 257)

YELLOWSTONE N.P.-
ISLAND PARK REGION
(Page 261)

McCALL
REGION
(Page165)

BOISE
REGION
(Page 181)

TETON N.P.-
EAST IDAHO
REGION
(Page 285)

FAIRFIELD
AREA: PART OF
HIGH
DESERT
MOSAIC
(Page 251)

ARCO-CRATERS
OF THE MOON
AREA: PART OF
HIGH DESERT
MOSAIC
(Page 254)

SUN VALLEY-
KETCHUM
REGION
(Page 229)

SAWTOOTH VALLEY-
STANLEY REGION
(Page 213)

SOUTHEAST
IDAHO
REGION
(Page 323)

TWIN FALLS-BURLEY
AREA: PART OF HIGH
DESERT MOSAIC
(Page 249)

POCATELLO
REGION
(Page 307)

93

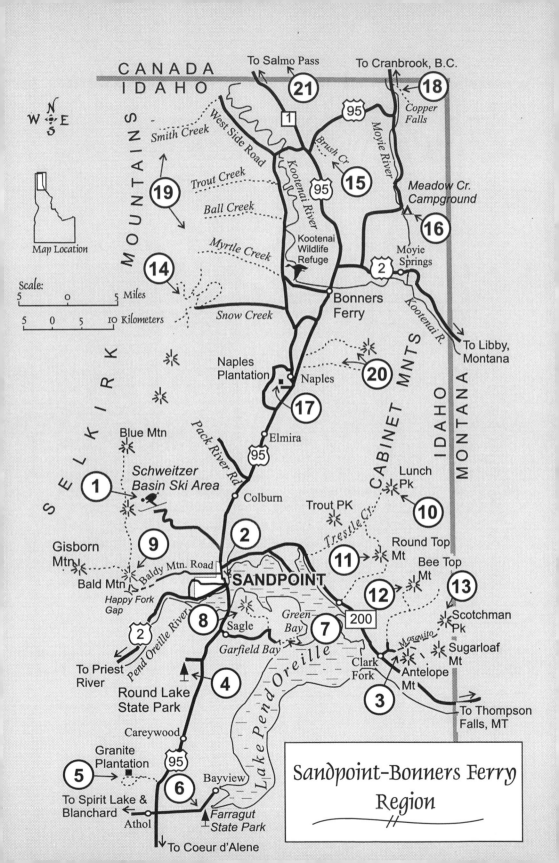

CHAPTER 6
SANDPOINT-BONNERS FERRY REGION

Area Covered: Idaho Panhandle including Sandpoint, Bonners Ferry, Hope, Clark Fork and nearby towns.

THERE'S a special sense of ownership among residents of North Idaho. My friends there and those that I've interviewed, don't just say they're from Idaho. They say that they are from *North* Idaho. It may be because the Panhandle is such a long, long way from the political power center of West Central Idaho and it's a subtle expression of independence. But there's more than just distance that is cause for a North Idaho identity. Certainly, landscape plays a role. The cool forested Selkirks and Cabinet Mountains are starkly different from the high desert of southern Idaho.

What an overpowering landscape it is in the winter. Reminiscent of a fjord in Norway, Lake Pend Oreille stretches between land which rises 4,000 feet on either side. Much of the skiing in this region takes place high in the Selkirk mountains, to the west of the lake. The one reliable access—and there is only one reliable plowed high access in the entire panhandle—is the Schweitzer Basin Ski Area, 11 miles (18 km) northwest of Sandpoint. Schweitzer maintains several kilometers of groomed cross-country ski trails and excellent backcountry terrain can be accessed from the area. Plus, of course, the Alpine, board and Nordic downhill couldn't be better at North Idaho's premier ski area.

Lower down, in midwinter, when there are several inches of snow in and around Sandpoint, the shoreline of Lake Pend Oreille, itself, offers some delightful cross-country skiing suitable for any ability. During the winter months, the lake level drops several feet creating a wide beach ideal for touring. Generally, the southern portion of the lake is not suitable because of the rocky cliffs along

the shore. The northern portion of the lake, however, offers many
locations. The most convenient access to the lake from Sandpoint
is the City Beach where parking is plowed. Other locations suggested by Sandpoint skiers include Garfield Bay, southeast of
Sandpoint; Sunnyside Area, on the north end of the lake; and the
David Thompson Game Preserve, northwest of Clark Fork.

North of Sandpoint near Bonners Ferry, one plowed road
provides access to the mid elevations. This is Snow Creek. The
Forest Service has been clearing the Snow Creek Road to a parking
area which serves as a trailhead to marked ski trails and snowmobile trails. The area, however, is not always a sure bet. Funding
from Park and Ski permits and snowmobile registrations hasn't
been reliable enough to support the high cost of plowing during
heavy winters, and you'll want to call the Bonners Ranger Station
before heading out.

There are other undeveloped low elevation areas that skiers
may want to try in the northern tip of the Panhandle. One is the
Kootenai National Wildlife Refuge just to the west of Bonners
Ferry or the Naples Plantation Area near Naples. The plantation is
especially attractive with its numerous small, open hills for practicing downhill techniques.

Snowshoeing is good throughout the region. In fact, because
of steep grades on many of the mountain roads and heavy trees and
underbrush in low elevations, snowshoes really come into their
own, and they are the ideal method for getting into the Panhandle
backcountry. Nearly all the trails suggested in this chapter, except
for the groomed ski trails at Schweitzer, make great snowshoe
trails.

For the long distance backcountry skier, West Side Road, west
of Bonners Ferry running along the eastern base of the Selkirks,
offers access to several snowbound roads which penetrate the
range. Smith Creek, near the Canadian border; Trout Creek, which
is the access to some of the highest peaks in the Selkirks; Ball
Creek, Myrtle Creek, and Snow Creek are all examples of tours off
the West Side Road. They can be utilized for day trips but are
particularly useful to the tourer planning overnight trips. Facilitat-
ing passage through the tangle of lower elevation brush, these
access roads lead the experienced tourer to the freedom of open
snowfields and off-trail skiing in the upper Selkirks.

From Schweitzer Basin, overlooking Lake Pend Oreille.

Besides Schweitzer Basin, the nearest high country backcountry touring to the city of Sandpoint is Bald Mountain, located just west of town. Bald Mountain's open ridges and high Alpine country overlooking Sandpoint and Lake Pend Oreille is fine fodder for free-heel skiing. Even though part of Bald Mountain Road is plowed, be prepared for a slog. It's still a long way up to the top.

From Bald Mountain, an advanced backcountry tour can be made by staying near the upper ridge of the Selkirks and traveling to the north, reaching Schweitzer and continuing beyond. It's the "continuing beyond" which has captured the imagination of Panhandle backcountry skiers. One of the great Idaho ski traverses is the route that follows the Selkirk crest from Bald Mountain to the north all the way to Salmo Pass in Canada. A part of the route was first attempted in 1975 by 65 year old Russ Keene, but he and his party were forced down by storms and high winds in the Sundance Burn area. Other attempts were made. Finally the whole route was completed in 1994 by Canadian skiers, but more about that later.

First, let's take a look further back in time, over a half of a century ago at a match up between skiers and snowshoers.

The Tales . . .

*T*O THE EAST of Sandpoint, in the Cabinet Mountains, the open bowls of 6,149-foot Round Top rise gracefully above forested lowlands. One of those who found a special attraction in Round Top was Ross Hall who, unarguably, had a keen eye for mountain landscapes. Ross was one of North Idaho's most famous and versatile photographers. He died in 1990, but his collection of photographs which span 50 years beginning with the depression, is a powerful and illuminating portrait of Panhandle life and the countryside which so influences that life.

In 1947, Ross Hall got a close look at the inviting slopes of Round Top.

"We were looking for an area to develop as a ski area," Ross explained to me in an interview. "Not knowing much about skiing ourselves, we invited two professional skiers from Washington to help us in our search."

The two men Ross invited from Washington would use skis, while he and five others from the Sandpoint area would use snow-shoes in their explorations of Round Top Mountain. At some point in the preparations, someone suggested making the outing a bit more interesting: how about a race, a race to the top, pitting skiers against snowshoers?

None in the party was going to back out of a little friendly competition, and before sunrise one morning in February of 1947, the race was on. Since the race was uphill, Ross figured that on snowshoes, his group could easily make better time than the skiers who would be forced to herringbone and side step their way up.

He hadn't counted on skins. The snowshoe team made a gallant attempt covering the 7-mile, 4,000-feet elevation gain in good time. But with climbing skins strapped to the bottom of their skis, the swift and experienced skiers reached the Round Top lookout tower 20 minutes before the first snowshoer.

Despite the outcome of the race, the skiers and snowshoers spent a beautiful day exploring the upper snowfields of Round Top

Mountain. The Washington skiers were impressed, finding some promising possibilities for a future ski area. In the coming years other areas were explored, and eventually, the site finally chosen was Schweitzer Basin.

What happened on the way down? Well, it wasn't too good for the snowshoers. The *Sandpoint News-Bulletin* reported later that "the pro skiers were probably in Spokane by the time the snowshoers got off the mountain by moonlight." ☐

Gene Klein

The Trails . . .

SANDPOINT AREA

1   **Schweitzer Basin Ski Area**—*Alpine Ski Area. Alpine, Nordic downhill and snowboarding. All abilities. All services: food, lodging, rentals, instruction, night skiing.* Alpine skiing in the Sandpoint area got started with a rope tow powered by an old Dodge motor on Pine Street Hill, 2 miles west of Sandpoint. Between 1947 and 1949, there was also some Alpine Skiing taking place on Talache Mountain. In both areas, however, the snow wasn't reliable, and while the Pine Street and Talache Mountain areas provided a temporary fix for skiers, the search was on for a better location with much more snow.

Mountains explored included Cape Horn near Bayview; Bald Mountain, west of Sandpoint; and Trestle Peak, Bee Top and Round Top, east of the lake. After extensive searching of the Selkirks and Cabinet Mountains, the area finally chosen for Idaho's northernmost ski area was right out Sandpoint's back door, Schweitzer Basin.

There's an interesting story behind the name Schweitzer. Schweitzer was a hermit of Swiss origins who lived in a cabin near where Schweitzer Creek crosses the Burlington Northern tracks. In the late spring of 1893, Mrs. L. D. Farmin, the wife of the first agent of the Great Northern Railroad, was riding home on her pony. Schweitzer, wearing a Swiss Army uniform and holding a gun, appeared from out of the brush and took the bridle. He walked the pony and the frightened woman for a quarter of a mile and then disappeared into the trees.

Mrs. Farmin reported the encounter, and when the sheriff visited Schweitzer's cabin, he found the walls of the cabin festooned with the skins of a number of neighborhood cats which over the past winter had turned up missing. One of the skins was identified as the pet cat of Mrs. Ignatz whose husband ran a general store.

Apparently, Schweitzer had a penchant for feline stew. Sometime later he was declared demented and committed to an institution.

As of this writing Schweitzer Basin has 2,400 feet vertical, 55 named runs consisting of 20% beginner, 40% intermediate, 35% advance and 5% expert. Average annual snow fall is 300 inches. The longest run is 2.7 miles and there are 2,350 acres of skiable terrain.

Schweitzer is located 11 miles northwest of Sandpoint. To reach it, drive north of Sandpoint on US 95. About one mile out of town, turn off on the ski area access road, well-marked with highway signs, and follow it to the ski area.

1 **Schweitzer Basin Cross-country Skiing Trails**—*Moderately difficult. Groomed cross-country trail system.* For a spectacular view and a cross-country ski workout, Schweitzer is the place. The ski area maintains 6 miles (10 km) of cross-country ski trails which are regularly groomed for skating and diagonal striding. At this writing, there was no charge for the users of the trails, but grooming is expensive and that could change. Whether there's a fee or not, it is a delight to have a place so close to Sandpoint with regularly groomed trails throughout the winter. The trails are accessed from the Alpine Village and begin near the base of chair 4. To help orient yourself, pick up a ski area map from the rental shop.

 Schweitzer Basin Backcountry—*Moderate to difficult backcountry terrain.* Schweitzer Basin doesn't condone it, but a good many people do start from the parking lot and ski and board in the backcountry surrounding Schweitzer. It is only natural that Schweitzer would become a sought out starting point since it is the only reliable high access in the Panhandle.

Backcountry skiers and backcountry boarders need to shift gears here. This is a high Alpine environment with all the attendant risks. Avalanche transceivers, shovels, maps, compass and basic survival gear should always be carried.

If you want to backcountry ski or snowboard here, you should first check with the ski area. If access is allowed, the **South Ridge** of Schweitzer serves as the route to the top. The distance from the base of the area to the top of Schweitzer Basin's Lift No. 1, via the South Ridge, is 2 miles (3 km) with an elevation gain of 1,700 feet (519 meters). From here, the Selkirk crest can be followed to the south or north. The route to the south drops 500 feet (153 meters) and follows a beautiful open ridge towards **Bald Mountain**, above Sandpoint. The route to the north drops to a saddle, climbs the **North Peak** of Schweitzer, falls off to another saddle and climbs to the top of **Blue Mountain** at an elevation of 6,662 feet (2,032 meters), 5 miles (8 km) from the start. Plenty of backcountry downhill can be found along either route.

2 **Shoreline of Lake Pend Oreille**—*Flat, easy terrain, suitable for families.* The water level of Lake Pend Oreille drops in the winter, opening

up a wide beach. In the midwinter when several inches have accumulated, the shoreline makes for a delightful ski tour—and is an especially beautiful tour on a moonlight night. The skiing is **easy** and suitable for families and seniors.

The shoreline can be accessed at several locations, but the most convenient to Sandpoint is the **City Beach**. To find it, simply watch for the sign on US 95 near the business district of Sandpoint or ask someone in town. The road is plowed and parking is available.

The idea of the tour is to ski from City Beach to the north, following the beach along Lake Pend Oreille. Right off the bat, there is one obstacle. On the north edge of the City Beach property is a narrow spit of land which serves as the City's water intake. You'll have to walk or ski around it *on the shore side.* Once around the spit, however, the skiing is straight forward and you can continue to contour around the lake as far as desired.

Other examples of locations of tours along the lake suggested by area skiers include the **Sunnyside** area, 6 miles east of Sandpoint on Idaho 200, and the **David Thompson Game Preserve**, 7 miles northwest of Clark Fork on Idaho 200.

3 **Antelope-Sugarloaf Area**—*Snowbound road. Easy to moderately difficult. Dogs OK.* This area is located 2 miles northeast of Clark Fork. Drive out of Clark Fork on **Mosquito Creek Road** (which also provides access to Scotchman Peak) to its junction with snowbound road leading to **Antelope** and **Sugarloaf Mountains**. The tour follows the snowbound road. The area seems to accumulate greater snow depths than other valley areas and is suitable for skiers and snowshoers of **all abilities**.

4 **Round Lake State Park**—*Groomed cross-country ski trail. Easy terrain, suitable for families. Toilets.* The turnoff to Round Lake State Park is located 9 miles south of Sandpoint on the west side of US 95. Snow conditions vary, but skiing is good when several inches of snow accumulate in midwinter. The trail encircles the lake and is groomed when there's enough snow. This is a wonderful place for **families** and also has winter camping, ice skating, ice fishing and a sledding hill. A Park N' Ski pass is required or pay the park entrance fee.

5 **Granite Plantation**—*Easy terrain. Snowbound roads and off trail skiing and snowshoeing. Dogs OK.* The Plantation is located 2.6 miles north of the junction of US 95 and Idaho 54 at Athol, or 22 miles south of Sandpoint on the west side of US 95. This is a pretty area suitable for **beginners** when covered with several inches of snow. The tour follows the snowbound road into the ponderosa pine stands making up the Granite Plantation. Off-trail skiing and side trips are possible.

6 **Farragut State Park**—*Easy to moderately easy terrain. Marked and groomed cross-country ski trail system. Toilets.* The park is located 25 miles south of Sandpoint or 20 miles north of Coeur d'Alene. The turnoff to the park is well-marked with highway signs. At the junction of US 95 and Idaho 54 at Athol, follow Idaho 54, 4 miles to the east to the park.

The park's 10 km (6 mile) trail system lies on the south side of Highway 54 and begins from the park headquarters. The trails are marked and groomed. Snow conditions are variable, but during times of sufficient snow accumulation, Farragut has some excellent track skiing.

7 **Mineral Point-Green Bay (Also known as Lost Lake Trail)**—*Snowbound roads. Moderately difficult. Dogs OK.* Mineral Point used to be a marked ski trail, but because of unreliable snow the Forest Service no longer maintains it. Nevertheless, the trails have great views of the lake, and when there's sufficient snow pack, skiers and snowshoers should keep this on their list of places to go.

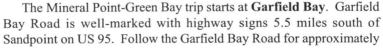

The Mineral Point-Green Bay trip starts at **Garfield Bay**. Garfield Bay Road is well-marked with highway signs 5.5 miles south of Sandpoint on US 95. Follow the Garfield Bay Road for approximately

8 miles. Watch for the first left turn after Garfield Bay Campground. The old ski parking area was located up this road .2 miles in a gravel pit. The route begins across from the gravel pit on the snowbound Camp Bay Road (No. 532). The parking situation may change, but you should be able find a place to pull off in the general vicinity.

Approximately 2.8 miles (4.5 km) from the start of Camp Bay Road is a 1.9 mile (3 km) loop that can be taken into Lost Lake Road. Since logging occurs in this area, roads can change and it is advisable to carry a recent Forest Service map.

8 **Gold Hill Road**—*Snowbound road. Moderately difficult. Great snow-shoe trip. Dogs OK.* Access to Gold Hill is off **Garfield Bay Road**.

The turnoff to Garfield Bay is located 5.5 miles south of Sandpoint on the east side of US 95. Drive another 5.5 miles east of Garfield Bay Road from its junction with US 95. Watch for a switchback in the road just before Garfield Bay Road begins to drop down into Garfield Bay on Lake Pend Oreille. Gold Hill Road (No. 2642) joins Garfield Bay Road at this point.

A couple of residences are found along the first 2 miles of Gold Hill Road, and you'll want to find a place to park out of their way. The route follows the snowbound portion of Gold Hill Road to the north along a ridge and eventually climbs to the summit of **Gold Hill** where you are treated to a scenic view of Lake Pend Oreille. Several inches of snow accumulation in valley regions are necessary in order to under-take this trip.

9 **Bald Mountain**—*Access via snowbound roads, then open off-trail high country. Moderate to difficult backcountry.* The trip to Bald Mountain is made via **Baldy Road**, located on the north edge of Sandpoint. To reach the road, drive from Sandpoint to the west on Cedar or Division Street. Take a right on Division and continue a short distance until reaching Baldy Mountain Road where you take a left. Drive to the west on Baldy Mountain Road as far as the road is plowed. Note that the last section of Baldy Mountain Road is plowed for local residence traffic, and it is wise to check in town about road conditions before heading up. Moreover, once you reach the end of the plowed portion of the Baldy Mountain Road, make sure you find a parking spot so that you are out of the way.

The route follows the snowbound Baldy Mountain Road to the west, until reaching the main access road leading to the top of Bald Mountain just after **Happy Fork Gap**. Follow the main access road to the sum-mit. From the summit and associated ridge system, you'll find plenty of **downhill terrain** for cutting turns.

Gene Klein

High on the crest of the Selkirks at sunrise.

You'll also find at the top high Alpine conditions with associated strong winds and cornice buildup. Avalanche dangers exist and shovels and transceivers should be carried..

Bald Mountain is the starting point for two longer trips. The first, and one of the most interesting high backcountry routes near Sandpoint, is a trip that can be made towards the top of Schweitzer Basin by following the ridge system to the northeast.

Another interesting trip, best done as an overnighter, follows the Baldy Ridge system to the northwest towards **Gisborne Mountain** within the Priest River Experimental Forest. The Experimental Forest is accessible by vehicle in the winter months via Priest River, and you'll need to arrange to have a shuttle vehicle pick-up.

10 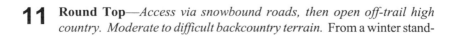 **Lunch Peak**—*Access via snowbound roads, then open off-trail high country. Moderate to difficult backcountry.* Lunch Peak at 6,414 feet (1,955 meters) is in the Cabinet Mountains on the east side of Lake Pend Oreille. Access to Lunch Peak is via **Trestle Creek**, 13 miles east of Sandpoint on the north side of Idaho 200. Drive up Trestle Creek until it is no longer plowed. Park where your vehicle is out of the way. The tour leads into beautiful subalpine fir country, but it is a very long trip into Lunch Peak and is best done as an overnight excursion.

11 **Round Top**—*Access via snowbound roads, then open off-trail high country. Moderate to difficult backcountry terrain.* From a winter standpoint, Round Top (6,149 feet or 1,874 meters) has an interesting history. Early on there was some occasional snowshoe travel in the area by trappers. In 1931, its winter charms captured a wider audience when Matt Schmitt snowshoed up Strong Creek and brought back the first winter photographs of the area. His interest piqued and eager to take some of his own photographs, Ross Hall and two other men accompanied Schmitt to the top of Round Top on snowshoes in 1933. It was frigid day and one of the cameras froze but more spectacular photographs came back. Later, it was explored as a possible Alpine ski area and was the site of the famous snowshoer-skier race held in 1947 which was described earlier in this chapter.

Obviously, with all the interest by photographers and its potential for an Alpine ski area, Round Top holds a special attraction for skiers and snowshoers.

Be prepared, however, the climb is steep and taxing. The **Strong Creek** access, the traditional access to the mountain, is a 4,000 foot (1,219 meters) ascent over an 8 mile (13 km) distance. To reach Strong Creek, drive to Hope, east of Sandpoint on Idaho 200. One home is at the beginning of Strong Creek Road, and Bob Norton of the Panhandle Forest Service suggests that you park near the cemetery in Hope and walk up to Strong Creek Road to avoid blocking the road.

Trestle Creek, 13 miles east of Sandpoint, also provides access to Round Top. Skiers and snowshoers utilizing this route have the added advantage of beginning the climb to Round Top at a higher elevation. Once at Round Top, a traverse can be done by following the **Round Top-Bee Top Trail** which follows a Cabinet ridge system to the south and southeast from the summit. The traverse, of course, requires the trip to be done as an overnighter, but it is an aesthetically appealing route overlooking Lake Pend Oreille and is the eastern counterpart of the Bald Mountain-Schweitzer route on the west side of the lake.

12 **Bee Top Mountain**—*Access via snowbound road, then open off-trail high country. Moderate to difficult backcountry terrain.* Located to the southeast of Round Top, Bee Top Mountain (6,212 feet or 1,893 meters) was also reconnoitered for a possible ski area and is considered by some of the old-timers as the area's number two ski mountain in Bonner County. Access is obtained north of Clark Fork, via the remote and rugged Bee Top Trail.

13 **Scotchman Peak**—*Access via snowbound road, then open off-trail high country. Moderate to difficult backcountry terrain.* Scotchman Peak, located in the front range of the Cabinet Mountains, is an impressive peak rising to an elevation of 7,009 feet (2,138 meters). Access to the summit is via the steep **Mosquito Creek Road**, located 2 miles northeast of Clark Fork. The upper part of the plowed portion of the road is a single lane serving private homes along the road. Unless you are able to work out arrangements with a home owner, it's probably best that you either walk the road or undertake the trip in the spring when the road has melted out opening up better parking.

While it's possible to do the trip in one, long day, Russ Keene (see page 68 for Russ's story) highly recommends doing it as an overnighter. He nearly killed a military friend of his who insisted on doing the trip in one day. On another trip that Russ Keene took to Scotchman Peak, the

hut on the summit of the mountain was so completely encased in rime that it seemed like it was just an extension of the mountain. Russ leveled out a spot on top of the hut, piled up a few snow blocks and spent the night out in the open with a member of the party he referred to as "the hippie." It was a beautiful clear night, but the next morning the wind was roaring and "the hippie" and other members of the party nearly had to crawl off the summit on their hands and knees. Russ, of course, loved it.

BONNERS FERRY AREA

14 **Snow Creek**—*Marked and occasionally groomed cross-country ski trails. Easy to moderately difficult terrain. Park N' Ski area.* To reach

Snow Creek, drive north from Sandpoint on Highway 95. Exit the highway at Naples (located on the left or west side of the highway), and drive straight through Naples and continue west for approximately 5 miles

until reaching West Side Road. Turn left (west) onto the West Side Road and follow it for two miles until coming to Snow Creek Road (No. 402). The winter recreation parking area, shared with snowmobilers, is located 9 miles up Snow Creek Road.

The Forest Service marks and occasionally grooms two cross-country ski trails in the area. One is a fairly **easy loop**, and the other is an out-and-back trail of **moderate difficulty** which goes to **Cooks Lake**. The trails pass through meadows, heavy forest and offer views of the high Selkirk crest.

This wonderful area may not always be open, however. It's expensive to plow the road, and revenues from the Park N' Ski and snowmobile funds don't always pay the bill. It's a good idea to give the Bonners Ferry Ranger Station a call before heading up to Snow Creek to check on its status.

15 **Brush Lake Road**—*Snowbound road. Easy to moderately easy terrain. Dogs OK.* This tour is located on the east side of US 95, approximately

1 mile north of the junction of US 95 and Idaho 1. The **moderately easy** tour follows a snowbound road for a 2 mile (3 km) tour into Brush Lake.

Gene Klein

The Selkirks from the Twins to Chimney Rock.

16

Meadow Creek Campground Area—*Campground and other snowbound roads. Easy to moderately easy terrain. Good area for families. Dogs OK.* Skiing friends of mine from Bonners Ferry, Berneice and Chuck Morgen, who I met when researching the first version of *Ski Trails*, really enjoy the Meadow Creek Campground area for family skiing. It's limited in size, but it's just right for **children**. Plus, it's a pretty place with the scenic Moyie River adjoining the campground

To reach the area, drive north out of Bonners Ferry on US 95. At the junction of US 95 and US 2 just out of Bonners Ferry, take a right on US 2 heading east toward Moyie Springs. Drive 2 miles, watching for signs which indicate the road leading to Meadow Creek Campground on the left (north) side of the highway. Turn onto Meadow Creek Road and drive 11 miles to the Forest Service sign marking Meadow Creek Campground. The snowbound campground access road is located on the right just past the point where the railroad tracks cross the plowed road. Park nearby.

For a look at the Moyie River, one can ski down into the campground. The beautiful setting of the river, flowing through the thickly forested canyon, provides a splendid location for lunch. For a longer trip, you can ski out the snowbound roads leading out of the campground.

17 **Naples Plantation**—*Snowbound roads and off-trail exploring. Easy to moderately easy terrain. Great area for families. Dogs OK.* This is

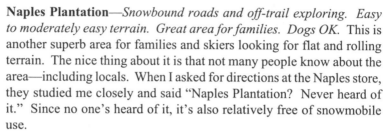

another superb area for families and skiers looking for flat and rolling terrain. The nice thing about it is that not many people know about the area—including locals. When I asked for directions at the Naples store, they studied me closely and said "Naples Plantation? Never heard of it." Since no one's heard of it, it's also relatively free of snowmobile use.

To reach the area, look for County Road 11, which is located .3 miles south of the turnoff to Naples on US 95. If you are heading to Bonners Ferry, County Road 11 enters the highway from the left (west) side of the highway. Turn onto the road and drive west for .8 mile. At this point, there should be an access road on the right (north) side of the county road. This road leads to one of two parts of the Forest Service land making up Naples Plantation. There is no developed parking and you need to pull your vehicle off the side of the road so it doesn't block the path of any residents that live in the area.

The tour follows the snowbound roads which wind through the plantation. There are occasional open hillsides, and since the trees are kept thinned, off-trail skiing and off-trail **snowshoeing** is possible.

You can access another portion of the Plantation by continuing down the county road another .3 miles. A spur road leads off to the left (south) which leads into an area with the same type of **rolling terrain**.

18 **Copper Falls**—*Snowbound road. Moderate terrain.* Copper Falls is located 1 mile south of the Canadian Border on the east side of US 95. The tour follows the snowbound road for a 3-mile (5 km) trip into the falls.

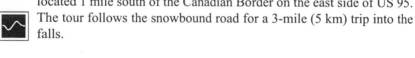

19 **Selkirk Mountains Access**—*Access via snowbound road, then open off-trail high country. Moderate to difficult backcountry terrain.* Access to the northern Selkirks is found off West Side Road. To reach it drive west of Bonners Ferry, 6 miles on the Riverside Road until reaching the West Side Road. Snow Creek, Myrtle Creek, Ball Creek, Trout Creek and Smith Creek off West Side Road allow high access into the Selkirks. Trout Creek, in particular, provides entrance to some of the highest peaks in the Selkirks.

20 **Cabinet Mountains Access**—*Access via snowbound road, then open off-trail high country. Moderate to difficult backcountry.* **Twenty Mile**

Creek, 1 mile north of Naples on US 95 and Brown Creek Road, 2 miles north of Naples on US 95, both provide access into the Cabinets. **Brown Creek Road** climbs to the summit of Black Mountain at an elevation of 6,096 feet (1,859 meters).

OTHER AREAS

21 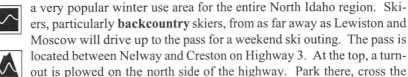 **Salmo Pass**—*Terrain for all abilities. Often good snow conditions and terrific backcountry skiing.* Salmo Pass in southern British Columbia is a very popular winter use area for the entire North Idaho region. Skiers, particularly **backcountry** skiers, from as far away as Lewiston and Moscow will drive up to the pass for a weekend ski outing. The pass is located between Nelway and Creston on Highway 3. At the top, a turnout is plowed on the north side of the highway. Park there, cross the highway and ski to the south, following a snowbound road. It won't take long before you find yourself in some mighty fine ski country.

Stoneridge—Stoneridge is a resort and condominium complex in Blanchard near the Idaho-Washington line, southwest of Sandpoint. When sufficient snow builds up, the resort grooms a system of trails for cross-country skiing. Information is available from Stoneridge, Blanchard, ID 83804. Phone: (208) 437-2451.

Gene Klein

Highway to heaven: Salmo Pass. Just over the border in Canada, it's a great area for all abilities and has easily accessible backcountry terrain.

Baldy Mountain Jim: Keeper of the Faith

THE IDEA of a traverse of the Selkirks from Sandpoint to the Canadian border has always held a fascination among Panhandle skiers. The trip wasn't done in its entirety until 1994, but of all the early exploratory Selkirk traverse trips, one of the most memorable was the one that took place in 1985. The 1985 party consisted of skiing and climbing guide, Gene Klein, and one of North Idaho's most dedicated ski traditionalists, Baldy Mountain Jim.

Baldy Mountain Jim, as described by Klein, is a person transposed from another era. With a long beard, a back-to-the-land ethic and a weakness for Harley Davidson T-shirts, Jim could have been a mountain man in a previous life. There is certainly no doubt that he is one of the last of a dying breed who has remained steadfastly true to skiing's roots.

For years he has skied on wood skis. Klein figures that was the reason they became skiing companions. When he first arrived in Sandpoint, Klein was using wood skis and the two men hit it off well.

As Klein spent more time perfecting his skills at the Schweitzer Basin Ski Area and the surrounding backcountry, he switched to new and more responsive fiberglass skis. Baldy Mountain Jim, however, never strayed from his wood skis. Sometime much later, Jim called Klein and explained to him that he had just bought a new pair of skis.

"Oh, what are they?" Gene asked, excited that his good friend had finally moved into the modern age of skiing.

"They're Holmenkollens," Jim replied.

"Holmenkollens!" Gene's level of excitement dropped a notch. Holmenkollens were wood skis. But then he became hopeful again. Maybe his friend had bought a more contemporary model with a fiberglass base or perhaps he had decided upon a model with metal edges. Surely Jim would want the extra security of metal edges when he was out skiing on an exposed frozen ridge somewhere. Gene asked expectantly, "What kind of edges do they have?"

"Walnut," Jim replied laconically.

Gene sighed.

On one of their outings, Gene and a few friends talked Baldy Mountain Jim into leaving his wood skis and old worn, flexible boots behind, and they outfitted him in fiberglass skis with a nice pair of rigid boots. Jim made the best of it, but when the trip was over he couldn't wait to get back in his old equipment. On future trips when asked if he'd like to try some new high-tech equipment, he would respectfully decline, saying that it would be "cheating."

On the 1985 attempt to traverse part of the Selkirks, Gene and Baldy Mountain Jim drove up the Pack River Road as far as they could. It took two days to ski to an east-facing bowl high on Mt. Harrison. The route from there to the north was no picnic. It led through steep, precipitous country and Gene realized that they lacked the skills to travel through it. Exhausted from carrying heavy packs, they stopped at the base of the bowl on Harrison near a stand of huge hemlock trees.

"We went into this grove of trees," Gene remembers, "The branches were arching over and creating this little serene pocket of refuge. It was almost like going indoors."

Outside of the hemlocks, it was the typical stormy, Panhandle weather. They looked longingly at the refuge of the trees, and then Baldy Mountain Jim made a pronouncement: "There's no reason to go any place else. This is the perfect place to ski. This is the perfect place to live."

And so they got no further, and for the next several days, the protective stand of Hemlocks became their idyllic home. They'd ski the bowl during the day and warm themselves beside a fire at night. The fire worked it's way into the snow, and around it, they built terraces. From the terraces protruded sticks, festooned with drying mittens and hats.

Once while tucked into their refuge, Gene mused about the weather outside. Baldy Mountain Jim ambled away, poked his head out of the ancient trees looking around and reported back: "snowing lightly."

Gene hasn't seen a lot of Baldy Mountain Jim lately. As far as he knows, he still skis on his Holmenkollens and dresses in woolen pants and Mackinaw. Gene is long past the wood and wool stage, happily layering himself in Patagonia and Goretex and cutting turns on state of the art skis. Over a cup of coffee one morning in Sandpoint, Gene pondered over why he and Baldy Mountain Jim hadn't done any recent skiing adventures together, and coming to a conclusion, he grinned: "He probably thinks I've been corrupted." □

Gene Klein

Baldy Mountain Jim and Gene.

Resources . . .

National Forest Lands in the Sandpoint Area
Sandpoint Ranger District of the Panhandle National Forest—Office located in the Federal Building in Sandpoint. Address: 1500 Highway 2, Sandpoint, Idaho 83864. Phone: (208) 263-5111.

National Forest Lands in the Bonners Ferry Area
Bonners Ferry District of the Panhandle National Forest—Office located on US 95 on the south edge of Bonners Ferry. Address: Route 1, PO Box 390, Bonners Ferry, Idaho 83805. Phone: (208) 267-5661.

Farragut State Park
Park Headquarters, Farragut State Park— Address: 13400 E. Ranger Road, Athol, Idaho 83801. Phone: (208) 683-2425.

Round Lake State Park
Park Headquarters, Round Lake State Park—Address: PO Box 170, Sagle, Idaho 83860. Phone: (208) 263-3489

Alpine Ski Area
Schweitzer Mountain Resort—Address: PO Box 815, Sandpoint, Idaho 83864. Phone: (208) 263-9555 or 1-800-831-8810.

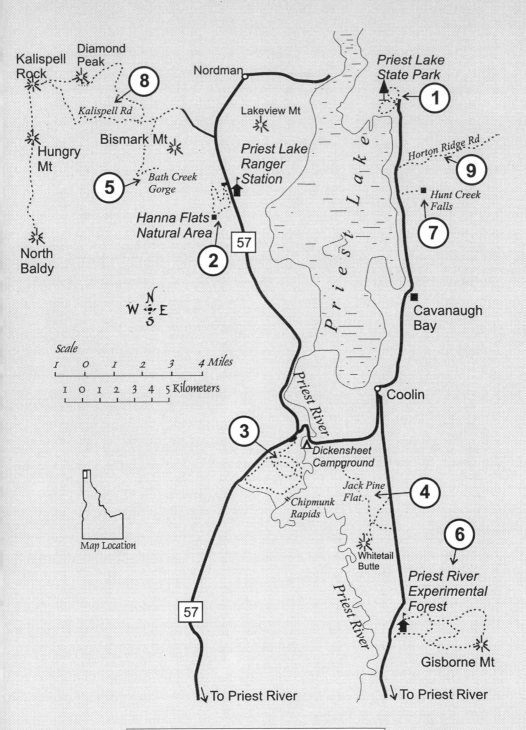

Kalispell
Rock

Diamond
Peak

⑧

Kalispell Rd

Nordman

Lakeview Mt

*Priest Lake
State Park*

①

Bismark Mt

*Priest Lake
Ranger
Station*

Hungry
Mt

⑤

*Bath Creek
Gorge*

Priest Lake

Horton Ridge Rd

⑨

*Hunt Creek
Falls*

*Hanna Flats
Natural Area*

②

57

⑦

North
Baldy

Cavanaugh
Bay

W N E
S

Scale

1 O 1 2 3 4 Miles

1 O 1 2 3 4 5 Kilometers

Coolin

Map Location

③

Dickensheet
Campground

Priest River

*Chipmunk
Rapids*

*Jack Pine
Flat*

④

⑥

*Priest River
Experimental
Forest*

Whitetail
Butte

57

Priest River

Gisborne Mt

↓To Priest River

↓To Priest River

Priest Lake Region

CHAPTER 7
PRIEST LAKE REGION

Area Covered: Priest Lake Area of the Idaho Panhandle including the towns of Nordman, Coolin and Priest River.

PRIEST LAKE was named by missionaries in the 1880s for Father John Roothaan, the superior of the Society of Jesus. The name's etymological roots are as appropriate as the character of the country for it is very much a place blessed by nature. In the center is the lovely 24 mile long Priest Lake and radiating out in all directions, mountains and vast cedar-hemlock forests. The land which rolls out like a wave from the lake valley and then splashes upward into steep mountains couldn't be better for traditional cross-country skiing, and at least three cross-country trail systems have been established with room for much more.

This is also snowshoeing country. Indeed, prior to plowed roads and snowmobiles, snowshoes—and dog sleds—were the most common way to move around in the winter. When Priest Lake froze over, it formed a perfect firm snowshoeing and dog sledding highway allowing direct travel from point to point instead of the longer and slower path around the lake shore. The trip from one end of the lake to the other would often take two days by ice and as much as four by the shore trail.

Established cross-country ski trail systems include the Hanna Flats Trail starting near the Priest Lake Ranger station, 32 miles north of the town of Priest River. The trail, occasionally groomed and suitable for all abilities, passes through open meadows, young pine plantations and a humbling stand of ancient cedars.

Another established trail system is near Chipmunk Rapids. This system is located south of the lake and along the Priest River. Along with picturesque overlooks above the Priest River, gentle terrain and the absence of snowmobilers, it is a fine place to take a snowshoe or ski tour. The area is, however, dependent upon snow conditions, and because snow packs are sometimes less than reliable, the Forest Service is looking at developing an alternative area. In the future, the Chipmunk Rapids area may not be officially designated as a ski trail, but it's still a wonderful place to visit in midwinter.

On the east side of Priest Lake, Priest Lake State Park, the Indian Creek Division has over 5 miles of marked and groomed cross-country ski trails which wind through the quiet forests of the park. Tours are suitable for beginning and intermediate skiers. By the way, if you're planning to do a little overnight camping, the park offers reduced winter camping rates.

Besides the marked cross-country trail systems, all other touring and snowshoeing takes place on the extensive forest road system. Beware, though, the roads are heavily used by snowmobiles. The Kalispell Road may be used by ambitious skiers to visit the edge of the striking Bath Creek Gorge. Three miles south of the Priest Lake Park, a short and sweet moderately difficult tour can be taken to Hunt Creek Falls. Also near Priest Lake State Park is the Horton Ridge Road, which, for backcountry skiers, provides the main access to Mt. Roothan and Chimney Rock of the spectacular Selkirk Mountains.

The Tales . . .

*P*AMPERED movie actresses and actors need not apply here. This film is not for the faint of heart—or body. In the winter of 1923 on a steep ledge on the side of Lookout Mountain, Dorothy Overmyer tried to keep her balance as the wind howled. Her precarious position was high above the north end of Priest Lake in the midst of the Selkirks with snowy summits stretching north and south. The cameras rolled as she went through the action called for in the script.

There were no boom microphones, no sound technicians. This was the era of silent films. And she, quite by chance, was the supporting actress to one of the stars of silent films, Nell Shipman. Dorothy Overmyer's brief journey into the fairyland world of movies is told in Claude and Catherine Simpson's book, *North of the Narrows*, a collection of stories of the men and women of the Priest Lake country.

Nell Shipman who was starring in and directing the film was a woman far a head of her time: writer, producer, promoter and actress. Gritty, determined, and a chaser of dreams, she had a special talent for outdoor film making. Not content with artificial sets, she went to great lengths to create films in wild, natural places—summer or winter.

She made her mark. When you think of the actresses of the silent films, one film critic observed, Nell Shipman is the one you associate with "dog sleds, parkas, and canoes rushing toward rushing waterfalls." In her movies she is very much a self reliant woman, inventive and capable of overcoming the obstacles placed in her path and often emerging in the end as the hero.

Shipman began using the Priest Lake area for films in 1921. Compared to other outdoor locations, it was, Shipman said, "the loveliest, wildest, most perfect spot of all." She worked on movies both summer and winter at Priest Lake, filming outdoor scenes for *The Grubstake*, and the 1923 two reel thriller, *Light on Lookout*.

Overmyer, a pretty, Priest Lake local, was chosen by Shipman to play the supporting role in *Light on Lookout*. In the movie, she is Shipman's cousin from the city who comes for a visit at a remote lookout.

For five days while shooting on Lookout Mountain, the two women lived in a pup tent set up in the snow while the leading man and cameramen lived in a tent which doubled as a kitchen. Camera and supplies were shuttled to higher locations on the mountain with dog sleds and snowshoes. Appearing plainly in one of the photos taken during the filming for *Light on Lookout* is a pair of skis which must have also been used in Shipman's production activities.

It was a dizzying experience for the Priest River High School graduate. After the film was finished, it was shown in Priest River and nearby Spokane, but ironically Overmyer never got an opportunity to see herself.

Eventually, Shipman ran out of money, and the film camp on Mosquito Bay on the lake was abandoned in 1925. Many years later, however, the state honored Shipman's early achievements in the film world by naming a northern point on the lake Shipman Point, and creating the Lionhead State Park at the old site of the film camp. ☐

The Trails . . .

1 **Priest Lake State Park (Indian Creek Division)**—*Marked and groomed cross-country ski trails. Easy to moderately difficult terrain. Toilets.* Located on the east side of Priest Lake, the park is easily found by following signs 11 miles north of Coolin. The park has at least 5 miles (8 km) of marked cross-country trails, consisting of two main systems: the **Old Fume Trail**, 2.5 miles (4 km) long, beginning and ending at the Indian Creek Campground near the park office; and the **Lone Star Trail**, also 2.5 miles long which begins just north of the Indian Creek bridge. The Lone Star Trail follows a clearing and has a scenic vista point along the route.

Both of the trail systems are connected and regularly groomed. Skiers using the trails will need Park N' Ski stickers or pay the park entrance fee.

Snowshoers are asked not to use the groomed ski trails, but there's an alternative, the **Soaring Eagle Trail**. The Soaring Eagle is an old ski trail that was abandoned because it was too steep for skiing. As long as you don't mind some climbing, the trail is a good one for snowshoers and provides scenic views of the surrounding country. Stop in the park office, and they'll be happy to point the way.

2 **Hanna Flats**—*Marked cross-country ski trail. Easy, level terrain. Occasionally groomed.* Located on the west side of Priest Lake, Hanna Flats is, as its name implies, flat and ideally **suited for families**. Parking for the area is available at the north end of the airstrip, just beyond the Priest Ranger Station, 32 miles north of Priest River and 4.5 miles south of Nordman on Idaho 57. The trail goes across open meadows and patches of young pines, but the highlight of the area is the awe inspiring ski through the **Hanna Flat Natural Area** and its magnificent old cedar trees. The loop trail is 4 miles. Park N' Ski stickers are required.

3 **Priest River-Chipmunk Rapids Area**—*Designated cross-country skiing and snowshoeing area. Gentle, easy terrain.* Because this area does not always have reliable snow, the Forest Service is planning to develop an alternative site for cross-country skiing. Don't let that scare you away. This is a wonderful area when the snow is good.

To reach it, drive 22 miles north of the town of Priest River on Idaho 57. Watch for a sign indicating state gravel pit No. 057-022, .2 mile southwest of the Dickensheet Road Junction with Idaho 57. Turn southeast onto the gravel pit road, drive .2 mile, and park in the cross-country trail parking lot at the gravel pit. (With the change in trail system status, the parking situation may change, but you should be able to find parking in the vicinity.)

There are a number of old trails that can be followed. To get started, begin skiing or snowshoeing on the old road which heads west from the gravel pit. The old road curves around to the southwest and gradually descends a hill, leading to a large marshy area, approximately 1 mile (1.6 km) from the start. Named **Kaniksu Marsh**, it supports a wide variety of wildlife in the summer. To the east and south beyond the marsh, trails can be followed which overlook the lovely Priest River and eventually reach a point above **Chipmunk Rapids**, 3 miles (5 km) from the parking area.

The network of snowbound trails in the area provides plenty of other side trips and as many as 10 miles (16 km) of trails are possible.

4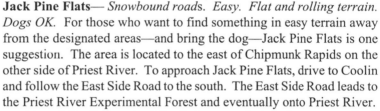

Jack Pine Flats— *Snowbound roads. Easy. Flat and rolling terrain. Dogs OK.* For those who want to find something in easy terrain away from the designated areas—and bring the dog—Jack Pine Flats is one suggestion. The area is located to the east of Chipmunk Rapids on the other side of Priest River. To approach Jack Pine Flats, drive to Coolin and follow the East Side Road to the south. The East Side Road leads to the Priest River Experimental Forest and eventually onto Priest River.

About 2.5 miles south of Coolin is a gravel pit and you can pull off anywhere between there to the Whitetail Butte area, 5.5 miles from Coolin. Keep watching on the right (west) side of the plowed East Side Road and pick out one of the snowbound logging roads which leads west into the Jack Pine Flats area. When you've found a suitable road, pull off and park. The East Side Road is not a major highway, and parking is fine as long as your vehicle is out of the way of traffic.

Skiing or snowshoeing is on snowbound logging roads and across **flat** or **rolling** terrain. There is one snowmobile route that passes through Jack Pine Flats, but generally the machines stay on route which leaves the area open for human powered explorations.

5

Bath Creek Gorge— *Snowbound road. Moderately difficult. Dogs OK.* Located on the west side of Priest Lake, Bath Creek Gorge is approached by following **Kalispell Road**, located 2.5 miles south of Nordman on Idaho 57. Two miles northwest of Idaho 57, take the snowbound road leading off to the left. This road leads into Bath Creek Gorge. Several spur roads are encountered and you should carry a recent Forest Service map. Bath Creek Gorge is a 10 to 12 mile round trip tour from Kalispell Road. You'll want to plan this one for a weekday. The area is heavily used by **snowmobilers**.

6   **Priest River Experimental Forest**— *Snowbound roads. Moderately difficult. Dogs OK.* To reach the Experimental Forest, take the East Side Road which leads south from Coolin situated on the southern tip of Priest Lake. Or, you can also get on the East Side Road turning north off of US 2 on the east edge of the town of Priest River. The Experimental Forest is located about midway between Coolin and Priest River. Plenty of snowshoeing and skiing exists on the network of roads in the area. Snowmobile use is light in this area.

 One destination tour that can be made is the long trip to the top of **Gisborne Mountain**. Of interest to backcountry skiers is the ridge system which leads from Gisborne to **Bald Mountain**, the predominant peak rising above Sandpoint. Described in more detail in the Sandpoint chapter, Bald Mountain is attractive because of its great downhill ski terrain and high open ridges and bowls.

7   **Hunt Creek Falls**— *Snowbound roads. Moderately difficult. Dogs OK.* A short, 2 mile (3 km) round-trip tour, located on the east side of Priest Lake, can be made to Hunt Creek Falls. The road to the falls is .3 mile south of the Hunt Creek Road, or 3.8 miles north of Cavanaugh Bay on East Shore Road. The snowbound road leads off to the east. Although snowmobile use may occur, it is not a main route. If you need help with directions, personnel at Priest Lake State Park are knowledgeable about the area and can help. A number of side roads branch off the Hunt Creek Falls route, and as always, be sure to bring a good map.

8 **West Side of Priest Lake**—*Access via snowbound roads, then open high country. Moderate to difficult backcountry.* On the west side of Priest Lake, **Kalispell Rock** is one **backcountry** area of interest. It is approached directly by following the Kalispell Road or by taking **Kalispell Road** to Indian Mountain Road to Diamond Peak Road and on to Kalispell Rock. From Kalispell Rock to the south, a skiable ridge system extends to **Hungry, Gleason, and North Baldy Peaks**. Kalispell Road is a main **snowmobile** route. Because of the distances involved, you'll need to plan this as a multiday trip or use a snowmobile shuttle.

9 **East Side of Priest Lake**— *Access via snowbound roads, then open off-trail high country. Moderate to difficult backcountry terrain.* On the east side of the lake is the very challenging backcountry of the Selkirk Range. The main access is **Horton Ridge Road**, 2 miles south of Priest Lake State Park (Indian Creek Division), or 5 miles north of Cavanaugh Bay. Access can also be gained by following Indian Creek Road, 1 mile north of the Park, but it does not provide as direct an access as Horton Ridge Road. Both roads provide access into the immediate vicinity of **Mt. Roothan and Chimney Rock**. Access roads are used heavily by **snowmobiles**. Because of the distances involved, you'll need to plan this as a multiday trip or use a snowmobile shuttle.

OTHER AREAS

Some exciting ski trail developments have occurred near Newport, Washington, just over the Idaho border to the west of Priest River. The Colville National Forest has put together two very nice cross-country ski systems which double as mountain biking trails in the summer. Both systems are suitable for skiers of all abilities, and they've quickly gained a reputation which draws skiers from Spokane and Sandpoint. One is called the **Geophysical Trail System**, so named because of the Geophysical Observatory, an earthquake monitoring station, which was located nearby. It has 7 loops and 6 miles (10 km) of trails and is regularly groomed for skating and diagonal striding.

To reach the Geo trailhead, drive east (towards Idaho) out of Newport and cross over the Pend Oreille River. Immediately on the other side of the river, take a left on Le Clerc Road and follow it for 7.5 miles. Turn right on Indian Creek Road and follow it 1.5 miles to the trailhead. Signs are posted to help guide the way to the trail. Washington Sno-Park or Idaho Park N' Ski permits are required.

The other trail system is called **Upper Wolf**. There are four loops for a total of 2.5 miles (4 km) of trails. Remarkably, the trails can be accessed right from the city limits of Newport. How would it be? From Newport, start driving north on highway 20. At the edge of town, turn left on Larch Street. Drive one block, take a right on Laurel-hurst and go .5 mile to the trailhead. Washington Sno-Park or Idaho Park N' Ski permits are required. The regularly groomed trails lie on land donated to the Forest Service by Fred and Maude Wolf for "quiet and peaceful use," and what a wonderful way to put that generous donation to its intended use.

Of Bugs and Snowstorms

DURING THE RESEARCH for the first version of this book, I used a 1964 Volkswagen Bug to get around the state. Bugs are getting rare these days, and before they completely pass into obscurity, I wanted to offer a couple of parting observations.

Volkswagen Bugs are like pets. There's never been an uglier car, but they grow on you, and not long after they come home, they've acquired a name and end up becoming more of an integral part of the family than you are. Mine was called Trolley—as in the Tooterville Trolley. I believe that Trolley was male, but having never done any serious repair work on the exhaust system, I'm not sure.

I've owned three different Bugs, and based on my experiences, I've come up with a list of three guiding principles of Bug owner-ship. The first principle is that all Bugs have their own personality, and if ignored for any period of time, they will misbehave. They generally can be nursed back to health, but not without a generous expenditure of time and money. The second, related to the first, is that all Bug owners, no matter how mechanically challenged or how resistant they are to getting their hands oily, eventually do get their hands oily and learn how to do their own repairs. I didn't know a thing about repairing cars when I purchased my first Bug, but by the time Trolley, my third Bug came around, I could stop down at Frank's Repair and actually engage in small talk about head gas-kets, piston rings, points and fly wheels.

The third principle? Let me come back to that. First, a quick skiing story. In 1976, I had been skiing all day in the Priest Lake area. As in most parts of Idaho, cross-country skiing was just starting to catch on and there wasn't much information floating around about the trail possibilities. I had talked to the Forest Service earlier at the Priest Lake station, and they had admitted that they didn't really have any ideas for cross-country trails, but if I found some good ones to let them know.

That day I skied a couple of different trails, the last one being the Chipmunk Rapids area which later was developed into a ski trail system.

I had spent quite a bit of time searching along the edge of the tree-covered embankment above Priest River for a view of Chip-munk Rapids. When I had finally found it and turned around, it had gotten dark, and I needed a headlight to guide my way back to the car. A storm had been brewing all day, and by the time I reached the Bug, snow was falling heavily.

Chilled and looking forward to returning to Sandpoint for a hot meal, I threw my pack in and lashed the skis to the outside rack. There's always an anxious moment for any Volkswagen owner before turning the key, especially during times when you really want it to start, like during a storm, but I heard the clicking of solenoid and . . . varrooom. Trolley started and I was off. It would take about 30 miles before the Bug warmed up, but I was used to that.

For a two wheel drive vehicle, Volkswagen Bugs are great on snow. With their high wheel base and engine positioned over the drive wheels, they can get through in some pretty bad conditions. Consequently, the several inches of snow which had by now accumulated on the highway didn't bother me.

It turned into quite a storm. Not a soul was on the road. Visibility was limited to only a few feet ahead and a narrow white band of snow flashing past the side windows. Snow was coming down so hard now, that the wipers weren't moving enough out of the way. I rolled down the window and while driving with my right hand, used my left hand to brush excess snow away.

I love the feeling of isolation that accompanies a snow storm. You know that there's a much larger world out there, but the wind and swirling snow compresses everything in that larger world to a small white space. As I was lost in thought, my nose detected a strange odor. It smelled like a plastic bag that someone had thrown in a campfire.

Something caught my eye: smoke was coming out of the front hood! Then, the headlights went black, and I couldn't see a thing. I quickly brought the Bug to a stop and got out to take a look.

I popped the hood and was engulfed in smoke and swirling snow. Tossing gear out on the highway, I cleared the front cargo space and stripped back the black vinyl covering. The problem and the source of the smell became immediately apparent. There in front of me was a mass of melted, steaming plastic where three or maybe four wires had shorted out.

I stood there looking at the mess for a long time. No cars had passed me. Even on a pleasant night, traffic is scarce in that country. I was pretty much on my own.

I rummaged around in my tool kit and couldn't believe that I had actually brought along a spool of wire. Then for the next couple of hours as the storm continued, I worked cutting away and replacing the wires. Miraculously—and it was miraculous since even though I was a Bug owner I wasn't much of a mechanic—the headlights came back to life.

The storm started letting up, and I hurried on to Sandpoint, still thinking about a warm meal. By the time I arrived, however, everything in town was closed, and I settled for a dinner of cheese and crackers from my day pack.

I should have known that I would arrive late. It relates to the third and last guiding principle of Volkswagen Bug ownership. And that is: If you're traveling in a Bug, never be in a hurry. You'll never be there on time anyway. □

Trolley

Resources . . .

National Forest Lands near Priest Lake
Priest Lake Ranger District of the Panhandle National Forest—Office located 4.5 miles south of Nordman on Idaho 57. Address: HCR 5, Box 207, Priest River, Idaho 83856. Phone: (208) 443-2512.

Priest Lake State Park
Park Ranger's Office—Office located at the Indian Creek Division, north of Coolin. Address: Priest Lake State Park, Indian Creek Bay #423, Coolin, Idaho 83821. Phone (208) 443-2200.

National Forest Lands near Newport, Washington
Newport Ranger Station of the Colville National Forest—Office located in Newport. Address: 315 East Warren, Newport, Washington. Phone 509-447-3129.

Guiding, Backcountry Shuttles in the Priest Lake Area
Guiding and backcountry shuttle service is available in the Priest Lake area. Since winter backcountry outfitting businesses sometimes have a history of coming and going in Idaho, it is best to call the Priest Lake Ranger station for the permittee's phone number and most current information.

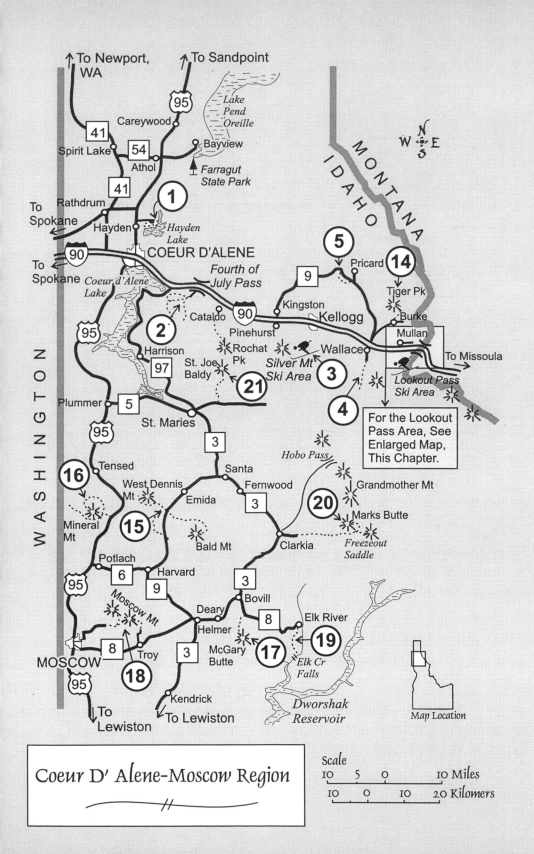

↑ To Newport, WA

↑ To Sandpoint

95

Lake Pend Oreille

Careywood

41

Bayview

Spirit Lake   **54**

Athol

↑ *Farragut State Park*

41

(1)

To Spokane   Rathdrum

Hayden

Hayden Lake

90

To Spokane

COEUR D'ALENE

Coeur d'Alene Lake

Fourth of July Pass

9

Pricard

(5)

(14)

MONTANA

IDAHO

Tiger Pk

Kingston

95

Cataldo

90

Kellogg

Burke

(2)

Pinehurst

Mullan

Harrison

Rochat Pk

Wallace

97

St. Joe Baldy

Silver Mt Ski Area

(3)

To Missoula

(21)

Lookout Pass Ski Area

Plummer   **5**

(4)

95

St. Maries

For the Lookout Pass Area, See Enlarged Map, This Chapter.

3

Hobo Pass

(16)   Tensed

Santa

West Dennis Mt

Fernwood

Grandmother Mt

Emida

3

(20)

Marks Butte

Mineral Mt

(15)

Bald Mt

Clarkia

Freezeout Saddle

Potlach

6

Harvard

3

9

Bovill

Moscow Mt

Deary

8

Elk River

(19)

Helmer

8   **MOSCOW**

3

Troy

McGary Butte

(17)

Elk Cr Falls

(18)

95

Kendrick

Dworshak Reservoir

↓ To Lewiston

↖ To Lewiston

Map Location

WASHINGTON

Coeur D' Alene-Moscow Region

Scale

10   5   0   10 Miles

10   0   10   20 Kilomers

CHAPTER 8
COEUR D'ALENE-MOSCOW REGION

Area Covered: North Idaho including Lookout Pass, Coeur d'Alene, Kellogg, Wallace, Moscow, St. Maries, Elk River and nearby areas.

IT WAS quite a 4th of July. Festivities included a patriotic speech, the firing of rifles and the blasting of dynamite. To the Indians who had been watching the event, the celebrating white men had lost their minds, and the natives fled the scene before a stray bullet caught one of them. The year was 1861, and the place was soon to be known as Fourth of July Pass. There, high above the crystalline blue waters of Coeur d'Alene Lake, a work crew led by John Mullan, an ambitious Irish first lieutenant in the army, was nearing the end of a three year road building project. Mullan's wagon road was rough, but it was a remarkable feat of engineering: 624 miles long from Fort Benton, Montana to Walla Walla, Washington, with the worst of it being the stretch across rugged North Idaho.

Fourth of July Pass is known also for a gathering of a colder and quieter kind: cross-country skiing and racing. Located 17 miles east of Coeur d'Alene on Interstate 90—a more modern version of Mullan's road—the pass at 3,070 feet is the Coeur d'Alene area's most convenient place to catch a quick ski tour or workout. The Panhandle National Forest in combination with local skiers has worked cooperatively to establish nearly 20 miles of marked and groomed cross-country ski trails here.

Beyond Fourth of July Pass in the Kellogg-Wallace area, the Forest Service has designated several cross-country ski and snowshoe trails. Like Fourth of July Pass, heavy timber in the Kellogg-Wallace area limits skiing to logging roads—unless you are willing to make a long climb to the subalpine zone of the higher mountains.

There is one exception. That exception is Lookout Pass (elevation of 4,725 feet) which offers some of the best, easy-to-reach backcountry skiing and boarding in the entire region.

One ride ski passes can be purchased at the Lookout Pass Ski Area and short descents can made off the backside of the area. Telemark skiers will find great practice slopes in and near the Alpine runs, and steeper slopes are available farther to the south-west. The St. Regis Lakes area, 3.5 miles from the ski area parking lot, is a destination for overnight backcountry trips, and from the general vicinity, you may strike out on longer traverses or ski mountaineering jaunts. Use great caution. Once away from the general vicinity of the ski area, you quickly enter severe avalanche country. The Forest Service provides avalanche warning information for the Lookout Pass area, and if you are planning to do any traveling off the marked trails, you should check the most recent forecast (see *Resources* at the end of the chapter).

There are more than just backcountry opportunities on Lookout Pass. A beautiful out-and-back ski tour, suitable for beginners, can be made by following a marked ski trail towards St. Regis Lakes. Moreover, Lookout Pass Ski Area is small and friendly, a perfect place for family skiing and boarding.

In the southern part of this region is Moscow which has long been a home to a committed cross-country ski community. Some of the closest skiing is Moscow Mountain, a cedar-covered mountain rising out of the rolling wheat fields a short distance to the northeast of town. Farther from Moscow are the Palouse Divide Trails which are north of the city on State Highway 6, near the site of the old North-South Ski Area. The trails, which follow a rolling route high along the crest, are designated and marked by the Forest Service for cross-country skiing.

The town of Elk River has thrown out the welcome mat to cross-country skiers. Beginning in Elk River a beautiful, marked cross-country trail winds through forests and occasional meadows to a scenic view point overlooking Elk Creek Falls. Snowshoers will also enjoy this trail and the abundance of snowbound roads in the Elk River area.

The closest backcountry skiing to Moscow is to the northeast in the Freezeout Mountain-Marks Butte area, near Clarkia. This is not, however, the kind of backcountry area where you drive up, step out and start cutting turns. The approach to Freezeout is a long haul up a snow bound road. Early season when lower portions of the road are still open is often a good time to visit the area. Whether it's early season or late season, the long trip is worth it. Once on Freezeout Saddle, the snow can be divine, and free-heel romantics won't want to miss out on making a few turns in an enchanting area on the side of Mark's Butte called the Crystal Forest.

The Tales . . .

*H*ISTORICALLY, the Wallace-Kellogg area is one of Idaho's worst areas for avalanche accidents. Mines and associated buildings and homes clinging to steep open hillsides all across the Coeur d'Alenes are a recipe for disaster. The *History of Northern Idaho* notes that the first fatal slide in the area occurred in 1886 on Willow Creek, east of Mullan. Two men, Andy Richards and Simon Christenson, were working in an area that had been burned the previous summer, and it was surmised that lack of cover contributed to the slide which caught and killed the two men. W.S. Harris who found their bodies in the avalanche went for help, but before he returned, another larger snow slide deeply buried the remains of the two men. The conditions continued to be dangerous, and searchers decided to leave the bodies for a later recovery.

In 1890, a deep snow pack had built up through the winter. Then in February, a Chinook wind blew in bringing with it a warm rain which triggered an unprecedented series of avalanches. A special dispatch from Wallace printed in *The Idaho Free County Press* read: "The town of Burke, Idaho in the Coeur d'Alene mining district, has been nearly destroyed by a disastrous avalanche. Half the business houses are in ruin. Tuesday morning, with scarcely a moment's warning, a tremendous mass of snow and rocks swept on the town. Five men were buried beneath the snow. Two were rescued, but the others are dead."

Then shortly after the Burke disaster, another avalanche came down on the Custer Mine along Nine-mile Creek, north of Wallace. This time the avalanche hit a boarding house that was full of miners. Six were killed.

The Burke Area continued to be a risky area during avalanche cycles. In 1894, the *Wardner News* reported that "Canyon Creek in the vicinity of the Black Bear Mine [2 miles from Burke] was the

Home destroyed when the 1910 avalanche hit Mace near Burke, Idaho. Thirteen people were killed.

scene of a fearful calamity on last Thursday morning when a succession of snow slides occurred causing death and destruction in their course." The first avalanche leveled four houses and killed a family of three. One of the slides left the Union Pacific telegraph line under 200 feet of snow. After it was over, 300 men helped to dig out what was left of the Black Bear settlement.

The worst disaster in the Burke area occurred 16 years later in 1910 when an avalanche swept down on Mace, a half mile to the east of Burke. Thirteen people were killed.

Not all avalanches in the Coeur d'Alenes caused fatalities. During the exceptionally heavy winter of 1889-90, Mike Sinclair was working at the Alhambra Mine two miles east of Kellogg. After avalanches buried part of the mining camp, two of Sinclair's fellow workers decided they had enough and snowshoed back to town. That left Sinclair and his partner.

One evening after dinner, Sinclair was doing the dishes while his partner was working outside. "I heard the most awful roaring sound that seemed like nothing I had ever heard before," said Sinclair. "Hurrying out of the cabin, I crawled over the snow up on the side hill and looking towards the summit saw the large stand of timber toppling over in all directions."

The big avalanche hurtled down through the camp, covering everything and leaving deep piles of snow. Sinclair was safe, but he feared for his partner. Hoping that he had been working in the mine tunnel, Sinclair grabbed a shovel and began to dig for the opening. Missing the entrance to the mine on the first try, he dug in another spot, only to miss the entrance again. He tried several more times, but with snow everywhere, he couldn't pin point exactly where it was.

Then he heard his name called and, turning, saw the head of his partner just above the snow. He was trying to extract himself. Fortunately, the partner had been in the tunnel when the avalanche had hit and had managed to dig himself out. The men needed no further prompting. Two days later Sinclair and his partner cleared out and didn't return to the area until spring. □

The Trails . . .

COEUR D'ALENE AREA

1 **English Point Trail System**—*Marked cross-country ski trails. Easy terrain. Toilets. Park N' Ski area.* To reach the trailhead, drive north from Coeur d'Alene on US 95 to Hayden. At the US 95 and Hayden

Avenue intersection, check your speedometer. Drive 1.5 miles farther north on US 95 to Lancaster Road. At Lancaster turn right (east) and drive 3.6 miles to English Point Road. The trails start here.

The trail system consists of three loops of 1 km, 2.5 km, and 5.1 km in length. One moderately steep hill on the 5.1 km loop may be a little difficult for some skiers, but otherwise the trails are gentle and suitable for families and beginners. Snow cover isn't always reliable, but when several inches of snow have accumulated in valley regions, this is a very pleasant area to visit. Depending on snow depth, the trails are occasionally groomed.

The English Point Trails have the distinction of being North Idaho's first marked cross-country ski trail system. Austin Helmers, whose home town is Coeur d'Alene, promoted the idea and designed the trail system in the 1970s. Our hats are off to Austin who recognized a need and helped get cross-country trail systems underway in North Idaho.

This is a Park N' Ski area and stickers on your vehicle are required.

2 **Fourth of July Pass**—*Marked cross-country ski trail system. Moderately difficult. Often groomed. Warming hut. Toilets. Park N' Ski area. No dogs.* Located 13 miles (21 km) east of Coeur d'Alene on

Interstate 90, Fourth of July Pass, at an elevation of 4,725 feet, is the closest reliable access for cross-country skiing near Coeur d'Alene. To reach the trailhead, take the Fourth of July Recreation Exit (Exit #28) off Interstate 90. Parking is located on the south side of the freeway, .4 miles from the exit. Park N' Ski signs point the way.

At the time of this writing, there are three marked trails: Elk Loop Trail at 5.2 miles (8.3 km), Cedar Loop Trail at 5.5 miles (8.8 km) and the South Fork Trail at 8.5 miles (13.7 km). A small A-frame warming hut is located .2 mile down the trail from the parking lot, and a picnic shelter is available for lunch stops halfway through the Elk Loop Trail. The trails twist and turn through a beautiful cedar forest with occasional places where you can catch a view of the Coeur d'Alene Mountains. This is not flat or rolling terrain, however, and even on the easier trails you'll want to be comfortable with downhill and uphill techniques.

Park N' Ski area. Stickers are required.

KELLOGG-WALLACE AREA

3 **Silver Mountain Ski Area**—*Alpine ski area. Alpine, Nordic downhill and snowboarding. All services: food, lodging, instruction, rentals.*

This impressive area has 1 gondola and 5 chairs which service 50 runs and 1,500 acres of skiable terrain. The vertical drop is 2,200 feet (671 meters). It is reached by taking the Kellogg Exit off Interstate 90 and following signs to the Gondola station.

Silver Mountain has gone through a session of name changes. It was originally known as Jackass, then changed to Silverhorn and now Silver Mountain. In past incarnations, skiers had to drive up a sliver of road which, hands down, was the hairiest access road to any ski area in the Western United States. Now, however, a Gondola picks up skiers in Kellogg and whisks them up to the Mountain Haus from which the entire mountain can be accessed.

For backcountry Alpine buffs, the ski area has designated Wardner Peak as a hiking and skiing area, but other than Wardner, it doesn't allow access to the backcountry from within the area's boundaries. In the 1970s things were a little looser. Jerry Johnson, a good friend of mine who grew up in Pinehurst, north of Kellogg, took me on an extraordinary 3,600 foot descent off the top of the ski area into Lynch Gulch near Pinehurst. It was a wild luge run down twisting, narrow mining roads and was nearly as hairy as driving up the road to the ski area. I described the descent in the first version of this book, but it never really seemed to catch on. Perhaps, it was because the white-knuckled drive from Kellogg was thrilling enough for a day of skiing.

4   **Experiment Draw Trail**—*Snowbound trail. First mile is moderately easy. Snowshoeing.* The Experiment Draw trailhead is located 2 miles south of Wallace on Placer Creek Road. Plowed parking is available.

The tour follows a snowbound hiking trail to the south along the creek bottom and is fairly gradual. The length of the trail is 1 to 1.5 miles (1.5 to 2.5 km). Avalanche hazard exists during periods of instability in some draws near the end of the trail, so use caution in this area. The trail also can be used to access backcountry ski country.

5   **Cedar Creek-Cinnabar Trail**—*Marked cross-country and snowshoeing trail. Moderately difficult.* This Forest Service marked trail is reached by taking the Kingston Exit (# 47) off Interstate 90. Head northeast on Forest Highway 9 toward Prichard for about 17 miles from the Interstate to a parking area at the junction of Forest Highway 9 and Forest Route 620. From here, signs point the way to the trail. The trail, which runs out for 5 miles, parallels the Coeur d'Alene River. Since you're near the river's riparian zone, wildlife sightings are likely.

6   **Beacon Light Trail (Hale Fish Hatchery Area)**—*Marked cross-country and snowshoeing trail. Moderately easy.* The trailhead is located 4 miles east of Mullan on the plowed county road commonly referred to as the Shoshone Park-Hale Fish Hatchery Road. The Hale Fish Hatchery is located .5 mile beyond the Shoshone Park Recreation Site. Plenty of plowed parking is available at the fish hatchery.

The trailhead is across the road from the fish hatchery. The 2.5 mile (4 km) trail is marked and follows old snowbound mining roads to the north of the fish hatchery along the **South Fork of the Coeur d'Alene River**. The area is suitable for **families**.

7 **Lookout Pass Ski Area**—*Alpine ski area. Alpine, Nordic downhill and snowboarding. All abilities. Rentals and lessons available.* Look-

out Pass Ski Area is one of those small, local areas with a pleasant family atmosphere and a lot of heart. It is reached by taking the exit (Exit # 0) off Interstate 90 on the top of Lookout Pass, 13 miles east of Wallace. The area has one double chair and one rope tow which services 12 runs. The vertical drop of the area is 850 feet (259 meters). The ski area sells a one-ride pass which can be used to access backcountry telemark skiing or to follow a descending cross-country ski trail which loops back to the parking area.

8 **Lookout Pass Trails**—*Marked cross-country ski trail. One easy, level trail and a moderately difficult descending trail. Ski lodge and toilets.*

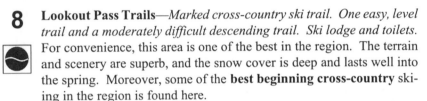

For convenience, this area is one of the best in the region. The terrain and scenery are superb, and the snow cover is deep and lasts well into the spring. Moreover, some of the **best beginning cross-country** skiing in the region is found here.

An easy 3.5 mile (6 km) round trip **beginner's tour** starts at Lookout Pass Ski Area. The exit ramp off the freeway (Interstate 90) to Lookout Pass Ski Area is clearly indicated with a sign (Exit No. 0) on the top of the pass.

The ski trail, which is marked, follows the snowbound old highway south towards Montana. The first part of the trail parallels a snowmobile trail and gradually descends. After approximately 1 mile (1.5 km), the road makes a sharp "U" bend. Just a few yards before the road starts to make the "U" bend, a trail takes off to the right (west). A Forest Service sign marks the trail as "St. Regis Lakes." At this point, you leave the snowmobile trail behind and follow the trail toward the lakes.

One mile from the "U" bend, the trail enters a beautiful, high Alpine valley. From here the avalanche hazard increases considerably, and it is recommended that only those who are comfortable with avalanche recognition skills continue beyond this point. You can return the same way. Or, if desired, the Forest Service has marked an **alternative return route** of moderate difficulty which may be followed back to the ski area parking lot.

From the top of the ski area a fun **descending** 2.5 mile long **moderately difficult** tour can be made which links up with the trail described above. To do the tour, take the lift to the top of the ski hill (the ski area sells a one ride ticket), and follow the marked trail. This run is not a particularly long one, dropping 1,000 feet (305 meters), and it is conceivable to do it several times in a day.

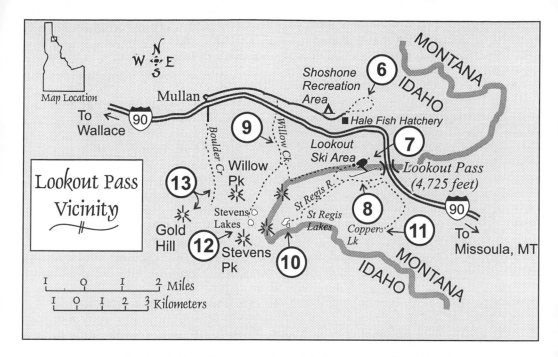

9   **Lookout Pass Backcountry**—*Moderate to difficult backcountry. Snowshoeing. Snowboarding.* Another **descending tour** that can be taken from Lookout Pass Ski Area follows what was at one time a designated Forest Service cross-country ski trail. It begins at the top of the lift and follows the Idaho-Montana Divide west and southwest to St. Regis Pass. From St. Regis Pass, the tour descends a steep, snowbound mining road (up to 25 percent downgrade) to Willow Creek. Skiers will find deep snow and superb scenery. Total length of the tour is 6 miles (9.5 km). A shuttle vehicle is required at **Willow Creek**, located 2 miles (3 km) east of Mullan on the south side of the plowed county road leading to Shoshone Park Recreation Site and Hale Fish Hatchery.

10   The main destination for overnighters and other backcountry excursions is **St. Regis Lakes**, located high on the drainage of the headwaters of the St. Regis River. To get there follow the beginners trail from the ski area parking lot and continue southwest all the way to the lakes, a distance of 3.5 miles. The lake basin sits in the midst of high, Alpine peaks and a variety of **backcountry** and ski mountaineering options are available. Avalanche hazard is significant and parties should be properly prepared and know how to travel safely.

11   **Copper Lake**—*Moderate to difficult backcountry.* The backcountry around Copper Lake (also called Sildex Lake) is reached by following Copper Gulch Trail. The trail is located a mile south of Lookout Pass. Park at the ski area, and ski following the old highway to the south until reaching Copper Gulch and the trail to the lake. Avalanche hazards exist.

135

Snowboarder shredding powder in the Lookout Pass backcountry.
Lookout Pass Ski Area is in the background.

12 **Stevens Peak-Alpine Lakes Area**—*Moderate to difficult backcountry.* The scenic Stevens Peak-Alpine Lakes Area to the southwest of Lookout Pass is reached by following the trail from Lookout Pass which leads over St. Regis Pass and onto Stevens Lakes. It can also be reached by ascending Willow Creek, east of Mullan. Avalanche hazard is high, and only experienced backcountry skiers should undertake tours in this area.

13 **West Willow Peak-Gold Hill Area**—*Moderate to difficult backcountry.* This high Alpine area which lies above 6,000 feet (1,823 meters) is just to the south of Mullan and is one of several areas that attracts the attention of **backcountry skiers** from Coeur d'Alene. To reach it, drive to the town cemetery on the southeast edge of Mullan and continue driving in a southerly direction until the road is no longer plowed. Ski 3 miles up Boulder Creek and pick out a descent line on the ridge between **West Willow Peak and Gold Hill**. Generally backcountry skiers are finding lines which will give them about 600 vertical (183 meters) before having to skin back up. Avalanche danger exists. Prepare properly and check the stability forecast.

14 **Tiger Peak**—*Access via snowbound road then open off-trail country. Moderate to difficult backcountry.* Tiger Peak at 6,625 feet (2,019 meters) is another backcountry area enticing skiers from the regional area. It is reached by driving from Wallace to **Burke**. From Burke, ski up the mining road heading north towards Tiger Peak and pick out a slope on which to leave a signature. Backcountry aficionados are reporting signature lines up to 1,500 vertical (457 meters) before having to stop and skin back up. As in any high Alpine environment, this is avalanche country and you should be well prepared.

MOSCOW AREA

15 **Palouse Divide Trails**—*Marked cross-country ski trail system. Easy to moderately difficult. Park N' Ski area.* The Palouse Divide system is a Forest Service designated cross-country ski area and is off limits to snowmobiles. Starting from the top of a pass on Idaho 6, 12 miles north of Harvard and 5 miles southeast of Emida, skiers have 18 miles (29 km) of marked trails to choose from. Parking is available in the plowed parking area on top of the pass.

The Palouse Divide trails lead off from either side of the pass. The trail on the west side of the highway follows a snowbound road westerly and contours around the south sides of **East and West Dennis Peaks**. If you're looking for **remoteness** and opportunities for more challenging skiing, this is the direction to go.

The trail on the east side starts on the entrance road to the old North-South Ski Area and is an ideal **beginner's tour**, gently rolling on top of the Palouse Divide. To get started on the tour, ski up the old North-South Ski Area entrance road. The trail begins .1 mile from the highway on the right (south) side and follows the snowbound road generally in an easterly direction. The old ski runs are also a nice place to practice telemark turns, but remember that the area is no longer controlled and avalanche precautions should be taken.

An ambitious ski tour can be made following the trail on the east side of the highway all the way from US 95A to **Bald Mountain**, a distance of 9 miles (14.5 km) one-way. Though it's a long journey, skiers will often be rewarded with good snow conditions on the north side of Bald Mountain, even when conditions elsewhere are poor.

Descending tours can also be made from either side of the Divide to points lower on Highway 6. In order to do the tours, you'll need to spot a shuttle vehicle unless you are a masochist and plan to trudge all the way back up to the top of the pass. One suggested **descending tour** is the **Sampson Jeep Trail** which forks off to the left (south) of the snowbound road leading to East and West Dennis Peaks. After some up and down, the snowbound Sampson Trail drops down and eventually joins Meadow Creek Road. The distance from the top of the pass to Highway 6 is approximately 6 miles (10 km).

The Palouse Divide Trail system is a part of the Idaho Park N' Ski system and permits are required.

16 **Skyline Trail-McCrosky State Park**—*Snowbound road. Easy terrain. Snowshoeing. Dogs OK.* This trail is located on top of a small pass between the towns of Potlatch and Tensed on US 95. More precisely it is located 10.5 miles south of Tensed on US 95, or 10 miles north of the junction of US 95 and US 95A near Potlatch.

The tour follows a snowbound road heading off from the west side of the highway. A private residence is located a short distance up Skyline Drive, and to keep from blocking the driveway, skiers' vehicles should be parked in the pulloff plowed along the highway. The tour, suitable for **beginners**, follows the snowbound **Skyline Trail** road through a heavy forest of cedar and white pine. The route generally heads west, staying high on the divide between Tensed and Potlatch.

From the Skyline Trail, **intermediate** skiers may enjoy the climb to the top of **Mineral Mountain** at 4,128 feet (1,259 meters). To reach Mineral Mountain, follow Skyline Trail to the northeast. Approximately 1 mile (1.5 km) from the start, a snowbound road branches off to the right (north). Follow this road, which winds around the Mineral Mountain and eventually reaches the top.

17 **McGary Butte**—*Snowbound roads. Easy to moderate. Snowshoeing. Dogs OK.* This area was a favorite of the late Jim Rennie, who started the University of Idaho Outdoor Program and who was of invaluable help when I was working on the first version of this book. It is located 4 miles south of Bovill on Idaho 8. **Beginning skiers** will enjoy the excellent terrain on the abandoned **railroad right-of-way** and the meadow nearby. The center of attraction here, however, is the 5-mile (8 km) **moderately difficult tour** following snowbound **McGary Butte Road** to the top of the Butte. The trip is highlighted by splendid views along the way.

18 **Moscow Mountain**—*Snowbound roads. Moderate to difficult. Snowshoeing. Dogs OK.* Because of the up and down terrain, tours in the Moscow Mountain Area are in the **moderately difficult** range and it is not a place for first time skiers. Nevertheless, it's close to Moscow and all in all, a pleasant place for a romp during midwinter.

There are several access points to the Moscow Mountain area. Mike Beiser, the Director of the University of Idaho Outdoor Program suggests the vicinity of the old **Tamarack Ski Area** as one of the best

since it provides the highest access to the area. To reach it, drive 12 miles east of Moscow on Idaho 8 to Troy. At Troy, take Randall Flats Road to Tamarack Road. Follow Tamarack Road until it's no longer plowed. The tour follows the snowbound road which continues to the

top of Moscow Mountain. During periods of sufficient snow cover, it is even possible to catch a few turns on the side of the mountain.

The closest access to town is **Moscow Mountain Road**. To reach it, start at Moscow's main street (US 95) and turn east on Sixth Street. Once on Sixth Street, follow it all the way out (approximately 1 mile) until it comes to a "T" near a church. This is Mountain View Road. Check your odometer and take a left on Mountain View Road. Drive 2.2 miles and turn right on Moscow Mountain Road. Follow Moscow Mountain Road to the point to where it is no longer plowed.

From the end of the plowed portion of Moscow Mountain Road, the tour follows the snowbound road. It begins to climb, immediately rising above the open wheat fields of the Moscow area. The snowbound road leads to the top of Moscow Mountain ridge which consists of a series of high points including **East and West Twin, Granite Point, Paradise Point** and, of course, **Moscow Mountain**. Of the all the points, Moscow Mountain, is the highest at 4,983 feet..

Snowmobilers use the area, but in recent years, their use has dropped off some.

19 Elk Creek Falls—*Marked and occasionally groomed cross-country ski trails. Moderately difficult. Services available in Elk River.*

Snowshoeing. Park N' Ski Area. It used to be that if you were planning a ski trip to visit Elk Creek Falls, you had better take along the latest

Forest Service map. I had one along when I first took a winter trip into the falls, but, nonetheless, I still managed to get side tracked for several hours, lost on the maze of snowbound roads in the area. Fortunately, however, that has all changed with a marked trail into the falls.

Even though marked, you should be aware this is not a beginner's

trip. **Moderately difficult** hills complicate the tour and you should have some experience under your belt before undertaking it. The trip to the falls starts in the town of Elk River, east of Moscow. To get there, follow Idaho 8 from Moscow to Bovill and continue another 20 miles east until reaching Elk River. Parking is located on the northeast edge of this remote backwoods community. While Elk Creek Falls is the most common destination of ski trips, the Elk River area boasts a total of 24 miles (39 km) of marked cross-country ski trails. Touring here in the upper drainage of the North Fork of the Clearwater is very typical of North Idaho cross-country skiing, with trails winding through the heavy forest and breaking out for a respite in an occasional meadow.

20 **Freezeout-Mark's Butte Area**—*Moderate to difficult backcountry. Access via snowbound road, then off-trail high country.* The Freezeout

area which includes Freezeout Saddle and Mark's Butte is the closest high elevation backcountry skiing to Moscow. Since elevations are at or close to 6,000 feet (1,825 meters), skiers (and snowboarders who are
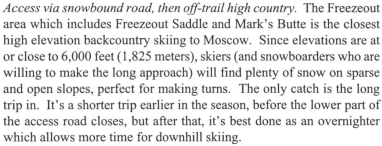
willing to make the long approach) will find plenty of snow on sparse and open slopes, perfect for making turns. The only catch is the long trip in. It's a shorter trip earlier in the season, before the lower part of the access road closes, but after that, it's best done as an overnighter which allows more time for downhill skiing.

To access the area, drive to Clarkia which is northeast of Moscow on Idaho 3. From the center of Clarkia follow Forest Road 301 to the east, past the school house. Stay on Road 301, the main road. Approximately 5 miles from Clarkia, you will reach the junction of Forest Roads 301 and 382. Forest Road 382 swings off to the right (south) and follows the Middle Fork of the St. Maries River, but you should remain on 301 which from this junction climbs steeply uphill, heading toward Freezeout Saddle. It's at 301-382 junction that you may need to park and start skiing. From this point it is about 7 miles (11 km) to the south slopes of Mark's Butte.

The skiing—and boarding—primarily takes place on **Mark's Butte**.

One noted area on the Butte which attracts skiers is an area called the **Crystal Forest**. It's a wonderland of ancient mountain hemlocks, often covered in a thick layer of rime. Skiers that frequent this area can't describe its exact location, just that it's on the back side of Mark's Butte and that you'll know when you've arrived.

For those interested in doing a multiday trip, a ski traverse is possible along the interconnecting ridge system running north from Mark's Butte to **Grandfather** and **Grandmother Mountains** and onto **Hobo Pass**. Hobo Pass is often plowed for logging operations. There's more about the traverse at the end of the chapter.

Avalanche danger exists. Be prepared.

21 **St. Joe Baldy**—*Moderate to difficult backcountry. Access via snowbound road, then off-trail high country.* The alluring high country around

St. Joe Baldy can be seen on a good day by looking to the east as you are driving through the Plummer area on US 95. It is on those open slopes, resplendent when the sun dips to the west, that backcountry skiers and snowboarders have found an equal to that of the Mark's Butte area.

To reach it, start at St. Maries which is southeast of Coeur d'Alene. Drive to the east along the St. Joe River Road heading toward Avery. Drive 7 miles from St. Maries until reaching **Phillips Draw**. There are residents that live up Phillips, and you'll need to make sure that you park out of their way. The trip to St. Joe Baldy is approximately 8 miles (13 km) long and follows the steeply climbing, switchbacking snowbound road to the north. There is also a more gradual approach to the area by starting at Cataldo which is located between Kellogg and Coeur d'Alene on Interstate 90 and following **Latour Creek Road** into the area. At this writing, a guide service was providing snowcat rides from Cataldo into the area. Check with the Coeur d'Alene District of the BLM (see *Resources* at the end of this chapter for further information).

The Freezeout Ridge Traverse

*F*REEZEOUT, for winter lovers, has a nice ring to it—and some nice snow fields on which to leave the temporal calligraphic marks of passing skis and boards. For a number of years, backcountry skiers had been discussing leaving more than just a few short marks, but rather one long sweep of the pen from Hobo Pass on one end of the high ridge system to Freezeout Ridge on the other end. It took a number of years before the traverse of the Freezeout Ridge system was done. Not because it was particularly difficult. It was just that no one got around to doing it. When it was finally done, however, it turned out to be one of those journeys that couldn't quite come to a sensible ending.

❄   ❄

*M*IKE BEISER watched as his friend Bart poked his head out of the tent which had been erected off the side of Hobo Pass, high on the divide between the St. Joe and St. Maries Rivers. The four skiers crowded into the tent had been startled by a weird popping sound outside: pop, pop, pop, pop . . .

Bart, in voice tinged with amazement, reported back to Mike and the others what he had seen. Then Mike, disbelieving, took a look. It was as he said. Big flakes were falling, and as they floated through the high voltage lines above their camping place, small charges of electricity arced between the flakes and the line. Pop, pop, pop. The sky was filled with snow falling and the repeated popping and flashing caused the draping lines to glow eerily in the dark.

That was the first night in a three day traverse of the high ridge that leads from Hobo Pass past Grandfather and Grandmother Mountains to Freezeout Saddle. Much of the ski and snowshoe country in the Moscow area is covered by heavy trees and brush, but this route is an open, high elevation traverse, and in good snow conditions, it has delightful downhill skiing. The three other members of the party with Mike were Bart Stryhas, Kay Garland and Mike's wife Teresa Beiser.

More snow fell on the second night of the trip while they were camped on the side of Grandmother Mountain. On the last day, their route took them across to Mark's Butte, where they figured it would be smooth sailing, all downhill to where they had spotted Bart's Toyota pickup truck, east of Clarkia. The snow, however, continued to fall with little let up.

"We were really looking forward to the downhill," recalled Mike, who directs the University of Idaho's Outdoor Program. "But three feet of snow had accumulated by then, and when we finally got to the downhill stretch, we had to break trail—*downhill*! It was backbreaking work."

After a long, long slog down the Freezeout Road, the exhausted party finally reached Bart's pickup truck. When they attempted to drive up to Hobo Pass to pick up Mike's 1980 Volkswagen Van, they found that the recent heavy snowfall had blocked the road. Not able to do anything that night, Mike decided to return the following weekend when the road was plowed. For the trip home, Kay, Teresa and Bart climbed in the cab of the pickup while Mike crawled in the back.

"It was the coldest ride I've ever had." Mike chillingly remembered. "By the time we reached Moscow, I was hypothermic and partly fumigated from all the exhaust fumes seeping through the back of Bart's old truck."

The next day, Mike had recovered somewhat from the ride in Bart's truck and started back to work. Despite all that had happened, the heavy new snow, arduous trail breaking and his abandoned van on Hobo Pass, he was gratified that the long, talked-about traverse had finally been completed. With the trip now over, he became absorbed in his work at the university and didn't think much about his van.

Somebody else, however, *was* thinking about the van: the sheriff of Shoshone County. The chapter on the trip wasn't quite closed.

The sheriff had become concerned when the Hobo Pass snow-plow driver reported to him that the skiers who had gone out last weekend had not returned to their vehicle. A lot of snow had fallen and it was possible that the ski party was caught someplace in the mountains beyond the pass. The county law officer ran a trace on the van's license, and turning up Mike's name, he started calling his home. For some reason, the sheriff only called during the day. And when he didn't reach Mike, he began making a preliminary search of the Hobo Pass area.

Finally on Thursday night, Mike who had no idea that he and his party were now the subject of a search, got a call from an angry sheriff. "He gave me a good chewing out," Beiser said, vividly remembering the Sheriff's mood. Mike tactfully tried to explain that he worked during the day and wasn't home to answer the sheriff's earlier phone calls, but the explanations largely fell on deaf ears.

"Well after looking for you guys," the sheriff said, starting to cool off a little, "we determined that you probably weren't there."

Not anxious to have more dealings with the Shoshone County Sheriff, Beiser, the next weekend enticed a friend into driving him out to Hobo Pass, where he collected his vehicle and returned to Moscow. Once home, he was finally able to sit back and relax. He was certain that this time the trip really had come to a close. □

Resources . . .

National Forest Lands: English Point, Coeur d'Alene and Fourth of July Pass Areas
Fernan Ranger District of the Panhandle National Forest—Address: 2502 East Sherman Ave, Coeur d'Alene, Idaho 83814 Phone: (208) 664-2381.

National Forest Land in the Wallace-Kellogg Area
Wallace Ranger District of the Panhandle National Forest—Office located in Silverton, Idaho. Address: PO Box 14, Silverton, Idaho 83867. Phone: (208) 752-1221.

National Forest Lands: Palouse Divide, Skyline Trail, Freezeout, Elk River Areas
Palouse Ranger District—Offices in Moscow and Potlach: 1221 Main, Moscow, Idaho 83843, (208) 882-1152; and Route 2, Box 4, Potlach, Idaho 83855, (208) 875-1131.

Public Lands in the St. Joe Baldy Area
Coeur d'Alene District of the Bureau of Land Management—Address: 1808 North Third, Coeur d'Alene, Idaho 83814. Phone: (208) 769-3029.

Alpine Ski Areas
Lookout Pass Ski Area—Address: PO Box 108, Wallace, Idaho 83873. Phone: (208) 744-1392 or 888-333-3737.

Silver Mountain Ski Resort—Address: 610 Bunker Avenue, Kellogg, Idaho 83837. Phone: (208) 783-1111 or (800) 204-6428 (snow report).

Avalanche Information
Local information is available from the ranger stations listed above. Additionally, avalanche forecasts are issued for the Lookout Pass area. The forecasts are available on the Internet or via recorded phone messages. For the current Internet address and phone number, contact: Forest Supervisor, Lolo National Forest, Bldg. 24, Ft. Missoula, Missoula, Montana 59801. Phone: (406) 329-3750.

Educational Programs
University of Idaho Outdoor Program—Office located in the Student Union Building on the University of Idaho campus in Moscow. Sponsors a variety of public educational programs on cross-country and backcountry skiing, winter camping and avalanche safety and is one of northern Idaho's most important informational sources on non-mechanized outdoor activities. Address: Outdoor Program, Student Union Building, University of Idaho, Moscow, Idaho 83843. Phone: (208) 885-6170.

Guiding, Backcountry Shuttles
Currently, a guiding operation is providing snow cat rides for backcountry skiing and snowboarding on the high St. Joe-Coeur d'Alene River Divide. Check with the Coeur d'Alene District of the BLM, listed above, for the permittee's phone number and the most recent information.

Another world: Freezeout Ridge. (Mike Beiser photo)

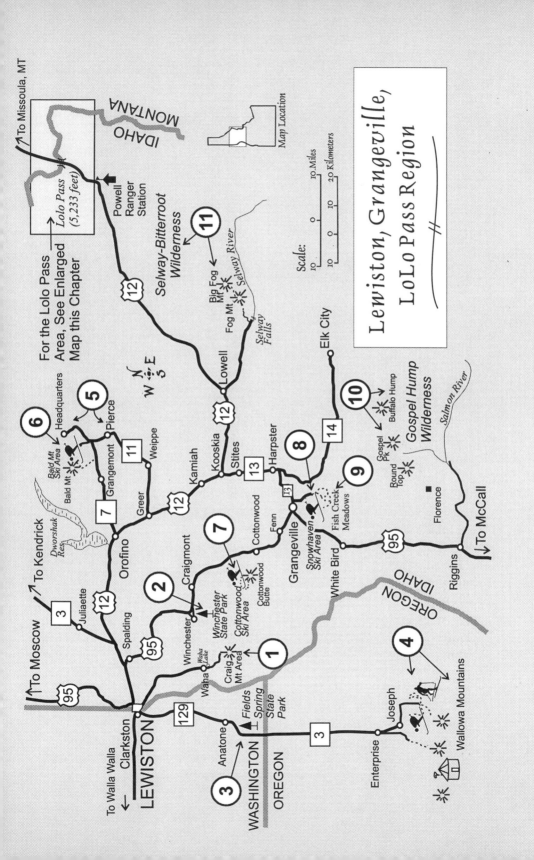

Lewiston, Grangeville, LoLo Pass Region

CHAPTER 9
LEWISTON-GRANGEVILLE-LOLO PASS REGION

Area Covered: North Idaho including Lewiston, Orofino, Pierce, Kamiah, Grangeville and Lolo Pass and nearby areas.

IT WAS in the central part of this region, in the Orofino and Pierce area, that skis were first used in Idaho, and like a wind fanned fire, their use quickly spread across the state with each new gold discovery. During the cold and stormy winter of 1861-62, skis were the only reasonable means of getting around. Supplies stacked up in Walla Walla—and Lewiston which was the area's newest outfitting and supply station established a few months earlier.

Packers with strings of horses waited impatiently for the snow to let up. They waited and waited. All winter, they waited. The snow never let up. What supplies that did get through were carried on men's backs.

While the packers bided their time, an incredible spectacle, the likes of which would never be seen again in the west, was playing out in the wilderness to the east. From Walla Walla and Lewiston to Orofino and Pierce, and across the rolling Camas Prairie to the present location of Grangeville, and on into the Salmon River Mountains to Florence, a steady migration was under way. Hunched over with canvas packs, men plodded away on skis, slowly moving black figures dwarfed by a landscape shrouded in white.

It has to be a rare winter, like the winter of 1861-62, for Lewiston to have snow to any degree. Yet, reliable snow is not far away. Twenty miles south of Idaho's lowest and warmest urban area is a pocket of high, snow covered country, the Craig Mountain area which is ideal for traditional cross-country skiing and snowshoeing. You'll need a 4-wheel drive vehicle to get up the steep and winding access road, but once there, you'll find lots of snow, undulating terrain and lovely trails passing through forests and open meadows. Also, very close to Lewiston is Winchester State Park, located east of town, off of US 95. Skiing here is snow dependent, but when several inches accumulate in the mid-valley locations, the park's marked trails are a delightful place to take the family.

Lewiston skiers, along with snow fiends throughout North Idaho, often strike out to neighboring Oregon and Washington. The Wallowa Mountains in Oregon are the most popular of destinations. They have all the ingredients for first rate cross-country skiing and snowshoeing: dry and abundant snow, marked and groomed trails, a hut system, wilderness trails and opportunities for ski mountaineering. The center of activity in this area is 15 miles south of Joseph, Oregon at Salt Creek Summit. Joseph is a reasonable 95 miles or 2 hours drive to the south of Lewiston. From Salt Creek Summit, an intricate system of trails leads off in all directions. Additionally, the Ferguson Ski Area adjoins the area and has its own Nordic trails and laid-back Alpine slopes on which to snowboard or practice telly turns.

On the way to Joseph, less than an hour south of Lewiston is Fields Spring State Park near the Washington-Oregon border. The park has a beautiful set of groomed Nordic trails and has become very popular among Idaho skiers.

The large region encompassed by this chapter extends eastward across Idaho all the way from Wallowas to Lolo Pass on the Montana border. In the midst of this expansive region is Grangeville on the northern edge of the Salmon River Mountains. The town was first established as a stopping place before the Florence and Elk City mines. Because of its location where the fertile Camas Prairie butts up against the grand fir forests of the Central Idaho wilderness, it evolved as an important regional center for farming and logging. From that amalgam of economies has come one of Idaho's gems of cross-country skiing. Cooperative efforts between the Forest Service, local skiers, business leaders and a logging company have created a Shangrila of Nordic trails eight miles south of Grangeville at Fish Creek Meadows. The area has exceptional rolling terrain, well designed trails, great views and notable off-trail possibilities. The icing on the cake is nearby Snowhaven Ski Area, Grangeville's homespun Alpine area.

On the far eastern edge of this region is Lolo Pass, located on US 12. The pass is a real hot spot for Missoula's sizable skiing and boarding community, but draws from northern Idaho towns as well. To meet the demand from both Montana and Idaho winter users, the Forest Service has developed a number of marked ski and snowshoe trails, and for the gravity inspired, there's also backcountry snowboarding and downhill Nordic on open slopes throughout the pass area.

The Lolo Pass area is steeped in the rich traditions of snowshoeing and trapping. Snowshoes were the only means to get around during the cold winter of 1936-37. It was winter that made a deep and lasting impression upon a teenager who was just beginning to cut his teeth in the trapping business. It was the kind of winter that the old, experienced Lochsa trappers called the Winter of Blue Snow.

The Tales . . .

In January of 1937, storms rolled across the Lochsa country one after another, leaving in their wake snow that piled 7 feet deep in the Lochsa valley and 14 or more on the high Bitterroots. Bud Moore, who the year before had taken up trapping to supplement his summertime Forest Service income, was on the move every day unburying traps and trying to keep the trails broken between line cabins. Moore's description of the winter of 1936-37 is found in his book, *The Lochsa Story*, a wonderful and sometimes poetic account of his life experiences in the Bitterroot Mountains.

"For twenty one days," Moore wrote, "I mushed each night into line cabins, leaving a deep trail through snow so loose its fluffy crystals looked blue in the wintertime light. For twenty-one mornings I climbed from the cabin's interior up to the snow's surface to find the trail buried by more snow that had fallen in the night."

He was at Papoose Camp when a storm had left yet another thick layer of loose snow on top of what was already on the ground. As he started off toward the next cabin at Cayuse Creek, he found his snowshoes sinking so deeply that his mittens would touch the snow's surface on either side of the trench that he was creating by

149

his passing. The deep snow slowed him down to a crawl. Near dark, he was reaching exhaustion and wondered if he could make it.

He struggled on, and when he finally felt that there was no possible way to continue, somehow he found the inner resources to move one snowshoe forward and then the other. During those interminable hours, he learned something. He wrote that "to discover the end of one's endurance was, I had supposed, a physical experience. But the mind, not the legs, gives up first."

"My world," he continued, "shrank to swirling snow, the blue glint where the webs broke the surface, and the herculean task of moving one snowshoe ahead the other. All else was instinct."

Darkness fell and yet he plodded onward in the blackness. Sometime during the long night, he felt something solid beneath his webs. It was the cabin. He had made it.

He got a fire going, fried up frozen elk meat and finished working on some skins. "Then I blew out the light," he wrote, "and crawled between the blankets on the mattress of beargrass where I slept while the snow piled deeper and the storm roared through the forest above the cabin's roof." □

The Trails . . .

1   **Craig Mountain**—*Snowbound roads and snowmobile trails. Easy terrain. Snowshoeing. Dogs OK. Four-wheel drive required.* In normal winter conditions, Craig Mountain is Lewiston's closest ski touring country. The edge of the plateau-like mountain is a mere 20 miles from the city limits. It's wonderful to have such an area close to a population center, but there are two caveats. The first is that you'll need a 4-wheel drive vehicle and a set of chains. The access road to Craig Mountain is narrow, steep and exposed and becomes treacherous in icy conditions. Secondly, the plowing of roads and parking are all paid through snowmobile funds and snowmobilers from Lewiston use this area extensively. While this isn't the most ideal of situations, Lewiston skiers gladly accept it and get along well with the snowmobilers, often using their groomed trails for skiing paths.

To reach it, drive south out of Lewiston on 21st Street. Follow 21st to Thain, and eventually Thain turns into County Road P-2. Continue on the county road. Once past the Waha Store, the road begins a long climb onto Craig Mountain. Snowmobile parking areas are found on top, and it is here where you start skiing. The groomed snowmobile trails can be followed or skiers can strike out on the other snowbound roads which traverse the area. The area is **rolling** with alternating open and timbered areas.

2 **Winchester Lake State Park**—*Marked cross-country ski trails. Easy to moderate terrain. Good family area.* The park is located .25 mile west of the town of Winchester, southeast of Lewiston on US 95. Three marked cross-country ski trails are available for varying abilities. The trails are all short with the longest being a mile long and running along the east arm of the lake. Snow conditions are variable at Winchester, and it is wise to give the park a call before driving there. When conditions are good, though, you'll be pleased with the skiing. Besides the picturesque trails, there are hills for practicing downhill techniques, and, the covered, frozen lake is an excellent surface for refining flat track techniques.

3   **Fields Spring State Park**—*Marked and regularly groomed cross-country ski trails. Marked snowshoeing trail. All abilities. Good family area. No Dogs.* Fields Springs has a wonderful set of groomed cross-country ski trails and is conveniently situated near the Lewiston-Clarkston area. When the roads are good, it can be reached in less than 45 minutes from Lewiston. It is located 4.5 miles south of Anatone, Washington on Highway 129.

The trails are for all abilities and wind throughout the 445 acre park. One of the ski trails and a snowshoe trail leads to the top of the 4,450 foot (1,356 meter) Puffer Butte from which you'll have an excellent view into the 3,000 foot deep Grand Ronde Canyon.

Washington Sno-Park or Idaho Park N' Ski permits are required.

4 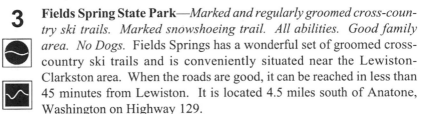 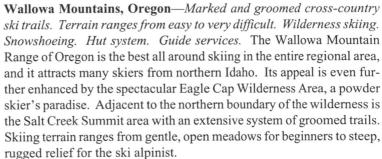 **Wallowa Mountains, Oregon**—*Marked and groomed cross-country ski trails. Terrain ranges from easy to very difficult. Wilderness skiing. Snowshoeing. Hut system. Guide services.* The Wallowa Mountain Range of Oregon is the best all around skiing in the entire regional area, and it attracts many skiers from northern Idaho. Its appeal is even further enhanced by the spectacular Eagle Cap Wilderness Area, a powder skier's paradise. Adjacent to the northern boundary of the wilderness is the Salt Creek Summit area with an extensive system of groomed trails. Skiing terrain ranges from gentle, open meadows for beginners to steep, rugged relief for the ski alpinist.

To reach the **Salt Creek** area, take Washington 129 (which turns into Oregon 3), 85 miles (137 km) south of Clarkston, Washington, to Enterprise, Oregon. At Enterprise, continue driving another 6 miles south until reaching Joseph. From Joseph, follow the signs the 17 mile distance to Salt Creek Summit parking area. This is Oregon Sno-Park area and you'll need either an Idaho or Oregon permit.

From the parking area, marked and groomed trails take off in all directions. A large portion of the area occupied by the trail system burned in a 23,000 acre fire in 1989. The burn has actually improved cross-country skiing, opening up views of the Seven Devils and allowing unlimited off-trail traveling.

Other skiing services in the Salt Creek vicinity include the **Ferguson Alpine Ski Area** with one T-bar and a rope tow. Ferguson has a vertical drop of 640 feet (195 meters), 6 runs and several miles of marked cross-country trails. Guided wilderness ski trips and a hut system are also available.

Another access into the Wallowas and Eagle Cap Wilderness is **Hurricane Creek**. Snowshoers and skiers with **moderate experience** will enjoy the first couple miles of touring on Hurricane Creek, while **backcountry** buffs will find terrain to their liking farther into the wilderness. To reach it, start at Enterprise and follow the signs leading to Joseph and Wallowa Lake. About .5 mile south of the center of town on Highway 3, the road splits. Take the right branching road in the direction of Hurricane Creek. Continue to follow the road toward Hurricane Campground, and 6.5 miles south of Enterprise, it crosses the Wallowa National Forest boundary. Continue driving until the road is no longer plowed.

Ski tours follow the snowbound Hurricane Creek hiking trail from the campground to the south. From Hurricane Campground, the trail is located on the west side of Hurricane Creek and remains on this side of the creek for the first several miles. There is some up and down skiing for the first mile of the tour which may give some beginners trouble,

but beyond this, the travel becomes fairly flat and easy skiing. An excellent destination for a beginning tour is **Deadman Creek** (1.5 miles or 2.5 km from the start). The tour leads through two large meadows,

offering views of Sacajawea Peak (elevation 9,839 feet or 3,000 meters) to the left of the Hurricane drainage, and the Hurricane Divide, the open

ridge line to the right of the drainage. Backcountry skiers may wish to continue further into the wilderness for a multiday trip.

For any trip in the interior of the Wallowas, skiers should be aware that severe avalanche dangers exist. Be prepared and check the latest avalanche forecast from the Eagle Cap Ranger District (see *Resources* for address and phone number).

5   **Pierce-Headquarters Area**—*Snowbound roads. Easy to moderately difficult. Dogs OK. Snowshoeing.* Located 70 miles east of Lewiston. A great network of snowbound logging trails in this area creates a variety of skiing opportunities for the **beginner** and **intermediate** skier.

6

Bald Mountain Ski Area—*Alpine ski area. Alpine, Nordic downhill and snowboarding. Rentals and instruction.* Bald Mountain, tucked away in the Clearwater Mountains, hasn't changed much since the late 1950s when it opened with a rope tow. It now has a T-bar, and has added some runs and replaced the old logging camp shacks with a real lodge, but it has preserved its character by not trying to become something that it isn't. Still run by the local ski club, it's the same ski area built with volunteers and a spirit of community cooperation.

Bald Mountain Ski Area is located 28 miles northeast of Orofino. From Orofino take Michigan Avenue to the east and drive towards Grangemont, following signs. The area has two lifts, a rope tow (which is free) and a T-bar. The vertical drop is 975 feet (297 meters), and it has 17 runs and 140 skiable acres.

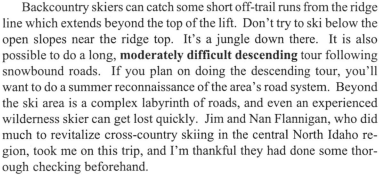

Backcountry skiers can catch some short off-trail runs from the ridge line which extends beyond the top of the lift. Don't try to ski below the open slopes near the ridge top. It's a jungle down there. It is also possible to do a long, **moderately difficult descending** tour following snowbound roads. If you plan on doing the descending tour, you'll want to do a summer reconnaissance of the area's road system. Beyond the ski area is a complex labyrinth of roads, and even an experienced wilderness skier can get lost quickly. Jim and Nan Flannigan, who did much to revitalize cross-country skiing in the central North Idaho region, took me on this trip, and I'm thankful they had done some thorough checking beforehand.

The Flannigan route leads into the Cow Creek drainage. Cow Creek crosses the Grangemont Road 6.1 miles west of the road's intersection with Highway 11. A shuttle car needs to be left here. From the ski area, the route works around to the south of Bald Mountain, crossing between it and Democrat Mountain. It continues across the top of the Ruby Creek drainage and then passes over into the Cow Creek drainage, which leads down to the shuttle vehicle. The total distance of the tour is 7 to 8 miles (11 to 13 km).

As with any tour originating within the boundaries of a ski area, be sure to notify ski area authorities of your plans. Otherwise, if they find your vehicle unattended at the end of the day, they may begin a search.

7

Cottonwood Butte Ski Area—*Alpine ski area. Alpine, Nordic downhill and snowboarding. Snowshoeing. Rentals, instruction and food.* Cottonwood is the western corner of a triangle of small, homey Alpine ski areas spread across the middle of this region. Like Bald Mountain, it has 1 rope tow and a T-bar lift. The vertical drop is 845 feet (258 meters), and it has 7 runs, a day lodge and night skiing. Known for its steep runs, it is located southeast of Lewiston, 8 miles west of the town of Cottonwood.

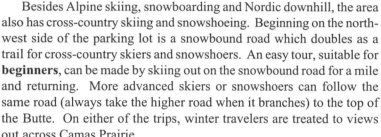

Besides Alpine skiing, snowboarding and Nordic downhill, the area also has cross-country skiing and snowshoeing. Beginning on the northwest side of the parking lot is a snowbound road which doubles as a trail for cross-country skiers and snowshoers. An easy tour, suitable for **beginners**, can be made by skiing out on the snowbound road for a mile and returning. More advanced skiers or snowshoers can follow the same road (always take the higher road when it branches) to the top of the Butte. On either of the trips, winter travelers are treated to views out across Camas Prairie.

8   **Snowhaven Ski Area**—*Alpine ski area. Alpine, Nordic downhill and snowboarding. Rentals and instruction.* Snowhaven is indeed a haven. Like its twin sister, Cottonwood, it has remained uncongested and has

retained the kind of local flavor that make such areas a pleasure to visit. The area has two lifts, a T-bar and rope tow. The vertical drop is 400 feet (122 meters) and it has 40 acres of skiable terrain. It's a great place to practice telemarks and is conveniently located near Fish Creek Meadows, Grangeville's premier cross-country ski area. The area is 7 miles south of Grangeville and is easily reached by following signs from downtown.

9   **Fish Creek Meadows**—*Marked and groomed cross-country ski trail system. East to moderate terrain. Toilets. Park N' Ski area.* The

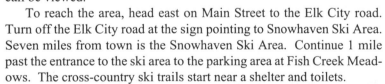

cross-country ski potential of Fish Creek Meadows was recognized by early Grangeville skiers, Jim and Nan Flannigan. It took a number of years before the area finally blossomed as a Nordic area. The impetus was the passage of the Idaho Park and Ski legislation which has done so much for Nordic skiing across the state. While many people, including Forest Service staff members, business leaders and skiers have helped make the area a reality, Dave Hayes needs to be singled out. He would be the first person to down play his role, but since 1982, he has been a constant and nurturing influence. Thanks to Dave and a few smoke jumpers stationed in Grangeville, the area even has a rustic log cabin along one of the trails from which the distant Gospel-Hump Mountains can be viewed.

To reach the area, head east on Main Street to the Elk City road. Turn off the Elk City road at the sign pointing to Snowhaven Ski Area. Seven miles from town is the Snowhaven Ski Area. Continue 1 mile past the entrance to the ski area to the parking area at Fish Creek Meadows. The cross-country ski trails start near a shelter and toilets.

The terrain in the Fish Creek Meadows area is ideal for cross-country skiing, and the trails make good use of it, winding through a forest of grand fir, Douglas fir and ponderosa pine. Open areas are scattered throughout, providing nice stopping places and offering views of the surrounding countryside. For the more adventurous, you can also take the lift up at Snowhaven Ski Area and follow a trail which connects with the Fish Creek system.

10  **Gospel-Hump Wilderness**—*Access via snowbound road, then off-trail high country. Moderately difficult to difficult backcountry terrain.* The snowbound hiking trail which leads across the crest of the Gospels to the Buffalo Hump is an unforgettable multiday ski traverse (see story about the traverse at end of this chapter). The area is accessed by start-

The Gospel-Hump Wilderness, looking down into the River of No Return.

ing from Fish Creek Meadows just past the Snowhaven Ski Area south of Grangeville and following the groomed snowmobile trail toward the **Old Adams Ranger Station**. From Adams, take the snowbound road up **Gospel Hill** and into the Gospels.

11 **Selway-Bitterroot Wilderness**—*Access via snowbound road, then off-trail high country. Moderately difficult to difficult backcountry.* Access to this wild, tangled wilderness can be gained from points along US 12 between Lowell and Lolo Pass, and along the Selway Falls road leading southeast from Lowell. The snowbound **Fog Mountain Road** is one of the better skiing access points from the Idaho portion of the wilderness, but nothing is easy about this wilderness, including getting into it. The long and steep Fog Mountain Road is located east of Lowell on the Selway Falls road near Selway Falls.

 Lolo Pass—*Marked and occasionally groomed cross-country ski trails. Marked snowshoe trail. Easy to moderate terrain. Toilets. Park N' Ski area.* Lolo Pass at 5,233 feet (1,595 meters) is the major pass on the state line between Idaho and Montana on US 12. It is located 45 miles southwest of Missoula, Montana and 170 miles east of Lewiston. A large parking area and a visitor center are located at the top of the pass. Since this is a Park N' Ski area, you'll need a permit. The marked and groomed ski trails start from the parking area and lead off to the east.

12 The **easiest** trail is the 2 mile **Glade Creek Loop** which is suitable for first time skiers and families. The trail, groomed on weekends, passes through stands of lodgepole and fir and open meadows. For a little more distance, you may want to try to the **Packer Meadows Loop** which is 6 miles long and encircles a beautiful, large meadow. The terrain on Packer Meadows Loop is a little more difficult than the Glade Creek loop, but skiers of **moderate ability** should have no trouble with it.

13 Another interesting trail which is of **moderate difficulty** is the descending **Lee Creek Trail**. Lee Creek Trail begins on the Packer Meadows Loop but then cuts off the north about 1 mile from the start. Leading down Lee Creek, the route follows a snowbound road and trail downhill to US 12 at Lee Creek Campground. The total distance is 6.6 miles (11 km). To do the tour, you'll need to leave a shuttle vehicle at the campground, located 5.9 miles from the top of the pass on the Montana side. There is also another alternative marked route to the campground which follows **Lee Ridge**. The ridge route is about a half mile longer and is a bit more difficult.

14 Another descending tour follows the **Pack Creek** drainage downhill to US 12, a distance of 8 miles (13 km). It is a **moderately difficult** trail and ends at Beaver Ridge Road, 5 miles from the top of Lolo Pass

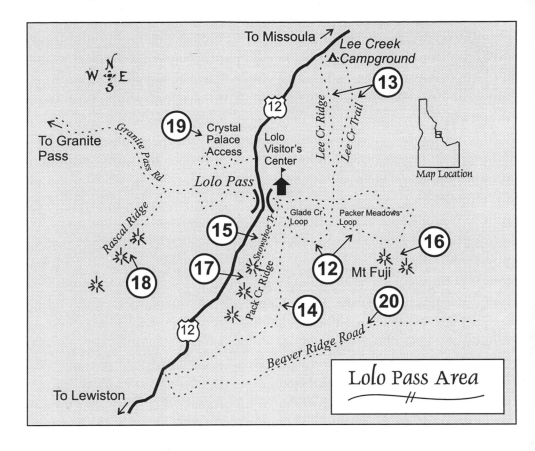

Lolo Pass Area

on US 12 on the Idaho side. While all the previously described trails are for skiing, this is a dual ski-snowmobile route.

 Lolo Pass also has a designated 3.5 mile **snowshoe trail** which heads to the south from the visitor center and climbs up on Pack Creek Ridge.

In the fall of 1913, Elers Koch was camped at Packer Meadows, the beautiful meadows which is a focal point of cross-country skiing on Lolo Pass. Franz Kube, an old trapper, stopped to say hello to Koch. With a string of pack horses and an inseparable dog, he was on his way to Lolo Pass. As he was leaving, he told Koch that it was to be his last trip out.

It *was* his last trip. He and his dog were never seen again. In the spring, friends searched his trap lines but found no sign of the trapper. Then, in the late 1920s a cook with a Forest Service trail crew reported seeing a wild man, naked with long hair and beard who fled when the cook spoke to him. Koch wasn't sure if there was any connection, but he hoped that the wild man was old Franz Kube who in the intervening years since his disappearance had become a part of the wilderness. "I'd like to think," wrote Koch, "that old man is still roaming his woods, matching wits against the wild animals for food and shelter."

Lolo Pass Backcountry—*Moderate to difficult backcountry terrain.*
Backcountry skiers and snowboarders will find Lolo Pass to their liking.
The most popular destination for backcountry enthusiasts is **Mt. Fuji**

16

which is located 2 miles to the southeast of the top of the pass. It appears
on topographic maps as points 6,372 and 6,388, and rises up from the
south side of the Packer Meadows Loop. The first time I skied on Lolo
Pass in the mid 1970s, Mt. Fuji hadn't been named yet, and it certainly
wasn't appealing from a skiing standpoint since at the time, it was heavily
timbered. Not too long afterwards, Plum Creek Timber Company came
to the rescue and clear cut the entire mountain. After the cutting was
over, the bare mountain top, when covered with snow, resembled Japan's
Mt. Fuji, and it picked up the cognomen. Besides attracting downhill
Nordic buffs, Mt. Fuji is also a popular place to snowboard. Enjoy it
while you can, though. The trees are already growing up, and eventually Mt. Fuji will revert to its old state.

17

   Pack Creek Ridge is another place of moderate difficulty where
backcountry skiers and snowboarders can find slopes for turns. To get
to it, start at the parking area and follow the Pack Creek Trail (a dual
snowmobile-ski trail) to south. Within the first mile, you'll notice a
ridge rises to the right (west) of the trail. This is Pack Creek Ridge.
Climb the ridge. Downhill runs off the ridge lead back into the Pack
Creek drainage.
   On the other side (west) of the pass, backcountry skiers and
snowboarders will find more downhill options. Like almost all
downhilling in the pass area, skiing and boarding are done in the open
areas created by clear cutting. For trips on the west side of the pass, it is
very helpful to have a special topographic map that the Forest Service
sells which has all the logging roads marked on it. The road system is
complex, and if you are unfamiliar with the roads, you can get terribly
lost without the map. One suggested backcountry area on this side of

18

the pass is **Rascal Ridge**. To reach it, take Granite Pass Road, which is
a dual use snowmobile-skiing trail, to the west. Turn left (west) on For-

est Road 5672 and then a .2 mile later, take a left (south) on Forest Road
75516. This takes you out on Rascal Ridge from which you can make
runs down toward the highway to the southeast.
   Another backcountry area on the west side of the pass is a place

19

called **Crystal Palace**. The access point is located in a small plowed
pulloff on the west side of US 12, 1.7 miles from the top of the pass on
the Montana side. Usually, a skin track leads up from the parking area

into the Crystal Palace area. This area has some of the best vertical
drops with descents of up 1,500 feet (457 meters) possible.
   It's also avalanche country as is all the backcountry in the Lolo Pass
area. Carry shovels, transceivers and check the avalanche forecast. Forecasts are posted at the visitor center or it is available by phone or the
Internet (see *Resources* at the end of the chapter).

Other Backcountry in the Lolo Pass Area—*Moderate to difficult backcountry terrain.* **Lolo Peak**, located on the northeast boundary of the Selway-Bitterroot Wilderness, is one of the most popular spring ski and snowboard descents in the Lolo Pass area. Access to the mountain is via **Mormon Peak Lookout Road**, located on the south side of US 12, 4 miles west of Lolo. In the late spring it is possible to drive up Mormon Peak Lookout Road. You can usually get within 6 miles of the peak. The route in follows the ridge line that leads in a southwesterly direction from Mormon Peak to Lolo Peak. Lolo Peak was at one time considered as a possible ski area and you'll find plenty of terrain on which to lay tracks.

Another spring skiing and boarding area includes the high country up **Beaver Ridge Road**, 5 miles from the top of the pass on the Idaho side of US 12. There's much more spring skiing, of course. As the roads into the high country melt off, they offer close access to the higher peaks which isn't possible during midwinter, and you'll want to keep your skis or board ready for those glorious spring days.

Sunset on Lolo Pass.

The Hump n' Thunder

I'D HAD ENOUGH. For 15 miles, the plastic sled dragging behind me by a rope and loaded with gear and food had been jerking me back and forth as I skied down the trail. On side hills, the sled would slide downhill and twist my body in unnatural and contorted positions. It was a great idea, but it didn't work, and I couldn't stand the torture any longer. I stopped and threw off the ropes that had been tied to my waist belt and transferred all my gear out of the sled and into my pack.

When I had finished, I looked at the sled. It was a borrowed sled from a friend of a friend in Moscow. Since it had been loaned to me, I wanted to make sure it was well taken care of. However, there was no way I could carry it with me. We had another 170 miles to go through rugged, mountainous terrain. I walked over to the side of the snowbound road that we were skiing along and started lashing it high in a tree.

"I'll pick it up next spring," I assured my companions who were watching. They nodded understandingly. I consider myself a fairly responsible person, and they knew that I'd follow through with my promise. I made a mental note of its location, and we skied off down the road heading to the Gospel Mountains.

It was the beginning of a month long ski traverse which took us through the Gospel-Hump Wilderness, then deep into the Salmon River Canyon and finally across the River of No Return Wilderness.

A couple of years later, I was sitting around with a few friends reminiscing about trip, when suddenly I remembered . . . the sled! It was still out there!

❋   ❋

*N*INE OF US started from Fish Creek Meadows, south of Grangeville in February of 1979. It was the year of the total eclipse of the sun, and we had planned to be high on Gospel Mountain in the Gospel-Hump Wilderness to watch it. When the day of the eclipse came, we had only made it to the side of Gospel Hill, short of our intended viewpoint. As it turned out, it didn't matter that we hadn't reached the perfect location to observe the heavenly spectacle. We wouldn't be able to see it anyway. The sky was heavily overcast and when the eclipse actually did occur, the day simply darkened a little more than it was. So much for the eclipse part of the trip.

Members of the party included Jim Flannigan from Grangeville who worked for the Forest Service and had helped establish some of the first cross-country trails in the area. From Moscow was publisher, Ivar Nelson and photographer, Phil Schofield; from Pocatello was biologist, Scott Finholdt and Peter Casavina who worked in an outdoor shop; from Boise was artist, Sandy Gebhards who also worked in an outdoor shop; and from McCall was smoke jumper, Jerry Dixon and Linda Burke who managed Youth Conservation Corps work groups in the summer.

I had to do quite a bit of talking to get Linda and Jerry interested in the ski traverse across the Gospel-Hump. They had been planning a trip to warm and sunny Baja, Mexico as a respite from the long winter in McCall. But I kept at it, telling them about the wonderful time we'd all have, and fabulous powder snow that we'd find high in the Gospels, and, oh yes, the eclipse.

What a wonderful place to view the eclipse, I told them, high up in the crystal clear air of Gospel Peak.

True, the eclipse part of the trip didn't quite go as planned—and, to be honest, some of the other parts of the trip didn't quite go as planned either.

The heavy overcast skies which obscured our view of the eclipse were just the beginning of a series of storms. It began snowing that day on Gospel Hill, and it didn't stop except for one day near the far edge of the Gospel-Hump. The clouds and blowing snow settled in and obscured the route which led across the high divide between Idaho's two great river systems: the Salmon to the south and the Clearwater to the north. Visibility at times dropped to a few feet. We gingerly skied to the east, using compass bearings and trading off the trail breaking duties through snow becoming deeper by the hour.

One day, mid way across, Jerry was skiing down a short pitch when he hit a drift of particularly resistant snow which threw him forward, face first. His heavy pack held his head into the snow and he flayed with skis and poles.

I skied up to him about the time he finally wiggled himself free. He threw off his pack, shot a look at me and said: "I could be in Baja right now!"

We had planned about six days to get across the Gospel Hump, but by the time we finally reached Dixie, stormy conditions had stretched the trip into ten. One mistake we made was dropping down Lake Creek and following the Lake Creek-Crooked Creek trail. The trail is located near the bottom of the steep-sided Lake Creek Canyon, and the canyon was filled with the debris of hundreds of avalanches that had come down two weeks earlier. Since nearly anything that could slide, had slid, we were safe from avalanches, but it was maddening and tiresome work, picking our way through the miles of frozen blocks of snow and ice.

Slipping further behind schedule because of the avalanche debris, we started rationing food, and by the time we finally skied into the town of Dixie, we were tired and hungry. No roads were plowed into Dixie at that time, and the Dixie restaurant isn't normally open in the winter. Yet, when we arrived, skiing down Dixie's main street, the owners flung open the doors and fired up the grill.

Jerry, whose mood had improved greatly upon reaching the restaurant, sat back and with great relish, dictated his order. By the time he had finished, he had consumed two steaks, two baked potatoes, two salads, several glasses of milk and several deserts. The prices for a cafe being that far back in the Idaho backcountry were very reasonable, but by the time Jerry had finished, he had racked up a bill of $74.52 which figuring for inflation would have been well over a hundred dollars today.

After replenishing lost calories and restocking supplies, four of us continued from Dixie to the south, making a 4,000 foot descent into Salmon River Canyon.

The Hump n' Thunder crew finally makes it to Dixie. Back row: Peter Casavina, Linda Burke, Scott Finholdt, Ron Watters, Sandy Gebhards, Jerry Dixon (after two steaks). Front row: Ivar Nelson, Phil Schofield and Jim Flannigan.

Phil Schofield

The rest of the trip down into the Salmon and across the River of No Return is another story, but before ending this one, I should make mention of what happened to the sled.

For some reason, the friend of the friend who owned the sled never asked about it when we had returned from the trip. And when a couple of years later, I finally remembered that the sled was still tied somewhere to the south of Grangeville to a tree, I decided after considerable thought that, perhaps, it was best to let sleeping dogs lie. Or, in this matter, let sleeping sleds lie.

One of these years, I might just have a quick look for it. Who knows? After all this time, it may still be out there. ☐

Resources . . .

Fields Spring State Park
Located 4.5 miles south of Anatone, Washington on Highway 129. Address: PO Box 37, Anatone, Washington 99401. Phone: (509) 256-3332.

Wallowa Mountains and Eagle Cap Wilderness Area
Eagle Cap Ranger District—Address: 88401 Highway 82, Enterprise, Oregon 97828. Phone: (541) 426-4978.

Winchester Lake State Park
Headquarters Winchester Lake State Park—Address: Winchester, Idaho 83555. Phone: (208) 924-7563.

National Forest Lands in the Grangeville Area
Supervisor's Headquarters of the Nezperce National Forest—Located in Grangeville at 319 Main Street. Address: Box 475, Grangeville, Idaho 83530. Phone: (208) 983-0460.

National Forest Lands in the Lolo Pass Area
Powell Ranger Station—Located in Powell. Address: Powell, Idaho 59847. Phone: (208) 942-3113. And, *Missoula Ranger District*. Address: Building 24A, Fort Missoula, Missoula, Montana. Phone: (406) 329-3814.

Alpine Ski Areas
Bald Mountain Ski Resort—Clearwater Ski Club, PO Box 1126, Orofino, Idaho 83544. Phone: (208) 464-2311 (Mountain phone) or (800) 794-8742.

Snowhaven Ski Area—Grangeville Chamber of Commerce, PO Box 212, Grangeville, Idaho 83530. Phone: (208) 983-0460 or (208) 983-2299 (snow report).

Avalanche Information
Avalanche information is available for the Wallowas from the Eagle Cap Ranger District, listed above. Forecasting work is also done on Lolo Pass. For the latest Internet address and number for recorded phone messages, contact the Powell Ranger Station, above.

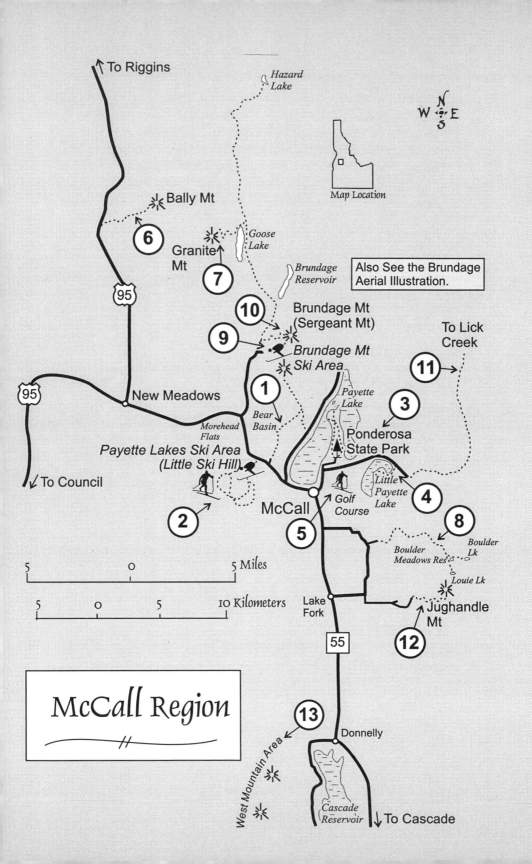

CHAPTER 10
McCALL REGION

Area Covered: West central Idaho including New Meadows, McCall, Donnelly, Cascade and nearby towns.

---

*M*cCALL BILLS ITSELF as Ski Town USA, and it isn't too far off the mark. It certainly has the history to back up the name. Skiing in Ski Town dates back to the early 1900s when Carl Brown used self-made long snowshoes to carry the mail to Burgdorf and Warren. The industrious and well-liked Brown eventually left the mail carrying business and built the Brown Tie and Lumber Company and its mill on the shore of Payette Lake. Although preoccupied with the lumber business, Brown always had a soft spot for skiing and, in 1937, gave McCall the land to build the Payette Lakes Ski Area.

What makes McCall such a desirable place for skiing and other winter sports is its cool climate and exquisite beauty. Throughout the winter, snow from frequent storms piles up and snowbanks get so high that businesses and homes are hidden behind them. Off the main highway in the residential areas of McCall, the streets become a maze of interconnected trenches.

The Payette Lakes Ski Area, Carl Brown's largesse, is the smallest of McCall's two Alpine ski areas and is also known as the "Little Ski Hill." The area is operated by the nonprofit Payette Lakes Ski Club and has a T-bar which takes skiers and snowboarders to the top of the 405 foot hill. The Little Hill is probably best known for its extensive and finely manicured Nordic trail system. Early on it established itself as one of Idaho's centers of competitive Nordic and Alpine skiing, and through the years, many fine athletes, including several Olympians got their start here. It has over 50 kilometers (31 miles) of Nordic trails, but the area is not solely for racers. It welcomes general tourers and even has a trail known as the dog loop, on which pets are welcome.

McCall's other Alpine area is the 1,300 acre Brundage Mountain. Brundage's gentle beginning and intermediate slopes makes it one of Idaho's most family friendly ski mountains. The slopes are ideal for telemark skiers and some days on the mountain, telemark skiers nearly outnumber Alpine skiers. Backcountry can also be accessed from the top of Brundage. Sergeant Mountain is the most popular, but experienced backcountry skiers also make a descending tour down the backside of Brundage toward Bear Basin.

Ponderosa State Park is the third gem in McCall's skiing crown. Located just northeast of McCall, the park has an outstanding trail system which is groomed for both classic and skating. Winter days are short, but Ponderosa has something to make skiing possible well into the evening: Idaho's first lighted Nordic trail, appropriately named Northern Lights.

Rounding out the selection of groomed cross-country trails, is the system maintained by the McCall Recreation Department on the Municipal Golf Course. It's a popular place for seniors and families and also boasts an ungroomed snowshoe trail on which dogs are allowed.

But not all skiing takes place on the groomed and marked trail systems. At times, it's nice to get away to untracked areas. For trips on easy terrain, you can ski or snowshoe around the edge of Little Payette Lake, just to the east of McCall or take a spin into Bear Valley, northwest of McCall.

McCall also sits in the midst of some fine backcountry skiing terrain, but getting to it is a problem. The most convenient backcountry skiing is Sergeant Mountain which is accessed easy enough by taking the lift at Brundage Ski Area. Jughandle Mountain to the south of McCall, however, isn't quite as convenient. Reaching the southern bowls on Jughandle involves a long, sustained climb through brushy and timbered slopes. The other mountain which attracts McCall backcountry skiers is Granite Peak, north of the Brundage area. The trip in and out of Granite is a 14 mile round trip journey, and even the fittest of skiers will want to plan to do it as an overnight trip or hitch a ride with a snowmobiler.

There's much more backcountry, of course, in the snow covered mountains which stretch for miles and miles to the east of McCall. Other than its fringes, this vast country is rarely ever skied or snowshoed. In the late 1800s and early 1900s, however, it was different. Miners or homesteaders that needed to buy supplies, pick up the mail or visit friends, strapped on skis or snowshoes and headed out on the trails that networked the area.

No one thought much of it. It was just a part of living in the backcountry. That's exactly how Forest Service Ranger Graham McConnell felt about it in 1920. His 50 mile ski trip out from the Middle Fork of the Salmon wasn't anything out of the ordinary. Yet, by the time it was all over, it was one trip he'd never forget.

Little Payette Lake: a nice place for easy off-trail cross-country skiing and snowshoeing in McCall.

The Tales . . .

IN DECEMBER of 1920, reports of a forest ranger missing some where in the wilderness to the east of McCall made front page news in Idaho newspapers. Apprehensive about the lost ranger, the Supervisor of the Payette National Forest hurriedly left a meeting in Boise to take personal command of the search. Along with the Forest Service, volunteers from McCall, Cascade and other areas started combing the mountains to the east looking for some sign of the lost man.

They were looking for Graham McConnell. McConnell had been assigned to a remote Forest Service outpost at the junction of the Middle Fork of the Salmon River and Marble Creek. Earlier, he had been asked to attend a ranger's meeting in Boise, the same meeting from which his supervisor had hastily left. It was a long trip out to the nearest plowed road, over 50 miles, through country heavily blanketed with snow, but McConnell was eager for a break from the monotony of the Middle Fork's long winter.

McConnell's route took him up the Middle Fork to the Pistol Creek Trail where snow quickly deepened. He was using snowshoes, but a pair of skis in a trapper's cabin along way caught his eye. Although, he was inexperienced in the use of skis, he chose to take them. Perhaps, he wanted a change of pace or perhaps he thought it was time for him, a proficient woodsman in other areas, to learn how to use skis. Whatever the reason, his decision turned out to be a mistake. Being unfamiliar with long snowshoes, he shuffled along awkwardly, expending far more energy than necessary, and his progress up Pistol Creek slowed considerably.

Later that afternoon, clouds settled in, and mist and blowing snow obscured nearby ridges and mountains. Trying to make up for lost time, he attempted a short cut. But after traveling for awhile the terrain around him didn't look right. He had expected to find a familiar meadow at the head of Johnson Creek, but the meadow was no where in sight. All around were trees and mountains and clouds. He searched and searched, but the meadow could not be found. Slowly it dawned on him that he had seriously miscalculated. He was lost. Night was upon him.

McConnell had made two mistakes, using skis without having prior experience and attempting a risky short cut in poor weather conditions. Yet he did do one thing right: he was prepared and had the ability to build a fire. That night and the following night, he was able to stay alive and keep from freezing by waking frequently and keeping the fire burning.

By the third day, long without food, and while many people throughout Idaho were wondering about his fate, he was nearing a state of utter exhaustion. He lunged forward in the snow, still searching vainly for some feature he could recognize. As he worked his way down an unknown drainage, the rugged terrain on either side of him eased up and began to flatten. He knew he must be reaching familiar country. If only he could find something to pinpoint his location.

Then he saw it. The sign read "Burnt Log Creek," and strung above the snow nearby was his lifesaver: a telephone line. The line linked ranger stations in the remote area. If he could manage to keep going, it would lead him to safety.

He staggered along the line, his energy ebbing. Night once again overtook him and snow from another storm started swirling around him. Slipping into a semiconscious state, he lost track of the phone line in the dark. As he wandered aimlessly in a meadow, he thought how ironic it was that he would end up perishing so close to his goal. Suddenly, he was shaken out of his stupor when something caught his ski.

It was a fence. He must be close. Struggling on, he followed the fence. A few minutes later McConnell stumbled through the door of the Penn Basin Ranger Station. He was alive, and his long ordeal was over. □

The Trails . . .

1 **Bear Basin**—*Easy terrain. Snowbound roads and off-trail. Snowshoeing. Dogs OK.* Access to Bear Basin isn't as easy as it was in the past. Homes have been built at the beginning of the road and skiers or snowshoers will have to walk down the single lane plowed road to the point where it is no longer plowed. To reach the trailhead, start at the junction of Warren Wagon Road and Idaho 55 on the western edge of McCall. Watch your odometer and drive 1.4 miles to Bear Basin Road, branching off to the right (northeast) side of the highway. Park off the highway.

From the highway, carry your skis or snowshoes down Bear Basin Road to where it becomes snowbound. Starting here, the tour follows the road which leads to the north into Bear Basin. The Basin, reached within 2 miles (3 km) of the highway, is crisscrossed with logging roads. It's a pretty area with **gentle** terrain changes and a nice mix of open meadows and timbered areas. Snowmobiles will be encountered.

2 **Payette Lakes Ski Area ("Little Ski Hill")**—*Alpine and Nordic ski area. All abilities. Instruction and night skiing. Dogs OK on special trail.* The Little Ski Hill is Idaho's second oldest ski area opening in 1937, the year after Sun Valley. It has one T-bar lift, a vertical rise of 405 feet (123 meters) and offers night skiing.

Little Ski Hill's main attraction is its network of 50 kilometers (31 miles) of Nordic trails. In the past, the area was known as primarily a training and work out center for ski racers, but the nonprofit club that oversees the area has been trying to broaden its appeal and has thrown out the welcome mat to everyone. They now have family programs, a special trail for dogs—and Nordic skiers over the age of 65 can ski for free. Trails are for all abilities and are beautifully groomed for skating or classic skiing.

The ski area is located 3.5 miles northwest of McCall on Idaho 55. Hot drinks and refreshments are available at the lodge.

3 **Ponderosa State Park**—*Marked and groomed cross-country ski trail system. Easy to moderately difficult terrain. Lighted trails for night skiing. Heated restrooms. Park N' Ski area.* Heavenly is one of the adjectives which can be used to describe Ponderosa State Park. Situated on a broad and long indentation of land which nearly splits Payette Lake, the park has a 10 mile (16 km) trail system ranging from **easy to moderately difficult**. The park's rolling terrain is unequaled for cross-country skiing. If beautiful terrain and location wasn't enough of an attraction, Ponderosa has also developed the first lighted Nordic trails in Idaho, enabling skiers to catch a quick tour after work. Maps of the trail system may be picked up in the visitor center.

The park, a short drive northeast from McCall, is easily located by following signs from the business district of McCall. A heated restroom is always open and plenty of parking is available. Park N' Ski permits are required.

4 **Little Payette Lake**—*Easy terrain. Off-trail skiing. Snowshoeing. Dogs OK.* For an easy ski or snowshoe away from heavily used areas, you may enjoy a jaunt around the edge of Little Payette Lake. The skiing is off-trail, but it's on **flat terrain**. It is located 3 miles east of McCall on Lick Creek Road. Parking is available in turnouts near the end of the plowed road. This area is also good for **snowshoeing**. One moderately difficult snowshoe trip that you might want to try is to head to the north from one of the pulloffs into the block of state land between Little Payette Lake and the main Payette Lake.

5 **McCall Golf Course**—*Flat, easy terrain. Groomed trails. Snowshoeing trails. Dogs OK on snowshoe trails.* McCall's golf course is located

northeast of McCall on the way to Ponderosa State Park. In past years, the golf course was the traditional place to go for the first cross-country skiing of the season. Once the snow was deep enough elsewhere, the

golf course was forgotten about. The McCall Recreation Department has changed all that by adding something new: 3 miles (5 km) of groomed trails for cross-country skiing and 3 miles of marked trails for

snowshoeing. This is the **easiest of all of McCall's** splendid **touring areas** and it is a good choice for seniors and families with small children.

To get to the starting point, turn off of Idaho 55 at the sign indicating Ponderosa State Park. Go .6 miles from Idaho 55 and turn right on Reedy Lane which leads to the parking area.

6 **Bally Mountain Road**—*Snowbound road. Moderately difficult. Snowshoeing. Dogs OK.* If you're looking for something a little dif-

ferent out of the McCall area, Bally Mountain is one possibility. Located on the east side of Idaho 95, 9 miles north of New Meadows, Bally Mountain can be climbed by following the snowbound road and

trail to the summit. The skiing is **moderately difficult**. Several side roads are encountered, and the topographical map *Bally Mountain* is helpful.

7 **Granite Mountain**—*Access via snowbound road and off-trail downhill skiing. Moderately difficult backcountry.* The base of Granite Moun-

tain is located 7 miles beyond Brundage Ski Area. While it's possible to ski in and out of the mountain in one day, it's best done as an overnighter. To get there, follow the snowbound **Goose and Hazard Lake Road** which takes off .2 miles below Brundage Mountain parking lot. Follow the snowbound road (which is a groomed snowmobile trail) into Goose Lake. Granite Mountain is behind Goose Lake, rising up from its west shoreline. It is on Granite's slopes, on the north end of the lake, where most of the skiing takes place.

To get as much downhill time as possible, some McCall backcountry skiers have been using snowmobiles. Behind the machine, two or three others hold onto ropes and are towed into the base of the area. What takes a half of a day to ski can be done in 20 minutes with a snowmobile.

It is a wonderful idea, but snowmobiles aren't always peaches and cream. "Their horrible and cranky," said Rick Freudenthal who has been a member of one of the groups using the snowmobiles. "Every time you go out, you're praying that nothing will go wrong."

On two occasions, backcountry skiers on broken-down machines were rescued by the president of the local snowmobile club. On another occasion, a skier being towed by a snowmachine tripped and got his arm caught in the tow rope. He ended up being rushed out with a broken arm. A newer, more reliable machine was purchased by one group of backcountry skiers. They had just taken it for a trial run at the beginning of the winter and had only driven it a quarter of a mile when a cloud of dark oily smoke poured out and the machine died. The mechanic who did the $1,500 in repairs found a clump of mud and dried grass in the engine. It had been left by a bird which had nested there the previous summer.

If you don't want to deal with a cranky snowmobile and you don't want to attempt the 14-mile round trip on skis, there may be one other option. At this writing, Brundage Mountain was operating a snowcat shuttle and guide service to Granite Mountain and **Slab Butte** directly across the north end of Goose Lake to the east. Backcountry operations like this come and go, and you'll want to check with the ski area beforehand to see if the service is still offered.

8 **Boulder Meadows Reservoir-Louie Lake Area**—*Snowbound roads. Moderately difficult. Dogs OK.* Usually the tour to Boulder Meadows Reservoir or Louie Lake is done as an overnighter, although it is possible to make the trip in a day. To reach the trailhead, drive .9 mile south of the McCall airport on Highway 55 and turn left (east) on Elo Road. This used to be called the Farm to Market Road. Once on the road, check your odometer and drive 2.8 miles to the east, around four right-angle corners and across the Lake Creek Bridge. Just beyond the bridge, turn left on Boulder Lake Road. Park where Boulder Lake Road is no longer plowed.

The first part of the tour is of **moderate difficulty** across **rolling hills** on a wide, mountain road. The upper portion of the tour narrows and **becomes steeper**. Approximately 3 miles (5 km) from the start, a jeep trail branches off to the right (south), which leads to **Louie Lake** (5.5 miles or 9 km from the start). Or you may continue on the main road to Boulder Meadows Reservoir (4 miles or 6.5 km from the start) and on beyond to **Boulder Lake** (1.5 miles past the reservoir).

9 **Brundage Mountain Ski Area**—*Alpine ski area. Alpine, Nordic downhill and snowboarding. Food, rentals, instruction and daycare.* With lots of **beginning and intermediate terrain**, this is Idaho's premier family mountain. Brundage is serviced by 4 chairs and 2 rope tows. It has 1300 acres of skiable terrain, 40 runs and 1,800 feet (549 meters) of vertical.

When the ski area opened for the 1960-61 season it was owned by three familiar names in Idaho: Industrialist Jack Simplot, Payette mill owner Warren Brown, and ski hall of famer Corey Engen. The Brown family has had much to do with the progress of skiing in McCall. As mentioned earlier, Carl Brown, Warren's father, donated the land for the Little Ski Hill, and Warren, of course, played a key role in developing Brundage. In Brundage's case, Brown and Simplot were lucky to have such a conscientious partner as ski coach Corey Engen. For two years before development on the mountain commenced, Engen skied it and even held a couple of races on it. He was taking no chances. He wanted to make sure that the lifts and runs made the best possible use of the mountain.

10 **Brundage Mountain Backcountry**—*Moderately difficult backcountry. See aerial illustration below.* **Backcountry skiers** have a couple of options starting from the Brundage Mountain Ski Area. One is an area called **Sergeant Mountain**. Sergeant is actually a local name which is called "Brundage Mountain" on the U.S. Geological Survey Map (point 7,803 on the *Brundage Mountain* topographic map). It is reached by taking one of the lifts which start just above the parking area to the top and skiing north along the Brundage ridge line. From the top of the lift to the top of Sergeant is about 1 mile. The backcountry slopes are located on the northwest side of Sergeant and descent lines up to 1,000 feet (305 meters) of vertical are possible. Just below these slopes is Goose Lake Road which can be followed back to where it intersects the ski area access road .2 mile below the parking area.

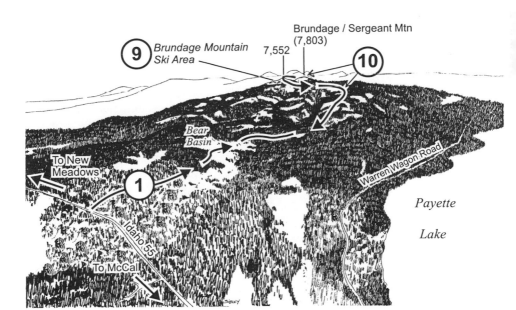

Aerial illustration of the Brundage Mountain area, viewed from the southeast.

The other option for backcountry skiers is a **descending tour** off the backside of Brundage Mountain Ski Area into **Bear Basin** (see aerial illustration on previous page). The tour starts with a lift ride to the top of the ski area, and drops to the southeast, eventually arriving in the basin. Either Brundage Mountain Road can be followed which is reached by following the main ridge south to the Brundage Mountain Fire Lookout—or an off-trail ski route is possible. A shuttle vehicle is necessary. Be careful with this one, particularly with the route which is off-trail. Make sure you've become thoroughly familiar with the area in the summer before attempting it in the winter and carry emergency overnight equipment. Avalanche hazard exists. The Brundage Mountain Ski Patrol should be notified of your plans, but remember the ski area is not responsible or liable for skiers who go beyond their boundaries. This tour, like any backcountry tour, is done at your own risk.

11   **Lick Creek Road**—*Snowbound road. Moderately difficult. Dogs OK.* Long, multiday tours are possible to the scenic Lick Creek Summit area northeast of McCall by following the snowbound Lick Creek Road. Several side trail options are available off the road, along with access to backcountry terrain. Snowmobiles also use the road. Avalanche hazard, especially beyond Lick Creek Summit, is extreme.

12   **Jughandle Mountain**—*Off trail. Moderate to difficult backcountry. See photograph on facing page.* Next to Brundage Mountain, Jughandle Mountain is the second most popular area for **backcountry skiers**. Backcountry **snowboarding** can also be done, but be prepared for some work getting to the top.

Driving there is also a bit complex: if driving towards McCall on Idaho 55, turn right on East Lake Fork Road at the town of Lake Fork. Keep an eye on your odometer and drive 1.7 miles, turning right on the Farm to Market Road. Go .2 mile and turn left on Ashton Road. From here, drive 1.2 miles to a "Y" in the road and take the right branch of the "Y." Park where the right branch is no longer plowed. One caution: constant building is occurring in the residential area at the base of Jughandle. The starting point and parking may change depending on new roads and development in the area.

From your parked vehicle, ski or snowshoe up. There's usually a skin trail to follow which winds its way upward to the south ridge of the mountain. Once above the lower timbered area, you can pick out a slope on which to leave a few signatures. Avalanche danger exists and shovels and transceivers should be carried.

13 **West Mountain Area**—*Snowbound roads and off-trail. Difficult terrain.* The West Mountain Area is located west of the Cascade Reservoir. Access to the area is obtained from the 30-mile long West Side

Jughandle Mountain. The backcountry skiing and boarding is on the south ridge (the long ridge extending to the right edge of the photo).

Recreation Area Road, which is reached either out of Donnelly or Cascade—or from the west side near Council. With the exception of No Business Canyon Road, the trails are very steep and there is considerable avalanche hazard in the higher elevations.

 Compared to past years, this area has been receiving a lot of attention from snowmobilers, and several groomed snowmobile trails now traverse the area. Nevertheless, it remains an option for backcountry skiers with the principle attraction being the big powder bowls on the upper slopes of the mountain. It's a long trip to the bowls and once there, the **backcountry skiing** is **moderately difficult** to **difficult**. As would be expected, avalanche hazards exist. Those few skiers that have explored the area have mostly concentrated on **Council Mountain** which is approached from the **west side** of the area, via from **Cottonwood Creek**, 2.5 miles south of Council. On the **east side**, some access trails leading to the higher portions of West Mountain include Campbell Creek (8 miles from Cascade), Hazard Creek (11 miles from Cascade), Evans Trail (13 miles from Cascade), and Poison Creek Trail (20 miles from Cascade).

OTHER SKIING AND SNOWSHOEING TRAILS

In the first edition of this book, I had listed **Morehead Flats** as a nice beginning and intermediate ski tour. It's now being used as snowmobile trail, but if you catch it in the early morning before the machines

175

get on it, the Morehead Flats Road is a very pleasant tour of moderate difficulty. Some skiers also use this snowbound road to access the **open slopes** on the **north edge of the New Meadows Valley** for telemarking. You'll want to plan this for the morning as well, since the slopes face south and can crust up quickly.

The trailhead is near the Brundage Mountain Ski Area turnoff, 5.5 miles northwest of McCall. One-quarter of a mile (.4 km) south of the Brundage turnoff on the west side of the highway is the snowbound Ecks and Morehead Flat Road. There usually is a plowed pulloff in the vicinity where your vehicle may be parked.

Several Park N' Ski areas were developed in the Cascade area, but as of this writing, all of them had been abandoned. One area which is no longer marked but remains a nice area for ski touring or snowshoeing near Cascade is in **Scott's Valley.** To reach it, turn left (east) onto

Warm Lake Road just north of Cascade. Check your odometer and drive 6.9 miles. The old trail leads off to the left (north) side of the highway into open and scattered timber areas. When I visited the area,

there was a small turnoff to park vehicles on the right (south) side of the highway .2 mile from the trailhead. If you like exploring, there's also some other possibilities farther east on Warm Lake Road.

Also, on the way to Scott's Valley is **Horsethief Reservoir.** The snowbound access road is located approximately 6 miles from the junction of Idaho 55 and Warm Lake Road on the right (south) side of the road. The skiing or snowshoeing is **easy to moderately easy.**

Finally, **Cougar Mountain Lodge,** which is a store and restaurant located at Smith's Ferry 45 miles south of McCall, at one time had developed a trail system. There wasn't enough use on the trails to justify continuing the grooming program, but you can still park at the restaurant and ski to the south for a short **easy** tour along a placid stretch of the **North Fork of the Payette.** Stop in the restaurant for hot drinks and a meal afterward.

LONG BACKCOUNTRY TRIPS

The McCall area is a good starting (or ending) point for a number of long, multiday journeys, and if you enjoy backcountry skiing and camping, you might be interested in a summary of some past routes.

In the 1970s, the most common long trip was the ski trip on snowbound roads into Burgdorf Hot Springs, a commercial hot springs to the north of McCall. Since it is a heavily used snowmobile route, it's not done much anymore.

McCall's Art Troutner has put together a series of long trips. One that he and friends have done a couple of times is the snowbound road trip from Warm Lake to Landmark, to Deadwood and on to the plowed portion of Idaho 21, west of Stanley. This route is also used by snowmobilers but use tapers off greatly during the week.

Further to the south, Troutner, Steve Passmore and Brad Stein skied a backcountry route from Grand Jean, up the South Fork of the Payette and down the Queens River to the old mining town of Atlanta. They were relieved to make it to Atlanta, having had some anxious moments near avalanche prone areas along the route. Troutner remembers skiing into the isolated town and walking into the town's bar, wearing the ski clothes that he had worn for the past several days. "None of the old miners batted an eye," said Troutner. "They told us it was pizza night and everyone was adding something to the pot. So we threw in our left over cheese and salami and they made up a pizza. We sat there drinking beer and eating pizza with them. It was like we had been living there all of our lives."

Humming Duck

WE HAD JUST SETTLED into our sleeping bags. Jerry's bag was huge. It took up a sizable portion of the available floor space in the North Face dome tent. My headlight illuminated the inside of the tent which was full of vapors from our breaths and warm bodies. Gregg, peering out of his bag, squinted as I flashed it in his direction. I shut off the headlight.

"Pals," Jerry said as the rustling of nylon bags quieted, "Tonight, I want you to think of me as a brown, crispy piece of toast."

Jerry was obviously proud of his new sleeping bag. It was one of those -40 degrees bags with 8 inches of loft. When he awoke the next morning, he had the smug, pleased look of one who had slept in luxurious comfort the night before. Jerry Dixon's sleeping bag was to be put to good use as we skied from McCall up Lick Creek Road, for unknown to us when we had started the trip, a particularly prolific storm had entered the state and would pound much of western and southern Idaho for the next several days with little let up.

With Jerry and I was long distance hiker Gregg Eames, a compact, perpetual motion machine who was doing much of the trail breaking. Part of the reason Gregg may have enjoyed being in front was that he didn't have to listen to the uninterrupted string of stories that Jerry and I passed back and forth, some of which I'd have to admit were already on the second telling within 24 hours of starting the trip. Our plan was to ski to the top of Lick Creek, make

a camp in the Hum and Duck Lakes area, and from there attempt a
winter climb of North Loon Peak. At some point later in the trip
when it was obvious we weren't going to even make it to Duck and
Hum Lakes, Jerry announced that henceforth the trip would be
known as the Humming Duck Expedition.

The second night we camped off the side of Lick Creek Summit. Even as we prepared the tent site, snow was coming so fast
that if you laid anything down, such as a mitten or stuff sack, it
would be quickly covered and lost.

The snow continued unabated all night. The next morning we
awoke to tent poles bent and walls collapsed around us. I forced
my way out, partly tunneling through a drift by the door and looked
back. The tent was just another mound in the snow, covered by at
least two-and-a-half feet of new snow.

And still it snowed. The avalanche danger was so high that
small side hills, only four or five feet high would send down slabs
of snow and miniature avalanches, triggered by the imperceptible
vibrations of one of us passing nearby. Obviously, there was no
way we were going to climb anything in those snow conditions.

During the next day, we built a snow cave and an igloo and
weathered another night. The snow continued. In a two day
period, 40 inches of new snow fell. I've never seen so much snow
come down so fast in Idaho.

For all intents and purposes, the trip was over. Gregg, anxious
to get back to a warm cabin and not relishing a slow amble back
with his pattering companions, sprinted off down the road. No
doubt that he was also looking forward to missing Jerry's nightly
and lengthy discourses on how warm and toasty he was in his new
sleeping bag. Gregg skied from the summit all the way back to
McCall in one day, a remarkable feat considering the amount of
fresh snow. Jerry and I took two days.

The temperatures began to moderate, and when Jerry and I
prepared our campsite for the night, wet snow was falling. Once
the tent was up, Jerry crawled into the luxurious fluff of his sleeping bag. A satisfied look spread across his face as the soft nylon
covered goose down settled gently around him and he began to
warm up. He repeated his nightly mantra about being a warm,
crispy piece of toast and drifted off to sleep.

During the night, the temperature rose even more, and I could
hear rain splattering against the tent. Since it was winter, I hadn't

brought along a storm fly, but as the rain continued beating against the tent, I wished that I had. We were bound to get wet without it.

When I awoke in the morning, I gingerly turned in my sleeping bag expecting to feel cold, wetness where water had seeped through the tent from last night's rain storm. I turned but felt no water. I was pleasantly surprised. My bag was dry. I was perplexed, however, wondering how I could have possibly stayed dry after a night like that.

I peered through the opening in my sleeping bag at Jerry. Then all at once, I realized what had happened. Jerry's sleeping bag, so full and lofty the night before, had been reduced to a couple of wet pieces of nylon material. Staring at me with wet hair, and a few drops of water running down his forehead was a very sorry looking tent mate. During the night, his sleeping bag had become a giant sponge, soaking up any water which had leaked into the tent.

I was just about to say something about crispy toast becoming soggy toast when he glared at me. Although sorely tempted to have a little fun, I went easy on him and filed it away—for a couple of hours anyway. This was one story that Gregg wouldn't mind hearing. □

Resources

National Forest Lands in the Area
Payette National Forest Supervisor's Headquarters—Office located in McCall. Address: Box 1026, McCall, Idaho 83638. Phone: (208) 634-0700.

National Forest Lands in Cascade and West Mountain Areas
Cascade Ranger District of the Boise National Forest—Office located in Cascade. Mailing address: PO Box 696, Cascade, Idaho 83611. Phone: (208) 382-4271.

National Forest Lands in the New Meadows Area
New Meadows Ranger District of the Payette National Forest—Office located in New Meadows. Address: PO Box J, New Meadows, Idaho 83654. Phone: (208) 347-0300.

Ponderosa State Park
Ponderosa State Park Visitor's Center—Located on the northeast edge of McCall. Address: Box A, McCall, Idaho 83638. Phone: (208) 634-2164.

Winter Recreation Programs
McCall Recreation Department—Schedules of events are available. Address: Box 1065, McCall, Idaho 83638. Phone: (208) 634-3006.

Alpine Ski Area
Brundage Mountain Ski Area—Address: Box 1062, McCall, Idaho 83638. Phone: (208) 624-4151 (offices) or (888) 255-7669 (snow report).

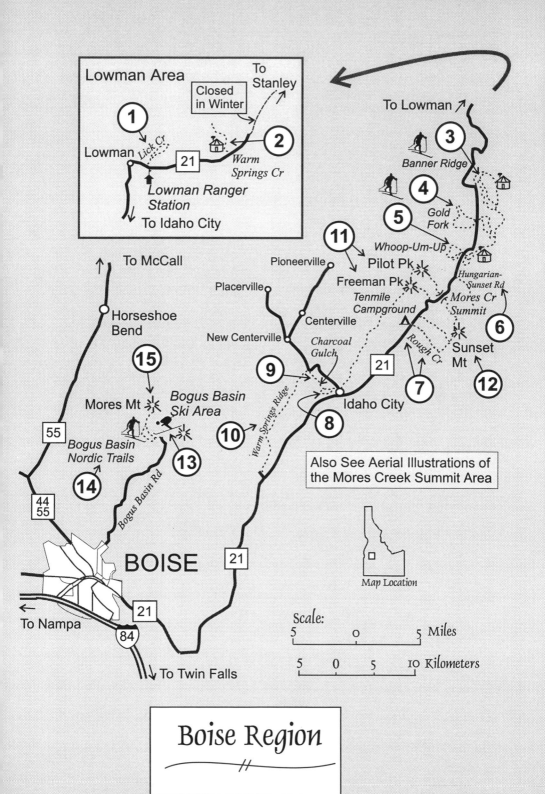

Lowman Area

To Stanley

Closed in Winter

(1)

Lowman

Lick Cr

21

Warm Springs Cr

(2)

Lowman Ranger Station

To Idaho City

To Lowman

Banner Ridge

(3)

(4)

Gold Fork

(5)

Whoop-Um-Up

Hungarian-Sunset Rd

Mores Cr Summit

(6)

To McCall

Pioneerville

Placerville

(11)

Pilot Pk

Freeman Pk

Tenmile Campground

Centerville

Charcoal Gulch

New Centerville

Rough Cr

(7)

Sunset Mt

(12)

Horseshoe Bend

(15)

(9)

Warm Springs Ridge

21

Mores Mt

Bogus Basin Ski Area

(8)

Idaho City

Also See Aerial Illustrations of the Mores Creek Summit Area

55

(10)

Bogus Basin Nordic Trails

(14)

(13)

Bogus Basin Rd

44 55

BOISE

21

Map Location

21

To Nampa

84

Scale:

5 O 5 Miles

5 0 5 10 Kilometers

To Twin Falls

Boise Region

CHAPTER 11
BOISE REGION

Area Covered: West Idaho including Boise, Idaho City, Lowman, Owyhee Mountains and surrounding areas and communities.

*I*T *QUICKLY* became obvious that gold discoveries in Idaho City were something out of the ordinary. By the fall of 1863, one year after the first discovery had been made, Idaho City had a population of 6,267 and had become the largest city in the northwest, surpassing the population of Portland. The trails were crowded with miners, merchants and packers traveling in and out of the basin. In the winter, a considerable amount of the travel took place by skis, particularly to the mines to the northeast. After silver and gold was discovered at Banner, men and women often used long snowshoes to travel between the two towns when the snow was too deep for other means.

Someone who knew a lot about skiing in the Idaho City area was Charley Magee who ran a stage and held the mail contract between there and Banner. The November 27, 1881 issue of the *Idaho World* advised readers that Magee's stage coach had stopped running between the two towns. "From the way the snow came down yesterday," the *World* reported, "it looks like snowshoes [skis] will soon have to take the place of the bronco." Magee was skilled on skis and used them often. During some snowy winters, he had to use them nearly all winter to get the mail back and forth between Banner and Idaho City.

Skiing still continues in the Idaho City area. It is, in fact, Cross-country Skiing Central for Boise and much of the skiing takes place in the high country that Charley Magee skied through over a hundred years ago on his way to Banner.

In 1972, Forest Service Ranger Don Reed established the first marked system of cross-country ski trails in the Idaho City area. While the system has changed considerably, the foundation that he established still remains today. The foundation was shored up when in the 1990s the State Parks and Recreation Department and an army of volunteers from Boise expanded the system and began a grooming program.

The centerpiece of the new, expanded system is a cluster of three trail systems, 20 miles to the northeast of Idaho City on Idaho 21: Whoop-Um-Up, Gold Fork and Banner Ridge. The trail systems are marked, well groomed, and most of them are in the intermediate or moderately easy range of skiing difficulty. Although beginning ski trails are lacking in the area, trail organizers hope to develop at least one new area with more gradual terrain.

The Idaho City systems are not just for those seeking a groomed experience. Nice telly slopes can be reached from both the Gold Fork and Banner Ridge systems. In addition to Nordic downhill opportunities, there are even more enticements. A yurt (with plans for more in the future) and the Forest Service Beaver Creek Cabin are available for cozy, overnight stays in this corner of winter paradise.

There's also skiing right from the town of Idaho City. You can walk to the beginning of a Forest Service maintained loop which starts at the airport. The 2.5 mile loop, called Buena Vista (or sometimes Airport Loop) has a few hills, but it is largely oriented to beginners. To get to it, walk or drive west on Wall Street, past the Community Center and head on to the airport. When you're not skiing, it's fun to poke around in Idaho City. It still has a rustic allure with its boardwalks and old tobacco-chewing residents frequenting local saloons.

The closest track skiing to Boise is the groomed trail system at Bogus Basin Ski Area, 16 miles north of the city. With its Nordic trails, marvelous Alpine skiing and snowboarding, Bogus is a priceless part of the Boise recreational landscape. That landscape will improve even more as Bogus goes through several expansion phases. The Nordic trails, since they are perched on the side of a mountain, are of intermediate difficulty, but they are well cared for, and it is close enough to Boise that if you have a couple free hours, you can run up and catch a workout.

Also included in this region are the Owyhee Mountains, a lone range rising up from a desert of gnarled sage and tawny cheat grass.

Since approaches into the area are long, it is most appropriately classified as a backcountry area. One general tour, albeit a long one, which will interest some skiers, is the visit to the old ghost town of Silver City. Whether it's Silver City or other parts of this range, you'll find that the Owyhees are a completely different skiing experience.

The Tales . . .

THE YEAR was 1880 and Idaho City's newspaper, the *Idaho World*, was keeping its readers entertained by carrying occasional stories on skiing. One of the stories concerned a party of six that was on their way from Idaho City to the Yankee Fork, a 150 mile journey to the northeast. It was spring, but there was plenty of snow in the mountains and they had taken skis along with them. Since some members of the group were badly in need of some training in the use of skis, they paused at Mores Creek Summit.

"Four of the boys," explained the *Idaho World* with relish, "were giving a snowshoe exhibition for the edification and instruction of the inexperienced, and succeeded well enough until they started down the summit. Here they struck up the 'Sweet Bye and Bye,' and slid off, at lightning speed, down the mountain. This daring quartet didn't 'Land on the beautiful shore' but were landed headfirst in a huge drift of the 'beautiful snow.' "

About this time, Charley Magee, the mail carrier between Idaho City and Banner, was coming over Mores Creek when he ran into the quartet. The *Idaho World* continued: "The first thing that met his astonished gaze was six wiggling legs projecting from the bank. The unfortunate snow-shoers were soon pried out with snowshoe poles. Their vanity was all knocked out, but they were otherwise uninjured."

The *Idaho World* also kept its readers appraised of the ski times between the two towns. A couple of weeks earlier that same year, the *World* reported that James Monroe and James Irwin had skied the distance between Banner and Idaho in a remarkable 7 hours and 45 minutes, proudly announcing as the best time ever recorded. As far as I can determine, the record still holds.

But the times were not always so blistering. Before Charley Magee, Jimmy Emerson had a short career as the Idaho City-Banner mail carrier. During one period of deep, unconsolidated snow during the winter, it took him five days to travel the distance between the two towns.

Things didn't get any better for Jimmy. He left Idaho City with the Banner mail on a Monday early in March. On Tuesday, exhausted, he returned with the Banner mail undelivered. Struggling for two days, he had only reached a point 8 miles beyond town. Jimmy had enough. He resigned as mail carrier and began to look for more sensible work. □

The Trails . . .

LOWMAN AREA

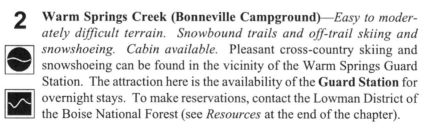

1 **Lick Creek**—*Snowbound road. Easy to moderately difficult terrain. Snowshoeing. Dogs OK.* Parking for snowshoe or ski trips on the Lick Creek trail is found at the **Lowman Ranger Station** located on Idaho 21, 1.1 miles east of the junction of Idaho 21 with the Banks-Garden Valley Road. From the ranger station walk through the little residential area on the other (north) side of the highway from where you've parked. Start skiing or snowshoeing where the road becomes snowbound. The old logging road that you are following forks 1.5 miles (2 km) from the start. If you really want some exercise, a 12 mile (19 km) loop can be done from this point. Otherwise, an up-and-back trip can be made on the first 2 miles (3 km) of the road which serves as an easy outing, suitable for **all abilities**.

2 **Warm Springs Creek (Bonneville Campground)**—*Easy to moderately difficult terrain. Snowbound trails and off-trail skiing and snowshoeing. Cabin available.* Pleasant cross-country skiing and snowshoeing can be found in the vicinity of the Warm Springs Guard Station. The attraction here is the availability of the **Guard Station** for overnight stays. To make reservations, contact the Lowman District of the Boise National Forest (see *Resources* at the end of the chapter).

To reach the area, drive approximately 19 miles east of Lowman on Idaho 21. Just after the highway bridge crossing from the south to north side of the Payette River (immediately before reaching Warm Springs Creek), a small pulloff is plowed. From here a snowbound road leads back to the west along the north side of the river and within .5 mile comes to the Guard Station. The touring, suitable for **all abilities**, takes place on and off the snowbound trails in the Guard Station area.

IDAHO CITY AREA

3 **Banner Ridge**—*Marked and regularly groomed cross-country ski trail*
system. Moderately difficult. Yurts available. Park N' Ski area. The
Banner Ridge parking area is located 22.4 miles northeast of Idaho City
on the left (west) side of Idaho 21. The system consists of three trails
with a total of 15 miles (25 km) of skiing possible. Except for one 2.4
mile (4 km) section, the trails are groomed and are of **moderate** difficulty. From the trails and nearby overlooks, skiers are treated to beautiful views of the South Fork of the Payette Canyon and the Sawtooths
in the distance.

A **descending tour** can be made from **Banner Ridge to the Whoop-
Um-Up** trail system, and some tourers may be interested in giving it a
try. It requires a shuttle vehicle be left at the Whoop-Um-Up parking
area, 5.5 miles south of Banner Ridge on Idaho 21. The tour follows
Beaver Creek Trail and descends 800 feet (244 meters).

There's also some terrific **telemark** skiing that can be accessed from
the trail system. To get to these fine slopes, travel clockwise 1.2 miles
(2 km) on the Elkhorn Loop to Banner Ridge. The slopes are located to
the north of the groomed trail. Remember that even though the slopes

are in the vicinity of a groomed trail system, it doesn't mean they're
somehow magically safe. Prepare adequately and take along shovels
and avalanche transceivers. Also, for a beautiful overnight experience,
Banner Ridge Yurt is located in this area and is available for rent (see
Resources for more details).

The original Banner Mine is located about 4 miles east of the Banner Ridge parking area. It is through this area and onto the top of Mores Creek Summit that the Idaho City mail carriers would pass through wearing their long snowshoes.

Leo Hennessy

Home in the mountains: Banner Ridge Yurt.

4

Gold Fork—*Marked and regularly groomed cross-country ski trail system. Moderately difficult. Park N' Ski area.* The Gold Fork parking area is located 20 miles northeast of Idaho City on the left (west) side of Idaho 21. Skiers can choose from trails on either side of the highway. On the **east side,** is a groomed loop trail that is 4.3 miles (7 km) long and has connector trails to both the Banner Ridge and Whoop-Um-Up trail systems.

On the **west side** of the highway is one long groomed loop of 5.1 miles (8 km) which has two shorter cutoff loops for those who don't want to go the full 5 miles.

Telemark slopes can also be accessed from the Gold Fork trails on the west side of the highway. To reach them, ski in a clockwise direction on the main Gold Fork Loop for 1.6 miles (2.5 km) to the turnoff to Double Dip, the second of the two smaller cut off loops. From here, turn left and ski to the west 1 mile until reaching the open slopes. Have fun, but remember to carry the usual emergency overnight and avalanche safety equipment with you.

5 **Whoop-Um-Up Creek**—*Marked cross-country ski trail system. Moderately difficult. Toilets. Dogs OK. Snowshoeing. Park N' Ski area. See aerial illustration below.* The Whoop-Um-Up Creek parking area is located 16.9 miles northeast of Idaho City on the right (east) side of Idaho 21. If you happen to pass a sign that indicates Edna Campground, you've missed it. Stop, backtrack .7 mile (1.1 km) and look for the entrance to the large parking area. The parking area is shared with snowmobilers, but the ski trails are restricted to human powered travel only.

Ski trails are located on both sides of the highway. Two loop trails totaling about 4 miles are located on the **west side** of the highway, and three loop trails totalling 3.5 miles are located on the **east side** of the highway. The east side also has a trail leading to the **Beaver Creek Cabin** which can be rented for overnight stays. Reservations for the cabin are made through the Idaho City District Ranger Station (see *Resources*).

All of the Whoop-Um-Up trails are ungroomed and you can take your dog here. Trail organizers ask that dog droppings be removed from the trail.

Aerial illustration of Pilot Peak and Whoop-Um-Up Creek, viewed from the east.

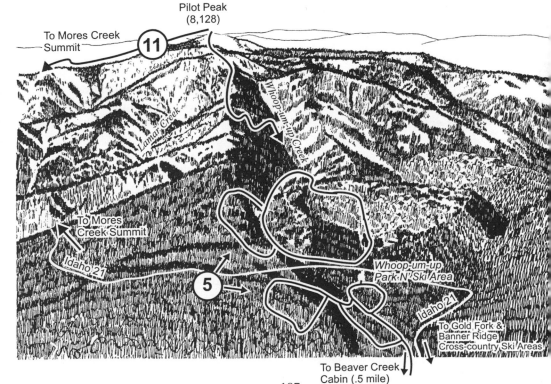

187

6   **Hungarian-Sunset Road**—*Snowbound road. Easy to moderately easy terrain. Snowshoeing. Dogs OK.* Parking for this trail is available at the Ee Da How Handicap Children's Camp entrance. Usually a small pulloff area is plowed here, but not always. Ee Da How Children's Camp is marked with a sign 2.1 miles northeast of Mores Creek Summit on the southeast side of the highway. Mores Creek Summit is 13.1 miles northeast of Idaho City on Idaho 21. From the parked car, walk to the northeast on the plowed highway through a road cut. Shortly after the road cut, a snowbound road leads in from the right (southeast) side of the highway. The tour, suitable for **beginners**, follows this road for as many miles as one desires.

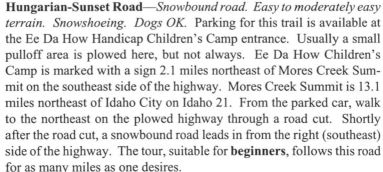

7   **Rough Creek, Bad Bear, Tenmile and Campgrounds**—*Snowbound roads. Easy but limited skiing in the campground area. Moderately easy trip up snowbound road. Snowshoeing. Dogs OK.* For an overview of the campground area see the Sunset Mountain Aerial Illustration on page 191. Touring suitable for beginners can be found around Bad Bear and Tenmile Campgrounds. Tenmile Campground is locate 8.7 miles from Idaho City on the right (southeast) side of the Idaho 21. The campgrounds are marked with Forest Service signs. Rough Creek Road takes off from the southeast side of the highway, .2 mile northeast of Tenmile Campground. The Rough Creek tour starts out with a hundred-yard, moderately steep climb and then eases up for some **gentle**, beginning touring on the snowbound road.

8   **Buena Vista (Airport Loop)**—*Marked and occasionally groomed ski trail. Moderately easy. Can be accessed from the town of Idaho City.* This is a Forest Service marked and occasionally groomed cross-country ski trail with regularly plowed parking provided at the **Community Center** on the western edge of Idaho City. The 2.5 mile (2.5 km) loop starts at the northeast edge of the airport, which is approximately 300 yards west of the Community Center. To get to the beginning of the trail, walk up the plowed road leading west from the Community Center, watching for a snowbound road and sign indicating the airport to the left. The trail is well-marked and is ideal for **beginners**, with its level terrain distinguished with an occasional hill.

9   **Charcoal Gulch**— *Marked ski trail. Moderately difficult. Shuttle required.* This is a fun—often hair raising—**descending ski trail**. It is marked by the Forest Service. The trailhead is located 3 miles northwest of Idaho City on Centerville Road. Warm Springs Ridge trail (see next) also begins here, and a plowed parking area is provided for both trails at this location. A shuttle vehicle will need to be left in Idaho City at the Community Center. The trail descends Charcoal Gulch to Airport Loop Trail, an approximate 1,000-foot (300 meters) drop over 3

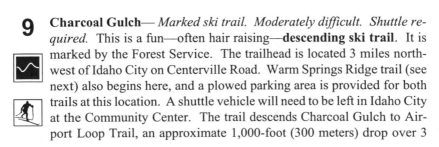

miles (5 km). Because of the lower elevation, this trail gets icy fast, and you'll want to do it during cold, dry spells or after new snow falls.

10 **Warm Springs Ridge**— *Marked ski trail. Moderately difficult. Snowshoeing. Dogs OK.* Warm Springs Ridge is a remnant of the original 1972 system of trails marked by the Forest Service for cross-country skiing. Fortunately for those skiers and snowshoers that like uncrowded trails, the Forest Service intends to keep it marked. The trailhead is located 3 miles (5 km) northwest of Idaho City on Centerville Road. You can do an out-and-back trip on the trail. Or, if desired, do a long descending tour by spotting a shuttle vehicle. It is a workout. The long descending tour follows Warm Springs Ridge 18 miles (29 km) to the southwest with terminus of the trail on Idaho 21, 10 miles southwest of Idaho City. This trip is best when the valley has a good layer of snow—and during cold spells. In the right snow conditions, open slopes along the trail provide some excellent powder skiing. At several points along the ridge, descents can be made to Idaho 21.

11 **Pilot & Freeman Peaks**—*Moderate to difficult backcountry skiing. Backcountry snowboarding. See the Pilot and Freeman Peaks aerial illustrations (next page) for an overview of the area.* Access to Pilot and Freeman Peaks can be gained from the top of **Mores Creek Summit**, 13.1 miles northeast of Idaho City on Idaho 21. Unfortunately, limited parking exists, and skiers and snowboarders planning tours in this area should arrive early in the morning to be assured a place to park. The ascent route to the summit of Pilot Peak follows the snow-bound **Pilot Peak Road** from the north side of Idaho 21. The total distance to the top is 4 miles (6.5 km). From the summit of Pilot Peak, skiers and boarders can descend the south facing slopes of Pilot Peak to Mores Creek Summit. Since the slopes are of an intermediate grade, this is a good choice for those just **learning** how to telemark or snowboard. Snowmobilers will be encountered.

This used to be pretty much a skiing area, but starting in the 1990s snowmobilers with more powerful hill climbing machines started taking a greater interest in it. As a result, a number of skiers have shifted to parking in a couple of plowed pullouts below the top of the pass on the Idaho City side. The pullouts are found just above and below the last switchback on Idaho 21 (at Mores Creek) before Mores Creek Summit. The first pulloff is 12.2 miles from Idaho City (.9 mile from the summit), and the second is 12.7 miles from Idaho City (.4 mile from the summit). From either of these pulloffs backcountry skiers can put skins on and climb **Freeman Peak**. The main areas which are skied or snowboarded are the east-facing slopes of Freeman towards the Mores Creek drainage. (See aerial illustration, page 191.)

Avalanche hazard exists and you should carry shovels and avalanche transceivers. Avoid the area during periods of instability.

In the 1970s some Boise skiers were making descending tours from Pilot Peak to points lower on Idaho 21. Such tours are rarely done these days, but from an historical standpoint, I'll briefly summarize them. One descending tour started at Pilot Peak and dropped to the northeast and then east into the Whoop-Um-Up drainage. This route is shown on the aerial illustration on page 187. The other followed the high southwest ridge that parallels Mores Creek and Idaho 21 towards Idaho City. At several locations along this ridge, descents were made to the highway. It is possible to follow the ridge all the way to Idaho City, but be aware that this route is also used by snowmobilers.

12 **Sunset Mountain**—*Snowbound road. Moderately difficult. Snowshoeing. Dogs OK. For an overview of the area, see the Sunset Mountain aerial illustration on the facing page.* The access to Sunset Mountain is located on top of **Mores Creek Summit**, the same access used by those going to Pilot Peak (described on the previous page). The tour to the summit of **Sunset Mountain** follows the snowbound road from the top of Mores Creek Summit to the south. This road is not as steep as Pilot Peak Road, and it is within the ability of an intermediate skier. The summit is 4.5 miles (7 km) from the parking area.

While Sunset Mountain does have some short telemark slopes, it's more of a **touring mountain** than it is a place to cut turns. It's also a wonderful place to take a snowshoe trip. The advantage of Sunset is that it is fairly uncrowded, having much less use by skiers and snowmobilers. Those that ski or **snowshoe** here generally go up the mountain for a nice tour, have a look around and return the same way.

Like Pilot across the road, Sunset Peak during the 1970s was used as a jumping off point for descending tours. Such tours are rare, if ever done, these days, but they are interesting Idaho City curiosities. The routes are shown on the aerial illustration on the facing page. One of the descending tours dropped into the Hayfork drainage, attained by following the snowbound jeep trail located on the right (west) side of Sunset Mountain Road approximately 1.5 miles (2.5 km) from the start. The trip was 4.5 miles (7.5 km) long and ended at Hayfork Campground on Idaho 21. Another tour started from the summit of Sunset Peak and followed the southwest ridge. Within 1.7 miles (3 km) of the summit, descents were made at several different locations along the ridge into the Hayfork drainage to the northwest. The tours ended at Hayfork Campground. Finally, Rough Creek, the next drainage to the southwest of Hayfork, was also utilized. The southwest ridge of Sunset was followed until dropping into the Rough Creek drainage and eventually ending near Bad Bear Campground.

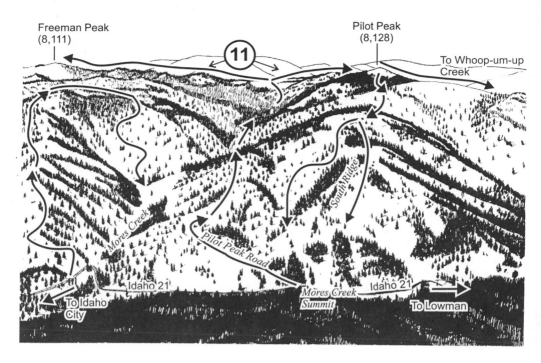

Aerial illustration of the Pilot and Freeman Peaks area from the southeast.

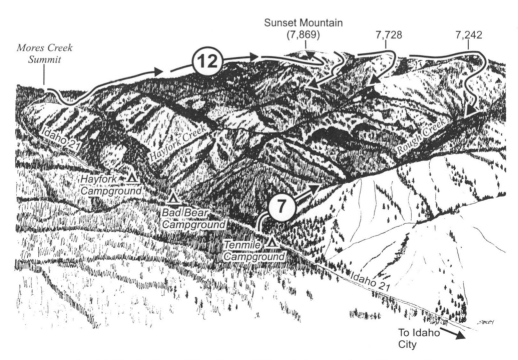

Aerial illustration of the Sunset Mountain area from the west.

191

Another day in paradise: the view along Banner Ridge.

BOISE GENERAL VICINITY

13

Bogus Basin Ski Area—*Alpine ski area. Alpine, Nordic downhill and snowboarding. All services: food, lodging, rentals, instruction, night skiing.* Bogus Basin almost seems like a mirage, a misplaced pocket of snow just peaking above the dry hills surrounding the Boise valley. But it is no mirage. It is a full-scale ski area with 48 runs of varying difficulties, 2,600 acres of skiable terrain and the second largest night skiing facility in the U.S. The number of runs and size of the area will be increasing as Bogus Basin progresses through a several phase expansion program. Presently, it has 6 chairs, 4 rope tows and a vertical drop of 1,800 feet (549 meters). It is located 16 miles northeast of Boise on the Bogus Basin Road.

14

Bogus Basin Nordic Trails—*Regularly groomed cross-country ski trail system. Moderate difficulty.* The system of Nordic trails at Bogus Basin is Boise's closest reliable cross-country skiing. To reach the area, start in Boise and follow the Bogus Basin Road 16 miles to the ski area. Park in the second parking lot where the Nordic trails begin.

Presently there are 30 kilometers (19 miles) of trails, and as Bogus expands, there are plans to add several more kilometers and to construct a Nordic lodge. The area is close enough that you can catch a quick tour and be back in town within a couple of hours. Boise Nordic diehards will even drive up after work and use headlights to do an evening workout on the trails.

15

Mores Mountain—*Access via Nordic trail, then off-trail backcountry. Moderate to difficult backcountry.* To get to the telemark slopes on Mores Mountain, you'll need to buy a pass for the Bogus Basin Nordic Trails and follow the trail to Shafer Butte Campground. From there, the summit of Mores Mountain can be gained by climbing its south side.

Backcountry skiers generally work the north slopes of the mountain. Watch for avalanche danger on the steep east side of the mountain.

OWYHEE AREA

 Silver City Historic Old Mining Town—*Snowbound road. Moderately difficult. Best done as an overnight trip.* The long 10 mile (16 km) ski into Silver City is most sanely done as an overnight trip. At one time, the historic Silver City Hotel was open for skiers who wished to stay the night, but unfortunately it is now closed in the winter. If you don't mind camping for a night, the city is an interesting place to visit in the winter.

To reach the beginning of the tour into Silver City, drive to Murphy, Idaho, which is south of Nampa on Idaho 45. Continue beyond Murphy in the direction of Oreana and Grand View. After about 5 miles beyond Murphy, watch for the Silver City turnoff on the right (southwest) side of the road. Turn there and proceed until snow prevents you from driving any further. Normally, the farthest you will be able to drive is 17 miles from Idaho 45 to a place known as the "Lower Transfer," a wide area in the road on top of a ridge. In the early days of Silver City, it was here that stagecoach passengers would switch to a horsedrawn sleigh or horseback for the remainder of their winter journey. Find a place to park. Ski following the snowbound road into Silver City.

Once in Silver City, day trips can be taken in the surrounding mountains. Snowmobilers often frequent the Silver City area, but normally not beyond the headwaters of Jordan Creek where skiers will find some enjoyable touring terrain. For backcountry skiers, Long Gulch provides access to the higher elevations of the Silver City Range

 Owyhee Range—*Access via snowbound roads, then off-trail travel. Moderate to difficult backcountry.* Most skiing in the Owyhees is centered around Silver City. Access into other parts of the range is difficult. The main access into Silver City is the Ridge Road turnoff, 5 miles southeast of Murphy described above. A longer access to Silver City is from the north. Vehicles can be driven to a place called Democrat, south of Reynolds. From Democrat, the ski route follows snowbound roads over a pass and into the old ghost town of Dewey. From Dewey, it's on to Ruby and Silver City.

Once in the Owyhees, the range offers some interesting backcountry ski routes and descents. Use caution. Avalanche hazards exist. Every so often newspapers of the late 1800s carried reports about people who were killed in avalanches or lost in blizzards in the Owyhees.

The Owhyee Boys

*L*IKE IDAHO CITY, Silver City's newspaper had great fun in describing the antics of local skiers. Appearing in the January 6, 1866 issue of the *Owyhee Avalanche* was this short piece describing a man who had dropped off a news item to be published: "One day this week, an odd looking biped tumbled off a pair of shoes of Norwegian cut, at our door, and flung in the following note, got aboard and was gone again before we had time to get his pedigree."

In a list of the most popular "amusements" during the winter of 1867, the *Owyhee Avalanche* listed skiing as number two. Number one was sleighing, and numbers three and four were "playing drinking games" and "discussing matters of state."

A few years later, the paper announced that some photographs had been taken of Silver City's number two amusement, and they were for sale. The photos are "an elegant present to one's friends at home, by which they can get a correct idea of snow-shoe riding in the mountains," said the *Avalanche*, suggesting that readers should buy some. There was no mention of photographs of Silver City's number three winter amusement: playing drinking games.

When skiers in Silver City really wanted to get a good ski run, they climbed up and schussed down Florida Mountain into Ruby City. Some had the descent down to an art. The Owyhee Boys issued a challenge to all in the territory to a ski race and offered a purse of $1,000 to $2,000 to the winner. The *Avalanche* bragged that some of the "Boys" could make the Florida to Ruby City descent in 28 seconds.

That's some pretty fast skiing. Figuring that the descent is about a 1,500-foot drop over at least a mile, their speed would well exceed a hundred miles per hour. It all goes to prove that the Owyhee Boys were not only good skiers but good at spinning yarns as well. □

Resources . . .

Bureau of Land Management Lands in the Owyhee Mountains
Lower Snake District of the Bureau of Land Management—Address: 3948 Development Ave., Boise, Idaho 83705. Phone: (208) 384-3300.

National Forest Lands in all Areas
Supervisor's Headquarters of the Boise National Forest—Address: 1750 Front Street, Boise, Idaho 83702. Phone: (208) 384-1516.

National Forest Lands in the Bogus Basin Area
Boise District of the Boise National Forest—Address: 5493 Warm Springs Avenue, Boise, Idaho 83712. Phone: (208) 384-1572.

National Forest Lands in the Idaho City Area
Idaho City District of the Boise National Forest—Office located Idaho City on Idaho 21 in Idaho City. Address: PO Box 129, Idaho City, Idaho 83631. Phone: (208) 392-6681.

National Forest Lands in the Lowman Area
Lowman Ranger District of the Boise National Forest—Address: HC 77, Box 3020, Lowman, Idaho 83637. Phone: (208) 259-3361.

Alpine Ski Area
Bogus Basin Ski Resort—Address: 2405 Bogus Basin Road, Boise, Idaho 83702. Phone: (208) 336-4500.

Backcountry Cabins
Both the Idaho City District and Lowman Districts of the Boise National Forest have cabins available for cross-country overnights. Addresses and phone number listed above.

Yurt System
Reservations for the yurts in the Banner area may be made through the Idaho Department of Parks and Recreation, 5637 Warm Springs Blvd., Boise, Idaho 83720. Phone: (208) 334-4199.

Owyhee Boys beware: the Silver City Girls in the 1920s.

Idaho Historical Society

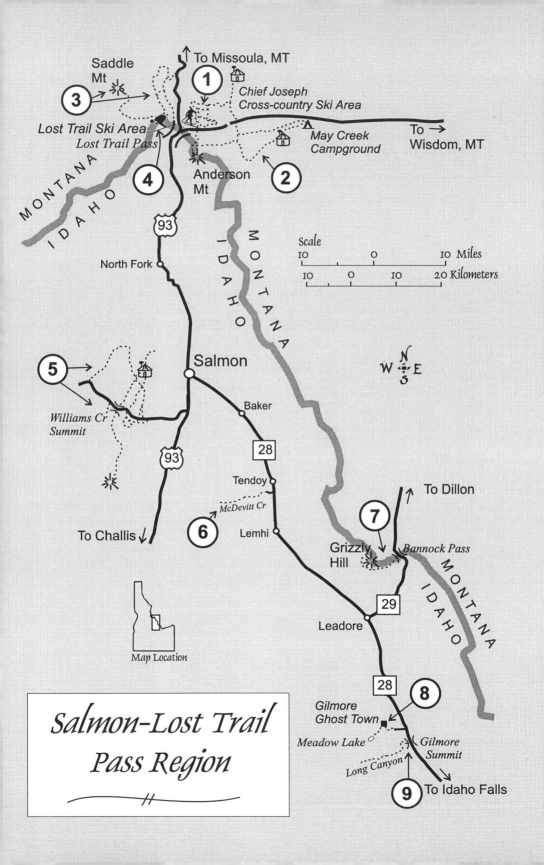

Saddle Mt

③

Lost Trail Ski Area
Lost Trail Pass

MONTANA

IDAHO

④

① To Missoula, MT

Chief Joseph
Cross-country Ski Area

May Creek
Campground

To Wisdom, MT

②

Anderson Mt

93

North Fork

MONTANA

IDAHO

Scale

10   0   10 Miles

10   0   10   20 Kilometers

N
W   E
S

⑤

Williams Cr
Summit

Salmon

Baker

93

28

Tendoy

McDevitt Cr

⑥

Lemhi

To Challis ↓

To Dillon

⑦

Bannock Pass

Grizzly
Hill

29

Leadore

MONTANA

IDAHO

Map Location

28

⑧

Gilmore
Ghost Town

Meadow Lake

Long Canyon

Gilmore
Summit

⑨ To Idaho Falls

*Salmon-Lost Trail
Pass Region*

CHAPTER 12
SALMON-LOST TRAIL PASS REGION

Area Covered: East Idaho including Salmon, Leadore, Lost Trail Pass, Gilmore Summit and surrounding areas.

---

*H*OOTING AND HOLLERING, the Rebels from Leesburg came flying down the mountain behind Salmon. Down they came, their skis doped, riding snowshoe poles and looking like a group of prancing children on wooden horses. In town, it was drinks with the boys and dancing with what few women there were—and if there were any Yanks in town, they better, by gum, be watching their backs.

From Leesburg earliest's days, starting around the time of the Civil War until today, skis have been an essential tool for winter travel. For skiers, there is much to be explored in this area of open valleys, sparse forests and snow draped mountains. One place to start is the pretty Lemhi Valley, south of Salmon. Along Idaho Highway 28 starting at Salmon and continuing 70 miles to Gilmore Summit, a number of roads branch off and provide access into the Beaverhead and Lemhi Mountains. Snowbound in the winter, the first several miles of most of the roads make good cross-country ski or snowshoe trips. McDevitt Creek is an example of one of these trips, but skiers and shoers will enjoy exploring many others.

Gilmore Pass is a primary point of interest. Here the highway swings close to the Lemhis, and for backcountry skiers it is a short hop from the pass to open telemark slopes. For general cross-country skiing, there's also a moderately easy tour that can be taken on a snowbound road which slips behind the hills into a hidden away valley. Just down from the pass, you can have a look around in the old ghost town of Gilmore that was a once-active mining community of 500 people.

In addition to snowbound roads and off-trail skiing, Salmon has two choice marked cross-country trail systems. One is the Williams Creek Summit area to the southwest of Salmon. In 1986, the Salmon Nordic Ski Association went to work with the Salmon National Forest Service to develop this fine system. At this writing, there are 20 miles (32 km) of trails, ranging from beginner to intermediate. The trails can also can be used to access open powder slopes for telemarking. One of the beauties of the Williams Creek Trails is its uniqueness among Idaho trail systems. The system has taken on the personality of the local community, has a wilderness feel to it and a free and unconfined pattern to its trails. Moreover, it is a shining example of Western can-do attitude and teamwork between a small community and the Forest Service.

The other trail system is found at the top of the 7,264 foot high Chief Joseph Pass, less than a mile from Lost Trail Pass on US 93 north of Salmon. The Chief Joseph trail system is a bright star in the Salmon cross-country scene, and like Williams Creek it is the result of close cooperation between skiers, local communities and the Forest Service. In this case, it is a remarkable group of senior citizens from Montana, organized as the Bitterroot Cross-country Ski Club, who made it all happen. What they created is a masterpiece, a stunning canvas of groomed and ungroomed trails.

The entire system, along with trails in the Lost Trail area, totals an incredible 100 km (62 miles). On weekends, the trails are busy with seniors and families, some standing chatting along the trails and others stopped for picnics at the top of hills. There is something more that goes on here, something more than people having fun, more than just simple outings on cross-country skis. Indeed, if there is really an elixir of life, then skiing here, in the crisp, rarefied air of Chief Joseph Pass, comes as close as anything to the real thing.

There's more. For those who want to spend a night in the magical air of the Chief Joseph-Lost Trail Pass area, the Forest Service rents out cabins located on remote corners of the trail system. Four other cabins available to cross-country skiers are scattered on Salmon National Forest lands nearer to Salmon. And, finally, there's plenty of fodder for backcountry enthusiasts. In particular, on the slopes above Lost Trail Pass on the way to Saddle Mountain, backcountry skiing and snowboarding doesn't get much better. A lot of hooting and hollering can be heard from the direction of those slopes. Just who's doing all the hooting and hollering, it's difficult to tell. But if there're any Yanks up there, well, by gum, they better watch their backs.

The Tales . . .

IN THE SPRING of 1866, five prospectors left Bear Gulch, Montana and sampled streams from the Big Hole to the Salmon Valley. Finally, behind the mountains rising above the confluence of the Salmon and Lemhi rivers, they struck pay dirt. When reports of their find leaked out, a frantic rush ensued, and the meadow along Napias Creek near the discovery site was filled with rows and rows of white tents.

Miners who were confederate sympathizers named the main camp Leesburg. Union sympathizers took offense and established another camp a short distance away called Grantsville. Eventually Grantsville lost out, as the rebels in Leesburg said it would, and the entire community became known as Leesburg.

Salmon City grew out of a need for a supply point for gold discoveries in the mountains to the east. It was also the place to hold up when the snow on the mountain above was too deep for horse travel. In April of 1866 winter snows were still blocking the path to Leesburg, and as a result, a large number of gold seekers had stacked up there, impatiently waiting to get on to Leesburg. Likewise, the residents of Leesburg on the other side of the mountain were anxious for the trail to open to allow pack teams in with needed supplies.

Finally, tired of sitting around, a large number of men, more than a hundred, set out on the trail and started shoveling it out by hand. It must have been a magnificent spectacle with men digging and tossing snow out of the way, and a narrow, trenched trail slowly creeping up to the summit of the mountain and down the other side. When it was finally open, a toll was charged. One gold seeker recalled paying 50 cents to ride his saddle horse over it, and he remembered passing by walls of snow that were in places 10 feet deep.

When the trail wasn't broken out—or shoveled out—skis were used to get back and forth to Salmon. In the 1870s, Lorton Prince used skis to make regular trips between Leesburg and Salmon. Lorton, originally from Kirtland, Ohio, was one of Leesburg's longest residents, spending 51 years of his life there. He was a sensitive man who loved the forests and wildlife of the mountains. Using skis most of the winter, Lorton loaded his pack full of mail—sometimes as much as 70 pounds—and each week made his journey to and from Salmon.

Skis were also used for trips of longer distances. Bill Richardson used skis to travel all the way from Florence to join his brother at Leesburg, a trip of about 140 miles. A few years later, he made the trip in reverse, this time starting at Leesburg and ending in Florence. "He traveled directly," said Orion Kirkpatrick who wrote of his trip, "through the dense forest, wilderness, often at night sleeping on the ground by his campfire." Using his long ski trip as an example, Kirkpatrick described Richardson as one of the "hardy, courageous, intrepid men who laid the foundation of civilization at Leesburg and in Lemhi County." William Richardson, pioneer and long-distance skier, is buried in the Salmon cemetery. □

The Trails . . .

1

Chief Joseph Cross-country Ski Area—*Marked and groomed cross-country ski trail system. All abilities. Toilets.* This marvelous area is located near Lost Trail Pass. To get there, drive to the top of Lost Trail Pass, 46 miles north of Salmon on US 93. At the top of the pass turn right (east) on Highway 43. It is exactly 1 mile from Lost Trail Pass to the Chief Joseph parking area located on the left (north) side of the highway. From here, skiers have a plethora of trails to choose from: 7 **easy** trails**,** 7 **moderately easy** trails and 2 **moderately difficult** trails.

The Chief Joseph Cross-country Ski Area is a recreational trail system, and the trails, which are nicely groomed by volunteers, are tracked for **classic skiing**. Donations are accepted—and this is one place that you don't want to forget to leave a **donation**. The trail organizers deserve all the support they can get for putting together such an outstanding Nordic resource. It is a place that truly has it all: wonderful trails, rolling terrain, reliable snow, open areas for picnicking and unforgettable vistas overlooking Idaho and Montana's splendid mountains. No matter what kind of skier you are, this is a place to put on your "must see and ski" list.

Chief Joseph Trails: A busy Saturday in Nordic heaven.

2 **North Big Hole Mountain Touring Trails**—*Marked cross-country ski trail system. Moderate difficulty. Snowshoeing. Dogs OK.* Along with the Chief Joseph trail system, volunteers and the Forest Service have marked an additional system of trails that provide skiers with a wilderness touring slant. The trails are **moderately difficult.** You can bring the dog and ski farther back into the mountains. One of the trails starts right from the Chief Joseph parking lot (see description above). To get to the trailhead, cross Highway 43 to its south side and ski following the trail markers. The trail follows the high ridge of the Continental divide to the 8,034 foot (2,449 meter) **Anderson Mountain**. From the parking lot to Anderson Mountain is 6 miles (9.6 km) one way.

Additionally, trails in this system can be reached from two other plowed pulloffs. One pulloff is located at the **Richard Creek Trailhead**, 3 miles east of the main Chief Joseph parking lot on highway 43, and the second is located at the **Cabinet Creek Trailhead**, 3.7 miles from the main parking area. All the trails are interconnected. It's likely there will be even more in the future. The Bitterroot Cross-country Club keeps coming up with new ideas and their members willingly put in many volunteer hours to bring those ideas to fruition. Two cabins are also available for rent and are accessible from the trail system

This is a good place to **snowshoe**. Out of courtesy for skiers, please snowshoe off to the side of the ski tracks.

While many trails in the North Big Hole are marked with the typical blue diamonds, some of the trails are marked in the traditional manner of using **axe blazes**. As an aside, I hope that the practice of blazing of trails is revived for use on summer hiking trails. Many hiking trails these days are no longer marked in this way. Yet, it's a simple method; it's inconspicuous and harmless to the tree, and it lasts years and years.

Most importantly from a skiing and snowshoeing standpoint, blazes on hiking trails are extremely helpful to backcountry winter travelers.

3   **Lost Trail Pass-Saddle Mountain**—*Marked cross-country ski trails and off-trail backcountry. Backcountry snowboarding. Snowshoeing.* As if the trail systems at Chief Joseph and North Big Hole weren't enough, there is even one more system of trails. These trails start from Lost Trail Pass and they access some terrific backcountry downhill terrain. Lost Trail pass is located 46 miles north of Salmon on US 93. Park at the Lost Trail Ski Area on the west side of the pass.

The most interesting of the trails starts at the ski area, climbs to the top, and heads northwest to **Saddle Mountain**. A fun way to do this trip is to buy a one ride ski pass from the ski area and take the lift up. The trail which is marked continues from the top of the lift.

Most skiers and snowboarders spending time on this side of the pass are primarily interested in the off-trail downhill terrain. The most common of the slopes that are skied are the northeast facing slopes dropping towards the **East Fork of Camp Creek** drainage. This is the big drainage which US 93 contours along on the Montana side of the pass. The upper part of the East Fork of Camp Creek drainage was burned extensively during the Saddle Mountain Fire which torched 4,000 acres in 1960.

Most telemark skiers, and the occasional snowboarder, work the top 500 or 600 feet, repeatedly climbing back up and skiing or boarding down. It is also possible to make a descending tour to a point lower on US 95. One marked trail is called **Wildfire Wahoo** on which you can

Lost Trail Pass, viewed from the east and looking up the Saddle Mountain Burn. A number of downhill route variations are possible through the burn. Lost Trail Ski Area, the starting point for backcountry trips, is to the extreme left and top of the photo.

cut telemark turns on the way down. All trails that descend from Lost Trail collect and end at the **Saddle Mountain Burn Trailhead** (Trail #411), 2.4 miles down on the Montana side of the pass on the left (west) side of the highway. A small pulloff is plowed here.

4 **Lost Trail Powder Mountain Ski Area**—*Alpine ski area. Alpine, Nordic and snowboarding. All abilities. Food, rentals, and instruction.* This is one ski area where you'll never have to worry about snow. No matter how shaky the conditions may be elsewhere, skiers and boarders at Lost Trail will be cutting and shredding away. The ski area is located on top of Lost Trail Pass, 46 miles north of Salmon or 90 miles south of Missoula, Montana on US 93. It presently has two lifts, 18 runs and a vertical drop of 1,200 feet (366 meters). The abundance of **intermediate terrain** at Lost Trail makes it a wonderful telemark area and it comes to no surprise that its ski school has some terrific telemark instructors.

5 **Williams Creek Summit**—*Marked cross-country ski trail system. Easy to moderate terrain. Backcountry downhill terrain accessible from trails. Overnight cabin available. Snowshoeing.* Maps of the cross-country trail system on the 7,814 foot (2,382 meter) Williams Creek Summit can be picked up at the Salmon National Forest Supervisor's Headquarters. The office is conveniently located on the edge of town along US 93 on the way to the pass.

To reach Williams Creek, drive 5.5 miles south of Salmon on US 93 until coming to the road leading to Cobalt. Turn right (west) on the Cobalt road and continue driving. The top of Williams Creek Summit is 14 miles from the turnoff, but there are several parking areas which access ski trails on the way to the top of the pass and on the other side. Williams Creek Road is narrow, winding, and it's a good idea to carry chains and a shovel with you.

If you are new to the area, one suggested starting place is the **Meadow Trailhead**, 1 mile below the top of the pass on the Salmon side. Starting from the south side of the Williams Creek Road is a short loop called the **Wapiti Meadows Loop** which is a 1.5 miles long and suitable for **beginners**. It meanders through meadows and lodgepole forest.

When the Salmon Nordic Association was laying out trails on Williams Creek, the idea of making them fun was utmost on their minds. As a consequence, much of the skiing is the enjoyable kind which starts high and descends to points lower on Williams Creek Road. At least 6 marked cross-country ski trails on the pass are designed to be descending tours. The main access for descending tours is to start on top of the pass and ski out on what is called **Ridge Road** to the north. Ridge Road is a snowmobile trail, and you'll need to maintain a watchful eye. Even so, it is commonly used by **beginning skiers** for an easy out-and-back tour since the grades on the snowbound road are gentle.

One descending tour that you might want to try is the **moderately difficult Buckhorn Trail**. To get to it, ski to the north on Ridge Road for 2.5 miles (4 km). The Buckhorn Trail turns off to the right (east) at this point and descends 700 feet (213 meters) coming out at the **Meadow Trailhead** (described above.) The trail is marked.

Some nice backcountry turning slopes can be accessed from the Ridge Road. Two miles (3 km) north of Williams Creek Summit, Ridge Road crosses an open hillside facing to the east and overlooking the main Salmon River country. Locals called this **Telemark Hill**. This area makes a nice place to take a break and catch a little telemark skiing. A larger, open hillside is found 2 miles (3 km) farther which is even a better slope for practicing telly turns. Additionally, the Forest Service has an **A-frame cabin** located another .6 miles beyond Telemark Hill which can be rented for an overnight stay (see *Resources* at the end of the chapter)

The most scenic skiing from Williams Creek Summit is found by following **Ridge Road** from the top of the pass to the **south**. It begins with a quick climb, but soon the steep climb ends, and the snowbound road rolls along the high ridge of the **Salmon River Mountains**. Within a mile (1.5 km), skiers or snowshoers are treated to superb views across the **Panther Creek** drainage. On a good day, you should be able to see the **Yellow Jacket Mountains** and **Big Horn Crags** to the distant west. In addition to rubbernecking, skiers will also find beautiful open hillsides for practicing turns.

This is a great area for **snowshoeing**. Generally the trails have quite a bit of up and down, and you won't have to worry about the trail courtesy of walking to the side of ski trails. Skiers using a snowplow to slow down as they come down the trails pretty much take care of the tracks. However, if you do come across trails on rolling terrain on which skiers have set in a nice set of tracks, then, to be polite, walk so you don't obliterate the trail.

6   **Beaverhead and Lemhi Access Roads**—*Snowbound roads. Easy to moderate terrain. Snowshoeing.* A number of snowbound roads provide skiing access into the Beaverhead and Lemhi Mountains. These roads lead off of Idaho 28, south of Salmon. The first few miles of these roads work well for **beginning** tours. Depending on snow cover in Lemhi Valley, one may drive part way up the selected road and gain higher access. Examples include Haynes Creek and McDevitt Creek.

McDevitt Creek is located 2 miles south of Tendoy on the west side of Idaho 28. The tour, suitable for beginners, passes through open sagebrush country, and the scenery may not be appealing to some tourers, but I found the loneliness and desolation of the surrounding country

The Lemhis.

 pleasing. There is a ranch 1.2 miles from the highway on McDevitt Road, and skiers or snowshoers should park so their vehicles do not block the path of people coming in and out of the ranch. The tour follows the snowbound McDevitt Creek Road from this point to the west. When you've reached singularly named Dipping Vat Road, you've gone 2.9 miles (4.6 km) from the ranch. Note that this is a tour that you'll want to do in midwinter when sufficient snow has built up in the valley regions.

7 **Bannock Pass**—*Snowbound road tour of moderate difficulty. Off-trail backcountry. Backcountry snowboarding. Snowshoeing.* Bannock Pass is a pass between Idaho and Montana, 13 miles northwest of Leadore on Idaho 29. From the top of the pass, a tour of **moderate difficulty** can made following the **Continental Divide** to the left as you look from the pass towards Montana. The divide takes a jog in this location. You would expect the divide to run north, but from Bannock Pass, it runs southwest for several miles before turning and heading back north. The tour follows a snowbound road which parallels the divide on the Idaho side. The road can be followed all the way to **Grizzly Hill**, 4 miles from the start. Since the country is open and sparsely treed, off-trail skiing is also possible for many miles along the divide.

There's also a place off the side of the pass to catch a few turns. 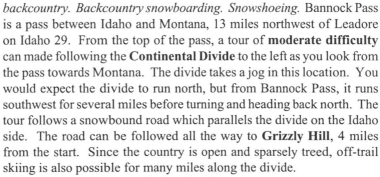 Within .2 mile of the top of pass, on the left side, you'll find a slope which can be used for practicing telly turns or making short runs on snowboards.

8   **Gilmore Ghost Town**—*Snowbound road. Easy to moderate terrain. Snowshoeing.* The Gilmore town access road is 1.9 miles north of Gilmore Summit. Gilmore Summit is 20 miles south of Leadore and is marked with a highway sign. Things have changed at Gilmore over the last few years. There is now a small housing development along the old townsite, and the access road will likely be plowed to the edge of town. Because of private lands in the area, it is best to confine your skiing or snowshoeing to the snowbound public access road which leads around the north edge of the old town.

From the townsite, a long tour of moderate difficulty can be made by following the public access road onto the **Meadow Lake Campground**, which sits high in the Lemhis. Be prepared for this one. In the 5.5 mile (9 km) distance, the road climbs 2,000 feet (600 meters).

Gilmore was named after John Gilmer, an owner of a stage and freight company in the Lemhis. Somewhere along the line when the new post office was established in the town, the name "Gilmer was changed to "Gilmore." The altered spelling stuck. In May of 1910, the Gilmore and Pacific Railroad was completed to the town, and Gilmore became the shipping point for the all of the area's mines. Gradually, however, ore production petered out, and in 1939, the line was closed. That was it for Gilmore. Within a few years, the town's remaining residents had packed up and moved elsewhere.

9   **Gilmore Summit and Long Canyon**—*Easy to moderately easy snow-bound road tour. Off-trail backcountry. Backcountry snowboarding. Snowshoeing.* From the top of Gilmore Summit, you can't see **Long Canyon**, but it's there. It lies behind intervening hills, a hidden away treasure for skiing and snowshoeing. The Long Canyon tour is suitable for all abilities and starts on the top of Gilmore Summit, approximately 20 miles south of Leadore on Idaho 28. Parking is found on the summit.

Immediately to the west of Gilmore Summit are some low lying, sage-brush covered hills. Long Canyon is approached by skiing or snowshoeing around the base of the northern side of the hills. Approximately 1 mile (1.5 km) from the highway, look for a small, narrow canyon which cuts through the hills to the left (south). A snowbound road leads through this gap, and once on the road, it's easy.

Ski or snowshoe through the gap, and on the other side you'll find a lovely, protected valley. The snowbound road gradually climbs up the valley, and along the way, you'll find great open downhill areas for play-ing. Even if Gilmore Summit is windy, which it often is, Long Canyon is likely to be quiet and calm.

For **backcountry** skiers, Long Canyon provides access to downhill slopes. Additionally, there are some short convenient slopes for **telemarking or snowboarding** directly to the west of the parking area on the top of Gilmore Pass.

Frank Daniels Collection

Time for a break and some fun at the McDaniels Saw Mill, southwest of Salmon, 1944.

Across the Idaho Primitive Area

I'M NOT THE sort of person that puts a lot of effort into organization. I find that sometimes you can get so caught up in the details that you miss out on all of the fun of life. But there have an occasion or two when I've learned that some details are important. Take, for instance, a ski trip that I had planned across what at the time was called the Idaho Primitive Area. It's now called the River of No Return Wilderness. The trip was to start at the confluence of Panther Creek and Clear Creek near the Main Salmon River, 30 air miles to the northwest of Salmon and end in Cascade on the other side of the state.

The one thing I hadn't planned for was having to carry our skis early in the trip. If I had checked out the details I would have learned that the mouth of Clear Creek lies at a low elevation, and the snow is pretty skimpy there even in midwinter.

When we arrived and discovered this fact, my good natured companions brushed it off as an oversight, and we proceeded to lash skis to our packs. With the addition of our heavy wood skis, the packs were unwieldy. Mine was so wobbly that I couldn't keep it balanced correctly to get it on. Then I spied the hay wagon. I set the pack in an upright position on the wagon, and I backed into it, slipping my arms through the straps and stood up.

Ah! It felt . . . well, it felt decent. At least I was standing. I walked a couple of steps when all of a sudden I felt my feet slip out from underneath me, and I was down fast and hard on my back.

I had hoped that no one saw me, but when I looked up, my companions stood there, staring at me with half amused and half horrified looks. They were probably thinking the same thing as me. How were we ever going to make it from here, 175 miles to other side of the state with these monstrous packs?

It was February of 1973. With me were Blake Knoll, an Idaho State University student and track athlete, John Lowry who is now a math teacher in Pocatello and Mark Collie, an ornithologist and photographer. They helped me back to my feet, and somehow, with far greater grace than me, managed to get their owns packs on. We started walking up the Clear Creek trail.

The first part of the journey was to take us into the high country of the Big Horn Crags. It was the crux of the whole trip, and we felt if we could just make it across the Crags, then we could complete the rest of the journey reach Cascade.

We hadn't gone very far when a tangle of downed timber forced us to cross Clear Creek. Clear Creek is not the kind of creek that can be jumped, and we could find no snow bridges. Searching around, we finally found a big tree that had toppled across the creek. Considering how well I had done with my pack on level ground, no one wanted to risk walking and balancing their way across the log wearing a pack.

Blake had an idea. He straddled the log like he was settling down in a saddle on a horse, and he slid forward, removing the snow in front of him with one of the shovels we carried. After a two foot section of snow had been removed, he slid forward again, removing more snow and repeating the process until he reached the other side.

We all followed one another, straddling the log as Blake had done, and pushing with our hands, each one of us scooted across. It was fun at first, but when terrain changes and downed timber forced us to do the same thing the sixth and seventh time, the fun started wearing a little thin.

It was another one of those small details. I had thought that the dotted line along Clear Creek on the Forest Service map was really a trail. In theory it was a trail, of course, but not in practice. We guessed that the last time it had been cleared was sometime around World War I. The total mileage that first day was a whopping three miles. It was about that time that I began to sense growing tension among the group.

But the tension went away quickly. Things got much better. We eventually reached higher country where the snow was deep. The heavy skis came off our packs, and we started into the beautiful Big Horn Crags. Our route took us through the Crags to a pass on its western edge, high above the Middle Fork of the Salmon River. The two day journey from the pass in the Big Horn Crags, a world dominated by white, to the Middle Fork Country, a world of golden browns, yellows and grays, was one of the most spectacular ski descents that any of us had ever done or will ever do on skis.

At the river, we caught the Middle Fork Trail, and during the next several days as we worked our way up the river, we eagerly looked forward to stopping at one of the river's famous hot springs to soak and to clean off a couple of weeks of sweat. But as anyone who hikes the lower Middle Fork Trail knows, all of the hot springs are on the opposite side of the river from the trail.

Except one. It was a hot springs near Hood Ranch that I hadn't known about before. And when we found it, it was like finding a little bit of heaven. We stripped off our clothes, soaked long and luxuriously in the hot springs, and then with our bodies warm and pink, we ran about, completely naked, free of any cares and celebrating being alive in such a beautiful place. Mark, of course, captured it all on film.

When I returned from the trip, I was asked to do a slide show for a friend of mine who taught at the local high school. She thought her students would enjoy the story of our trip, and at the same time, she hinted to me that I might be a good role model for the students. My chest puffed out.

Role model? Sure, I told her. I'd be happy to do it.

The show was going well, and I was absorbed in the telling of it when I flashed one of Mark's photos from the hot springs. It took me a moment to realize what I had done. It was, I have to admit, another one of those times when a little advance planning and attention to details would have been the best course of action. I had quickly thrown the slides together that morning, and somehow, the slide appearing on the screen had accidently gotten mixed in with the rest of the show.

It was on the screen long enough for the class to realize that the person who was facing them without a stitch on was their narrator—and would-be role model. The class erupted in laughter and cat calls. The teacher was still trying to bring the uproar under control as I was quietly slipping out the door. □

Resources . . .

National Forest Lands throughout the Salmon Area
Supervisor's Headquarters of Salmon-Challis National Forest—Office located on US 93 just west of Salmon. Address: Box 729, Salmon, Idaho 83467. Phone: (208) 756-2215.

National Forest Lands in the Lost Trail Pass Area
North Fork District of the Salmon-Challis National Forest—Address: PO Box 780, North Fork, Idaho 83467. Phone: (208) 865-2383.

Wisdom Ranger District of the Beaverhead National Forest—Address: PO Box 238, Wisdom, MT 59761. Phone: (406) 689-3243

Sula Ranger District of the Bitterroot National Forest—Address: 7338 Highway 93 South, Sula, MT 59871. Phone: (406) 821-3201.

National Forest Lands in the Lemhi Valley Area
Leadore District of the Salmon-Challis National Forest—Address: PO Box 180, Leadore, Idaho 83464. Phone: (208) 768-2731.

Backcountry Cabin Rental
For the A-frame cabin located on Williams Creek Summit (and other cabins), contact the *Salmon Ranger District*, PO Box 729, Salmon, Idaho 83467. Phone: (208) 756-3724. For the Hogan cabin located in the Chief Joseph Area, contact the *Wisdom Ranger District* (address and phone number above)

Backcountry Guiding
Winter backcountry guided trips are available in the Salmon area. Check with the Salmon National Forest for the phone number of the current permittee.

Avalanche Information
Avalanche forecasting work is done at Lost Trail Pass. The forecasts are available on the Internet or via recorded phone messages. For the current Internet address and phone number, contact: Forest Supervisor, Lolo National Forest, Bldg. 24, Ft. Missoula, Missoula, Montana 59801. Phone: (406) 329-3750.

Alpine Ski Area
Lost Trail Powder Mountain Ski Area—PO Box 311, Conner, Montana 59827. Phone: 406-821-3211 or 406-821-3508.

Opposite Page: Chamberlain Basin, River of No Return Wilderness

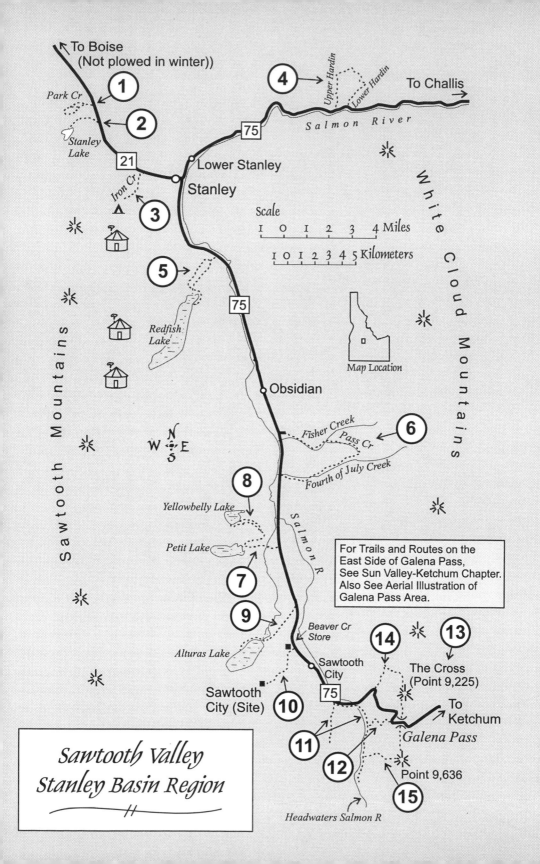

To Boise
(Not plowed in winter))

1

Park Cr

2

Stanley
Lake

21

4

Upper Hardin
Lower Hardin

To Challis

75

Salmon River

Lower Stanley

Iron Cr

Stanley

3

Scale

I O I 2 3 4 Miles

I O I 2 3 4 5 Kilometers

5

Redfish
Lake

75

Map Location

Obsidian

Fisher Creek

Pass Cr

6

White Cloud Mountains

Sawtooth Mountains

Fourth of July Creek

8

Yellowbelly Lake

Petit Lake

Salmon R

W N E S

7

9

For Trails and Routes on the
East Side of Galena Pass,
See Sun Valley-Ketchum Chapter.
Also See Aerial Illustration of
Galena Pass Area.

Beaver Cr
Store

Alturas Lake

14

13

The Cross
(Point 9,225)

Sawtooth
City

Sawtooth
City (Site)

10

75

To
Ketchum

11

Galena Pass

12

Point 9,636

15

Sawtooth Valley
Stanley Basin Region

Headwaters Salmon R

CHAPTER 13
SAWTOOTH VALLEY-STANLEY BASIN REGION

Area Covered: Sawtooth Valley and Stanley Basin of Central Idaho.

IT WASN'T the most eloquent of descriptions. But from the pen of a trapper who had some hard traveling ahead of him through a piece of country that looked like it had been turned upside down once or twice, it wasn't bad. "An interesting prospect," he called the view from Galena Summit across the Sawtooth Valley. "[It] repaid us well for our troubles."

Alexander Ross was on a trapping exploration in the interior of an unknown region identified on one 1814 map with the note: "These Mountains are Covered with Snow." His journal entry for September 18, 1824 was the first written description of the Sawtooths and the valley below.

Both the 1814 map and Ross had it right. These mountains, the Sawtooths, *are* covered with snow, and the snow is particularly deep in the winter. And they *are* an interesting prospect, particularly for those with a passion for winter. Nonetheless, the Sawtooth Valley is a cold place for warm passions. The cold air from the Sawtooth Range on one side and the White Clouds on the other, sinks in the valley and the temperatures recorded here are among the coldest in Idaho. Consequently, the snow stays cold and powdery for weeks at a time.

The gentle terrain of the valley—and its cold and powdery snow—offer lots in the way of easy cross-country ski tours or snowshoe trips. The lakes sprinkled at the base of the Sawtooths are common destinations for such trips. The lakes include: Stanley, Redfish, Pettit, Yellowbelly and Alturas. Skiers or snowshoers who want a bit more of a challenge, yet avoid avalanche areas, will enjoy the trips up Rough Creek, Fourth of July Creek and the Headwaters of the Salmon River.

Currently, there is only one trail system in the valley marked specifically for cross-country skiing. It is the small Park Creek system which is located 5 miles east of Stanley on Idaho 21 and is occasionally groomed. More may be created in the future. Proposals have been floated to extend the Wood River Valley groomed trail system to the north into the Sawtooths.

While primarily known for its scenery, the Sawtooth area is also prime habitat for roaming backcountry bipeds and monopeds, often spotted on the slopes of Galena Pass leaving curious scalloped tracks. From either side of the pass—to the north or south—backcountry skiers and snowboarders have a wealth of downhill options. For those just learning how to telemark, the slopes below Galena Overlook on the Sawtooth side of the pass have gentle slopes ideal for practicing tellys. More advanced skiers and snowboarders, often climb and access downhill terrain from The Cross, a high point directly to the north of the pass. And there is equally inspiring backcountry terrain to the south of the pass.

Backcountry skiing and snowboarding is found throughout the area, but another popular area—particularly among Boise skiers because it's reasonably accessible from the city—is Copper Peak located 24 miles west of Stanley on Idaho 21. This section of Idaho 21 is closed in midwinter, but early in the season or when the road opens in late spring, good turning terrain is found on the mountain.

Just to the east of Copper Peak, Idaho 21 makes a sharp "V" shaped bend in an area known as Cape Horn. A few miles to the north of Cape Horn is Bear Valley which in years past was good trapping territory. Early one spring in the late 1920s, someone entered Jack Seagraves's trapping cabin. The intruder helped himself to most of Seagraves's food, his furs and his .30-06 rifle, and then disappeared. Seagraves, who was off on a trip to Challis, would soon find out that he had been the victim of a robbery.

The Tales . . .

JACK SEAGRAVES arrived in Stanley after a jarring trip from Challis on the stage. It was nearly spring and the Stanley-Challis road was broken out for horse travel, but from Stanley to Seagraves's trapping cabin in Bear Valley, the roads and trails were still under several feet of snow. He would use skis from here, and it would be a much smoother and quieter ride.

His 11-foot skis were fitted with a housing made from belting material, fashioned in the shape of a boot and nailed to the ski. On the top of the housing was sewn canvas which was tightened around the calf of his leg with a draw string. There was no leather binding. Attachment to the ski was accomplished by the housing which was loose enough so the heel of his boot could go up and down and yet snug enough that his boot wouldn't easily pull out.

He explained all of this to me when I interviewed him in the late 1970s in his small room in the Woodstone Manor, a Twin Falls Rest Home. He was 97 years old at the time. Seagraves came to Idaho in 1897 when he was 17 years old. He worked as sheep-herder, had a mine on Rough Creek, a ranch at the base of Galena Pass, and trapped for a number of years in the winter. One of his trapping cabins was located in Bear Valley at the head of the Middle Fork of the Salmon.

After a long journey on skis, he arrived at the cabin. Once inside, he stopped dead in his tracks and stared. The inside of the cabin was bare.

"My furs were gone," Seagraves said, "all the butter, a lot of beans, all the meat, my .30-06 rifle . . . everything!" Furious as a treed cougar, he grabbed his .30-30 rifle and skied to Cape Horn, 20 miles to the southeast. At Cape Horn he told his friend McCallister what had happened, and asked McCallister if he'd seen anyone recently.

"Yep," McCallister told him, "I seen somebody. That charac-ter Love. He passed by here one night with his dog sled."

"Well, that's where my furs went," said Seagraves.

Love's place was three to four miles away, and after spending the night at McCallister's place, Seagraves left early the next morning to have a look around. He skied quietly to Love's cabin, but soon realized that the cabin was unoccupied. Slipping out of the canvas housing of the skis, he stepped in the cabin and immedi-ately found what he was looking for: his furs. Upon looking around more, however, he could find no sign of his rifle or other things.

Seagraves decided to wait for Love. Skiing away from the cabin, he found a place to hide. He wasn't sure how long he would have to wait, but he intended to stay as long as necessary to get his gear and his grub back.

Later that day, he heard the sound of Love's webs stepping across the crusty snow. Seagraves stayed hidden until Love was beyond him, and then he slowly moved out of his hiding place. Pointing his .30-30 steadily at Love, he said, "Tell me where it is, or I'm going tie you up and start a fire."

The startled Love turned around and faced the barrel of the rifle.

"Your gun's right in there," Love stammered, pointing to the cabin. Seagraves followed Love into the cabin and watched him peel back some floorboards.

Seagraves was amazed by what he saw. "He had all kinds of stuff in there," said Seagraves, "All kinds of fishing tackle, all kinds of guns. He was a regular, damn thief."

Among Love's cache of stolen goods were the rest of Seagraves's supplies and his rifle. Thinking it over, Seagraves decided to come back later to collect his belongings, but his first priority was to get Love out of the territory. With Love in front wearing webs and Seagraves behind with his .30-30 handy and wearing skis, the two men marched all the way back to Seagraves' ranch at the base of Galena Pass. Love stayed the night in a back room while Seagraves stayed in the front. "He slept," said Seagraves, "and I stayed awake."

The next morning, Seagraves ushered Love to the top of the pass.

"I brought him up there," Seagraves said, "And I told him to get out, and that I didn't want any damn thieves like him around."

That was the last Seagraves ever saw of him. Sometime later, he heard that Love showed up in the Middle Fork Country, but his stay there was short lived. "One day he just fell over dead," Seagraves said. He never learned the cause and didn't much care. ☐

The Trails . . .

1 **Park Creek Ski Trails**—*Marked and occasionally groomed cross-country ski trail system. Easy to moderately easy. Dogs OK.* This is a marked ski trail system with stunning views of the Sawtooths. The parking area is located 5 miles east of Stanley on Idaho 21. At this writing it has about 4 miles of trails which pass through rolling, open meadows. Dogs are allowed.

2 **Stanley Lake**—*Snowbound road. Flat, easy terrain. Dogs OK. Snowshoeing.* The snowbound road leading into Stanley Lake is located on the south side of Idaho 21, 5 miles west of Stanley. The 3-mile (5 km) tour into Stanley Lake on the snowbound road is a flat and **easy** tour. Snowmobile use occurs.

3 **Iron Creek**—*Snowbound road. Flat, easy terrain. Dogs OK. Snowshoeing.* The snowbound Iron Creek Road is located 2.5 miles west of Stanley on the south side of Idaho Highway 21. It is a 3-mile (5 km) **easy** tour to the Creek Campground. Snowmobile use occurs.

4 **Upper and Lower Hardin Creek Loop**—*Snowbound road and off-trail travel. Moderately difficult. Dogs OK. Snowshoeing.* Upper and Lower Hardin Creeks drain into the Salmon River, 10 miles east of Stanley on Idaho 75. Parking can be a problem. Sometimes there is a small pulloff plowed across from the Rough Creek Bridge, 10 miles (16 km) east of Stanley, from which the Upper Hardin tour begins. Lower Hardin is located .4 mile (.6 km) east of Upper Hardin along US 93.

A 6-mile (9.5 km) loop tour involving some **off-trail** travel can be made by following Lower Hardin snowbound road. Once on the upper portion of Lower Hardin, one can follow a trailless route, cutting across to the west and dropping into Upper Hardin drainage. Once in the Upper Hardin drainage, a trail is reached and followed downhill. The trail is narrow and overgrown in spots, but it eventually arrives at Idaho 75.

5 **Redfish Lake**—*Snowbound road. Flat, easy terrain. Also a moderately difficult alternative tour. Dogs OK. Snowshoeing.* The turnoff to Redfish Lake is clearly marked with a Forest Service sign 4.5 miles south of Stanley on the west side of Idaho 75. The 2 mile (3 km) tour follows the **gradual**, snowbound road to Redfish Lake. Snowmobile use occurs.

An alternative to the snowbound road is to follow a **low ridge** into the lake. Start skiing down the snowbound road until reaching the small ranger hut, located a few hundred feet from the highway. The route crosses over the Redfish Lake outlet via a bridge and contours southwest along the outlet and **Little Redfish Lake**. Climb to the top of the ridge on the northwest side of Little Redfish Lake and continue to ski along the ridge to the southwest until reaching **Fishhook Creek**, approximately 2 miles (3 km) from the highway. Fishhook can be followed .5 mile (.8 km) downstream until coming to Redfish Lake.

6 **Fisher Creek-Fourth of July Creek Loop**— *Snowbound road. Moderately easy terrain, but some route finding involved. Dogs OK. Snowshoeing.* **Fisher Creek**, the starting point for the loop trail, is located 1.7 miles south of Sessions Store in Obsidian on Idaho 75. Fisher Creek Road branches off the east side of the highway and is marked with a Forest Service sign. **Fourth of July Creek Road** is the end of the tour, and if there is an available plowed pulloff, a shuttle vehicle can be left there, 1.7 miles south of Fisher Creek on Idaho 75.

The loop begins on Fisher Creek. Follow the snowbound Fisher Creek Road into the canyon. Two miles (3 km) from the start, the snowbound Fisher Creek Road enters a large clearing. At its entrance, a Forest Service sign (if it is not covered by snow) indicates **Pass Creek**. Pass Creek joins Fisher Creek from the right (east) side of the clearing. Cross over Fisher Creek and ski toward the small Pass Creek Canyon on the eastern edge of the clearing.

The skiing up Pass Creek is mostly gentle, and here and there you'll pass through small meadows which make lovely places to stop for a snack or lunch. Eventually you break over a small ridge looking into the Fourth of July Creek drainage. From here, ski down to Fourth of July Creek Road and follow it out to the highway. The loop is 9.5 miles (15.3 km) long. If the section along Idaho 75 between Fisher Creek and Fourth of July is eliminated by spotting a shuttle vehicle, the length of the tour is 7.8 miles (12.6 km). No snowmobile use occurs on Pass Creek.

7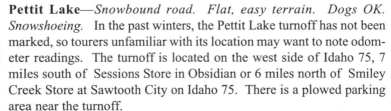

Pettit Lake—*Snowbound road. Flat, easy terrain. Dogs OK. Snowshoeing.* In the past winters, the Pettit Lake turnoff has not been marked, so tourers unfamiliar with its location may want to note odometer readings. The turnoff is located on the west side of Idaho 75, 7 miles south of Sessions Store in Obsidian or 6 miles north of Smiley Creek Store at Sawtooth City on Idaho 75. There is a plowed parking area near the turnoff.

The tour follows the gradual snowbound Pettit Lake Road to the west, eventually arriving at Pettit Lake, 2 miles (3 km) from the highway. Open hillsides are available for practicing downhill turns, and optional tours are possible on side trails. The tour is **flat and easy**. Snowmobile use occurs.

8

Pettit-Yellowbelly Tour— *Snowbound roads. Moderately easy terrain, but requires some route finding. Dogs OK. Snowshoeing.* This 9-mile (14.5 km) loop is one of the most pleasant tours in the area. It's not marked and you'll need to take the *Alturas Lake* and *Snowyside Peak* topographical maps along. It begins on the snowbound Pettit Lake access road (see above). Follow **Pettit Lake Road** to a side snowbound road branching off to the right (north) .5 mile before reaching Pettit Lake. This turnoff is near the fish barrier dam on Pettit Lake Outlet. The side road crosses a bridge over the Pettit Lake Outlet and

The Sawtooths and Sawtooth Valley: for those with warm passions for cold places.

then splits—one road, left, leading to a backpacker transfer camp and the other, right, leading over sagebrush hills and across a large open area.

Take the right road and follow the road over the sagebrush hills. Because it cuts across an open area, you'll have to look closely for signs of the road. This is where it helps to have a map. If all goes well, you should be able to reach **Yellowbelly Lake**, approximately 4.5 miles (7 km) from the start.

A delightful return trip can be made by following the **Yellowbelly hiking trail** back. The Yellowbelly trail is not marked well, but it can be recognized by the thin swatch it cuts through the trees. To pick up the trail, ski the Yellowbelly Road almost to its end on the western side of the lake. There, a sign indicates Yellowbelly Trail, which contours closely around the shore of the lake back toward the east.

Once on the trail, follow it downhill to where it comes out into the large, open area. Here one may return to Pettit via the original trail. The total length of the tour, round-trip, is 10 miles (16 km).

9 **Alturas Lake**— *Snowbound road. Flat, easy terrain. Dogs OK. Snowshoeing.* The Alturas Lake turnoff is not usually marked in the winter. Tourers unfamiliar with the area can locate it by driving 3 miles (5 km) north of Smiley Creek Store in Sawtooth City and watching for the snowbound access road leading from the west side of Idaho 75.

The ski tour follows the **Alturas Lake access road** to the west, passing by **Perkins Lake**, 1.8 miles (2.9 km) from the highway and arriving at Alturas Lake, 2.3 miles (3.7 km) from the highway. Snow-mobile use occurs. As a side trip, skiers may enjoy the lovely tour along the Alturas Lake outlet flowing north out of Alturas and Perkins

Lakes. In the past, the Sawtooth Ski Club has sometimes groomed a loop trail along the road and back along the north side of Outlet Creek.

10 **Sawtooth City Ghost Town**—*Some off-trail and snowbound road. Flat, easy terrain. Dogs OK. Snowshoeing.* Start the tour at the **Beaver**

Creek Store, located 1 mile (1.6 km) north of the Smiley Creek Lodge in Sawtooth City on Idaho 75. Be sure to check with the caretakers at Beaver Creek Store for permission to park.

From Beaver Creek Store, ski across the open area to the west, cross-

ing over the stream (Beaver Creek), and follow the main branch of the stream in a southerly direction. Approximately 1 mile (1.5 km) from the start, tourers will leave the open area and upon entering the trees,

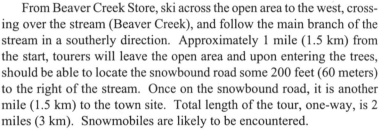

should be able to locate the snowbound road some 200 feet (60 meters) to the right of the stream. Once on the snowbound road, it is another mile (1.5 km) to the town site. Total length of the tour, one-way, is 2 miles (3 km). Snowmobiles are likely to be encountered.

Only a portion of one cabin still stands in Sawtooth City, its walls lean and are supported by pines growing on either side. The lone cabin and a few scattered foundations are the only remains of a once flourish-ing, mining settlement of 600 people. Silver was discovered in 1878 by the prospector Levi Smiley at the head of Smiley Creek, a few miles to the south. A year later, the town of Vienna was established on Smiley Creek, and it eventually grew to a population of almost 1,000. Sawtooth City came into existence shortly after Vienna when other mining dis-coveries were made at the head of Beaver Creek.

11 **Frenchman Creek-Headwaters of the Salmon River**—*Snowbound road and off-trail. Easy to moderately easy terrain. Dogs OK.*

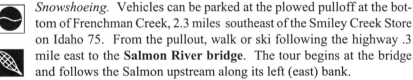

Snowshoeing. Vehicles can be parked at the plowed pulloff at the bot-tom of Frenchman Creek, 2.3 miles southeast of the Smiley Creek Store on Idaho 75. From the pullout, walk or ski following the highway .3 mile east to the **Salmon River bridge**. The tour begins at the bridge and follows the Salmon upstream along its left (east) bank.

You'll have to cross a couple of side drainages along the way, but usually, there are sufficient snow bridges to make the crossings. One side hill along the river bank is encountered, but with caution, begin-ning skiers should be able to pass it easily. For the first mile (1.5 km), a gentle ridge parallels the left bank, and, if desired, you can follow the ridge instead of staying on the road. Once past the mile point, those on the ridge can rejoin the road again. The snowbound road climbs gradu-ally, and all along the way the scenery is spectacular. Snowmobiles use the area.

From the parking area, you can also make an easy up-and-back tour on the snowbound **Frenchman Creek Road**. It is even possible to do a short loop by skiing up Frenchman Creek and looping back around the west. The loop is of moderate difficulty, but you'll want to have the *Alturas* 7.5 minute topographic map along for route finding.

Galena Pass Introduction—*Off-trail backcountry skiing or snowboarding. Some easy telemarking slopes. Mostly moderately difficult to difficult backcountry terrain.* Galena Pass, located 30 miles north of Ketchum on Idaho 75, has a little bit of everything for backcountry skiers and snowboarders. A number of possible descents and tours on the **Sawtooth Valley side** are described in the next couple of pages. Also see the Sun Valley chapter which describes a number of backcountry skiing and snowboarding on the Wood River side.

Before going up be sure you have a compass and the *Galena, Horton Peak, Alturas Lake* and *Frenchman Creek* topographic maps. Except for the Galena Pass Overlook and historical marker trails, avalanche potential in the pass area is high, and skier and snowshoers should **carry transceivers** and shovels, and check the avalanche forecasts provided by the Ketchum Ranger District. Ketchum area forecasts are some of the best forecasts in the U.S., and it's a serious oversight not to avail yourself of this information before undertaking backcountry skiing and snowboarding trips (see *Resources* at the end of the chapter for more information).

12

Galena Pass Overlook and Historical Marker Descents—*Off-trail backcountry. Moderately easy slopes for telemarking and snowboarding. See aerial illustration next page.* The **Galena Pass Overlook**, 1 mile north of the top of the pass on the Sawtooth side, is a good place to get started. It has sizable pulloff plowed for parking. From the overlook a relatively easy descending tour can be made to the valley below. It's a wonderful place for skiers just **learning how to telemark**— and there's little avalanche hazard. Two options exist for ending the tour. Once at the base of the pass, the large, open flat can be skied across to the northwest to reach the plowed highway (see the aerial illustration). A shuttle vehicle can meet skiers here and return them for another run if desired. Or you can put skins on and climb back up. The vertical drop of the overlook tour is 1,000 feet (300 meters). Total length of an average tour that ends at the highway is 2 miles (3 km).

A shorter and much quicker version of the overlook tour is to start from the **historical marker**, approximately 1.5 miles farther down the highway from the overlook. The slopes are a bit steeper and the vertical drop is around 400 feet (122 meters). The ski out to the highway is short and sweet.

13 Galena Pass: The Cross—*Off-trail backcountry skiing and snowboarding. Moderately difficult to difficult. See aerial illustration.*

On the **north side** of the pass is a high point (Point 9,225 on the *Horton Peak* topographic map) which is called The Cross. From The Cross, ski and snowboard descents can be done on the Sawtooth or Wood River sides. The Cross is accessed by parking in the plowed pulloff just beyond the top of the pass on the Sawtooth side. Ski to the north up the snowbound road and climb to the high point, The Cross. If you have a shuttle vehicle, descents can be made down to plowed pulloffs along the highway on the Wood River side or the Sawtooth side. Or you can use skins and work in one area. There's a lot of avalanche danger on Galena. Check the forecast and carry transceivers and shovels. Excellent **avalanche forecasts** are provided by the Ketchum District Office of the Sawtooth National Forest and are available via recorded phone message or on the Internet (see *Resources* at the end of the chapter).

14 Galena Pass to Barr Gulch— *Off-trail backcountry skiing and snowboarding. Moderately difficult to difficult. See aerial illustration.*

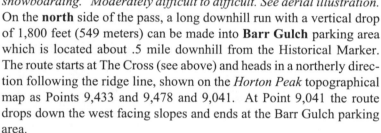

On the **north** side of the pass, a long downhill run with a vertical drop of 1,800 feet (549 meters) can be made into **Barr Gulch** parking area which is located about .5 mile downhill from the Historical Marker. The route starts at The Cross (see above) and heads in a northerly direction following the ridge line, shown on the *Horton Peak* topographical map as Points 9,433 and 9,478 and 9,041. At Point 9,041 the route drops down the west facing slopes and ends at the Barr Gulch parking area.

15 Galena Pass: Humble Pie— *Off-trail backcountry skiing and snowboarding. Moderately difficult to difficult. See aerial illustration.*

Backcountry skiing and snowboarding is also available on the **south side** of the pass. Many of the descents on this side drop into the Wood River side and are described in the Sun Valley-Ketchum chapter, but there is one descending tour that should be mentioned that drops into the Sawtooth side. This is called **Humble Pie,** and it is a beautiful trip, particularly in spring conditions. It starts from the parking area on top of the pass and heads south along the ridge serving as the divide between the Wood River and Salmon River drainages. Follow the ridge 1 mile from where you've parked to point 9,636 (on the *Galena* topographic map). From this point, ski to the west following the predominate ridge into the Headwaters of the Salmon River.

There's abundant avalanche hazard on this side of the pass. Make sure you're prepared and check the avalanche forecast before heading out.

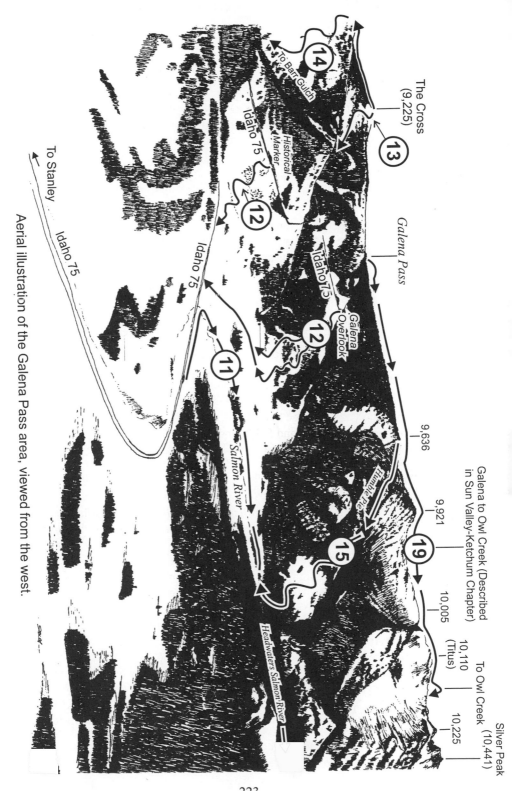

Aerial illustration of the Galena Pass area, viewed from the west.

223

OTHER AREAS

Copper Peak. *Off-trail backcountry skiing or snowboarding. Moderately difficult to difficult backcountry terrain.* Copper Peak is a popular backcountry mountain on the east side of Idaho 21 near Banner Summit. To access it, drive 24 miles west of Stanley on Idaho 21 and park in the **Bull Trout parking area**. If you reach the end of the plowed road at Banner Summit, you've gone about .5 mile too far. Starting at the Bull Trout parking area, walk .2 mile back up the highway towards Stanley. From this point, the route follows a small drainage to the east and onto the peak. Kirk Bachman, the owner of Sawtooth Mountain Guides, warns that some maps have Copper Peak mislocated and mislabeled as Cooper Peak. Copper is the proper name, and it is located almost directly east of the parking area. The summit of the peak is over 9,000 feet. The snow there is often dry and the downhill terrain excellent.

Sawtooths— *Access via snowbound trails and then open off-trail high country. Difficult backcountry terrain.* The Sawtooths can be entered via any of the summer hiking trails off the west side of Idaho 75 in the Sawtooth Valley.

Because of the **extreme avalanche danger** in the Sawtooths, ski traverses across the area are infrequent. Peanut McCoy, Ken Dickens, and Ed Flood made one of the early crossings of the Sawtooths in February of 1972. Their route started at Clark Miller Guest Ranch and followed trails beyond Yellowbelly Lake to Toxaway Lake, over the pass to Veron Lake, and out the South Fork of the Payette to Idaho 21. They were plagued by snowstorms and avalanches for most of the trip. At one point along the South Fork of the Payette, they were so apprehensive about an avalanche surprising them during the night that they spread out over a wide area and camped out individually. Their hope was that if an avalanche did come down, one of the group might be spared and could dig the others out. No avalanches hit them that night, and they eventually reached safety. None of them have since repeated the trip.

White Clouds— *Access via snowbound trails and then open off-trail high country. Difficult backcountry terrain.* Access to the White Clouds can be gained from Idaho 75 along the Sawtooth Valley via any of the summer hiking trails. Access also can be obtained along the stretch of Idaho 75 from Stanley to Clayton or off East Fork Road just east of Clayton. Backcountry terrain is **difficult,** and there is plentiful **avalanche hazard**.

Like the Sawtooths, the interior of the White Clouds does not receive very many winter visitors. Dale Gelsky, one time owner of Galena Lodge, was on one early south-to-north traverse of the range. His party was caught in a blizzard as they climbed across the side of Blackburn Peak.

At one point, when visibility had dropped to a few feet, Gelsky stopped in his tracks. Something felt funny to him. He didn't feel the usual resistance of the deep, new snow against his skis. Looking more closely through a momentary break in the blinding snow, he found that his skis were teetering on the edge of a cornice overhanging a deep void plunging off the side of Blackburn. Gelsky crept slowly back away from the edge of the cornice and cautiously continued skiing on a less terrifying but more secure route. Their route, which took six days in 1974, started at Galena Lodge and concluded at Robinson Bar.

The Origin of the Yurt as a Winter Backcountry Shelter

IT WAS in the Sawtooth Valley that the first yurt was used as a backcountry winter shelter. That tradition continues today with a yurt system available in the Sawtooths which is operated by one of Idaho's top mountain guides, Kirk Bachman.

Few people realize that Kirk was the person who originated the idea of using yurts as winter backcountry shelters. He built his first Yurt in the Craft Shop at Idaho State University when he was a senior. After graduating, he spent the next winter living in his yurt near Stanley and working as a guide for Joe Leonard, who owned the earliest ski guiding business in the Sawtooths.

During evenings of that first winter, Kirk and his girlfriend, sat, comfortably ensconced in the yurt, reading and discussing passages from Peter Matthiessen's, *The Snow Leopard*. No matter how much snow fell or how cold it was outside, the yurt worked wonderfully. Kirk had come up with an approach to winter shelters which was poetically simple and aesthetically harmonious with the outdoor environment. The following year, a yurt was placed in the Sawtooths to be used as a backcountry hut. People who used the yurt came back raving about it, and it wasn't long before other yurt systems began appearing throughout the west. □

Cowboys and Hippies

IF YOU WERE A FRIEND or relative and were planning on dropping in on Peanut McCoy and spending the night, you'd better bring your winter camping gear. His place in Triumph, east of Hailey, was an old sheepherder's wagon. The window was gone and a piece of cardboard had been taped in its place with a towel added for a little insulation. "It was pretty chilly," Peanut said, recalling his Bohemian days in the early 1970s, "In the morning, it was just as cold inside as it was outside."

Peanut had a wonderfully simple life then. (Things are a bit more complicated now. He is married and has a family.) Every day, he and his friend Ed Flood would ski and explore the surrounding mountains, averaging as many as 10 miles a day.

But it was the long ski trips, of several days of duration that he really savored. He had cut his teeth in the Sierras. In March of 1970, along with mountaineer, Doug Robinson, Peanut did a 36 day ski traverse of the Sierras from Mt. Whitney to Yosemite Park. Later, making Idaho his home, the White Clouds is where he set his sights.

"Some places, like the White Clouds, are so special," he said, "that if we lose them, the whole planet suffers." In fact, there was danger of losing the White Clouds. In the early 1970s he became involved with a group of conservationists trying to protect the White Clouds from a large molybdenum mine that was planned at the base of Castle Peak in the very heart of the area. (Mining activity in the White Clouds has been temporarily averted, but the area is still not safe. You can help in the fight to save this beautiful area by joining the Boulder-White Clouds Council, PO Box 3719, Ketchum, Idaho 83340.)

In January of 1971, Peanut McCoy and Ed Flood started at Galena Summit and skied into the White Clouds. For four days in the upper Chamberlain Basin area they were pinned down in their cramped 48" high A-frame tent by a furious blizzard. Another time during the trip, the winds were so great that they had to crawl on their hands and knees to cross from one side of a ridge to another. Eventually they arrived on the East Fork of the Salmon.

To get back, they had to hitchhike. They managed to get to a bar and restaurant along the Salmon River called Torrey's and were standing out front, trying to thumb a ride back to Hailey. "We looked pretty ragged," said Peanut. After being in the mountains for a considerable time, their long hair was greasy and their beards had grown. They both wore baggy wool clothing.

During the seventies in much of the West, there was something of a cultural tension between rural blue-collar workers and young, free-spirited baby boomers. It was a given that Idaho rednecks and cowboys automatically didn't like anyone resembling a hippie— which meant anyone with long hair and a beard.

The cultural tension was heating up that winter day outside Torrey's. "There was a guy taunting us," said Peanut. "He was standing out in front of Torrey's and pounding on top of a car and pointing at us."

"Lookie what we got here," the man yelled. "Dirt bag hippies!"

Both Peanut and Ed were getting nervous about the situation. They were on a remote stretch of highway, and of the few cars that passed, no one was interested in picking them up.

The man continued beating on top of the car and announced loudly to his companions who had gathered outside: "There's only one thing I dislike more than one dirty hippy, and that's two of the dirty sonsofbitches at the same place and the same time."

The two skiers, were now quietly discussing among themselves how they might defend themselves, when a Chevy Camero screeched to a stop with two cowboys in it. Peanut caught a glimpse of the antagonist standing in front of Torrey's. He had a smug look and was smiling broadly. Things had suddenly gone from bad to worse. With the two new cowboys, Peanut and Ed were now far outnumbered and outgunned.

"Both of them were pie-eyed," said Peanut, "and they wanted to know where the hell we were going," Peanut replied politely that he and Ed were trying to catch a ride back to Triumph where they lived.

"Hell, are you Peanut?" one of them asked. Peanut nodded. It turned out they had friends in common. "Well, git on in here," said the cowboy.

Peanut loaded his pack, and as he got in, he looked back at Torrey's. His antagonist was incredulous, and he stood with an open mouth as the cowboys, and the two hippies, drove off down the highway. □

Resources . . .

National Recreation Area Lands in the Sawtooths
Headquarters, Sawtooth Recreation Area—Office located 8 miles north of Stanley on Idaho 75. Address: Star Route, Highway 75, Ketchum, Idaho 83340. Phone: (208) 726-8291.

Yurt System and Guide Services
Sawtooth Mountain Guides—Address: PO Box 18, Stanley, Idaho 83278. Phone: (208) 774-3324.

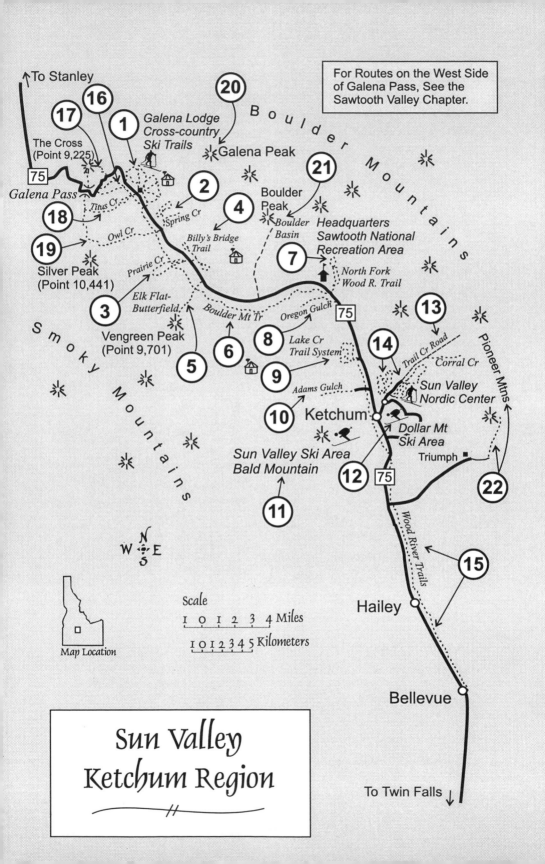

For Routes on the West Side of Galena Pass, See the Sawtooth Valley Chapter.

↑To Stanley

16

17

1

Galena Lodge Cross-country Ski Trails

20

Galena Peak

B o u l d e r

The Cross (Point 9,225)

75

Galena Pass

Titus Cr.

18

Owl Cr.

Spring Cr.

2

4

21

Boulder Peak

Boulder Basin

Headquarters Sawtooth National Recreation Area

19

Silver Peak (Point 10,441)

Prairie Cr.

Billy's Bridge Trail

7

North Fork Wood R. Trail

M o u n t a i n s

3

Elk Flat-Butterfield

Boulder Mt Tr

Oregon Gulch

75

13

S m o k y

Vengreen Peak (Point 9,701)

5

6

8

Lake Cr Trail System

14

Trail Cr Road

Corral Cr

Pioneer Mthns

9

Sun Valley Nordic Center

M o u n t a i n s

Adams Gulch

10

Ketchum

Dollar Mt Ski Area

Triumph

22

Sun Valley Ski Area Bald Mountain

12

75

11

W ✦ E
N S

Wood River Trails

15

Hailey

Map Location

Scale
1 0 1 2 3 4 Miles
1 0 1 2 3 4 5 Kilometers

Bellevue

Sun Valley
Ketchum Region

To Twin Falls ↓

CHAPTER 14
SUN VALLEY-KETCHUM REGION

Area Covered: Central Idaho including the surrounding areas of Sun Valley, Galena, Ketchum, Hailey and Bellevue.

*W*HAT HAS HAPPENED in the Ketchum-Sun Valley Nordic scene over the last few years is nothing short of a miracle. Track skiing—the kind of cross-country skiing that the area is so well suited to—reached a nadir in the early 1990s when the trail systems at Galena Lodge and Busterback Ranch, just over Galena Pass, shut down. A group of inventive and enterprising skiers came to the rescue, and working through the Blaine County Recreation District has, in a few short years, put together a cross-country trail system which ranks among the best in the U.S.

Welcome to a place where Nordic skiing is a passion. Welcome to skiing heaven. Nordic skiers have their choice of almost 200 kilometers of groomed trails in the Wood River Valley. Trails are groomed for both classic and skating. Special trails are available to skiers with dogs and others designed for snowshoeing. And, just beyond the groomed trails, in the surrounding mountain ranges, backcountry skiing and snowboarding is rich and abundant. Can it get any better than this?

Groomed trails in the Wood River Valley are grouped into three networks. Farthest to the south are the Wood River Trails, which follow the old Union Pacific railroad bed. The railroad tracks have long been taken out and in their place is a paved non-mechanized corridor, which in the summer is a wonderful trail for biking, roller blading and hiking, and in the winter, an equally wonderful trail for cross-country skiing. The trail is 30 kilometers (19 miles) long and connects the communities of Bellevue, Hailey and Ketchum.

The next network is the Sun Valley Nordic Center. The Sun Valley trails start just off Sun Valley Road, a short distance beyond the main Sun Valley village. The trails wind around the Sun Valley Golf Course and on the open hillsides on either side of Sun Valley Road. At this writing it has 40 kilometers (25 miles) of groomed trails. Ski passes for the Sun Valley system can be purchased at the Sun Valley Nordic Center's office where the trails start.

The third, and largest, network is called the North Valley Trails which includes trail systems along a 19 mile stretch of Idaho 75 from just north of Ketchum to Galena Lodge. The first set of trails is 3 miles north of Ketchum on Idaho 75 at Lake Creek. Lake Creek is where the Sun Valley Nordic team practices, but the trails are available to everyone.

From Lake Creek north on Idaho 75 there's a 4.5 mile gap, but the trails start again at the Sawtooth National Recreation Area Headquarters, with the North Fork, Billy's Bridge and Prairie Creek trail systems.

At the northern most end of the Wood River Valley is the last of the North Valley Trails, the Galena Lodge System. Galena Lodge, the final jewel in the Wood River crown, has 50 kilometers of groomed trails. The trail system starts from the rustic lodge which serves meals, rents skis and snowshoes, and whose managers can always be relied upon for the best of skiing advice. The lodge also rents out a couple of yurts which, reached from the groomed trail system, are designed especially for those looking for a tamed overnight experience.

The Wood River Valley is, of course, the home of the world famous Sun Valley Ski Area. There are few mountains with fall lines as true and grooming as meticulously done as at Bald Mountain. The mountain has two access points: Warm Springs on the north side and River Run on the east side. Also, don't forget about Dollar Mountain Ski Area. It is a small area, but its gradual slopes are great for families and those learning how to ski. The lift starts at the small village of Elkhorn over the hill from Sun Valley or at Dollar Mountain Cabin, on the southeast edge of Sun Valley.

Besides all this, great opportunities exist for backcountry skiing and snowboarding. This was the stomping grounds of Idaho backcountry skiing pioneer Andy Hennig, the Sun Valley Ski School instructor who was one of the most prolific backcountry skiers of the pre and post war era. He explored and skied elegant descent lines throughout the three ranges encircling the area: the

Pioneer Mountains to the south and east of Sun Valley, and the Boulder Mountains which parallel the right or east side of Idaho 75 driving north, and the Smoky Mountains which parallel the west side of Idaho 75.

Hennig also spent quite a bit of his time skiing the slopes of Galena Pass. But even before Hennig, skiers travelling between mines in the Sawtooths and the Wood River were skiing the slopes of the pass. One of those skiers was Ann Sullivan who skied over the pass in 1919 and left us a written account—and her insights—on what that journey was like.

The Tales . . .

BY THE TIME that 20 year-old Ann Sullivan reached Galena, where the present day Galena Lodge lies, she was pretty well spent. On the descent off Galena Pass coming from the Sawtooth Valley she had taken a spill and sprained her ankle. Exhausted and her ankle swollen, she was relieved to be down and near shelter.

"Skiing up to the cabin," Sullivan wrote, "we noticed the snow was level with the eaves. The boys had to dig down to find the hatch on the door and taking our turn, we practically fell in onto the floor. Hooray! There was a stove here with plenty of wood."

Sullivan was in a party of thirteen, eleven men and two women, who had left the Vienna Mine in the Sawtooths two days earlier and were on their way to Hailey. New to skiing, she had only two days of practice before leaving Vienna. By making the long 50 mile trip in 1919, Sullivan became one of a long line of venerable women skiers from the Wood River Valley. Wood River women were particularly distinguished among the fellowship of long snowshoers. During the 1880s the skills and racing exploits of one group of Bellevue women was known as far away as Silver City in the Owyhee Mountains south of Boise.

Along with the party was a Siberian Wolfhound named Rags that was harnessed to a sled. The next day, Rags and the party of skiers worked their way down along the Wood River. (Modern day skiers can retrace an approximation of the journey by following the Boulder Mountain Cross-country Trail, described on page 236.)

Sullivan worried about Rags: "He would try to ride my brother's skis. My heart ached for Rags pulling that heavy sled." That night, their third, they spent at Fleming's sawmill. "Rags was more tired than hungry," wrote Sullivan, "and had an opportunity to rest up. He ate a good breakfast the next morning before we pulled out."

Rags survived and Sullivan finished the trip by skiing down the main street of Ketchum. She didn't have to worry about the sort of traffic that can be found on Main Street these days. Back then, Ketchum was practically a ghost town. She stayed a night with friends and then took the train from Ketchum to Hailey. In her account, Sullivan touches upon the bonds that often form between individuals when faced with the challenges of travel through wild country: "Being associated with a group for five, hard strenuous days, it was difficult to say goodbye. They had all been so fine and courageous."

Sullivan also described an event which happened at the end of the trip. Some of the "boys" had gone ahead of her, and decided to ski all the way to Hailey. They ended up "facing a genuine blizzard," Sullivan wrote. As they were bent over in the wind, following one another, the one in the lead all of sudden gave a yell and sprang up the hillside. Pandemonium broke out behind him as the others realized what was happening and they too leaped off the trail as best they could in their long snowshoes.

The "boys," it seems, had been finding their way along the snow covered railroad tracks of the Union Pacific and had been surprised by the Ketchum bound train. □

The Trails . . .

1 **Galena Lodge Trail System**—*Groomed cross-country ski trail system. Snowshoe trails. All abilities. Food, instruction, rentals, backcountry huts and yurts. Passes required. See the aerial illustration on the facing page* . The publicly owned Galena Lodge is one of the great success stories of the revival of Nordic skiing in the Ketchum area. After being closed in the early 1990s, it finally reopened in 1994 after a community wide, "Save Galena" fund raising campaign.

The lodge lies at the base of Galena Pass and is the starting point of an elaborate network of groomed trails. Presently, over 50 kilometers of groomed trails are available. With trails for **all abilities**, the Galena system consists of a series of interconnecting pathways throughout the drainages of **Gladiator, Senate and Cherry Creeks** on the east side of the highway and **Titus Creek** on the west side of the highway. It's a beautiful area, highlighted by gentle, open ridges and picturesque views of the surrounding mountains.

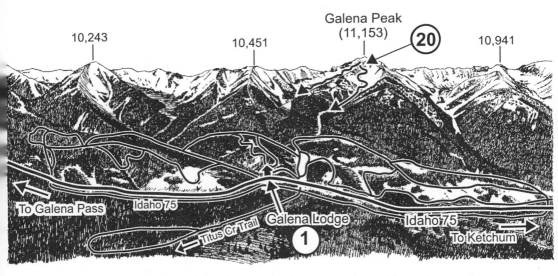

Aerial illustration of the Galena Lodge area, viewed from the west. The Galena cross-country ski trail system and the spring descent route off of Galena Peak are shown.

Galena has special trails for **snowshoeing** and trails on which you may take your dog. Meals and hot drinks may be purchased at the lodge. Instruction and rental skis are available, and **yurts** and **ski huts** may be rented for overnight stays. If you don't want to cook, you can even order out. Dinner will be delivered right to the yurt. Indeed, life is very good here.

The Galena trail system is part of the North Valley Trails and you'll need to **purchase a pass** before using them. Passes are available in the lodge, at the Sawtooth National Recreation Headquarters, or in cross-country ski stores in Ketchum. The pass is good on all the groomed public trails, including those to the south of Galena.

2 **Owl Creek-Spring Creek**—*Snowbound roads. Easy to moderately difficult. Snowshoeing.* From the Owl Creek pulloff, ski or snowshoe trips can be made on both the **unmarked** and snowbound Owl Creek and Spring Creek roads. The pulloff is located 2.7 miles south of Galena Lodge on the west side of Idaho 75. Passes are not required here.

The snowbound **Owl Creek Road** is located on the west side of the highway and is a **gradually rising** route, paralleling Owl Creek to the right (north) side. One mile (1.5 km) from the start, the first of several slide paths is encountered in Owl Creek Canyon. Beyond the 2.5 mile (4 km) point, the avalanche hazard becomes significant and skiing or snowshoeing is only advised during stable snow conditions. Current avalanche information is available from the Sawtooth National Recreation Area Headquarters.

233

On the other side (east side) of the highway is **Spring Creek Road**. From the road, a number of **unmarked** snowbound roads or trails branch off, all of which make good tours. It's also a good area for snowshoeing. One of two trails can be taken into the **Cherry Creek** drainage, just to the north of Spring Creek. Avalanche hazard is low as long as you stay in the lower reaches of the Spring Creek-Cherry Creek area. Skiing difficulty ranges from **moderately easy** to **moderately difficult**.

3 **Prairie Creek**—*Groomed cross-country ski trail. Marked snowshoe trail. Moderately easy terrain. Passes required.* The Prairie Creek

Loop is a part of the North Valley Trails, a public system of groomed trails. **Passes** are required. The plowed pulloff is located on the west side of Idaho 75, 5.1 miles south of Galena Lodge, or 10.2 miles north of the Sawtooth National Recreation Headquarters.

Prairie Creek area has long been popular for cross-country skiers in the Ketchum area, and in 1977, Frank Rowland of the Sawtooth National Recreation Area, first initiated a grooming program on the trail. Forest Service grooming funds eventually ran out, but fortunately Prairie Creek has since become one of the trails groomed by the Blaine County Recreation District.

The trail follows the north side of Prairie Creek, passing through islands of timber and open areas which provide nice views of the Smoky Mountains to the west. Approximately 4 kilometers from the start, the trail turns and crosses over to the south side of Prairie Creek for the

return trip. Total distance of a round-trip tour is 7.5 kilometers (5 miles). The skiing is **moderately easy**. The Prairie Creek area also has a separately marked **snowshoe trail** accessed from the same parking area as the ski trail.

4 **Billy's Bridge Trail**—*Groomed cross-country ski trail. Easy terrain. Passes required.* Billy's Bridge Trail is a part of the system of trails groomed by the Blaine County Recreation District. The trail starts from a pulloff on the east side of Idaho 75, 5.6 miles from Galena Lodge or 9.7 miles north of the Headquarters of the Sawtooth National Recreation Area. **Passes** are required.

The trail leads east a few hundred feet to a small bridge over the Wood River. The original bridge was built by Bill Smith, a wood artisan from Ketchum and for whom the trail is named. The trail splits after the bridge, and a ski tour can be taken either to the southeast or northwest along the meandering Big Wood River. In either split, the trail makes a small loop and returns on itself. Eight kilometers (5 miles) of trail are available.

It is a beautiful tour and excellently suited to **beginners**. Those skiers wishing to get off the trail and catch a little downhill skiing may enjoy climbing up on the broad, flat, sloping ridges which lie between the drainages of the foothills of the Boulder Mountains to the east of the Billy Bridge Trail. The tops of the ridges are, in some cases, several hundred meters wide and are perfect for **telemarking**.

5   **Elk Flat-Butterfield**—*Snowbound road then off-trail backcountry. Moderately difficult.* This is a moderately difficult tour that follows the snowbound Elk Flat Road. Passes are not required here. It begins from a plowed pulloff on the west side of Idaho 75, 6.7 miles south of Galena Lodge or 8.6 miles north of the Sawtooth National Recreation Area Headquarters. Some of the lower slopes near the road are good for **practicing telemarks**. The distance to **Elk Flats** is 3.5 miles (6 km) and the total vertical rise is 1,800 feet (549 meters). **Vengreen Peak** (appearing as point 9,701 on the *Easley Hot Springs* topographical map) is the mountain which rises up just to the west of Elk Flat, and can be climbed and descended for more difficult backcountry skiing. Avalanche potential is low on the road, but significantly higher on the peak.

6   **Boulder Mountain Trail (Harriman Trail)**—*Groomed cross-country ski trail. Easy terrain. Passes required.* The Boulder Mountain Trail approximates part of the route that was followed by long snowshoers passing between the Sawtooth and Wood River mines in the late 1800s and early 1900s. Its official status as a contemporary ski trail came about when it was used for a cross-country ski race called the Boulder Mountain Marathon, which has since become one of Idaho's most famous cross-country ski races. The ski race is still held, but the groomed trail is otherwise available for general touring throughout the winter.

What a spectacular and unique trail it is. The Boulder Trail begins at Galena Lodge and ends 27.5 kilometers (17 miles) to the south at the Headquarters of the Sawtooth National Recreational Area. It runs down the Big Wood River Valley with the **Smoky Mountains** on one side and the incomparable **Boulders** on the other. While it passes over several hills of intermediate difficulty, overall, the trail is a **gradual** and graceful **descent** downhill from start to finish.

The trail is the trunk of the North Valley Trails from which all other trail systems—Galena, Prairie Creek, Billy's Bridge and North Fork—branch off. You can access it from the parking areas at the trail system or occasional plowed pulloffs along Idaho 75. **Passes** are required and may be purchased at Galena Lodge, Sawtooth National Recreation Headquarters, or in cross-country ski stores in Ketchum.

7   **North Fork of the Wood River**—*Groomed cross-country ski trail. Marked snowshoe trail. Easy terrain. Passes required.* The North Fork Trail is one of the trails groomed by the Blaine Country Recreation District. Parking is at the headquarters of the Sawtooth National Recreation area, 8 miles north of Ketchum. The trail leaves the parking lot and leads to the north along the North Fork of the Wood River. Contrasting with other trails in the region, which are in conifer and aspen forests, part of the North Fork trail goes through a riparian zone of large cottonwoods and willows. **Skiing is across easy terrain.** Total length of the tour is 4 kilometers (2.5 miles). Also, a **separate marked snowshoe trail** leaves from the parking lot. **Trail passes** are required and can be obtained from the Sawtooth National Recreation Area Headquarters or from cross-country ski shops in Ketchum.

8 **Oregon Gulch**— *Snowbound road. Easy terrain. Snowshoeing.* This is an **easy** tour and is **unmarked and ungroomed**. It begins on the west side of Idaho 75 at the North Fork Store, 7.5 miles north of Ketchum. The tour follows the snowbound Oregon Gulch Road to the west. Avalanche hazard increases significantly after the 2.5 mile (4 km) point. Snowmobiles will be encountered.

9

Lake Creek Trail System—*Groomed cross-country ski trail system. Moderately easy to moderately difficult. Toilets. Passes required.* The Lake Creek system is a part of the North Valley Trails groomed by the Blaine Country Recreation District. The parking area is located on the west side of Idaho 75, 3.4 miles north of Sun Valley Road and Idaho 75 intersection in Ketchum. A total of 15.5 kilometers (10 miles) of trails are available. The area is used by the Sun Valley Nordic Team but is open for public use. In the 1970s, Butch Harper who for many years was the Bald Mountain Snow Ranger, was the first to put together a cross-country ski trail system in the area. His handiwork is evident in some of the trail names: Harper's Hump on the way up and Butch's Blitz—on the way down. Trails range from **moderately easy to moderately difficult**. Trail **passes** are required and can be obtained from the Sawtooth National Recreation Area Headquarters or from cross-country ski shops in Ketchum.

10

Adams Gulch—*Snowbound road. Easy terrain. Snowshoeing.* The turnoff to Adams Gulch is located on the west side of Idaho 75, 1.5 miles north of the Idaho 75 and Sun Valley Road intersection in the middle of Ketchum. Turn onto Adams Gulch Road and drive until it is no longer plowed. The tour follows the **gradual** snowbound Adams Gulch Road to the west into a picturesque canyon. Located conveniently close to Ketchum, Adams Gulch provides an option for snowshoers and skiers looking for **ungroomed and unmarked** trails. Avalanche hazard increases beyond the 2.5 mile (4 km) point.

11

Sun Valley Ski Area: Bald Mountain—*Alpine ski area. Alpine, Nordic downhill and snowboarding. All services: food, lodging, rentals, instruction, etc.* Averell Harriman, Union Pacific Chairman, had been eyeing Bald Mountain ever since Sun Valley opened in 1936. Finally, on a horseback ride up the mountain in 1939, he instructed two of his engineers and a steel and cable expert to come up with an estimate of what it would cost to build a chairlift from the base of the mountain up to where the Roundhouse is now located. By six that night, the group gave Harriman their estimate of $205,000. That's all that Harriman needed. He gave the project the green light, and the lift was completed well under budget before the year was out.

Harriman wanted something to rival the resorts of Europe, and with Bald Mountain and the best lifts in the world, he got it. To this day, Bald Mountain is still a world class mountain, and it is one of those places that every skier must visit at least once in their lifetime. Bald Mountain currently has 13 lifts, 64 runs, a vertical drop of 3,400 feet and 2,067 acres of skiable terrain.

12 **Sun Valley Ski Area: Dollar Mountain**—*Alpine ski area. Alpine, Nordic downhill and snowboarding. All services: food, lodging, rentals, instruction, etc.* Dollar Mountain and nearby Proctor Mountain, a short walk from the Sun Valley Lodge, is the location of Sun Valley's first Alpine ski slopes, and where in 1936 the world's first chairlifts were used. The early lifts have long been retired and have been replaced with far safer and more reliable lifts. The ski area has two access points: one from Elkhorn Village and the other from Dollar Cabin, on the northeast edge of Sun Valley Village. Dollar Mountain has 4 lifts, 13 runs and 638 vertical feet of skiing. It's a good area in which to learn skiing and is ideal for families.

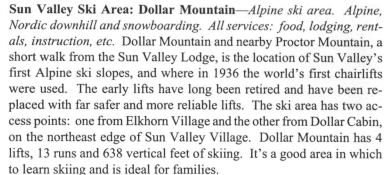

13 **Trail Creek**—*Snowbound road. Easy for the first couple of miles.* Trail creek is reached by driving from Ketchum to Sun Valley on the Sun Valley Road (also called Trail Creek Road). Continue driving approximately 2 miles (3 km) past Sun Valley Village until the road is no longer plowed.

This is an **unmarked and ungroomed trail**, but is **easy** and relatively flat, following the snowbound Trail Creek Road to the northeast. Trail Creek also provides access for longer moderately difficult tours on the snowbound **Corral Creek Road** joining from the east, approximately 3.5 kilometers (2 miles) from the start. For backcountry skiers, Corral Creek is one access to the **Pioneer Mountains**.

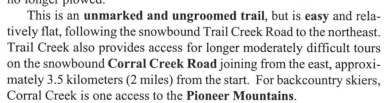

14 **Sun Valley Nordic Center**—*Groomed cross-country ski trail system. All abilities. Rentals, instruction, wax room.* The Sun Valley Nordic Center is located on the east side of the Sun Valley Road, just past the Sun Valley Garage in Sun Valley Village. The immaculately groomed trails begin at the Sun Valley Touring Center and meander across the gradual terrain of the Sun Valley Golf Course and into the open hills on either side of the Sun Valley Road. The trail system has a nice range of trail difficulties from **easy to moderately difficult**. Over 40 kilometers (25 miles) of trails are available. A popular tradition at the Sun Valley Nordic Center is to take a 3 kilometer trip into **Trail Creek Cabin** where a fire is always roaring and hearty lunches are served. Lessons and rentals are available. Purchase **trail passes** in the touring center.

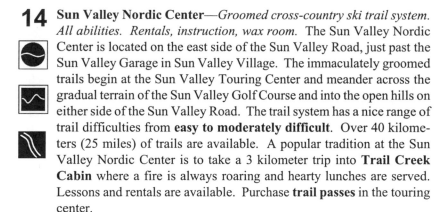

15 **Wood River Trails**—*Regularly groomed cross-country ski trails. Level, easy terrain. Dogs OK.* This trail system is one of Blaine County's pride and joys. It follows the old railroad line, paralleling Idaho 75 from just north of Ketchum to Hailey and onto Bellevue, a distance of 30 km (17 miles). You can jump on the trail at any of the towns or from several parking areas between Ketchum and Hailey. Dogs are allowed. Passes are required (see *Resources* for more information).

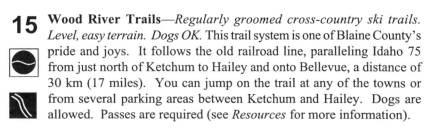

Two skiers finish up a tour at the venerable Sun Valley Nordic Center.

Galena Pass Introduction—*Off-trail backcountry skiing or snowboarding. Some easy telemarking slopes. Mostly moderately difficult to difficult backcountry terrain.* Galena Pass, 30 miles (48 km) north of Ketchum on Idaho 75, is a common jump-off place for backcountry downhill skiing and snowboarding. In addition to the material presented in this chapter which covers the **Wood River side of the pass**, also see the Sawtooth chapter for a run down of descents which are found on the Sawtooth side of Galena Pass. Everything on the Wood River or Ketchum side of the pass except for the old Galena Pass Road is moderately difficult to difficult backcountry. Before going be sure you have a compass and the *Galena* and *Horton Peak* topographic maps. As you would expect, this is avalanche country. **Carry shovels and transceivers** and check the **avalanche forecasts** provided by the Ketchum Ranger District (see *Resources* at the end of the chapter for more information).

16 **Galena Pass: Old Galena Pass Road**—*Old road bed. Moderate easy backcountry.* A good first time backcountry tour on Galena Pass is the descending trip down the old Galena Pass Road. In order to do the trip, a shuttle vehicle needs to be left at Galena Lodge. The old Pass Road begins from a plowed pulloff on the Wood River side of the highway, 1 mile from the top. The skiing is **moderately easy** backcountry and follows the old road bed downhill. For the first mile, the old road parallels the plowed highway, and then it turns and drops down into the Big Wood River, coming close again to Highway 75 in the Emma Gulch area. It is eventually followed all the way to Galena Lodge.

The distance following the Old Galena Pass Road is 3.5 miles (6 km) and the vertical drop is around 1,150 feet (335 meters).

16 **Galena Pass to Big Wood River**—*Off-trail backcountry skiing. Moderately difficult backcountry.* Another similar descent to the Old Galena Pass Highway route is to drop into the **Big Wood River drainage**. Big Wood River is the obvious drainage on the left (southeast) side of the highway as one drives to the top of the pass from the Ketchum side. The trip may begin from one of the three or four pulloffs on the upper part of the highway before the top of the pass. The route descends in any number of ways into the drainage and then follows it downstream, eventually coming out on the plowed highway near **Galena Lodge**. The total distance of an average tour is 3.5 miles (6 km). Avalanche hazard exists on the route.

17   **Galena Pass: The Cross and Avalanche Bowl**—*Off-trail backcountry skiing and snowboarding. Moderately difficult to difficult backcountry.* Ski and snowboard descents are commonly made from **The Cross** which is point 9,225 (on the USGS topographical map, *Horton Peak*). Descents from the Cross can be made to either the Sawtooth Valley side or the Wood River side. To reach The Cross, park in the pullout on the north side of Idaho 75, just beyond the top of the pass on the Sawtooth side. From this parking area, a snowbound road heads up toward to highest point (The Cross) just on the north side of the pass. Skiers and snowboarders on Cross routes either spot shuttle vehicles at the plowed pulloffs lower on Idaho 75 or use a skin trail and work in one area.

Beyond The Cross, a ridge line leads to point 9,433 (on the *Horton Peak* topographic map). Descents from this point may be through what is called **Avalanche Bowl** to a plowed pulloff near a steep cut in the highway about 2.4 miles down from the top of the pass on the Wood River side.

Routes in The Cross area are **steep** and cut across open snow fields which are dangerous in unstable snow conditions. Be prepared and check the avalanche forecast provided by the Ketchum Ranger District (see *Resources* at the end of the chapter).

18 **Galena Pass to Titus Creek**—*Off-trail backcountry skiing and snowboarding. Moderately difficult to difficult backcountry.* Galena Pass is also the starting point for the descending tour to Titus Creek. This moderately difficult backcountry tour begins at the top of the pass and follows Titus Lake Trail to the south. The route passes around the head of Wood River and reaches **Titus Lake,** 1 mile (1.6 km) from the start. From the lake, the trail descends Titus Creek and eventually comes out at **Galena Lodge**. The total length of the tour is 5 miles (8 km). Avalanche hazard exists on the route.

19 Galena Pass to Owl Creek— *Off-trail backcountry skiing and snowboarding. Difficult backcountry terrain. See aerial illustration on page 223 in the Sawtooth Valley Chapter.* Galena Pass to Owl Creek

is a long, classic route which was pioneered by Andy Hennig of the Sun Valley Ski School in the late 1930s. Extreme **avalanche hazard** exists, and it should be done in **late spring** when slopes have become stable. A summer reconnaissance is helpful to plan a safe route. It begins at the top of the pass and follows the prominent ridge line to the south (see aerial illustration on page 223 for a view of the ridge). At point 10,110 as indicated on the *Galena* topographical map, the ski route drops to the southwest to the saddle between point 10,110 and point 10,225. From the saddle, the beautiful east-facing bowl is skied, dropping into the Owl Creek drainage. Once in Owl Creek, the main drainage is followed to Idaho 75, coming out 3 miles (5 km) south of Galena Lodge. The total length of the tour is approximately 8 miles (13 km).

This tour and ski descent was first described in *Sun Valley Ski Book* by Andy Hennig. The book has long been out of print, but it is available in Idaho libraries. If you do check out the book, and it is a worthwhile read, you may find it difficult to transpose the Owl Creek route description from the book to the *Galena* topographical map. The reason is the difference between the names given by Hennig and those printed on the map. Hennig calls the point 10,110 (labeled "Titus" on the USGS map), Bromaghin Peak. Hennig also refers to an unnamed peak which is point 10,225, but this is the point that USGS map names Bromaghin Peak. Farther to the south is point 10,441. Though unnamed on the map, this mountain is referred to by Hennig, and generally accepted in Sun Valley, as Silver Peak.

According to Hennig, Bromaghin Peak was named after Captain Ralph Bromaghin, a ski instructor at Sun Valley who died in World War II while fighting with the 10th Mountain Division.

20 Galena Peak— *Off-trail backcountry skiing and snowboarding. Difficult backcountry terrain. See aerial illustration on page 233.* Galena

Peak is a difficult descent. It should be attempted only by **very skilled skiers** and **snowboarders** in safe **spring** conditions. Although difficult, Galena Peak is considered the best of Sun Valley's grand old ski

descents. Louis Stur who was well known for his numerous climbs of the Pioneers and Sawtooths would whole heartily agree. In the late 1970s when I interviewed him, he told me that he had made the Galena descent practically every year since 1952. Before that, of course, it was skied often by Sun Valley ski instructors including Idaho's father of backcountry skiing, Andy Hennig.

A west ridge divides the face of Galena Peak into two huge bowls. Draining from each of the bowls are the two main tributaries of **Senate Creek**. The bowls, by the way, are also huge **avalanche** collection areas leading down into impressive avalanche paths. In the spring, when the snow has stabilized, these bowls offer some of the finest downhill skiing accessible from Idaho 75.

The ascent route follows Senate Creek to the point where it splits, draining from each of the bowls. From here, the **west ridge** is ascended to the summit. The ski or snowboard descent, however, does not actually begin at the summit, but rather on the west ridge, several hundred feet below the final ridge crest which leads to the summit. From this point, either one of the two sensational bowls can be skied or boarded. The vertical drop of the descent is not bad. It's in the neighborhood of 3,500 feet (1,068 meters).

21

Boulder Basin—*Off-trail backcountry skiing and snowboarding. Moderately difficult to difficult backcountry terrain.* Boulder Basin was a popular **late spring** and **summer** area for early Sun Valley skiers. The reason becomes obvious as one gazes at the **five** huge **bowls** surrounding the basin. For spring skiing or boarding this area is unparalleled.

Access to Boulder Basin is via a rough jeep trail, located 12 miles (19 km) north of Ketchum on the north side of Idaho 75. Each of the five bowls has a variety of different descent routes, and there's enough to keep a backcountry skier or snowboarder busy for a long time. What's the best descent? Willie Helming, a Sun Valley ski instructor who at one time was a frequent visitor to Boulder Basin, recommends **Boulder Peak**. Boulder Peak, at 10,981 is not the highest point in the Basin, but according to Helming the bowl below the summit is the "finest" of the fine.

22

Pioneer Mountains— *Off-trail backcountry skiing and snowboarding. Moderately difficult to difficult backcountry terrain.* There are several winter access points to the Pioneers. One access is **East Fork Road**, which is located 6 miles south of Ketchum on Idaho 75. From East Fork Road, the snowbound **Hyndman Creek Road** is followed to the north to a snowbound trail and then into the Pioneers proper.

Access can also be gained from **Trail Creek Road** (described earlier) which leads northeast past Sun Valley Village. **Corral Creek** is the principal point of access off Trail Creek Road. Additionally, access to the Pioneers can be gained via **Wildhorse Creek**, which is reached by driving southwest on Trail Creek Road from US 93 north of Mackay.

Andy Hennig, of the Sun Valley Ski School, spent many springs during the 1930s and 1940s exploring routes in the Pioneers. Hennig loved the Pioneers and spoke in glowing terms of their magnificent summits and the graceful descents down their faces. If you were to ask Hennig for suggestions, he'd point to **Handwerk Peak, Goat Mountain, Duncan Peak, Cobb, and Hyndman** as all being fine and honorable mountains. It's a full day getting into the interior of the range, and skiing and snowboarding excursions are best planned as multiday trips.

In a Nightshirt

*T*HE OLD STORIES of skiing are filled with drama, of men and women facing formidable tests of endurance. In 1919, Ann Sullivan skied for four days with a badly sprained ankle on long, heavy wooden skis after falling on Galena Pass. When Sullivan's party arrived at Galena, there were no phones—and if there were, no one in the deserted town of Ketchum could run up on a snowmobile and pick her up. She had to get out, and she get out on her own.

But how tough were they? Aren't things being stretched a little to think that they were any tougher than outdoorsmen and women these days? That's probably not a fair question and there's certainly no definitive answer. But it is certain that they viewed and talked about their ski journeys and close calls in a different manner than we do now. Events that today would be reported in Idaho newspapers or written up in outdoor magazines, in the old days wouldn't have warranted much more than a passing remark. As an example, let me share a couple of stories that were told to me by 97-year-old Jack Seagraves when I interviewed him 20 years ago from his cramped room in a Twin Falls rest home. Jack was first introduced in the Sawtooth chapter of this book.

One of Jack Seagraves's longest ski trips followed the same route taken by Ann Sullivan's party a few years before him. He had been working at the Vienna Mine and hadn't been paid in some time, and he and a friend, Frank May, stomped off into Hailey to file a lien against the mining company. On the return trip, the temperatures plunged to -50 degrees below. "It took us one day to get back." Seagraves said. "Near the end, I looked over at Frank and his ear was frostbitten and had swelled up to the size of my hand."

After telling me this, Seagraves started into another story. I interrupted him and asked him what had happened to his friend. "Oh," he said. "It hurt for a while, then he got better."

Seagraves trapped in the winter, and on his frequent forays in the mountains, he now and then found himself in some precarious positions. "I've seen some awful slides," he said. The largest avalanche that he had ever seen was in the Smoky River drainage to the west of Ketchum, a slide that he estimated to be two miles long. In one particularly bad winter, he talked of the stretch of the highway along the Salmon River just below Stanley as being a fantastic scene: "Seventy-five slides came down there below Stanley for two days and nights. Seventy-five slides came off the hills, some a half mile wide."

Seagraves was never caught in a slide which is telling of his winter acumen, but he did tell me of an acquaintance of his that had. Jack McCarvey was caretaking a mine west of Ketchum near the South Fork of the Boise River. He was asleep when an avalanche crashed into his cabin. Surrounded in snow and blackness, he felt around him and found a tin cup. Using the cup, he started digging, and sometime later that night, he managed to climb out on top of the rubble of broken boards and snow.

All of his clothes were buried in the avalanche. He was barefoot, and the only thing he had on was a nightshirt. He started running downhill. For four miles he struggled through the snow, his feet becoming numb and bruised. Finally, he reached a cabin located below his where two miners took him in. They warmed him up, gave him some clothes, and by the next day McCarvey was feeling much better.

Amazingly, according to Seagraves, McCarvey never got frostbite out of the experience. Most people having gone through what McCarvey had, would have been anxious to call it quits and get out of there, but not McCarvey. He intended to stay and finish out the winter. His cabin, however, was buried and wouldn't be of use to him, so his two rescuers who were headed out for the winter let him stay at their place.

After the story, I told Seagraves that I thought McCarvey must have had incredible fortitude and endurance, being able to dig his way out of an avalanche with a cup and make it four miles through the snow to safety. "Yeah," Seagraves replied, giving his slant on it. "It's pretty tough for a man to travel that far in a nightshirt, but he was all right." □

Resources . . .

National Forest Lands in the Ketchum-Sun Valley Area South of the Boundary of the Sawtooth National Recreation Area
Ketchum Ranger District of the Sawtooth National Forest—Office located on Sun Valley Road in Ketchum. Address: Sun Valley Road, Ketchum, Idaho 83340. Phone: (208) 622-5371.

Sawtooth National Recreation Area, North of North Fork
Sawtooth National Recreation Area Headquarters—Office located 8 miles north of Ketchum on Idaho 75. Address: Star Route (Highway 75), Ketchum, Idaho 83340. Phone: (208) 726-8291.

Cross-country Ski Centers
Galena Lodge—Located 24 miles north of Ketchum on Idaho 75. Address: HC 64, Box 8326, Ketchum, Idaho 83340. Phone: (208) 726-4010.

Sun Valley Nordic Center—Located immediately off of the Sun Valley Road, past the Sun Valley Garage in the village of Sun Valley. Address: The Sun Valley Company, Sun Valley, Idaho 83353. Phone: 1-800-786-8259.

Alpine Ski Area
Sun Valley Ski Resort (Bald Mountain and Dollar Ski Areas)—Address: Sun Valley Resort, Sun Valley, Idaho 83353. Phone: 1-800-635-4150.

North Valley Trail Passes and Trail Maps—Main Office
Blaine County Recreation District—Located at 308 North Main in Hailey. Address: PO Box 297, Hailey, Idaho 83333. Phone: (208) 788-2168.

Other Outlets for North Valley Trail Passes
North Valley Trail passes are also available at the Sun Valley Ketchum Chamber of Commerce, cross-country ski shops in Ketchum, Sawtooth National Recreation Area Headquarters and Galena Lodge.

Avalanche Information
Avalanche forecasts are available via phone or through the Internet. For the most current number and web address, contact the Ketchum Ranger District or the Sawtooth National Recreation Area listed above.

Guide Service, Yurt System
Sun Valley Trekking—PO Box 2200, Sun Valley, Idaho 83353. Phone: (208) 788-9585. Also, check with the Sawtooth National Recreation Area Headquarters for a list of current permittees.

Further Reading
The Sun Valley Ski Book, by Andy Hennig (New York: Barnes and Co., 1939) is an excellent book written in the late 1930s which describes the old Alpine ski runs and spring ski tours that were a normal part of skiing at Sun Valley. The book is out of print but can be found in some libraries in Idaho.

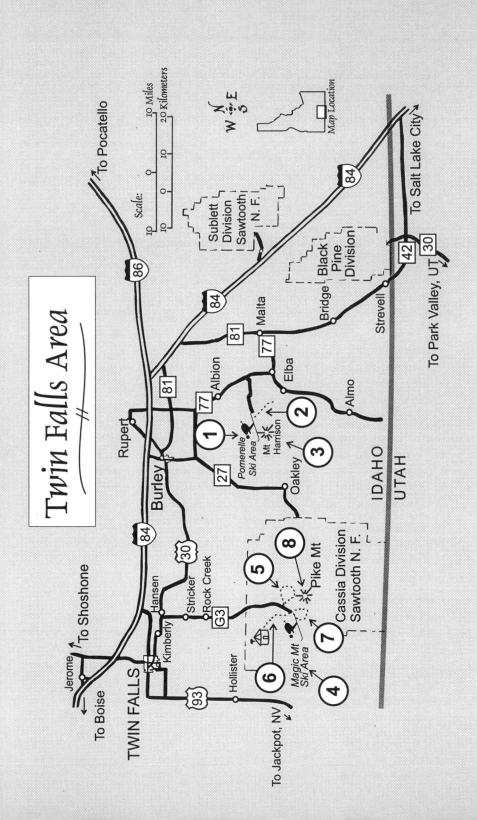

Twin Falls Area

To Pocatello

Scale:

10 Miles

20 Kilometers

N
W — E
S

Map Location

86

84

84

Sublett
Division
Sawtooth
N. F.

Black
Pine
Division

Bridge

To Salt Lake City

42

30

Strevell

81

Malta

77

81

To Park Valley, UT

IDAHO

UTAH

Rupert

77

Albion

Elba

Almo

1

2

3

Pomerelle
Ski Area

Mt
Harrison

Oakley

27

Burley

84

30

Hansen

Stricker

Rock Creek

G3

Kimberly

5

8

Pike Mt

Cassia Division
Sawtooth N. F.

7

6

Magic Mt
Ski Area

4

Hollister

93

TWIN FALLS

Jerome

To Shoshone

To Boise

To Jackpot, NV

CHAPTER 15
HIGH DESERT MOSAIC

Area Covered: Twin Falls, Burley, Fairfield, Arco, Craters of the Moon, Big Southern Butte, Spencer and Kilgore.

THE MOUNTAINS which rise from the high desert of the mid Snake River drainage are as deceptive as the dry but rich volcanic soils lying at their base. Outdoor dilettantes living outside the region think of it as being a blank spot on the map, a wasteland from a winter standpoint. Indeed, it is true that skiing and snowshoeing is different here, but it is no wasteland. It is quite the opposite.

Winter recreation in the Snake River Country takes place under big open skies where you can see for miles and where backcountry travel is free and unhindered across naked expanses of sagebrush lands. One example is Magic Mountain Ski Area, which sits high above the flat breadth of the Snake River Plain. It's located only an hour south of Twin Falls, and from the access road and parking area, cross-country skiers can take tours on such trails as Walstrom Hollow, Rock Creek or Penstemon. In addition, cooperative efforts between the Sawtooth National Forest and Nordic skiers in the area, have resulted in the placement of a backcountry yurt in the Magic Mountain area which is available for overnight use.

Neighboring Pomerelle Ski Area, south of Burley, is one of the most snow-blessed ski areas in all of Idaho. Falling directly in the path of prevailing storms, it often has snow before any other ski area in the region, including such well known places like Sun Valley and Targhee. It has lots of intermediate slopes, and if there's new snow, you can almost always count on there being powder at Pomerelle. For general touring, the Connor Flat cross-country ski trail is located nearby, and backcountry skiers and snowboarders will find excellent downhill terrain on Mt. Harrison.

To the north is the Fairfield area. Like Pomerelle and Magic Mountain, the country is big and open. Soldier Mountain Ski Area is located here, and even though overshadowed by nearby Sun Valley, it holds its own. It has 35 runs and a respectable vertical drop of 1,400 feet. Below Soldier Mountain, primarily around the Lawrence Creek area, cross-country skiers will find telemark slopes, backcountry downhill and plenty of places to explore in the network of draws and ridges.

Craters of the Moon is also part of this region. It, too, deceives. But let it be known that, indeed, there is skiing and snowshoeing here. The monument gets loads of snow, and a memorable ski or snowshoe trip can be made on the loop trail which encircles some of the area's most famous volcanic features. While you're out on the trail, be sure to try a few turns. The telemark skiing is terrific on the smooth surfaces of the cinder cones.

The final portion of the mosaic of lands making up this region includes a treat for the backcountry skier or snowboarder. Just behind Craters of the Moon is a big dome of a mountain called Blizzard Mountain which has one of the friendliest fall lines found anywhere in the Idaho backcountry. It is a wonderful place to go in the spring and an outstanding mountain for backcountry skiers or snowboarders of all abilities.

Last is Big Southern Butte. Rising up out a sea of sagebrush, the butte is a remnant of an old volcano and is the Snake River Plain's most prominent landmark. This is one place in Idaho where skiing and snowboarding stretches the limits of believability. In April when the desert roads open, you can make an exhilarating descent down a bowl on the butte's northern side. When the last turn has been made, and the skis or snowboard lashed back on your pack, the strangeness of it all becomes clear when you walk away from the snow and suddenly find yourself . . . in the midst of a desert. □

The Trails . . .

TWIN FALLS-BURLEY AREA

1 **Pomerelle Ski Area**—*Alpine ski area. Alpine, Nordic downhill and snowboarding. Rentals and instruction.* Pomerelle is South Idaho's great secret. If there's only one cloud somewhere in Idaho's sky, it's probably sitting south of Albion sprinkling powder snow on Pomerelle. This fun and homey area can be reached by taking the Declo-Albion Exit (#216) off Interstate 86 and head south on Idaho 77. Watch for the turnoff to Pomerelle on the right (west) of Idaho 77 about 6 miles past Albion. The ski area has 2 chairlifts, 17 runs and 1,000 feet (305 meters) of vertical. Ski and board rentals are available and meals can be purchased at the lodge.

2

Connor Flat Nordic Trail (Pomerelle Area)—*Marked and occasionally groomed cross-country ski trail. Moderately difficult.* The Connor Flat Ski Trail can be accessed from the parking area at Pomerelle Ski Area, south of Burley (see description above). The marked trail leads to the southeast, climbing about 90 vertical feet (27 meters) to Connor Flat, a narrow canyon between two hillsides. The elevation at Connor is just shy of 8,000 feet (2,438 meters), and as you can imagine, the snow on nearby slopes is often very good for telly skiing. The skiing is **moderately difficult**, and a total of 7 miles (11 km) of marked trails are available with 3.5 miles (5.5 km) of the total being occasionally groomed.

3

Mt. Harrison Backcountry (Pomerelle Area)—*Off-trail backcountry. Moderately difficult backcountry.* Near Pomerelle, backcountry devotees can follow the snowbound road which leads past **Cleveland Lake** to the top of Mt. Harrison (9,265 or 2,824 meters). On the way to the top and from the summit of Harrison, skiers or snowboarders have their choice of a great range of slope angles. There's everything from mellow telemark hills to steep boarding slopes. This is excellent spring skiing country and the snow lasts into June. Normal avalanche precautions should be taken, including carrying avalanche transceivers and shovels.

4

Magic Mountain Ski Area—*Alpine ski area. Alpine, Nordic downhill and snowboarding. Rentals and instruction.* Magic Mountain is located 28 miles south of Hansen. The ski area is easily reached from Interstate 86 by taking the Hansen exit (#182), a few miles east of the Twin Falls exit. Head south through Hansen and follow the Rock Creek Road and signs to the ski area. Magic Mountain has no pretenses. It is a place where everyone is made to feel welcome. The area has 2 chairlifts, 20 runs and a vertical drop of 700 feet (213 meters).

5

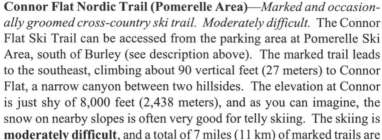

Dry Flat-Walstrom Hollow Nordic Trail (Magic Mountain Area)— *Marked cross-country ski trail. Moderately difficult.* This **moderately difficult** trail is marked for cross-country skiing. It is located along the access road to Magic Mountain Ski Area, .9 mile before reaching the ski area parking lot (see description above). The Walstrom Hollow Trail is on the left (east) side of the plowed road. Following the snowbound Walstrom Hollow Road, the trail climbs immediately, traversing across a steep, side hill. The first .5 (.8 km) is the most difficult part of the entire tour, and those making it beyond this point will find easier skiing ahead. The snowbound road continues to climb for approximately 1 mile (1.5 km) until reaching a broad ridge, a lovely place with lots of opportunities for side trips and **downhill** runs. The loop trail is 4 miles (6 km) long.

6 **Penstemon Nordic Trail (Magic Mountain Area)**—*Marked and occasionally groomed cross-country ski trail. Moderately difficult.* The Penstemon Trail can be reached from the Magic Ski Area parking lot or from a pulloff just below the ski area. The trail consists of two parts: the **Lower** Trail which is the portion of the trail that leads north from the ski area parking lot, and the **Upper** Trail which starts from the far end of the Lower Trail near some private cabins. The marked loop on Lower Penstemon Trail is 3.2 miles (5 km) and involves one leg that is shared between snowmobilers and skiers. The longer loop on Upper Penstemon Trail is 8 miles (13 km) long and also has a section shared with snowmobilers. A yurt can be accessed from the north end of the Upper Trail (see Resources for more information). The trails are occasionally groomed and are **moderately difficult**.

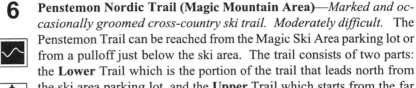

7 **Rock Creek Nordic Trail (Magic Mountain Area)**—*Marked and occasionally groomed cross-country ski trail. Moderately difficult.* The Rock Creek Trail also starts from the Magic Mountain Ski Area parking lot and forms two loops to the south of the ski area. One loop is 1.8 miles (3 km) long and the other is 2.6 (4 km) long. Both of the loops involve climbs of 350 to 400 feet (91 to 122 meters) and are **moderately difficult**.

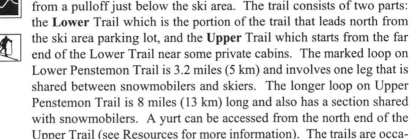

8 **Pike Mountain (Magic Mountain Area)**—*Off-trail backcountry. Moderately difficult backcountry.* The backcountry skiing in the Magic Mountain Area is on Pike Mountain (7,710 feet or 2,350 meters) directly east of the ski area. It can be accessed from the ski area parking lot. Because of the openness of the area and its exposure to wind, conditions can be tricky. When the snow is good, however, you can hear the hollering all the way back in Twin Falls. Normal avalanche precautions should be taken, including carrying avalanche transceivers and shovels.

FAIRFIELD AREA

The town of Fairfield is located on US 20, 37 miles southwest of Hailey and 60 miles north of Twin Falls. The mountains north of town are open, devoid of most tree cover and are an off-trail skiers' paradise with lots of downhill options. Also nearby is excellent Alpine skiing and snowboarding at Soldier Mountain Ski Area. The *Phillips Creek* 7.5 Minute Topographic Map is useful for the following tours. Presently only the provisional version of the map is available, and unfortunately, it mislabels Williams Creek as Lawrence Creek. Both the aerial illustration and map of the area included within this chapter show the correct placement of Williams and Lawrence Creeks.

9 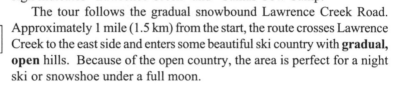 **Lawrence Creek**—*See aerial illustration. Snowbound road and off-trail. Moderately easy in lower areas. Dogs OK. Snowshoeing.* Cross-country skiers and snowshoers of all abilities will enjoy the tour up Lawrence Creek. The starting point of the trip is reached by driving north on the main street through the town of Fairfield. Follow the signs which lead to Soldier Mountain Ski Area. Approximately 9 miles from Fairfield, the snowbound Lawrence Creek Road enters from the right (east) side of the Soldier Mountain road. Normally a Forest Service sign indicates "Lawrence Creek" and "Camas Cow Camp."

The tour follows the gradual snowbound Lawrence Creek Road. Approximately 1 mile (1.5 km) from the start, the route crosses Lawrence Creek to the east side and enters some beautiful ski country with **gradual, open** hills. Because of the open country, the area is perfect for a night ski or snowshoe under a full moon.

10 **Williams Creek**—*See aerial illustration. Off-trail skiing or snowshoeing. Moderately difficult. Dogs OK.* Williams Creek is a moderately difficult tour and begins on Lawrence Creek, described above. Approximately .5 mile (.8 km) from the start of Lawrence Creek, Williams Creek adjoins from the east. Cross Lawrence Creek, and for the best skiing or snowshoeing, follow the north side of Williams Creek upstream. Approximately .7 mile (1 km) up Williams Creek, turn to the southeast and climb the **moderately steep** ridge (a rise of 600 feet or 183 meters) to the top of a small plateau at an elevation of 6,365 (1,940 meters). From the butte, a panoramic view reveals the surrounding ridges and Camas Valley below.

Aerial illustration of Lawrence Creek Area, viewed from the west.

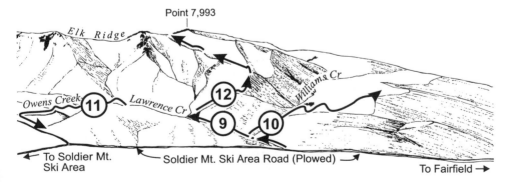

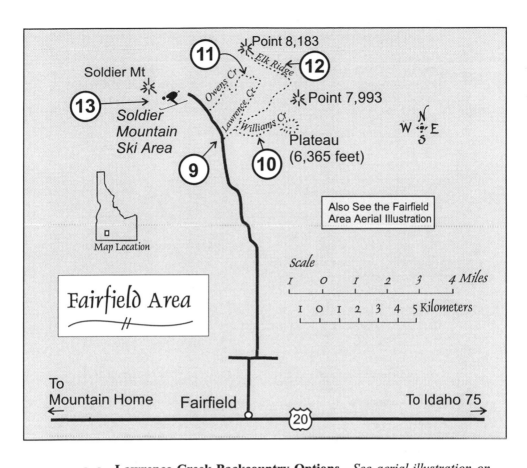

11 **Lawrence Creek Backcountry Options**—*See aerial illustration on facing page. Off-trail backcountry. Moderately difficult. Dogs OK.*
Dave Markham, who once ran a cross-country ski guiding business in the Fairfield area, has explored the area extensively and recommends it highly for **backcountry skiing**. One moderately easy backcountry trip that he suggests starts on Lawrence Creek. The **left branch** of **Lawrence Creek** is followed in a northerly direction until reaching a saddle between Lawrence Creek and **Owens Creek**, 2 miles (3 km) from the start. From the saddle descend into Owens Creek and pick up the road which leads 2.5 miles (4 km) back to the start of Lawrence Creek.

For more difficult backcountry skiing, the 8,000 foot (2,438 meter) **Elk Ridge** can be ascended. (See aerial illustration.) One route to the top is to climb the ridge between Lawrence Creek and Williams Creek. From the ridge, steep descents may be made into either the Lawrence Creek or Owens Creek drainages. This is avalanche terrain, and shovels and transceivers should be carried.

12

13 **Soldier Mountain Ski Area**—*Alpine ski area. Alpine, Nordic downhill and snowboarding. Rentals and instruction.* The open slopes of Soldier Mountain are a powerful attractant, drawing skiers from all directions: Boise, Twin Falls and, of course, from Ketchum and Sun Valley. The area has 2 lifts, 35 runs and a vertical drop of 1,400 feet (427 meters). It also has terrific backcountry adjacent to the area, and has been running snow cat trips for skiers and boarders. The area is located 12 miles north of Fairfield.

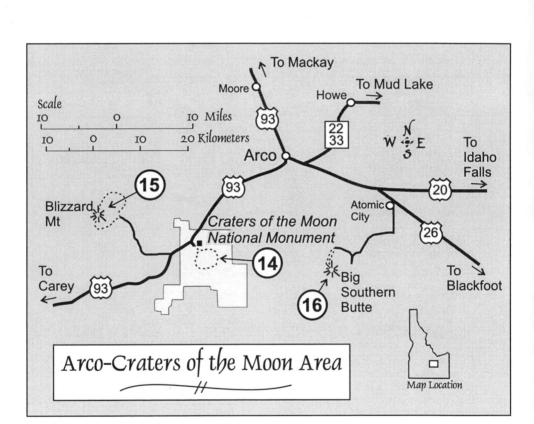

ARCO-CRATERS OF THE MOON AREA

14 **Craters of the Moon National Monument**—*Groomed cross-country ski trail. Easy, level terrain. Telemarking on cinder cones. Snowshoeing.* Craters of the Moon is located southwest of Arco on US 93. The visitor center is open during the winter, and you can pick up maps and obtain more information about skiing and snowshoeing.

The Park Service grooms about 5 miles (8 km) of trails for both classic and skating skiing styles. The trail follows the main snowbound road which leads to the south past the Visitor's Center. In the summertime, this road serves as the scenic loop through the monument. If desired, the entire 7-mile (11 km) loop can be skied. All skiing on the prepared tracks and snowbound road is very easy and suitable for skiers of **all abilities**.

 You'll also find good **telemarking** at Craters of the Moon. The cinder cones along the groomed trail or to the north of US 93 make great slopes on which to make turns.

15 **Blizzard Mountain**—*Spring ski or snowboard descent. Moderately difficult backcountry.* The **east face** of Blizzard Mountain is an outstanding area for **spring skiing**. Usually, the road accessing the area melts out towards the middle of May, and the skiing will be good until early June. Although you can get fairly close in a 2-wheel drive vehicle, a 4-wheel drive will assure that you get all the way to the base of the mountain.

 To drive there, start at Craters of the Moon and head south on US 93 toward Carey. As soon as you pass the southern boundary of the monument, start looking for the first dirt road coming in from the right (northwest). Turn on this road and follow it as it skirts around the edge of a lava flow. A couple of side roads branch off, but stay on the road which takes you into the base of Blizzard Mountain, the largest mountain in the area. After the road crosses a creek draining the east face of Blizzard Mountain, drive up another .5 mile and park.

Lash skis or snowboard to your pack and walk up the road to the top of the main **southeast ridge** of the mountain. Follow the ridge to the top. You may encounter some snow near the summit, but otherwise the ridge will be dry. Once at the summit, walk or ski down the gradual slopes to the south until reaching a saddle within .5 mile of the summit. From the saddle to the east, a bowl and wide gully leads all way to the base of the mountain. The fall line is perfect, and as long as you have corn snow, the skiing or boarding never gets too scary or difficult.

16 **Big Southern Butte**—*Spring ski or snowboard descent. Moderately difficult backcountry.* Big Southern Butte (7,517 feet or 2,291 meters) is one of Idaho's classic **spring** ski or snowboard descents. It has a limited season, however, and you'll want to plan to make the trip sometime in April. By the time May rolls around, the skiing is just about over. To get to the butte, drive to Atomic City, approximately 30 miles northwest of Blackfoot on US 26. Once in Atomic City, follow the well-marked and maintained road to Big Southern Butte. At the base of the butte, the road splits. One branch goes around the south side of the

Big Southern Butte from the north. The ascent route follows the right hand ridge and descends the snowfields just below the ascent ridge.

butte, and the other, the one you want, goes around the north side. This road is not nearly as in good shape as the other, and, although a 2-wheel drive can make it, you'll probably want the extra clearance of a 4-wheel drive.

As you drive around the north side, one road will branch off to the left. Continue driving until a second road branches off to the left and goes into a small canyon. Stop and back track 200 yards. Park here.

From where you have parked, walk up the dry ridge which leads to the left (east) of a prominent saddle on the west half of the butte. The ski or snowboard descent is down the bowl and gully to the left (east) side of the ridge. At the top, the slopes are **very steep**, but you can start wherever you feel most comfortable lower in the bowl.

SPENCER-KILGORE AREA

An Austrian Count by the name of Felix Schaffgotsch was employed by Averell Harriman, Chairman of the Board of the Union Pacific Railroad, to find a location for the Railroad's proposed ski resort. In the winter of 1935-36, Count Schaffgotsch searched all over the American West looking at such famous places as Jackson Hole, Lake Tahoe and Alta. He finally settled on a location near Ketchum that eventually grew into Sun Valley. Among his travels, however, Spencer was one of the areas that caught his eye. It was very attractive for skiing: open slopes, beautiful country and a long winter. Even though the Union Pacific's Alpine ski resort went elsewhere, the Spencer countryside which first aroused Schaffgotsch's interest is still there and remains as enticing as when the count visited it in the 1930s.

17 **Stoddard Canyon Cross-country Trail**—*Marked cross-country ski trail. Easy, suitable for families.* Maintained by the Dubois Ranger District, Stoddard Canyon is by far the most popular winter recreation area in the Dubois and Spencer area. It is used for tubing, sledding, cross-country skiing and snowmobiling.

To reach the parking area, take the Stoddard Creek exit off Interstate 15, 4 miles north of Spencer. Stoddard Creek is on the west side of the Interstate, and the parking area is located a short distance away from the interchange.

The cross-country ski trail is not groomed, but it is marked. It is an **easy** trail, forming a 3.8 mile loop (6 km) and is suitable for beginners.

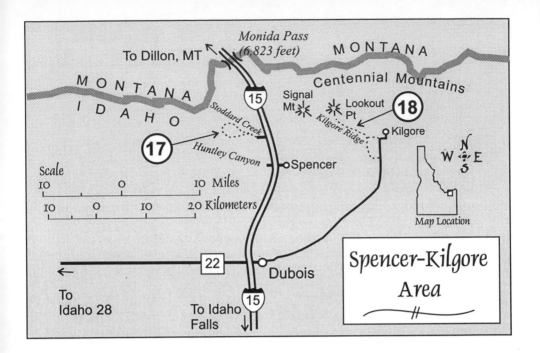

Spencer-Kilgore Area

Other Areas—*Moderately easy backcountry. Snowshoeing. Dogs OK.*
In 1986, the Forest Service established a cross-country ski trail in **Hunt-
ley Canyon,** just north of Spencer. However, forest officials were never
able to obtain a legal right of way and, as a result, it is no longer an
official ski trail. The trail is still used to some degree, but you should be
aware that it begins on **private land**.

18

For skiers or snowshoers looking for an off-trail experience, **Kilgore
Ridge** is just the ticket. This moderately difficult route follows a ridge
overlooking the **West Camas Creek** drainage. To reach the start of the
trip, follow the plowed road leading north out of Dubois to Kilgore.
From Dubois, it is a 25-mile drive to Kilgore on a gravel road. Chains
and a shovel are advised.

Stop the car at the sharp right-angled bend in the plowed road, 1.8
miles before reaching Kilgore. Looking to the west from the right-
angled bend, a ridge gradually rises above the flat, snow-covered culti-
vated fields and leads northwest. The tour follows this ridge.

This ridge can be gained by skiing directly from the right-angled
bend to the west, or it can also be approached via a snowbound road, 1
mile south of the bend on the west side of the plowed Kilgore Road.
Whichever way is chosen, climb to the top of the ridge, and remaining
on the ridge crest, follow it to the northwest. From a backcountry standpoint, the ridge is **moderately easy** and can be skied for many miles
along the West Camas Creek drainage. With snow lasting well into the
spring, this tour and others in the Kilgore area make excellent, spring-
time trips.

Resources . . .

National Forest Lands in Magic Mountain Area
Supervisor's Headquarters of the Sawtooth National Forest—Address: 2647 Kimberly Road East, Twin Falls, Idaho 83301. Phone: (208) 737-3200.

National Forest Lands in the Pomerelle Area
Burley District of the Sawtooth National Forest—Address: 2621 S. Overland Ave., Burley, Idaho 83318. Phone: (208) 678-0430.

Craters of the Moon National Monument
Craters of the Moon Visitor's Center—Located southwest of Arco on US 93. Address: PO Box 29, Arco, Idaho 83213. Phone: (208) 527-3257.

National Forest Lands in the Fairfield Area
Fairfield Ranger District of the Sawtooth National Forest—Address: Box 186, Fairfield, Idaho 83327. Phone: (208) 764-202.

National Forest Lands in the Spencer-Kilgore Area
Dubois District of the Targhee National Forest—Address: PO Box 46, Dubois, Idaho 83423. Phone: (208) 374-5422.

Alpine Ski Areas
Magic Mountain Ski Resort—Address: 3367 N. 3600 E., Kimberly, Idaho 83341. Phone: (208) 423-6221.

Pomerelle Ski Area—Address: Box 158, Albion, Idaho 83311. Phone: (208) 673-5599 or (208) 673-5555 (snow report).

Soldier Mountain Ski Resort—Address: Soldier Mountain, Fairfield, Idaho 83327. Phone: (208)764-2626.

Yurt Rental Near Magic Mountain
High Desert Nordic Association—Since this is a club comprised solely of unpaid volunteers, the club's address changes. The Sawtooth National Forest Supervisor's Office (address above) can provide you with the latest contact person.

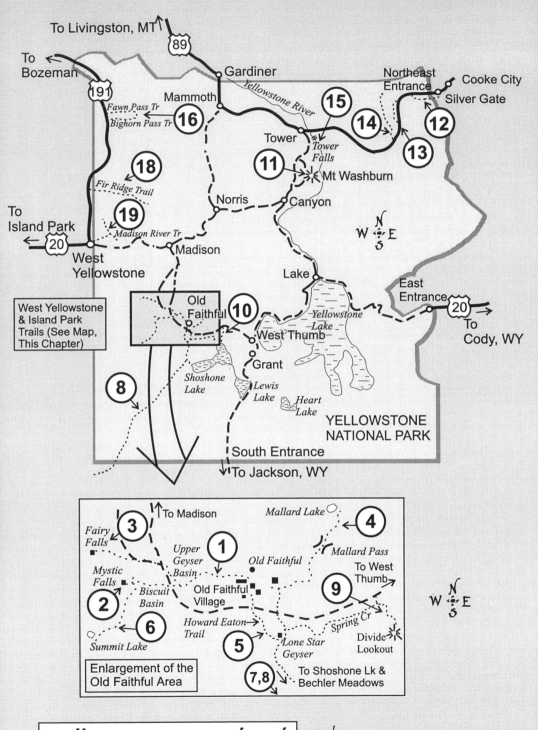

To Livingston, MT

89

To Bozeman

191

Gardiner

Mammoth

Yellowstone River

Northeast Entrance

Cooke City

Silver Gate

15

14

12

Fawn Pass Tr

Bighorn Pass Tr

16

Tower

Tower Falls

13

11

Mt Washburn

18

Fir Ridge Trail

Norris

Canyon

19

Madison River Tr

N
W · E
S

To Island Park

20

West Yellowstone

Madison

Lake

Yellowstone Lake

East Entrance

20

To Cody, WY

West Yellowstone & Island Park Trails (See Map, This Chapter)

Old Faithful

10

West Thumb

8

Grant

Shoshone Lake

Lewis Lake

Heart Lake

YELLOWSTONE NATIONAL PARK

South Entrance

To Jackson, WY

To Madison

Mallard Lake

4

Fairy Falls

3

Upper Geyser Basin

1

Old Faithful

Mallard Pass

To West Thumb

Mystic Falls

2

Biscuit Basin

Old Faithful Village

9

6

Howard Eaton Trail

5

Lone Star Geyser

Spring Cr

Divide Lookout

Summit Lake

7,8

To Shoshone Lk & Bechler Meadows

N
W · E
S

Enlargement of the Old Faithful Area

Yellowstone National Park

Scale
10   5   0   10 Miles

10   0   10   20 Kilomers

CHAPTER 16
YELLOWSTONE-ISLAND PARK REGION

Area Covered: Yellowstone National Park, West Yellowstone, Island Park, Targhee Pass, Raynolds Pass and Warm River.

---

*Y*ELLOWSTONE is one those places that every person who has a special affinity for the winter must sometime in their lifetime visit. There's nothing like it: ice-encrusted waterfalls, geysers spewing great clouds of mist in the cold air and ghostly, rime-encrusted trees near misty hot springs, appearing, as it sometimes seems, like tormented souls from an Edvard Munch painting

All roads in the park, with the exception of the road from Gardiner to Cooke City, Montana, are snowbound and closed to automobiles. Because you can't drive into the interior of the park, the way to get there is to use the regularly scheduled snowcoach service. Snowcoaches resemble vans—in some cases, they are vans—that are built with skis in the front and tracks in the back and can easily travel over packed snow surfaces. Snowcoaches leave from West Yellowstone at the West Entrance, Flagg Ranch at the South Entrance, and Mammoth at the North Entrance.

The coaches enable the skier or snowshoer to penetrate almost any portion of the park, but a primary destination for most cross-country skiing or snowshoeing vacations to the park is the Old Faithful area. Meals, overnight accommodations, rentals, interpretive and guide services are available.

The roads in the park are used by snowcoaches and snowmobiles, and yes, it is true that there is probably no other place in the world with a greater concentration of snowmobiles than on Yellowstone's roads in the winter. But the key thing for the non-mechanized user is that snowmobiles are strictly limited to roads, and the park service is ruthless in their enforcement of that rule.

With skis or snowshoes you can move away from the madness of roads and experience Yellowstone the way it should be experienced: with a sense of quietness that is so overpowering that it sometimes seems that you've been enveloped in great white, protective arms.

This region also includes the trails in the rolling lodgepole forest around West Yellowstone, Montana and Idaho's Island Park area. On the south edge of West Yellowstone is the Rendezvous cross-country ski trail system which is close enough that you can walk to the trailhead from any place in town. This 50 kilometer (31 mile) system, is one of the finest systems of groomed cross-country ski trails found anywhere. Since West Yellowstone is one of the most reliable places in the United States for snow and cold temperatures, the Rendezvous Trails are used by U.S. and European ski teams for training and racing. But they're not just for racing, the trail network is a terrific place for general touring and getting out and enjoying the surrounding countryside.

Further south on the volcanic highlands of Island Park, are several Park N' Ski trails which are marked by the Forest Service. One trail takes the cross-country skier along the rim of the Henrys Fork Canyon to viewpoints overlooking Lower and Upper Mesa Falls. Another trail meanders along the placid and soothing waters of the Buffalo River. The most scenic and varied trails of all are found at Harriman State Park. Here, trails go across expansive meadows, through silent lodgepole forests, around the bright white plane of Silver Lake and by the timeless, crystalline waters of the Henrys Fork. The park also rents cabins for overnight stays, but, as you can imagine, they go fast on weekends, and you'll want to make early reservations.

While the Yellowstone country is primarily known for its rolling terrain, backcountry skiers will find plenty here to their liking. Long multiday journeys can be taken across the Yellowstone backcountry to explore hidden away geysers and hot springs. The Targhee Mountains, which are most easily accessed from the top of Targhee Pass between Island Park and West Yellowstone, have much in the way of backcountry, including steep, spring descents. For milder backcountry, Raynolds Pass provides midwinter access to safe but inviting telemark country.

One of the nice things about all this country is the wildlife. In Yellowstone, in particular, you will see elk and buffalo while on ski trips. It's not any different than when at the turn of the century, skiers traveling in the park would see plentiful game. In the early 1900s, one small group of skiers working for the park was doing something more than just watching for game. They were trying to capture some, and as it turned out, it wasn't as easy as they had thought.

The Tales . . .

Skis have been used for all sorts of utilitarian purposes including carrying mail and supplies, conducting scientific research, hunting big game and they have even been used in fighting battles. But probably one of the most unusual uses of the long snowshoe took place in Yellowstone when skis were employed for calf wrestling— or to be more specific, bison calve wrestling.

It occurred during one of the more bizarre ski expeditions taken in Yellowstone, an expedition organized by a character by the name of Charles "Buffalo" Jones. A one-time buffalo hunter, Indian fighter and bumbling game manager, Jones was hired by the Park to supervise, among other duties, the rebuilding of Yellowstone's bison herd. Concerned at the alarmingly low numbers of bison at the turn of the 20th century, park authorities purchased from commercial breeders a small domestic herd which was fed and cared for at Mammoth.

In 1903, Jones organized a small ski expedition to capture two or more wild bison calves which were to be added to the domestic herd at Mammoth. Jones's bison expedition consisted of Peter Holte, a seasoned outdoorsman, and James Morrison, a Yellowstone scout, and Private John Minor. Along with the men were three "fox hounds" which Jones had used for tracking and killing mountain lions.

The party left May 5th and were greeted with warm, wet snow conditions which caused clumps of snow to stick to their skis, slowing their progress and making traveling intolerable.

After several days and several mishaps with a supply toboggan to which Jones had hitched his unruly and uncooperative dogs, the party eventually skied into the Pelican Valley to the east of Yellowstone Lake and located a herd of bison. Before attempting to capture any of the calves, the men dug out a nearby park patrol cabin and crowded in the tight quarters with Jones's three dogs to spend the night.

Jones's plan to capture the calves involved running the herd until the calves dropped behind, at which time the men would ski out and wrestle them to the ground. Things, however, didn't quite go as planned. Jones had sent Private Minor to drive the bison herd to him and the two others, but Minor became lost in a fog and wandered back in a circle. Finally, Morrison went out, found the herd and started them running with three shots.

As the herd passed by Holte, he sprinted off on his skis after two calves which lagged behind. "My speed carried me across their trail," wrote Holte in an article about the trip, "almost throwing me when I struck their wallows, but by braking hard with my pole I soon stopped and hurried back to them."

He slid in between two calves which had stayed close together and put one arm around each calf. "They seemed paralyzed with fear," wrote Holte, "and being unable to do anything in the snow, gave no struggle and lay still."

Everything was fine. Holte had two calves, but he had a problem. He couldn't tie up either of the animals' legs to immobilize them. One of the calves was sure to get away as soon as he let go to tie up the other. He looked around and could see no sign of Jones or the others. While he was puzzling over this, he looked back over his shoulder.

"I saw something that made me lose all interest in the calves. It was a buffalo cow coming back on the trail with head lowered and at a furious gallop."

Holte sprung in the air and clattered off on his skis as fast as he could to escape the charging cow. "Buffalo can make wonderfully fast time," Holte remarked.

"I ran, certainly for all that I was worth. With the skis strapped to my feet I was greatly handicapped."

To Holte's fortune, the cow stopped as soon as she reached the calves, nosing them and pushing them back on the trail.

Holte couldn't have been blamed if he let it go at that, but he was a tenacious person and saw his chance again when the cow left one of the calves behind. He caught the calf and this time he had the other hand free to tie it up. Then, later with the help of Morrison, he was able to catch the second calf and tie it as well.

What about Jones, the expedition leader, during all this? He had been missing and had been of no help in the capture. When he arrived and seeing that much of the work had been done by the others, he boasted that if he had been there, he would have been able to catch some of the full-grown bison. You can just see Holte and the others rolling their eyes at the comment. As it often is with men like Jones, he later showed his true colors when he made an inept attempt to catch a calf, only to have it get away.

The two calves were hauled back on the toboggan and eventually added to the captive herd in Mammoth. It is ironic, however, that with time and effective poaching prevention, the wild bison herd began to recover on its own, and it grew to such numbers that the domestic herd—and Jones's efforts to supplement it with wild bison—really made no difference in the bison's long-term survival in the park. ☐

The Trails . . .

YELLOWSTONE PARK-OLD FAITHFUL AREA

Old Faithful in Yellowstone National Park is reached by taking a snowcoach from West Yellowstone, Flagg Ranch or Mammoth. You can ride the coach in, take a quick tour, and ride the coach back out in one day—or, better yet, take a relaxing tour and stay overnight at the accommodations available at Old Faithful (for further information on snowcoaches and accommodations, see *Resources* at the end of the chapter).

1 **Upper Geyser Basin Trail**—*Marked trail. Easy, level terrain.* Suitable for **all abilities**, the Upper Geyser Basin Trail begins at Old Faithful and leads easterly. The well-marked trail passes beside **Grand**, **Riverside** and **Castle Geysers**, some of the most famous geysers in the park. At 1.2 miles (1.9 km), it reaches Morning Glory Pool.

Continuing another .8 mile (1.3 km) to the east beyond **Morning Glory Pool**, you'll cross the main road to Old Faithful and reach **Biscuit Basin**. Biscuit Basin is a large geothermal area with numerous steaming springs and pools. In addition to the thermal features, you may see bison and elk nearby. A small loop can be made by going to the far end of Biscuit Basin behind Avoca Spring and returning to Old

265

Castle Geyser

Faithful via the marked trail. The round-trip distance of this trip is 5 miles (8 km).

2 From Biscuit Basin, you can also make a **moderately easy** side trip by going another mile (1.6 km) to the lovely **Mystic Falls**. The trail leads west from Avoca Spring passing over rolling, timbered country, and traversing a side hill above Little Firehole River. The total length of the round trip tour from Old Faithful to Mystic Falls is 7 miles (11 km). All trails are well-marked and generally ski packed.

3 **Fairy Falls**—*Marked trail. Easy to moderately easy.* This is an enjoyable trip since you can catch a snowcoach ride to the Fairy Falls trailhead, ski up to Fairy Falls and then ski all the way back to Old Faithful. The terrain is gradual and skiing is **easy**. The total length of the trip is 11 miles (18 km). Park rangers and the snowcoach personnel can help skiers with maps and trail details.

From the snowcoach drop-off, it is a gradual rise of about 2.5 miles (4 km) into the falls. The falls is a thin ribbon of water that drops vertically for 200 feet (61 meters) and is often partially sheathed in ice.

If you wish to put in a few more miles, follow the trail leading beyond Fairy Falls to **Imperial** Geyser. The geyser is only .8 mile (1.3 km) past the falls and is constantly erupting to a height of 10 to 40 feet.

4 **Mallard Lake Trail**— *Marked trail. Moderate difficulty. Telemark slopes.* This tour involves a steady 600-foot (183 meter) climb and is of **moderate difficulty**. The trail starts from Old Faithful and leads in a northeasterly direction following a marked trail. Climbing steadily for 2.5 miles (4 km), the trail reaches a high point at **Mallard Pass**. From the pass, the trail continues another .5 mile (.8 km) to **Mallard Lake**. If desired, you can camp at the lake, but be sure to pick up a backcountry permit at the Old Faithful Ranger Station.

Much of the first part of the trail is in timber burned during the 1988 fires. When you reach the top of Mallard Pass, it's worthwhile to make a short detour. By skiing from the top of the pass to the south and climbing out on a rock abutment, you'll have an outstanding view— one of the best views in the area—of the Old Faithful area. Those looking for some **telemark** skiing will enjoy the descent down the steep bowl located to the south of the top of the pass.

5 **Lone Star Geyser Loop**—*Marked trail. Moderate difficultly.* This **moderately difficult** trail is a popular one in the Old Faithful area. The first leg of the trip follows the "Old Howard Eaton Trail" in a southerly direction from Old Faithful. The first 1.2 miles (1.9 km) climbs, and then, the next 2 miles (3 km) has a couple of short descents. In icy conditions, these descents can be a little hairy, but in powder snow, they're no problem. After the descents, the trail crosses the edge of a meadow and arrives at **Lone Star Geyser**, a total distance of 3.8 miles (6.1 km) from Old Faithful. Surrounded by an 18-inch high cone, the geyser erupts every 3 hours.

The loop continues to the north by following the Lone Star Geyser Trail along the Firehole River and back to Old Faithful. The total length of the loop is 9 miles (14.5 km).

6 **Summit Lake**— *Marked trail. Moderate difficultly.* This challenging trail involves steep climbing and long distance skiing. Round trip, it totals 20 miles (32 km), and you may want to do it as an overnight trip.

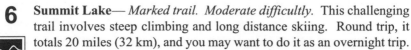

It begins at Old Faithful and follows the **Biscuit Basin Trail**. At the far end of Biscuit Basin, follow the Mystic Falls Trail .5 mile (.8 km) to its junction with the Summit Lake Trail. From the junction, the Summit Trail climbs very steeply to **Madison Plateau** (1,000 feet or 305 meters vertical elevation gain) where Summit Lake is located.

7 **Shoshone Lake-Shoshone Geyser Basin**— *Marked trail. Moderate difficulty.* To reach Shoshone Geyser Basin or Shoshone Lake, begin at Old Faithful. Follow the **Lone Star Geyser Trail**, for 3.8 miles (6.1 km) where the trail forks. Follow the right fork over Grants Pass to Shoshone Geyser Basin, 10 miles (16 km) one way from Old Faithful. This section of the trail has several **steep pitches** and is often wind-blown.

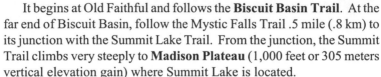

Those skiers wishing to go to **Shoshone Lake** can continue skiing beyond the Geyser Basin on the marked trail. Trail markers may be covered and having a topographic map is a must.

8 **Bechler Meadows**— *Marked trail. Moderately difficult backcountry.* This long, 42-mile (68 km) **multiday trip** starts at Old Faithful and follows the snowbound hiking trail to Bechler Meadows. From Bechler Meadows, the trail is followed to the south, coming out at Cave Falls Road, located east of Ashton, Idaho where a shuttle vehicle should be spotted. Trail markings may be covered by deep snows, and it is wise for skiers or snowshoers to have previous summer experience in the area. As with any winter trip in Yellowstone, backcountry travelers should be prepared to handle very cold temperatures which in midwinter can reach -40 degrees Fahrenheit or colder.

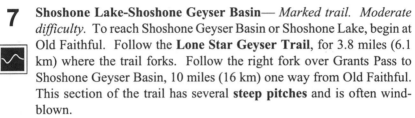

9 **Divide Lookout Trail**— *Marked trail. Moderately difficult. Telemarking.* In the first version of this book, I noted that this trail led to a lookout tower which could be climbed for a view of the surrounding country. In the early 1990s, the tower was removed. The view, however, is still there—and so is the delightful downhill run which takes you all the way back to Old Faithful.

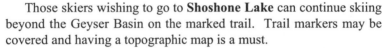

This is a **moderately difficult** trip, and if you have climbing skins take them along. While you can do the trip without skins, they will help make the steep uphill portion of the trail go much easier. The tour begins 1 mile (1.6 km) west of Craig Pass (6 miles east of Old Faithful) on the main road leading to West Thumb. Snowcoach transportation is necessary to reach the trailhead, and information on departure times are available at Old Faithful. The trail leads off from the south side of the highway and climbs .7 mile (1.1 km) to the old lookout site. It's only .7 mile, but Ron Dent, a past Yellowstone backcountry guide, calls it "the longest .7 mile in Yellowstone National Park." From the top, you'll have a spectacular view of Shoshone Lake, the Old Faithful area and the Tetons. Telemark skiers will also find **powder bowls** in the Divide Lookout area.

The return trip is one of those "must dos" in Yellowstone. It's all downhill and follows **Spring Creek Trail** back to Old Faithful. The total mileage from the divide trailhead to Old Faithful is 8 miles (13 km) and descends 550 feet (168 meters). The trails are marked and easy to follow. Skiing difficulty on Spring Creek Trail is moderately easy.

10 **Shoshone Lake From Craig Pass-Continental Divide**—*Marked trail. Easy, level terrain.* This beautiful and **easy** tour follows the **Delacy Trail** which is the shortest access to Shoshone Lake. The trail begins 2.5 miles east of the top of **Craig Pass** or 9.5 miles west of Old Faithful. To get to and from the trailhead, you'll need to take a snowcoach. Information on the trail and snowcoach schedules are available at Old Faithful. The trip into the lake is 3 miles (5 km) long

YELLOWSTONE PARK—OTHER AREAS

11 **Mount Washburn**— *Marked trail. Moderately difficult to difficult backcountry.* The road between Tower and Canyon usually opens around the middle of May. For the backcountry skier, the road provides convenient access to Mt. Washburn, a delightful spring skiing mountain. Located approximately half way between Tower and Canyon, Washburn can be ascended from the south side, following the snowbound road leading from the **Dunraven Pass picnic area**. The ascent to the summit simply follows the road. Descents can be made on the south side or the north side. Avalanche hazards exist and normal safety precautions should be taken.

If you don't want to climb all the way to the summit, you'll also find excellent skiing on the west side of Mount Washburn. Access is gained from the **Chittenden parking** area located part way up the access road which approaches the mountain from the north. Often in the spring, bighorn sheep can be seen in the area.

12 **Gardiner to Cooke City Road**— *Snowbound roads and trails. Most trails are easy to moderately easy. Snowshoeing.* The Gardiner to Cooke City Road in the north portion of Yellowstone National Park is open all year long. This road provides access to a number of snowshoeing and skiing trails. One example is **Bannock Trail**, beginning at Warm Creek picnic area, located 1 mile west of the Northeast Entrance on the south side of the highway. The trail is level and **easy** and follows an old snowbound road to the east. The tour is short. If you follow the road beyond 2 miles (3 km), it connects to a snowmobile trail outside the park at Silver Gate, Montana.

Another **easy** trail is the **Barronette Trail**. It can be accessed at

13 two locations: upper and lower Soda Butte bridges, 3 and 6.5 miles west of the Northeast Entrance to the park. The skiing or snowshoeing pathway follows an old snowbound road between the two bridges. The views are unhindered and magnificent. You can travel out and back, or if you have a shuttle vehicle, you can go from one access point to the other, a distance of 3.5 miles (5.6 km).

14

For a **difficult** snowshoe or ski trip, you may wish to try **Pebble Creek**. Located 11 miles west of the Northeast Entrance on the north side of the highway, the tour follows the snowbound Pebble Creek Trail to the north. The trail climbs steeply (climbing skins are recommended), rising over 1,000 feet (305 meters) in the first 1.5 miles (2.4 km) and eventually reaches a beautiful section of trail along Pebble Creek with **Cutoff** and **Barronette Peaks** rising up on both sides. During unstable conditions, avalanche hazards exist. Be sure to check with a park ranger about snow conditions.

15

One last suggestion is the rewarding ski or snowshoe trip which begins at the Tower Ranger Station at **Tower Junction**. From the junction, follow the snowbound Tower Falls Canyon Road 1.5 miles (3 to 5 km) to the Calcite Springs Overlook for a inspiring view of the **Grand Canyon of the Yellowstone**. From here you can continue, another mile to the majestic **Tower Falls**. The trip to Calcite Springs Overlook is **easy** and suitable for families. From Calcite Springs Overlook to Tower Falls the difficulty increases from **moderately easy** to **moderately difficult** depending on snow conditions. The Ranger Station is manned in the winter, and additional information is available there.

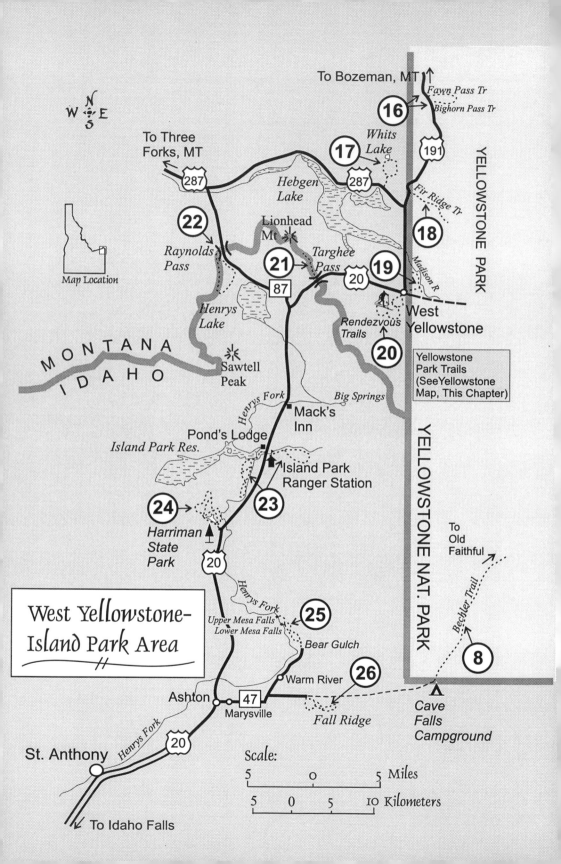

West Yellowstone-
Island Park Area

WEST YELLOWSTONE AREA

16 **Fawn Pass and Big Horn Pass Trails**— *Marked trail. Easy to moderately difficult. Snowshoeing.* Fawn Pass Trail is located 21 miles north of West Yellowstone on the east side of US 191. Big Horn Pass Trail is located 2 miles south of Fawn Pass Trail, also on the east side of US 191. Both trails are **easy**, suitable for families and lead east into Yellowstone National Park. No snowmobile use occurs.

 Fawn Pass Trail follows the drainage of **Fan Creek**, passing through open and **gently rolling** terrain. Pine marten, snowshoe hares, ermine, moose, elk and other wildlife may be seen along the way. This trail may also be used for long, overnight journeys. Use caution, however, on long trips since avalanche terrain is encountered on the upper portions of this trail and, most particularly, the Big Horn Pass Trail.

 A **moderately difficult** tour can be made by branching off to the south from Fawn Pass Trail and joining Big Horn Pass Trail. The Big Horn Pass Trail is then followed west to US 191, coming out 2 miles south of the parked vehicles at the Fawn Pass trailhead. One can walk, run, be met by a shuttle vehicle or hitch a ride back to the Fawn Pass trailhead. The total length of this loop tour is 10.5 miles (17 km).

Big Horn Pass Trail also makes an enjoyable up-and-back trip. Leading east and gradually ascending the valley of the Gallatin River, the trail is a wonderful trip, and along the way, you have spectacular views of the Gallatin Mountain Range.

 While in the area, skiers and snowshoers may also want to try the trip along the **Bacon Rind Trail**, located on the west side of US 191 across from Fawn Pass Trail, or the **Specimen Creek Trail**, located 4 miles north of Fawn Pass Trail on the east side of US 191. The first couple miles of either trail is **easy**, with more advanced terrain found farther from the start.

 Fawn Pass-Bannock Peak—*Marked trail. Moderately difficult backcountry. Snowshoeing.* **Overnight** ski trips can be made by continuing on Fawn Pass Trail, described above, to Fawn Pass. In the general vicinity of the pass, excellent telemark country is found. Backcountry skiers looking for long, downhill routes, can climb **Bannock Peak** (elevation 10,323 feet or 3,149 meters) via the ridge leading from Fawn Pass. Several descent lines are possible, but use caution since avalanche hazard exists.

 A popular **multiday ski trip** is to follow Fawn Pass Trail to the east, eventually ending the trip at **Mammoth**, south of Gardiner, Montana. The trip is 23 miles (37 km) long, and as with all overnight back country travel in Yellowstone, skiers should pick up a backcountry permit from a Yellowstone Park Ranger Office.

17 **Whit Lakes Trail**— *Marked trail. Moderately difficult. Snowshoeing. Dogs OK.* The trailhead of this **moderately difficult** tour is reached by driving north from West Yellowstone. Seven miles from town, take a left on the plowed road (US 287) leading toward Ennis, Montana. Drive 2.5 miles on US 287 and watch for the Whit Lakes trailhead on the right (north) side of the plowed road.

The tour follows **Whit Lakes Trail** to the northeast. Climbing 300 feet (50 meters), the trail reaches lower Whit Lake at 3.5 miles (5.5 km) from the beginning. Drinking water may be obtained at the lake from a spring which does not freeze during the winter.

If you want to make the trip more ambitious, ski or snowshoe from the lake to the northwest. After a steep .5 mile climb, you'll arrive at Upper Whit Lake. From here, a loop tour can be made by skiing east for approximately 1 mile to **Little Tepee Creek**. Tepee Creek Trail is then followed south and southeast connecting onto the original trail. Snowmobiles may be encountered.

18 **Fir Ridge (also known as the Duck Creek, Gneiss Creek or Campanula Springs Trail)**—*Marked trail. Easy to moderately easy. Telemarking. Snowshoeing.* Skiers and snowshoers of all abilities will enjoy Fir Ridge Trail, located 9 miles north of West Yellowstone on the east side of US 191. Park at the plowed pulloff on the right (east) approximately 1 mile beyond the turnoff to Ennis, Montana (US 387 and US 191 junction).

Extending to the east, the trail crosses the boundary of Yellowstone National Park .5 mile from the trailhead. Once in the park, the trail begins to gradually curve to the south. The trail is marked and usually broken.

Thea Nordling who was once a naturalist for Yellowstone National Park first told me about this beautiful trail. Thea recommends stopping for lunch at the 2 mile point, at the confluence of **Campanula Creek** and **Duck Creek**, where you may see elk or ermine—or, if you're really lucky, pine marten. Nice telly slopes are found on Fir Ridge and the views across to the surrounding mountains are splendid.

No snowmobiles are encountered once you are within the boundary of Yellowstone National Park.

19 **Riverside Ski Trail (Madison River Trail)**— *Marked and occasionally groomed trails. Easy, level terrain.* Conveniently located on the east edge of West Yellowstone, Riverside Ski Trail passes through nearly **flat, gradual** terrain. For a real treat, try a moonlight tour on this trail. The trail begins on the east end of Madison Avenue at the boundary of Yellowstone National Park. Popular among skiers, the route is marked and is usually always tracked. As one skis to the east toward the Madison River, the terrain is flat and covered with lodgepole pine. Located 1.6 miles (2.5 km) from the start of the tour, a small hill is descended to an open shelf 100 meters from the **Madison River**. From here, tourers have some nice views of the southern portion of the Gallatin Range. During early mornings, elk and bison can be seen browsing on the other side of the river, and frequently, geese and ducks inhabit the area. No snowmobile use occurs.

20 **Rendezvous Cross-country Ski Trail System**—*Marked and regularly groomed cross-country ski system. All abilities.* This beautiful system of groomed ski trails is conveniently located on the edge of West Yellowstone. To reach the trailhead, drive or walk to the parking area at the south end of Geyser Street. The trails begin here.

The trails are **groomed** by the West Yellowstone Chamber of Commerce and the Forest Service and go across **rolling terrain** and open meadows and through stands of lodgepole pine. The trail system is for **all abilities** and has 50 kilometers (31 miles) of trails. The trails and snow conditions are so good that U.S. and European Nordic ski teams often use the trail for training. At the current time, there is no fee, but donations are accepted.

ISLAND PARK REGION

21 **Targhee Pass**—*Off-trail backcountry skiing and snowboarding. Moderately difficult backcountry.* Targhee Pass at an elevation of 7,072 feet (2,156 meters) is located between Island Park and West Yellowstone on US 20, 4.2 miles north of the junction of US 20 and Idaho 87. A major snowmobile route passes through this area, and because of heavy snowmobile traffic, skiing or snowboarding in the area is not recommended during the cold winter months. In the **spring**, however, this is a wonderful place for **Nordic downhill** or **snowboarding**, and it also provides access to the steep slopes of the Targhee Mountains.

The destination of most tours in the Targhee Pass area is the **Lionshead Ski Area** which closed down years ago. It can be reached by starting from the top of Targhee Pass and following the broad ridge line (Continental Divide) 2 miles (3 km) to the north, until arriving at the top of the runs of the old ski area.

From here, you can see Lionshead Peak, the prominent peak to the northwest, and other high points in the spectacular Henry Lake Mountains. Below this point and draining to the southwest is Targhee Creek, which offers a descending ski tour to a point lower on US 20 at the base of the Idaho side of Targhee Pass.

The old ski runs and other nearby slopes are great for telly skiing or snowboarding. Avalanche hazard exists on the steeper slopes and transceivers and shovels should be carried.

22 **Raynolds Pass**—*Off-trail backcountry. Moderately easy backcountry skiing or snowboarding. Snowshoeing. Dogs OK.* The pass is located on the Idaho-Montana border north of the Island Park area. From the junction of US 20 and Idaho 87, it is approximately 9.5 miles northeast on Idaho 87 to the top of Raynolds Pass. Parking is available on the top of the pass.

From the top of the pass, the tour follows the ridge (the **Continental Divide**) to the southwest. Some great downhill slopes are found at the start of the tour, and when the snow is good, some skiers may never get beyond this first slope. The tour continues along the ridge. Most of the slopes are **moderate** and avalanche danger is, for the most part, low, except in some of the steeper or leeward areas. The views along the divide of the Targhee Mountains, Henrys Lake, and across the Island Park country is unmatched. Many route options exist, with some special hidden-away basins that will keep tourers exploring for hours.

On the return trip, any number of descents can be made to points lower on Idaho Highway 87. Once at the highway, skiers can walk or ski back up to the vehicles on top of the pass.

Snowmobile use is heavy throughout much of the Island Park countryside, but Raynolds Pass is normally a sanctuary away from the commotion of the machines. For mellow backcountry skiing and snowshoeing, it's a place to be treasured.

Robert and Bud: ready for another great day of skiing in Island Park.

23 **Brimstone-Buffalo River Trails**—*Marked and occasionally groomed cross-country ski trail. Easy to moderately difficult. Park N' Ski area.*

The Brimstone and Buffalo River Trails are made up of two systems. One, and the longer of the two, is called **Brimstone**. The trailhead is located .5 mile north of the Island Park Ranger Station on US 20. (The Island Park Ranger Station is about 4 miles to the north of Last Chance.) If you are driving towards West Yellowstone, turn left (west) just past the bridge over the Buffalo River.

The second of the two is the **Buffalo Trail** and it starts from the parking lot at the Island Park Ranger Station. Buffalo Trail is lovely loop, only 4.2 kilometers (2.6 miles) which heads in an easterly direction along the serene **Buffalo River**. Lots of waterfowl can be seen along the river banks. It heads back to the ranger station through lodgepole pine. It is **easy** and suitable for families and seniors.

The Brimstone system has several loop options with as many as 20 kilometers (12 miles) of skiing possible. Beyond the far end of the first loop, called the Moose Loop, you can cross Island Park Dam and access several more loop trails on the west side of the **Henrys Fork of the Snake** in the **Box Canyon** area. This side of the Brimstone system connects with trails in **Harriman State Park**, providing skiers with attractive long distance touring options. Trail difficulty ranges from **easy** to **moderately difficult**.

Both trail systems are made possible from Idaho Park N' Ski revenue and you'll need to purchase a permit for your vehicle.

24 **Harriman State Park**—*Marked and groomed cross-country ski trail system. Lots of easy terrain. Warming hut. Toilets. Cabin rentals.*

Park N' Ski area. Harriman State Park is located on the west side of US 20, approximately 20 miles north of Ashton or 7 miles south of Island Park. Watch for signs which direct skiers to parking and ski trail facilities.

The park is a gift to the state of Idaho from the famous Harriman

family, well known in connection with the Union Pacific Railroad. William Averell Harriman, one of the sons of Edward Henry Harriman who built the fledging Union Pacific Railroad into a prosperous enter-

prise, played an especially important role in Idaho's history when in 1935 and 1936, as Chairman of the Board of Union Pacific, decided to build and built the Sun Valley Ski Resort on a sheep ranch near Ketchum.

The 4,700-acre Harriman State Park has an outstanding cross-coun-

try trail system with 50 kilometers (21 miles) of trails routed across the **gentle**, open, and wooded terrain of the park and nearby Forest Service lands. The trails are **marked, groomed** and suitable for **all abilities**. This is a wonderful area for families and seniors or anyone who appreciates a traditional Nordic ski experience.

A warming hut is available, and cabins may be rented for overnight stays. No dogs. No snowmobiles. Park N' Ski permits required.

25 **Bear Gulch-Mesa Falls**—*Marked and occasionally groomed cross-country ski trail. One moderately difficult hill and then easy terrain*

thereafter. Park N' Ski area. The parking area for this trail is near the old Bear Gulch Ski Area which closed down in the 1970s. To reach it, follow highway 47 from Ashton to the Warm River Campground. Continue beyond the campground for another 3 miles and park in the plowed lot.

The trail starts on the north end of the parking lot and **climbs steeply**

before leveling out along the canyon rim. Be prepared for some company on this first part. A portion of the trail is shared with snowmobilers. Once up the hill, the skiing is **easy** and follows the edge of the canyon above the **Henrys Fork**. The trail leads first to a viewpoint of **Lower Mesa Falls**, 3.5 miles (6 km) from the start and then continues another 1.5 miles (2.5 km) to **Upper Mesa Falls**, the highest of the two falls, dropping 114 feet (35 meters).

It used to be when you made winter visit to Upper Mesa Falls, you had to take ice axes and crampons in order to climb out to a location from where you could get a good view of the falls. Fortunately, you can leave the ice axe at home. The new viewing points are far safer.

 The snowbound road is a popular snowmobile route, and although the ski trail is for skiing only, the overlooks are shared. The quietest time is in the early morning. This is a Park N' Ski area and permits are required.

26 **Fall River Ridge**—*Marked cross-country ski trail system. Moderately easy. Park N' Ski area.* To get to the trail, turn east on Highway 47 in Ashton. About 6 miles from Ashton, turn right (east) onto the Cave Falls Road and drive for another 5 miles to the parking area. The ski trail starts from the south side of the parking area.

 The Forest Service has marked three loop trials which are **moderately easy**. The longest of the loops is 10 kilometers (6 miles). Wildlife, moose in particular, can be seen along the trails. The trail system also provides access for longer trips in the National Forest backcountry to the south of Yellowstone.

This is a Park N' Ski area and permits are required.

Jim Berry: Man of All Seasons

I WATCHED the exhaust from the warming snowcoach pour upward, white and distinct against the blue of the sky and floating lazily. The coach driver was busy strapping on the last of the luggage to the top rack. Watching him cinching the load down, I wondered about him.

It wasn't hard to tell that all nine of his passengers were excited. We were all on vacation, looking forward to spending time at Old Faithful, but what about him? It was just another day of work for the coach driver, and probably not much in terms of a pay check at the end of the day. I relished the crisp, subzero air. It meant perfect ski conditions, powder snow and crystal clear air and skies, but to him it probably meant chilled feet waiting for his passengers and numb fingers while tying and untying gear.

We all piled into the snowcoach. Vapors from moist breaths and warm bodies created a fog in the coach.

The driver turned around. He had full, round cheeks, rosy from the morning subzero temperatures, and wore a baseball hat and a broad, disarming smile.

"Hello everyone, I'm Jim Berry," he bellowed over the motor noise. "I'll be taking you to Old Faithful this morning. I'm originally from Salt Lake City, but no, I'm not one of them. I'm an Irish Catholic." The smile broadened across his face. At least, he seems to be in a good mood, I was thinking.

As the tracks caught hold and the coach ground off towards the entrance of the park, our driver Jim Berry, lifted his eyes searching for our faces in the rearview mirror, and went on. He said he had lots of good Mormon friends in Salt Lake, and they had been fairly active in trying to get him to join the church.

"I'm not sure if it was so much me, though," he said. "I think it was my name that they really wanted. Can you imagine what it would be like to have an Elder Berry in your church?"

It didn't take too much more. By now I understood that this was someone who truly enjoyed where he was and what he was doing. In a previous life, he had been an Industrial Psychologist, and for years worked for the Caterpillar Corporation. He loved training and helping employees become better at their jobs, but late in his career, he found himself mostly consumed with counseling workers dealing with the effects of downsizing and chemical dependency.

Shortly before reaching retirement age, he had enough of it and said good bye to the corporate world and moved to Yellowstone to drive snow coaches in the winter and buses in the summer.

"There's one thing I've learned now that I'm an adult. And by the way, adults are over 50 and kids are under 50. When the last kid is gone from the nest, then it's time for you to *fly* and have some fun!"

All the way to Old Faithful, Jim regaled us with stories. He, like most the snowcoach drivers, had a wonderful grasp of the natural history and geography of Yellowstone, and his bits of wisdom and running commentary made a simple ride into the park, an event.

"I'm a motor mouth, I admit," he said. "I love to talk, and I love to make people laugh."

On one trip, however, he found himself talking to a Spanish family, and none of the family could speak English. He sat in silence, and it drove him crazy.

"Finally, desperate to get a laugh out of somebody," Jim said, "I turned to one of the fathers, a man probably about 35. I pointed out the window and said, 'look over there. Elephants come down that way to get to the water and then the elephants go back up.' "

But the father didn't respond, and he was greeted by silence in the rest of the coach. So Jim gritted his teeth and drove on.

When the snowcoach arrived in Old Faithful, the family unloaded and began carrying bags to the lodge. The father, however, stayed behind.

He approached Jim, and in very broken English, said, "*Señor* Berry, in my language, *Español*, 'Elephant' means 'Elephant.' And also in my language, *Señor* Berry," the father continued. " 'Bull' means 'bull.' "

❄   ❄

*A*S WE APPROACHED Old Faithful, he told one story of his summer experience in Yellowstone. He was driving the bus which Michael Dukakis was using to tour the park. Dukakis, who was running in the presidential campaign against George Bush, was on the campaign trail. The large Yellowstone fires were burning then, and he was using his visit to the park as a photo opportunity.

At one point, it was just Dukakis and Berry in the bus, and Dukakis, in a talkative mood, started telling Berry about his recent visit to the Montana State Mental Hospital in Warm Springs. Dukakis didn't realize at the time that he was visiting a mental hospital and as he walked around introducing himself, he was thinking that it was odd that all the patients in the hospital were sitting up and dressed and no one looked sick.

He introduced himself to an old character at the far end of the hallway: "Hello, my name is Michael Dukakis, and I'm running for President of the United States."

The old patient eyed Dukakis curiously.

"That's OK sonny," the old man replied, "in another couple of years, they'll have you cured of that." □

Jim Berry with trusty 706.

Resources . . .

Information on Cross-country Skiing and Snowshoeing in Yellowstone
Superintendent of Yellowstone National Park—Address: PO Box 168, Yellowstone National Park, Wyoming 82190. Phone: (307) 344-7381 or (307) 344-2109.

Yellowstone Snowcoach and Lodging Information
TW Recreational Services—Address: PO Box 165, Yellowstone National Park, Wyoming 82190. Phone: (307) 344-7311. (307) 344-5395 (TDD).

Yellowstone Park Publications and Educational Programs
Yellowstone Association and Institute—Address: PO Box 117, Yellowstone National Park, Wyoming 82190. Phone: (307) 344-2296.

National Forest Lands in the West Yellowstone Area
Hebgen Ranger District of the Gallatin National Forest—Address: PO Box 520, West Yellowstone, Montana 59758. Phone: (406) 646-7369.

National Forest Lands in the Island Park Area
Island Park District of the Targhee National Forest—Office located on US 20 near Pond's Lodge. Address: PO Box 220, Island Park, Idaho 83429. Phone: (208) 558-7368.

National Forest Lands in Bear Gulch and Mesa Falls Area:
Ashton District of the Targhee National Forest—Office located on US 20 in Ashton. Address: Ashton, Idaho 83420. Phone: (208) 652-7442.

Harriman State Park
Harriman State Park—Address: H.C. 66, Box 500, Island Park, Idaho 83429. Phone: (208) 558-7368.

Guiding
Guided backcountry trips are offered in Yellowstone Park and nearby Gallatin National Forest. For a list of current permittees, contact Yellowstone National Park and the Gallatin National Forest, addresses and phone numbers above.

Cross-country Ski Lodges
Lone Mountain Ranch—Address: PO Box 160069, Big Sky, Montana 59716. Phone: (406) 995-4670. (One of Montana's oldest cross-country lodges, Lone Mountain has overnight accommodations, meals, rentals, instruction and 75 kilometers of groomed trails.)

Wade Lake Resort—Address: PO Box 107, Cameron, Montana 59720. Phone: (406) 682-7560. (Quiet and isolated, the Wade Lake cabins and 35 kilometers of groomed trails are 6 miles from the nearest plowed road—shuttle provided.)

Further Reading
Cross-country Skiing in Yellowstone Country—By Ken and Dena Olsen, Abacus Enterprises-Falcon Press, 1992.

Yellowstone's Ski Pioneers: Peril and Heroism on the Winter Trail—By Paul Schullery, High Plains Publishing Co., 1995.

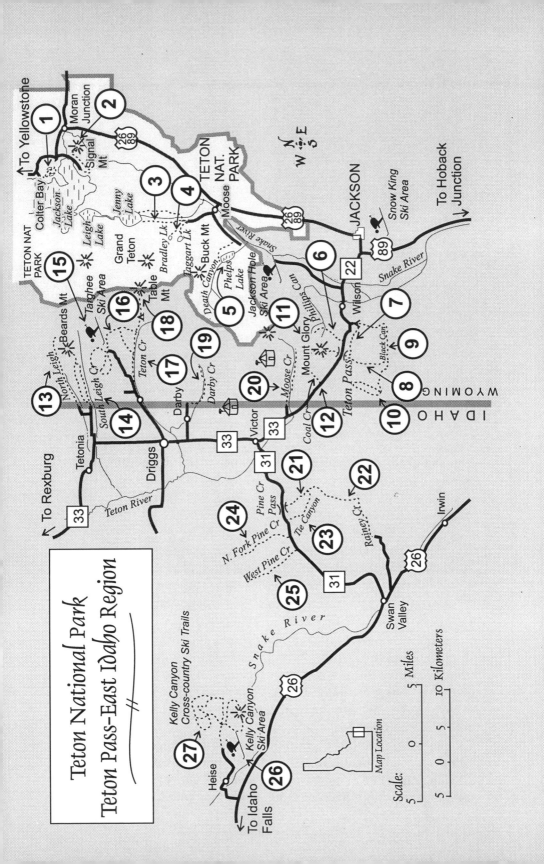

CHAPTER 17
TETON NATIONAL PARK
TETON PASS-EAST IDAHO REGION

Area Covered: Grand Teton National Park, Teton Pass, Pine Creek Pass, Kelly Canyon Area and Teton Valley including Driggs and Victor.

SOMETIMES it is best to leave descriptions of the Teton Range unexpressed. That's particularly true in the winter. When you ski around the curve of a ridge, beyond an opening in the trees and when you are suddenly faced with them, there is nothing intelligible that can be said that compares to what is felt. It is a momentary feeling of helplessness, of beauty so great that all you can do is stop and gaze. You can really only experience it by getting out and traveling through the snow-blanketed valley below, by stepping into its canyons, by gliding across its ridges or by climbing its high peaks. Then, and only then, do you really begin to understand the magic of the Tetons.

The most obvious place to begin experiencing the Tetons is Teton National Park. Near Colter Bay on Jackson Lake is an enchanting three-mile round trip tour on snowshoes or skis to Swan Lake and Heron Pond. It is a gentle trip with a rewarding view of the Tetons and Jackson Lake from the edge of Heron Pond.

Another similarly inspirational tour is the trip into Jenny Lake along Cottonwood Creek. Here, you are in the midst of the great cathedral of the Tetons, and as you glide down the aisle, great buttresses and spires loom above. The Jenny Lake tour is easy enough that it can be done by mere mortals as long as it is done in prayerful supplication.

Just over on the crest of the Tetons is the west slope, on the Idaho side. This is where Targhee Ski Area is located and where the quick uplift of moist air causes vast amounts of powder snow to fall. Powder skiing and boarding doesn't get much better than this.

The area also has a nice system of groomed trails for track skiing or catching a lazy afternoon tour. The several canyons (South Leigh, Teton, Darby, etc.) which penetrate the west slope make nice touring or snowshoeing trails—and, they provide access for hidden away bowls for backcountry skiing or boarding. West slope backcountry skiing is farther back in the mountains than in places like Teton Pass, but it's far less crowded.

This region also includes the Pine Creek Pass area which is popular among Idaho Falls skiers. Along the highway leading to the pass, skiers will find several nice beginning tours. There are also a couple of delightful descending tours off Pine Creek Pass to points lower in the valley. Speaking of Idaho Falls skiers, they have done a remarkable job of developing the trail system around Kelly Canyon, which is just 25 miles northeast of Idaho Falls. The area has a nice selection of Nordic trails ranging from beginning to advanced. Along with the cross-country trails, Kelly Canyon Ski Area is a pleasant family area, and with four chairlifts, it keeps skiers on the mountain rather than in line.

Finally, there is Teton Pass, lying on the south edge of the Teton Range. The pass is a true mecca for backcountry skiing, and on weekends, pilgrims from all around gather there. However, if you want a place to park, be there early. Parking certainly wasn't a concern earlier in the twentieth century. The few people that skied on the pass had it all to themselves. That was the situation in 1935 when two newlyweds were skiing over Teton Pass during the Christmas holidays. They were on their way to an isolated ranch in Jackson Hole where they were looking forward to a romantic and quiet winter. First, however, they had to get there.

The Tales . . .

*E*VEN FOR PAUL PETZOLDT, a big bear of man and soon to become one of North America's great mountaineers, it had been a long day. Finally, at 6 P.M. that night after breaking trail through fresh snow for 12 hours on skis, he and his wife Patricia reached the top of Teton Pass. The road winding up the pass was barely discernible from all the new snow, and in several places, they skied over piles of debris left by avalanches. At the top of the pass, with the great dark and empty bulk of Jackson Hole below them, they paused for a rest.

286

It was the second day of an incredible ski journey which had started in Ashton, Idaho. Newly married, Patricia and Paul Petzoldt had decided to spend Christmas and the winter of 1935-36 at a ranch near Moran at the foot of the Tetons in Jackson Hole. Patricia tells the story of that long ago trip in her book *On Top of the World*. She explains that before getting to the pass, they had been held up in Ashton for a week. A blizzard had been raging for days, and the train could not get through to Victor.

Marooned with the Petzoldts were the participants of the American Dog Derby, an event held each winter in Ashton. "The dog owners kept their dogs in the hotel," Patricia wrote, "and when we stepped out of our room into the hall we had to bypass great huskies who were prowling and sniffing about. At regular intervals there were dog fights in the lobby." To stop the dog fights, hotel guests would throw water on the dogs. That would quiet things down, until another fight would break out.

Finally tiring of waiting around and breaking up dog fights, Paul Petzoldt proposed to his wife that they ski from Ashton across the rolling farm country around Newdale and Tetonia, and up the Teton Valley by Driggs to Victor. From there they would ski over Teton Pass into Jackson Hole. "I had done some skiing in the Wasatch Mountains near Salt Lake," Patricia wrote, "but altogether I don't suppose I'd been on skis more than a half dozen times. However Paul assured me I could do it."

The next day was clear and sunny and the newlyweds struck out to the southeast. Petzoldt didn't follow the roads, but rather cut straight across the flats, trying to minimize the distance they had to travel. Darkness engulfed them, and at 7 p.m., it started snowing, and by 9, it had turned into a blizzard. Finally at 11 that night they skied wearily into Victor.

They managed to get a room, but Patricia described it as barely better than spending the night out: "The wind howled outside and blew through the room, fluttering the torn curtains. When I turned the covers back I discovered that the bedding consisted of two damp gray sheets, a ragged army blanket and a faded pink coverlet. So I took off my ski boots, pulled my cap snugly down on my head, wound my scarf about my throat, put on my mittens, and crawled into bed. In an instant I was sound asleep."

The next day after a long struggle through deep snow, they reached the top of Teton Pass. From Ashton, they had come 50 miles. By any measure, that's a lot of miles on skis through unbroken snow. Patricia hoped that from the summit of the pass it might be easier, a glide down into the Jackson valley, but two long days had left her with little reserve for the downhill run. Shoving off down the pass "my knees were so weak that I fell down every few feet," said Patricia.

Paul skied behind her and when she fell, he helped her to her feet. Down the pass they went with Paul picking Patricia up again and again. "After a while I hardly knew whether I was up or down, and cared less," said Patricia. Much later when she was writing about the account of her trip, Patricia joked that she must have been the "only woman who has fallen all the way down Teton Pass and lived to tell the tale."

Finally, near Wilson at the base of the pass, they reached a ranch owned by Gibb Scout, a friend of Paul's. Here they would stop and rest a couple of days before going the remainder of the distance to Moran. When they first arrived, Gibb ushered them into his big, warm kitchen, poured coffee and fried up some large elk steaks. Patricia was so tired that she took one bite of steak and promptly fell asleep at the table. □

The Trails . . .

GRAND TETON NATIONAL PARK

1 **Swan Lake-Heron Pond Loop**—*Marked cross-country trail. Easy, gradual terrain. Snowshoeing. No Dogs.* This is a pretty ski or snow-

shoe tour that has **gradual hills**, no snowmobiles and nice views. To reach the start of this trail, drive to Colter Bay Visitor Center off of US 89 in Teton National Park. Park in the parking area and start skiing or snowshoeing to the south. The trail is marked and follows a snow-bound road for the first .5 mile and then branches. By taking the right branch, you'll first go to **Heron Pond**, then **Swan Lake** and return again to the junction, completing the loop. The terrain is gentle and along the way are views of Jackson Lake and the north end of Teton Peaks. The total distance of the loop is 3 miles (5 km).

2 **Signal Mountain**—*Snowbound road. Moderately easy. Dogs OK.* This trail begins at the end of the plowed road near Signal Mountain Lodge. The Lodge is located 5 miles south of Jackson Lake Junction on US 89 in Teton National Park. The route follows the snowbound road for 1 mile until reaching snowbound **Signal Mountain Road** which branches off to the left (east) and leads through conifer forests to the summit of the mountain. From the top of Signal Mountain, you'll have a splendid view of Jackson Hole and the Teton Range. The round trip total is 10 miles (16 km) and the vertical climb is 900 feet (274 meters). Dogs are not allowed on Teton National Park hiking trails, but since this trip is on a snowbound road, they are allowed here. Park officials ask that they be kept on a leash. Snowmobilers also use the road.

On the flats in Grand Teton National Park

3 **Jenny Lake Trail**—*Marked cross-country ski trail. Moderately easy, gradual terrain. Snowshoeing.* This beautiful and **moderately easy** tour is a favorite of veteran Teton skiers and snowshoers. It begins at the Taggart Lake parking area. To reach the parking area, turn off of US 89 at Moose and drive past the visitor's center to where the road is no longer plowed. From the parking area, follow the snowbound road to the north .2 mile to **Cottonwood Creek**. Leave the road and ski the marked trail along the west side of the creek and continue to head north.

The trail crosses a series of meadows from which you are treated to a close and glorious perspective of the Tetons. Rising above are the members of the Cathedral Group: Teewinot Mountain, Mount Owen and the Grand Teton. Eventually the marked trail climbs a low ridge overlooking **Jenny Lake**. The total distance to the lake is 4.5 miles (7 km). Snowmobiles may be encountered on the first .2 mile, but otherwise the trail is for non-mechanized users only.

4   **Taggart Lake**—*Marked cross-country ski trail. Moderately difficult. Snowshoeing.* The Taggart trail is located beneath the central portion of the Teton Range including Mount Wister, Shadow Peak, Nez Perce, Disappointment Peak and the Middle and Grand Teton. To reach the start of this trail, drive past the visitor's center at Moose toward Jenny Lake. Park in the Taggart Lake turnoff just before the plowed road ends at Cottonwood Creek.

From the parking area follow the marked **Taggart Lake Trail** to the west (toward the Teton Range) and then to the north. This **moderately difficult** trail is very popular in the park, and it is likely that there will be plenty of ski tracks to follow into the lake. The trail forks after approximately 1 mile (1.5 km). The left fork leads to Taggart Lake, 1.6 miles (2.6 km) from the start. The right fork leads to the ridge between Taggart and **Bradley** Lakes, from which either lake can be approached. The round-trip tour to Bradley is 4 miles (6.5 km).

5   **Phelps Lake Overlook**—*Marked cross-country ski trail. Moderately difficult. Snowshoeing.* This is a **moderately difficult** trail to a portal between ancient Douglas firs overlooking Phelps Lake and the country beyond. To reach the trailhead, drive from Moose south on the Moose-Wilson road for 3 miles to a small parking area on the right (west) side of the plowed road. Ski or snowshoe following a narrow snowbound road which climbs gradually for 1.7 miles (2.7 km) to the **Death Canyon** trailhead. Follow the marked trail to the south to where the trail rises up to large, stately fir trees and a viewpoint above **Phelps Lake**. Skiing or snowshoeing beyond this point is not recommended because of avalanche hazard.

TETON PASS

Teton Pass (General Information)—*Backcountry skiing. Snowboarding. Snowshoeing.* Use on Teton Pass has skyrocketed over the last couple of decades. On weekends, over 100 vehicles will be crowded in the limited parking area on the summit. Use tapers off a little on weekdays, but even then as many as 50 to 60 vehicles will be parked there. Skiers and snowshoers looking for relaxed, easy trips on weekends will find smaller crowds by selecting one of the valley trails. By the same token, backcountry devotees looking for downhill terrain will experience far less traffic if they choose other off-trail areas in the Jackson and Victor-Driggs areas.

Nonetheless, when all is considered, the easiest accessible backcountry is found at the pass, and backcountry skiers and boarders will want to be there early to be assured of a place to park. Remember, also, that this is serious avalanche country. Before venturing out, check the most recent avalanche forecast (see *Resources*) and carry shovels and transceivers.

As you can imagine, Teton Pass has considerable winter history connected with it. Mail was carried over the pass by horse-drawn sleighs and, when the snow was too deep, by skiers and snowshoers. Avalanches have been and are a constant hazard to winter travelers, and through the years, many people have been caught.

A significant historical fact brought to light by Thomas Turiano in his book, *Teton Skiing,* is that the Pass was the stomping ground of an important woman backcountry skiing pioneer. In 1936, Betty Woolsey trained on Teton Pass when she was a member of the 1936 Olympic Ski Team. She fell in love with the powder bowls of the area, and in 1943 bought the Trail Creek Ranch just at the base of the pass on the Jackson Hole side. From the late 1940s through the early 1960s, she and Margaret Schultz took guests from Trail Creek Ranch on frequent backcountry ski trips to the pass. She also made some of the first explorations into the Granite Hot Springs area, made a ski descent of Flying Buttress and organized trips into the Wind Rivers.

6   **Phillips Canyon (Jackson Side of Teton Pass)**—*Snowbound hiking trail. Moderately difficult. Access to backcountry terrain.* The trailhead for this **moderately difficult** trail is 4 miles west of Wilson on Wyoming 22 before the summit of Teton Pass. The trail also provides access to slopes for backcountry skiing. As you drive to the top of the pass from Wilson, look for a sharp left curve on the highway. Park in the pulloff area (called **Big Bend Parking Area**) on the left side of the highway.

From the parked vehicle, walk up the highway 100 yards to where a snowbound road leads off from the right (north) side of the highway. The route follows this snowbound road to the north and then northeast. It is a moderately easy to moderately difficult 4-mile (6.5 km) tour to the edge of Phillips Canyon. Along the route are plenty of open hillsides for catching some turns.

Another option is to take the snowbound **Phillips Canyon hiking trail** which branches off to the left (north) about .5 mile from the start. After another .6 mile, a side trail leads to **Ski Lake** concealed in one of the small, east-facing cirques of the Teton Pass area. Ski Lake is about 2.5 miles (4 km) from the parking area.

7   **Teton Pass General Touring Options**—*Snowbound roads. Moderately difficult. Snowshoeing. Dogs OK. See aerial illustration, next page.* Teton pass is mostly a backcountry skiing and snowboarding area, but a couple of **moderately easy to moderately difficult** cross-country ski routes are available for general tours. One is a descending tour and follows the **old Teton Pass Road** from the top of the pass to its base on the Jackson Hole side. To do it, start on top of the pass, drop to the southeast, and descend the obvious snowbound road which roughly parallels the plowed Teton Pass highway. At approximately 2 miles (3 km) downhill from the top of the pass, the snowbound road crosses an avalanche chute, **Glory Slide.** This is not a place to stop and have lunch. The trip ends at the base of the pass near the Heidelburg Inn, where a shuttle vehicle can be left for the return trip to the top of the pass. Note that parking at the bottom is *very* limited.

8

The other relatively easy tour is to follow the **snowbound utility road**, just on the Idaho side of the pass, which leads from the top of the pass to the south. The snowbound road ends, but the ski route contin-

ues to follow the high ridge above the Jackson Valley. The normal ending point of this tour is **Pass Point** (point 9,279 on the *Teton Pass* topographic map) about 2 miles (3 km) from the parking area. This is an out-and-back tour and doesn't require a shuttle.

Teton Pass Backcountry-South Side—*Off-trail backcountry. Moderately difficult backcountry. Snowboarding.* The closest skiing and boarding to the parking area on top of the pass is just off the south side of the highway on **Telemark Bowl**. The bowl faces the Jackson Hole side of the pass. From 1947 until the late 1960s, a rope tow powered by a World War II vintage pickup truck would provide early season Alpine skiing here. By skiing along the south ridge of the pass beyond Telemark Bowl, you can also access other short open areas facing the Jackson side. Normally, skiers and boarders just work the top portion of the ridge which provides them with about 200 feet of vertical.

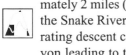

9

Black Canyon is a descending route that is occasionally done by some skiers. A shuttle is required. It is reached by skiing the ridge to the south from the top of Teton Pass. The ridge is followed approximately 2 miles (3 km) until it reaches Pass Point, where a plain view of the Snake River Range can be seen to the south. From here, an exhilarating descent can be made to the south and east into the obvious canyon leading to the east (Black Canyon). The tour ends at the town of Wilson. (See aerial illustration on facing page.) The avalanche hazard is high, and the tour should be undertaken during stable conditions.

10

Another popular powder field on the south side of the pass is **Edelweiss Bowl**. Edelweiss is the large, east-facing bowl which is visible from the highway several hundred yards before reaching the top of the pass as one drives from the Idaho side to the Wyoming side.

The top of Edelweiss is reached by skiing first on the snowbound utility road and then along the ridge line to the south from the top of the pass. The ridge curves to the west, and the bowl is located approximately 2.5 miles (4 km) from the start. Skiers will normally set in a

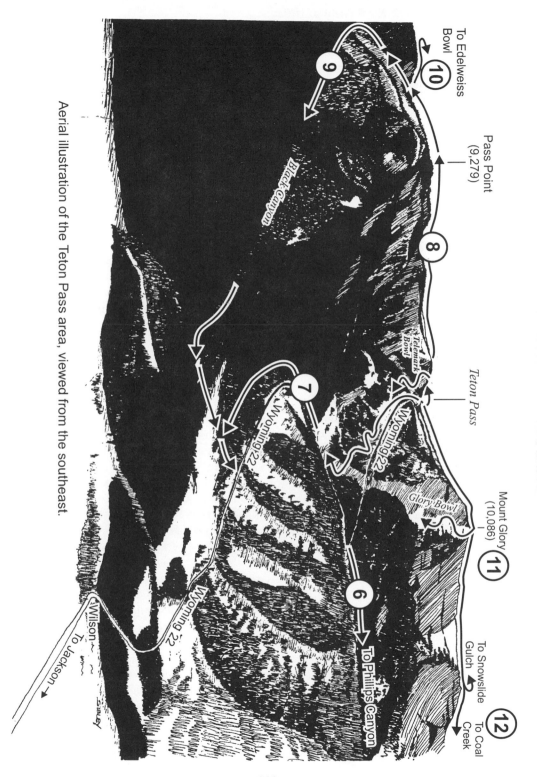

Aerial illustration of the Teton Pass area, viewed from the southeast.

293

skin track and make multiple runs. Edelweiss is an excellent early season run, usually skiable in November. Because of the grassy surface beneath the snowpack and the steep open slope, Edelweiss can slide. Check the avalanche forecast and carry proper safety equipment.

11 **Teton Pass Backcountry-North Side**—*Off-trail backcountry. Moderately difficult to difficult backcountry. Snowboarding. See aerial illustration on previous page.* Just to the north of Teton Pass is the 10,084 foot (3,074 meter) **Mount Glory**. Because of its access and steepness, this is a popular area for snowboarding—and backcountry skiing. There is plenty of avalanche hazard on this side of pass, and you should make every effort to be properly prepared, including checking the most recent stability forecast.

 Starting from Teton Pass, a boot trail is usually broken along the ridge line leading north to the top of Mount Glory. From here, you have several choices. One is the **difficult** descent down **Glory Bowl**, the big, steep bowl descending to the southeast from the summit. This magnificent and avalanche prone bowl drops 2,300 feet (703 meters) to the plowed highway below. Glory is best skied or boarded in the **spring** when you can better judge snow stability. However, it can even be tricky in the spring. Thomas Turiano in his book *Teton Skiing* notes that a "massive" avalanche came down Glory Bowl in early April of 1977. It was a great spring skiing day and quite a number of skiers had been on the bowl. Fortunately, none of the skiers were caught.

Moderately difficult backcountry descents can be made to the southwest into an area called **Snowslide Gulch** which has several variations which lead to the highway. The vertical drop is around 1,800 feet (549 meters). Once at the bottom, it is an easy walk to the top of the pass.

A descent which is **moderately easy** from a backcountry standpoint is to follow the ridge line from Mount Glory to the north to the second high point (just slightly over 10,000 feet on the *Rendezvous Peak* topographic map). Locally, this point is known as **Moby Dick**.

12 Descend from Moby Dick in a northwesterly direction into **Coal Creek** drainage. Coal Creek is followed out to the parking area lower on the Idaho side of the pass where a shuttle vehicle can be left. Coal Creek receives considerable touring traffic and the trail along the canyon bottom is often broken. Even though this is one of the easier backcountry descents off of Teton Pass, there's still avalanche hazard, and you'll want to take proper precautions.

The above information is just a sampling of the routes available. For more details on the backcountry options on the north side of the pass as well as skiing and boarding descents throughout the Tetons, you'll want to pick up a copy of Thomas Turiano's comprehensive book, *Teton Skiing*.

The West Slope of the Tetons.

TETON VALLEY (DRIGGS-VICTOR AREA)

13 **North Leigh Creek**—*Snowbound road. Moderately easy. Provides access to off-trail backcountry. Snowshoeing. Dogs OK.* Follow Idaho 33 north of Driggs for 6 miles until reaching the sharp, left-angled bend in the highway just before Tetonia. At the bend, turn right (east) off the highway, and follow signs toward South Leigh Creek. At 2.7 miles from Idaho 33, watch for a sign indicating North Leigh Creek. Take a left (north) on the North Leigh Creek road and continue until it is no longer plowed. You will probably have to park quite some distance back on the road in order to keep the road clear to the last private residence. The tour follows the snowbound North Leigh road.

The **gradual** snowbound road is a nice tour for beginners. At the end of the road is some wonderful telemark country, particularly up **Green Mountain Trail** to the southeast. The problem is that it is nearly a 5 mile (8 km) ski into the telly slopes, and by the time you've come that far, there isn't much time left to cut turns. In the middle of the winter, it is best done as an overnight trip.

14 **South Leigh Creek**—*Snowbound road. Easy. Provides access to moderately difficult backcountry. Snowshoeing. Snowboarding. Dogs OK.*

Follow Idaho 33 north of Driggs for 6 miles until reaching the sharp bend just before Tetonia. Turn off the highway here, and take the first right. Follow the signs to South Leigh Creek. Just before the road ends at a private residence, it turns sharply to the right. Park off the side of the road near the bend.

From the parked vehicle, ski on the snowbound road east into South Leigh Canyon towards the base of the Tetons. The tour is an enjoyable one, leading through lodge pole pines and a small, open area. Approximately 3 miles (5 km) from the start, **Beaver Creek** joins South Leigh from the left (northeast). Here the snowbound road ends, and two trails begin. One trail leads up South Leigh and the other up Beaver Creek. This is usually the turn around point for **beginning** tours.

An interesting **moderately difficult** touring loop can be made by skiing up Beaver Creek Trail until reaching **Commissary Ridge** Trail. Commissary Ridge Trail, then, can be followed back to the west arriving at a point near the start of South Leigh Creek Road. The total length of the tour is 9.5 miles (15 km). A **yurt** operated by Rendezvous Ski Tours is located on Commissary Ridge and may be rented.

South Leigh also provides access to backcountry skiing on **Beard Mountain** (9,466 feet or 2,885 meters). To reach the top of the mountain you can either ski up Beaver Creek Trail and gain the north ridge of Beard Mountain, or starting from the bottom of Beaver Creek, climb the southwest ridge of Beard Mountain to the summit. It's a 2,400 foot (732 meter) climb to the summit from lower Beaver Creek. There's considerable downhill skiing and snowboarding on Beard Mountain, but avalanche hazards exist. Check the avalanche forecast and carry proper equipment.

15 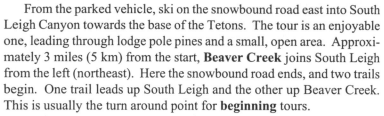 **Grand Targhee Ski Resort**— *Alpine ski area. Alpine, Nordic downhill and snowboarding. All abilities. All services: food, lodging, rentals and instruction.* Grand Targhee is one of the great powder ski areas of the west. Situated perfectly to reap the advantages of the orthographic lift of air flow over the Teton Range, it receives unimaginable amounts of snow, most of it dry and fluffy. It is located just over the Idaho border in Wyoming and is easily reached by following signs leading from Driggs to the east. The area has a lot of intermediate terrain and is popular among families and telemarkers. Grand Targhee has 5 chairs, 68 runs and a vertical drop of 2,200 feet (671 meters). It has lodging, restaurants, instruction and rentals.

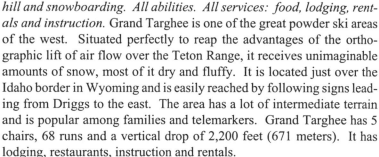 **Grand Targhee Nordic Trails**—*Regularly groomed cross-country trails. All abilities.* The Targhee Nordic Center has been around since the mid-1970s and grooms a nice set of Nordic trails in **Dry** and **Ricks** Basins at the base of Freds Mountain. The trails are for **all abilities** and

run through varied and open terrain, offering views across the valley to the Big Holes and Yellowstone country. Trails are groomed for both skating and classic skiing. Backcountry tours, instruction and rentals are available.

16 **Grand Targhee Backcountry**—*Moderately difficult to difficult backcountry. Permission required from ski patrol for uphill travel on cat tracks.* Backcountry skiing in the Targhee area has been contentious and as noisy as metal edges scraping against boilerplate. It didn't help that some of the earliest backcountry skiers such as winter hardman Gregg Amalong lived in a snow cave at the base of the ski area, and was observed by flabbergasted guests taking baths in Targhee's swimming pool and drying his wet socks by the fire in the lodge.

Targhee has always been known as one of the "cowboy" resorts. So it is not surprising that it was at Targhee that cattlemen's slang for sheep, "range maggots" was resurrected in a slightly altered form and applied to baggy wool-clad, backcountry skiers roaming the hillsides around the resort. During this latter-day range war, cross-country skiers were referred to by Targhee management as "mountain maggots," and Nordic downhill was banned from the hill. Targhee wasn't the only ski area where the relationship between skinny skiers and mountain managers was less than cordial. When the first version of this book came out, many other ski areas in the Intermountain West didn't allow cross-country skiing on their slopes. That, of course, has all changed now and the range war is in the distant past. Nordic skiers, and their dollars, are welcome at ski areas everywhere, including Targhee.

You can access backcountry terrain from Targhee, but because most access involves climbing cat tracks against ski traffic, you first must check with the Targhee Ski patrol to find out when uphill traffic is allowed. On busy days that may be in the early morning before lifts open.

In the past, the most popular place to backcountry ski at Targhee was on the west ridge of Peaked Mountain (Point 9,827 on the *Granite Basin* topographic map). Peaked is located just to the south of Freds Mountain on which the main part of the ski area is situated. Things, however, have changed. Now Peaked is within the boundaries of the ski area, is currently used for cat skiing, and will be developed for lift-serviced skiing. What that leaves for backcountry skiers is terrain which is mostly much more difficult than Peaked.

There is, however, one descent of **moderate difficulty** that is outside the boundaries of the ski area and is fair game for backcountry skiing. **Lightning Peak** (Point 8,452) is located to the southwest of Freds Mountain. Its south face was a popular route among the Mountain Maggots as a route to the valley floor and was shared with me by

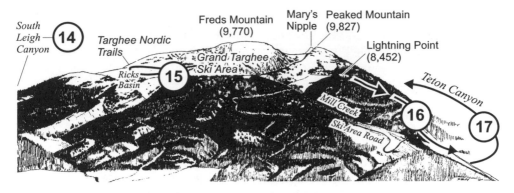

Aerial illustration of the Targhee area, viewed from the west.

Geno Foresyth in the mid-1970s. The descent starts on top of Lightning Peak and descends to the south. Midway down, a small knob is reached at the 7,640 level. Below this point to the south are some very steep, gnarly slopes, but they can be avoided by not dropping past the 7,600 level. From the knob, follow a ridge line to the west to where it intersects with **Mill Creek** and **Teton Canyon Road**. A shuttle vehicle needs to be left at the Teton Canyon at the bottom of the ski area access road.

    Other descents are considerably more **difficult** than the Lightning route and should be saved for **spring**. Two suggestions from Tom Turiano's *Teton Skiing* include the 3,000 foot descents of the **Southeast Face** of Peaked Mountain and the south face of **Mary's Nipple** (Point 9,920 on the ridge between Freds Mountain and Peaked). Both are very steep and should be done under stable early morning corn conditions. Both routes end near **Treasure Mountain Boy Scout Camp** on Teton Canyon Road.

17 **Teton Canyon**—*Snowbound road. Easy, level skiing. Snowshoeing. Dogs OK. Access for backcountry skiing.* Located 6 miles east of Driggs on the road to Targhee Ski Area. The snowbound Teton Canyon Road is marked with a Forest Service sign indicating "Treasure Mountain Boy Scout Camp" and "Teton Canyon Campground." Parking is limited.

    The tour follows the snowbound Teton Canyon Road to the east. The skiing is **flat and easy**. A 5-mile (8 km) ski or snowshoe trip can be made to Teton Campground. From the campground, hiking trails lead farther into the Tetons, but the traveling becomes more difficult and quickly enters avalanche country.

18 **Table Mountain**—*Backcountry off-trail. Moderately difficult backcountry.* Table Mountain is a delightful and entertaining spring

skiing mountain. The most popular—and safest—route to the top is to start from **Teton Canyon Campground** and follow the **west ridge**. The ridge climbs steeply at first but levels out for a long, lazy ascent

almost to the summit of Table Mountain. The last 200 or 300 feet of the ascent is an easy scramble to the summit platform. The airy view of the Tetons from the 11,106-foot (3,385 meter) summit is like floating in a hot air balloon with the Grand Teton so close that you can almost reach out and touch it, and for that reason alone, the climb is worth it.

One descent option from Table Mountain is to ski or snowboard the long gradual **west ridge**, the same as the ascent route. Another descent option is to ski the sublime **northwest face** which drops into the drainage of the North Fork of Teton Creek. Once at the bottom, follow the North Fork of Teton Creek Trail back to Teton Campground.

19 **Darby Canyon**—*Snowbound road. Easy touring. Snowshoeing. Dogs OK.* The turnoff to Darby Canyon is located 3 miles south of Driggs on

Idaho 33. Drive until the road is no longer plowed. The snowshoe or ski trip follows the snowbound Darby Canyon Road.

After a couple of miles up Darby Canyon, the road begins to cross

avalanche paths. From here, touring is not recommended during periods of unstable snow conditions.

20 **Moose Creek**—*Snowbound road and trail. Easy to moderately easy. Wildlife wintering area. No dogs.* Moose Creek is located 3.5 miles

southeast of Victor on the north side of Idaho 33. Drive until the road is no longer plowed. Usually a small pullout is plowed. This easy going, gradually sloping tour follows the narrow, snowbound Moose Creek Road to the east. Eventually the road turns into a snowbound trail.

Beginning ski tours and snowshoe trips usually go up a couple of miles and turn around.

A little over a mile from the parking area, you may see ski tracks cutting off to the left. The tracks lead across a flat open area and climb

Plummer Canyon to Rendezvous Ski Tours **yurt**. The yurt accesses some fine intermediate backcountry skiing terrain and may be rented (see *Resources* for more information).

Moose Creek is a wildlife wintering area. Stay on the main trail and leave dogs at home.

PINE CREEK PASS AREA

Pine Creek Pass is located on Idaho 31 northeast of Swan Valley, some 55 miles (90 km) east of Idaho Falls. Between Swan Valley and the pass, Idaho 31 provides access to a number of skiing and snowshoeing opportunities. Snowmobilers use the main snowbound road leading to the east from the top of the pass, but if you catch it early in the morning before snowmobile traffic picks ups, you'll find it a pleasant ski tour. It also provides access to some appetizing telemark slopes and a couple of invigorating descending tours.

21 **Pine Creek Pass to Tie Canyon**—*Snowbound road and off-trail backcountry. Moderately difficult. Dogs OK.* This is a **moderately difficult** descending tour which begins on top of Pine Creek Pass and ends at the mouth of Tie Creek (described below). When the powder is good, it's a wonderful trip highlighted with fine **telemarking** on the way down. The total length is approximately 4.5 miles (7 km). Plan at least a half day for the trip.

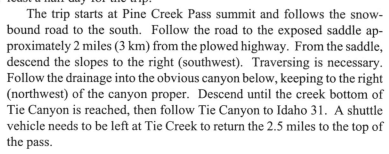

The trip starts at Pine Creek Pass summit and follows the snowbound road to the south. Follow the road to the exposed saddle approximately 2 miles (3 km) from the plowed highway. From the saddle, descend the slopes to the right (southwest). Traversing is necessary. Follow the drainage into the obvious canyon below, keeping to the right (northwest) of the canyon proper. Descend until the creek bottom of Tie Canyon is reached, then follow Tie Canyon to Idaho 31. A shuttle vehicle needs to be left at Tie Creek to return the 2.5 miles to the top of the pass.

22 **Pine Creek Pass to Swan Valley**—*Snowbound road and off-trail. Moderately difficult.* This is a long, moderately difficult **descending** tour which begins at the top of Pine Creek Pass and ends near the town of Swan Valley.

To do the shuttle, drive from Swan Valley toward Palisades on US 26, 1 mile to the southwest to a church. Turn left (east) at the church and follow this road toward the obvious major drainage (Rainey Creek) to the northeast. Two miles (3 km) from the highway, the road comes to a "T." Take a left and drive 1 more mile until the road is no longer plowed (at the last farm house).

The ski descent down Rainey Creek starts on top of Pine Creek Pass and follows the major snowbound road along the ridge and finally to the south. In approximately 6 miles (10 km), the snowbound road leads into the Rainey Creek drainage. Bushwhack your way down Rainey Creek for a few miles until a snowbound road is reached, which leads down Rainey Creek and eventually to the shuttle vehicle. There are two crossings of Rainey Creek and you may encounter some open water. Total distance of the tour is approximately 15 to 16 miles (24 to 26 km). The bottom portion of Rainey Creek is a wildlife wintering area and you should stay on the snowbound road.

23 Tie Canyon—*Snowbound road. Moderately easy. Snowshoeing. Dogs OK.* Located 12 miles northeast of Swan Valley or 2.5 miles southwest of Pine Creek Pass on the south side of Idaho 31. Normally, parking is plowed for this popular tour. The tour follows the snowbound road into the canyon to the southeast. The first portion of the tour is **gentle** and suitable for a beginner. It passes through forested areas and open meadows along the stream. The snowbound road, after approximately 1 mile (1.5 km), climbs the ridge to the right (southwest). Tourers can either follow this road or continue up the canyon, which eventually tops out at the Rainey Creek divide. The skiing or snowshoeing in the canyon is not on a trail, but traveling is not too restricted by undergrowth. There are plenty of open hillsides for practicing tellys.

24 North Fork of Pine Creek—*Snowbound road. Easy. Snowshoeing. Dogs OK.* Suitable for beginners, this trail is located 11 miles northeast of Swan Valley or 3.5 miles southwest of Pine Creek Pass on the north side of Idaho 31. The drainage is a picturesque setting offering long tours on relatively **level** terrain of the valley floor. It begins as a snowbound road which turns into a trail. Parking at the trailhead may or may not be plowed. Some snowmobile traffic.

25 West Pine Creek—*Snowbound road. Easy to moderately easy. Snowshoeing. Dogs OK.* Located 10 miles northeast of Swan Valley or 5 miles southwest of Pine Creek Pass on the north side of Idaho 31. The tour follows the snowbound road northwest to a church lodge approximately .5 mile (1 km) from the start. From the lodge, further touring follows summer hiking trails up the drainage. At approximately 3 miles (5 km) into the tour, the trail crosses a steep hillside and, in unstable conditions, can present a hazard to skiers. The trailhead may or may not have parking plowed. Snowmobile use can occur but is unlikely.

KELLY CANYON AREA

26 Kelly Canyon Ski Area—*Alpine ski area. Alpine, Nordic downhill and snowboarding. All abilities. Food, rentals, instruction and night skiing.* Kelly Canyon lies on the edge of a hilly, agrarian area where the great American novelist Vardis Fisher grew up. In one of his novels he described the hilly country of his boyhood as being surrounded by "great buildings of mountain, white and gleaming slides of rock, and deep black canyons, misty and still." Some of those "buildings" rising above the "misty and still" Snake River Canyon were undoubtedly the Kelly Mountains.

Kelly Canyon Ski Area, on the slopes of Kelly Mountain overlooking Vardis Fisher country, is a great family ski area located just off US 26, 25 miles northeast of Idaho Falls. It has 4 chairs, 26 runs and 938 feet (286 meters) of vertical. Rentals, instruction and night skiing are available.

27 **Kelly Canyon Cross-country Ski Trails**—*Marked and occasionally groomed cross-country ski trails. All abilities. Toilets. Warming hut.*

The cross-country ski trail system at Kelly Canyon has improved greatly since the first version of this book. Currently, it has 6 looped trails, some of which are groomed, and over 20 total miles (32 km) of skiing.

To reach the trailhead, drive to the Kelly Canyon Ski Area 25 miles northeast of Idaho Falls off of US 26. Park in the ski area parking lot and ski east on the snowbound road. Slightly more than a mile beyond

the parking area, is an area known as the **"Y" Junction**. Maps are available at a sign-in area as you approach the "Y" Junction.

All the trails begin from the "Y" Junction. For **easy tours**, you may want to try the 1 mile **Tryo loop** or the **Hawley Gulch** overlook. Both lead northeast from the "Y" Junction and are occasionally groomed. At the south end of Hawley Loop is a short trail that leads to **Hidden Vista** which overlooks the Snake River plains and Antelope Hills where several of Vardis Fisher's famous novels take place.

You may also want to take a spin up to the Idaho Falls Ski Club warming hut. The trip begins at the "Y" Junction and heads southeast on the **Kelly Mountain Logging Road**. The hut is maintained by Idaho Falls Ski Club, one of the most active ski clubs in the state and an important guiding force for Nordic and Alpine skiing in the area.

Most **backcountry skiing** takes place in the Kelly Mountain area. The trail leads south from the "Y" Junction and climbs a snowbound jeep trail eventually reaching the Kelly Mountain ridge near the top of a chairlift. The ridge line is followed to the southeast to the top of **Kelly**

Mountain. A descent can be made to the north into the warming hut. This is currently not marked, but it may be in the future. When the snow is good, there's fine telemarking on the route. Be aware, the Kelly Mountain ridge is high and exposed and shouldn't be attempted under adverse weather conditions. Carry basic survival equipment and take normal avalanche precautions.

Never Trust a Poacher

*T*O *GAME WARDEN*, George Green, Reade wasn't such a bad guy. He was an amiable sort and had made quite a hit at the St. Patrick's day party in Alta to which Green had taken him in 1910. Reade liked to slip out now and then to smoke his corn cob pipe, but George Green didn't worry much about him. That seems like odd behavior for a game warden who only a few days earlier had apprehended Reade for poaching.

Perhaps Warden Green thought he was a good influence on the prisoner and that Reade had turned the corner away from his criminal ways.

When Green made the arrest, Reade "was garrisoned," said the *Teton Valley News*, "with a battery of two twistbore Colt revolvers with a 45 caliber badger hole in each barrel." Despite his fire power, he put up no resistance to Green. "Fact is," reported the *News*, "he seemed to enter into the spirit of the occasion with a great deal of enthusiasm. He acted as though he had been looking forward to the event."

The poacher was good on skis, and in no time, he would put a mile between him and Green. He could have easily escaped from the slow and plodding Green, but Reade would stop, sit down and wait for Green to catch up. When they got back to Alta, Green decided to keep Reade at his house a while before taking him to jail. That suited the prisoner just fine: "He seemed to enjoy his captivity," said the *News*, "and acted as though he cared to lead no other kind of life."

But, as any game officer will tell you, poachers are never to be trusted, and despite Reade's amiability, the young man hadn't turned any corners. One night Reade slipped out of the house and disappeared, taking with him any charitable feelings that Green might have held for the prisoner—and Green's snowshoes. Not only did Green find himself hoodwinked by the wily Reade, but the town's newspaper was having a grand time reporting the whole affair.

"There is much agitation over the fellow's disappearance," said the *News*, "and the country is being scoured right and left in an effort to locate the fugitive. We suggest that the next prisoner be taken to the market in an elk cage." □

Resources . . .

National Forest Lands in the Pine Creek Pass Area
Palisades Ranger District of the Targhee National Forest—Address: 3659 E. Ririe Highway, Idaho Falls, Idaho 83401. Phone: (208) 523-1412.

Grand Teton National Park:
Grand Teton National Park Headquarters—*Address*: Moose, Wyoming 83012. Phone: (307) 733-2880.

Teton National Park Publications
Grand Teton Natural History Association—Address: PO Box 170, Moose, Wyoming 83012. Phone: (307) 739-3403.

National Forest Lands in Teton Pass and Jackson Hole Areas
Supervisor's Headquarters of the Bridger-Teton National Forest—Offices located at 340 North Cache in Jackson. Address: Box 1888, Jackson, Wyoming 83001. Phone: (307) 733-5400.

National Forest Lands in the Driggs Area
Teton Basin District of the Targhee National Forest—Address: PO Box 777, Driggs, Idaho 83422. Phone: (208) 354-2312

Yurt Rentals and Guide Services
Rendezvous Ski Tours and Guest House—Address: 219 Highland Way, Victor, ID 83455. Phone: (208) 787-2906. Note: a number ski and mountaineering guides are licensed in Teton National Park and other areas of the Bridger-Teton National Forest. For an up-to-date list contact Grand Teton National Park, address and phone above, or the Jackson Hole Chamber of Commerce at (307) 733-3316.

Alpine Ski Areas
Grand Targhee Ski Resort—Address: PO Box SKI, Alta, Wyoming 83422. Phone: 1-800-827-4433 or 1-888-766-7466 (snow report).

Kelly Canyon Ski Area—Address: PO Box 367, Ririe, Idaho 83442. Phone: (208) 538-6261 or (208) 538-7700 (snow report).

Avalanche Information
Avalanche forecasts are available via phone or through the Internet. For the most current number and web address, contact the Bridger-Teton National Forest, listed above.

Additional Reading
Teton Skiing: A History & Guide to the Teton Range—By Thomas Turiano (Homestead Publishing, Moose, WY, 1995). This outstanding work covers Alpine ski and snowboard descents in the Teton Range. It is one of the best of its kind and a must for anyone who is passionate about steep white bowls, rimed ridges and ragged skies.

Opposite Page: Near the summit of Mount Glory.

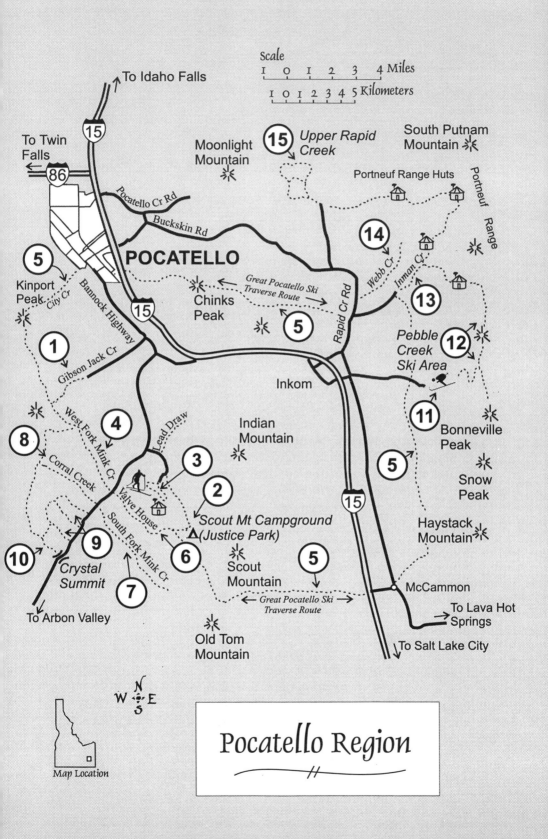

CHAPTER 18
POCATELLO REGION

Area Covered: Pocatello, Chubbuck, Inkom and McCammon.

SKIING'S ROOTS in Pocatello sink as deep as a Mt. Bonneville snow pack, going back to before the turn of the twentieth century. The earliest skiers used homemade skis, often fashioned with a draw knife out of one-by-four slats. By the 1920s, though, most Pocatello skiers had stored away their homemade boards and were using fancy store-bought models. A fine pair of hickory skis could be purchased through the Sears and Roebuck catalog. The fashionable Pocatello skier at this time wore skis with canvas tacked around the binding. The canvas surrounded the boot and served as a built in gaiter to keep the snow out and the skier's feet warm.

At the time of World War II, cable bindings were in use, and with increased control skiers were busy out exploring and descending the surrounding mountainous areas. The Mink Creek (Bannock) Highway just south of town was not plowed in those days, and winter travelers heading towards Arbon Valley followed Mink Creek and turned up West Fork, eventually crossing over the divide into Arbon. During the post war days, favorite tours included the ever popular West Fork to Elk Meadows, Valve House Draw to Blind Springs Canyon, and as the appeal of Alpine skiing became stronger, Mt. Bonneville was reconnoitered for the site of what has become the Pebble Creek Ski Area.

It comes as no surprise that skiing has such a rich tradition in Pocatello, for the open draws and hillsides allow free and unrestricted travel. The weather plays its tricks at times, but when the skiing is good here, it's good.

Take one look at all the options and it's obvious. Cross-country skiers and snowshoers looking for a relaxing Saturday afternoon tour have their choice of a cluster of marked and signed Forest Service trails along Mink Creek Highway including West Fork of Mink Creek, Valve House Draw, Corral Creek, Porcelain Pot and Crystal Summit. Those skiers who like long distance tours will enjoy the trip starting at Crystal Summit and ending on the West Fork of Mink Creek. For combined touring and telemarking, the descending trail between Crystal Summit and Corral Creek is delightful after a fresh snow fall.

The Pocatello area also sports the first publicly owned system of yurts in the U.S. Located in the Portneuf Range just to the east and south of town, each of the four yurts are positioned about a day apart. A skier or snowshoer can conceivably make a five day trip starting near the Pocatello city limits and travel almost all the way to Lava Hot Springs, staying in a cozy yurt each night. The system was designed for all users regardless of ability. Two of the yurts have been placed in locations where they're easy for families to reach, while others are located near the crest of the Portneuf Range where the backcountry skiing and snowboarding is excellent.

There's so much in the area that one could spend a lifetime seeking out the hidden away trails, powder runs and spring descents in nearby mountains. In fact, some have. And, if asked, they're quick to say that it's all been worth it.

The Tales . . .

*B*LAINE GASSER had been eyeing Scout Mountain for some time. It's hard to miss the mountain. From nearly any place in Pocatello, the mountain dominates the southern skyline, and in the winter when snow deeply covers the sharply angled face rising out of a band of conifers, it is a scene that, for a skier, is hard to resist. Finally in mid December of 1940, Gasser decided to do something about it.

Along with Jerry Turner, of Turner Insurance and Chuck Hibbard who later developed the Lost Trail Ski Area north of Salmon, they drove their car as far as they could on Scout Mountain Road. The day they had chosen was windy and stormy, very much like it had been the past several days, but it meant fresh powder on the mountain and the likelihood of some great skiing.

A pair of skis in those days was a pair of skis. The same pair could be used for lift serviced skiing as well as for trips to the backcountry. Most skiers did both. Gasser, Turner and Hibbard thought nothing of driving out of town, climbing up a likely looking hill under their own power and catching a nice run down.

They strapped on climbing skins, clipped into the metal bindings, and started up the open face of Scout visible from town. They stayed just to the right of prominent gully on its north edge. Near the saddle of the mountain, the terrain forced them to cut across the steep upper slopes of the gully.

"For some reason at that point," said Gasser recalling the journey, "we knew something wasn't right. Somewhere one of us had read that if you think the snow might have a chance to slide, you should cross the slope, one at a time, which is what we did."

First Chuck Hibbard skied across. Then Gasser.
"All of sudden, I heard a crack," said Gasser, "and Jerry yelled 'Follow me!'" Gasser swung around and was horrified at what he saw. Turner was on a three-foot thick slab of snow, in the midst of an avalanche, sliding down the steep gully. The slab of snow cracked like an egg shell and started breaking apart around him.

Gasser and Hibbard watched helplessly as Turner accelerated down the slope, snow churning about him. Three hundred yards down the gully, the remaining slab of snow on which Turner still clung bashed into a boulder and disintegrated, and Turner disappeared. Gasser and Hibbard reacted immediately, jumping into the gully before the snow settled and skiing after Turner with skins still attached to their skis.

"We got down to where the gully narrowed," said Gasser, "and then we saw Jerry. There he was. He had his arms wrapped around the limb of a pine tree."

They stepped up to Turner and pried his arms away from the pine tree. Other than being left temporarily speechless, he was fine. The three of them remained huddled together, catching their breaths and regaining their composure. Finally after about 30 minutes, they shakily crept off the mountain.

At the time, none of the men had any desire to ever ski Scout Mountain again, but they did return. In fact, they returned to ski the mountain a number of times. It was, nonetheless, the last time they ever went in the middle of the winter. After Turner's wild ride in the avalanche, they were taking no chances and all subsequent trips were made in late spring when the snow was firm and predictable. □

Rush hour traffic: Dave Arcano and "T." 5th Street, Pocatello.

The Trails . . .

1   **Gibson Jack**—*Snowbound trail. Moderately easy to moderately diffi-cult. Dogs OK. Snowshoeing.* Drive towards the Mink Creek-Scout Mountain area by following Bannock Highway to the south. Just across from the entrance to the Pocatello Country Club approximately four miles out of town, turn right on Gibson Jack Road. Drive until the road is no longer plowed. Parking may be a problem here. You'll need to park out of the way of the private residence at the end of the road and in a spot where you are not in line with their driveway.

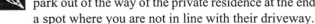

The route follows the snowbound trail, which climbs through the open country above Gibson Jack Creek on its north side. All along lower portions of the trail, you'll have nice views of the Portneuf Range across the valley. The early part of the trip is **moderately easy** and as you climb more, it becomes **moderately difficult**. Eventually the trail ducks out of the open country and continues along Gibson Jack Creek through stands of Douglas and subalpine firs.

Ambitious skiers or snowshoers can follow Gibson Jack Creek and cross a small saddle into the **West Fork of Mink Creek**. In good snow conditions, a skier can have a delightful glide all the way to the Bannock Highway and end at the West Fork trailhead (see West Fork of Mink Creek Trail description). This loop, which involves a short shuttle of cars, is one of several classic tours in the Pocatello areas. Most skiers start at West Fork, but either direction is enjoyable. Skiers attempting this route, however, should carry basic emergency gear, maps and com-pass. Be sure to carry the *Pocatello South* and *Clifton Creek* topographic maps since route finding can get a little difficult on the upper portions of Gibson Jack.

2   **Justice Park-Scout Mt. Campground**—*Snowbound roads and trails. Moderately easy to moderately difficult. Dogs OK. Snowshoeing.* If it's early in the season and you're anxious to dust off the skis, Scout Mountain Road is a good starting place. The turnoff to Scout Mountain is on the left (east) side of Bannock Highway 2 miles past the boundary of the Caribou National Forest. Turn left at the intersection indicating Camp Taylor or Scout Mountain Recreation Area. In early winter it is possible to drive most of the way to **Justice Park**, the campground at the top of the road.

At Justice Park, turn into the picnic area (to the right at the end of the road). From there, you can ski on the snow covered roads or hiking trails.

One Justice Park intermediate tour that skiers may enjoy follows the **East Fork Trail**, leading south from the day picnic area. This trail passes through the woods and eventually connects to trails that continue to the summit of Scout Mountain or to the **South Fork of Mink Creek**. The *Scout Mountain* and *Clifton Creek* topographic maps are helpful when going on this excursion.

3   **Scout Mountain Cross-country Ski Trail System**—*Proposed marked and groomed cross-country ski trail system. All abilities.* At the time of this writing, the Pocatello Parks and Recreation Department was working with Caribou National Forest to establish a system of groomed cross-country ski trails at the base of Scout Mountain. The Parks Department also intends to place a yurt in the area. If all goes to plan, access to the area will be the main Scout Mountain Road. To reach it, drive south of Pocatello on Bannock Highway. Watch for the sign indicating the boundary of the Caribou National Forest. Two miles past the boundary, turn left at the intersection indicating Camp Taylor or Scout Mountain Recreation Area. From there, follow the signs to the ski area parking area. For the latest information on the status of the area, contact the Pocatello Parks and Recreation Department (see *Resources* at end of the chapter).

4   **West Fork Mink Creek**—*Snowbound trail. Moderately easy to moderately difficult. Dogs not allowed. Park N' Ski area.* If you drive 4 miles farther up Bannock Highway from the turnoff to the Scout Mountain Road (see above) you'll see some low buildings on the left and a plowed parking area on the right. The West Fork comes in on the right side (west) of Bannock Highway. Park in the large plowed parking area on the right. Since part of Pocatello's water supply comes from here, dogs are not allowed

The ski or snowshoe tour follows the snow covered West Fork Road up a hundred yards, and once passing a tubular gate, the road turns into a trail which follows the creek. For 2-3 miles (3-5 km) the trail is protected by a good stand of firs, after which the trees open up into a meadow area with multiple beaver dams forming small ponds. The West Fork is a beautiful trail near Pocatello and is very popular with cross-country skiers. Snowmobiles are not allowed.

In the beaver pond area on the upper West Fork, one can take an old road to the south into the Elk Meadow area, or one can follow the West Fork farther up and cross a small divide into the Gibson Jack drainage.

Because it receives heavy use from skiers, the West Fork trail quickly becomes icy. Best skiing, especially for **beginning** skiers, is in early mornings or after a new snowfall. Park N' Ski stickers are required.

5 **The Great Pocatello Ski Traverse**—*Snowbound roads and trails. Moderately difficult backcountry.* A multi-day backcountry trip can be made which includes parts or all of Gibson Jack, West Fork of Mink Creek, Valve House Draw and other notable cross-country trails in the area. The trip was first done in December of 1974. That was the last time it was done, but it is worth a mention because it forms an elegant arc around Pocatello beginning and ending in the city limits. It starts at City Creek, west of Pocatello and climbs Kinport Peak. From Kinport it descends into upper Gibson Jack, then goes over the divide to the West Fork of Mink Creek. After descending the West Fork, it follows

Ike Gayfield on the Great Pocatello Ski Traverse, 1974.

Valve House Draw to the saddle between Scout and Old Tom Mountains. From here, it heads straight east, crossing I-15 at the McCammon Exit. From McCammon, the route can either contour around the base of the Portneuf Range or climb and follow the Portneuf Range Crest to the north. It ends with an ascent of Chinks Peak and a run down the snowbound access road into Pocatello.

6 **Valve House Draw**—*Snowbound road. Moderately easy to moderately difficult. Dogs OK. Park N' Ski area.* The trailhead to Valve House Draw is located along Bannock Highway. Follow the directions to get to the West Fork of Mink Creek. Park on the right (west) side of the road in the parking area. The trail starts on the east side of the road.

 Valve House Draw is similar to the West Fork. The trail follows the drainage. Skiing is **easy to moderate**, but can be difficult in icy conditions.

You can actually ski from Valve House Draw to Justice Park Campground (on Scout Mountain) or into the South Fork of Mink Creek. Route finding on either trail is challenging, and it is recommended that *Clifton Creek* and *Scout Mountain* topographic maps be carried. No snowmobiles are permitted in Valve House Draw. Park N' Ski stickers are required.

7 **South Fork Mink Creek**—*Snowbound road. Easy to moderately easy. Dogs OK. Park N' Ski area.* The South Fork road intersects the Bannock Highway about 1 mile beyond the parking lot from the West Fork-Valve House trails (see West Fork of Mink for directions). Park in the plowed area on the right (west) side of the highway.

The ski route follows the snowbound South Fork Road. There are no route finding problems since the South Fork Road is very wide and obvious. Skiing is easy and suitable for the complete **beginner**. It is, however, a very popular snowmobile route, and skiers are recommended to get their skiing done in the early morning if they wish to avoid the snowmobile traffic.

One side trip is to ski to Valve House Draw Trail by following **Box Canyon** out of the South Fork. Box Canyon is approximately 2.2 miles up the South Fork from Bannock Highway.

Another possible side tour off the South Fork Road is to connect with the **East Fork** hiking trail leading from Justice Park on the side of Scout Mountain. The *Clifton Creek* and *Scout Mountain* topographic maps are recommended. Park N' Ski stickers are required.

8 **Corral Creek**—*Snowbound trail. Moderately difficult. Access to telemark slopes. Dogs OK. Snowshoeing. Park N' Ski area.* Drive out Bannock Highway. One mile past the West Fork of Mink Creek, the

313

Corral Creek parking area is located to the right, opposite South Fork Road. Park in the small parking lot just below the entrance to the trail.

Corral Creek Trail leads westward and up through woods. The first part is suitable for **beginners**. It becomes quite steep at the upper end and traversing may be necessary to get to the crest. Once on the top, you can connect with the ski trail which originates at Crystal Summit (see Crystal Summit Trail). Good **telemarking** slopes are found in the upper portions of Corral Creek. Park N' Ski stickers are required.

9 **Porcelain Pot Trail System**—*Marked cross-country ski trails. Moderately easy to moderately difficult. Snowshoeing. Dogs OK. Park N' Ski area.* Two pullouts are plowed on the right (west) side of Bannock Highway in the two mile stretch of road between the South Fork and Crystal Summit (the highest point the Bannock Highway).

The trail system leading from either pulloff has been cleared and marked specifically for cross-country skiing. The Porcelain Pot System has something for everybody with trails ranging from **easy to difficult** and with a number of loop trips available. It is also possible to connect onto the Crystal Summit Trail, described next.

The Caribou National Forest, which has developed this fine system of trails, is to be commended for giving cross-country skiing a boost in the Pocatello area. Park N' Ski stickers are required.

10 **Crystal Summit**—*Marked cross-country ski trails. Moderately difficult. Snowshoeing. Dogs OK. Park N' Ski Area. Access to telemark slopes.* Crystal Summit is located two miles past the South Fork of Mink Creek. At 5,964 feet (1,818 meters), it is the highest point on the Bannock Highway, forming the divide between Arbon Valley and Mink Creek. Park in the plowed area on the right (west) side of the road.

Its name describes the area well. When the snow is good, Crystal Summit is one of the best all around ski touring areas in southeast Idaho. It's not for someone getting started on cross-country skis, but for those with a little touring experience this is a delightful place. It has a little of everything: pleasant trail skiing, **abundant telemarking**, invigorating ridge tours and on sunny days, sparkling snow fields and splendid views. Snowmobiles also use the area and some trails are dual-use.

From the parking area, follow the marked ski trail. If desired, you can connect with the Porcelain Pot Trail system. Most skiers, however follow the trail leading deeper into the Crystal area. The trail climbs and contours around the base of an open hill, called Corral Point. Within .7 mile (1 km) from the parking area, the trail descends into a forested area. It then gradually climbs for about 1 mile and breaks out on a broad ridge with views of Scout and Long Tom Mountains. All along the trail, one can make short jaunts to open slopes for telemark skiing.

Doctor Strawberry: he has the cure for the wintertime blues.

Eventually the Crystal trail links up with the top of the Corral Creek ski trail. From here, there are several options: ski on the nearby hill-sides, follow Corral Creek Trail downhill to a spotted vehicle, or join up with the snowmobile trail which goes to Elk Meadows.

Of course, you don't have to follow the trails. There's an cornuco-pia of backcountry skiing and delectable hillsides for practicing telemarking. Be careful on days of poor visibility; it's easy to become disoriented. However, as long as you're cautions and careful, you'll find a wealth of hidden away places. It's enough to keep you exploring for many winter days. Park N' Ski stickers required.

11 **Pebble Creek Ski Area**—*Alpine ski area. Alpine, Nordic downhill and snowboarding. Rentals and instruction.* Pebble Creek Ski Area is reached by driving to Inkom, just south of Pocatello. Follow the old Highway 30 south under I-15 and follow signs to the area.

Among Idaho skiing circles, it's often said that if you can ski at Pebble Creek you can ski anywhere. Pebble's reputation comes from a quirk of geography. The ski area is situated on the west slope of the Portneuf Range which makes it a short drive from Pocatello, but the west slope is steeper than the more moderate east slope. Considering what it has to work with, though, Pebble Creek has done a superb job making the area accessible to all skiers. A lower chair services a nice beginning area and a mid-level triple chair accesses intermediate slopes, while the remaining chair drops skiers above the steeper upper slopes.

315

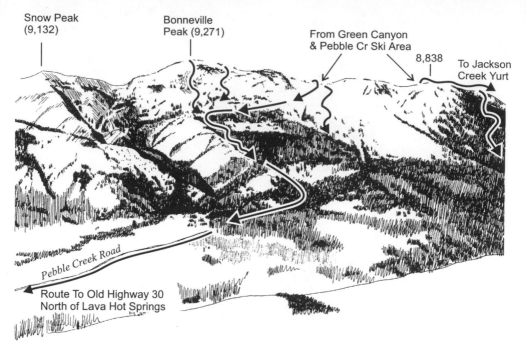

Snow Peak
(9,132)

Bonneville
Peak (9,271)

From Green Canyon
& Pebble Cr Ski Area

8,838

To Jackson
Creek Yurt

Pebble Creek Road

Route To Old Highway 30
North of Lava Hot Springs

Aerial illustration of the east side of Bonneville Peak.

Pebble Creek is one of Idaho's most progressive areas. Unlike some ski areas in the region, it has always welcomed Nordic skiers on its slopes and has never restricted access to the backcountry. It was one of the early supporters of handicapped skiing and offers many school and community programs. As you can imagine with that sort of background, Pebble Creek is a friendly and personable place to spend time skiing and boarding.

At this writing, Pebble Creek has 3 chairs, 24 runs and a vertical drop of 2,000 feet (610 meters). It has plans to build a new chairlift to the top and eventually access the moderate and powder-prone slopes on the east side of the mountain. It has a lodge with food service, instruction and rentals.

12 **Bonneville Peak-Pebble Creek Backcountry**—*Access via ski lift. Off-trail backcountry. Moderately difficult backcountry skiing or snowboarding. See aerial illustration.* Sometime in the future, the Pebble Creek Ski Area hopes to build lifts to the top and access the great powder slopes on the east face of Bonneville Peak, but until then, the backside is a backcountry skier's paradise.

Backcountry skiers and boarders normally access the Mt. Bonneville Ridge, above the ski area, by starting from the top of the **Upper Green** ski run which is on the northern most edge of the ski area. From there, either skin up to the Upper Green saddle which provides access to the east face of Mt. Bonneville, or make a long traverse to the north to point 8,838 (on the *Bonneville Peak* topographic map). Point 8,838 provides access to a series of descent lines north of area.

The Jackson Creek **Yurt** can also be accessed from Point 8,838. It is a matter of following the Portneuf Range crest 1 mile to the north. The yurt is tucked away on the west side of the ridge near Inkom Pass. For location maps and more information on reserving the yurt, see *Resources* at the end of the chapter.

One of the grand old runs on the backside of Pebble Creek Ski Area starts from Upper Green Saddle and drops to the valley floor. Once in the valley, the route follows the snowbound Pebble Creek Road for 8 miles (13 km) eventually reaching Old Highway 30, at a point 9 miles north of Lava Hot Springs. The run is rarely done these days, but in past years, it invariably included a stop at a bar name Mike's (also known as Whiskey Mike's) located conveniently along the highway at the end of the run. Mike's was the scene of some wild backcountry revelry. Though Mike's is no longer there, the tour is still a fun one to do, combining downhill turning with a long flat track out. Give it a try sometime, for old times sake—and be sure to stop at Lava for a soak on the way back. The aerial illustration on the facing page shows the route.

A cautionary note. The Portneuf Crest is exposed and often gets blasted by high winds. Combined with clouds that often collect on the ridge, traveling can get nasty and sometimes impossible. Because of its close proximity to a ski area, backcountry travelers are often not very well prepared. If you ski or snowboard in the Pebble Creek backcountry, carry survival equipment, a shovel and an avalanche transceiver. The Pebble Ski patrol keeps track of avalanche conditions and they're your best source of information before you venture out.

13 **Inman Canyon**—*Snowbound road. Moderately easy. Dogs OK. Park N' Ski area.* Drive to Inkom and take Rapid Creek Road. Two miles out of Inkom, Inman Road joins Rapid Creek Road on the right. Turn up Inman Road and drive to the parking area at the end of the plowed portion of the road. This is a snowmobile parking lot, and Park N' Ski stickers are required.

The Inman tour starts from the parking area and follows the snowbound road along Inman Creek. There is some limited avalanche danger along this road, but it usually occurs during major storms or in unusually unstable conditions. The skiing is fairly **easy** on the road. Please note that snowmobiles use the road heavily, and early morning tours are recommended.

Several alternative tours are possible. At 2.5 miles from the parking area, the **South Fork of Inman Creek** joins Inman Canyon on the right (south). A tour can be made on the snowbound hiking trail. It sometimes gets a little tangled in the heavily timbered drainage, but it is a lovely, quiet hidden away place and well worth exploring.

Telemark skiers may be interested in following the snowbound Inman Road to Inman Pass, three miles from the parking area. At the top of the pass, turn left (north) and follow the ridge line. **Telemark slopes** are found all along the ridge.

 The Inman Canyon **Yurt** can also be accessed from the parking area. For reservations and detailed maps, see the *Resources* section at the end of the chapter. Park N' Ski stickers are required.

14 **Webb Canyon**—*Snowbound road. Moderately easy.* The Webb Canyon tour starts on Rapid Creek Road, approximately 1 mile beyond the Inman-Rapid Creek Road Junction. Do not drive up Webb Canyon Road. This is a private drive. Park in the plowed pulloff on the Rapid Creek Road and walk up Webb Canyon Road to where it becomes snowbound. Since the tour crosses private land, everyone's cooperation is asked in respecting the property owner's rights.

The first part of the tour is fairly **easy** following the snowbound road. The snowbound road ends 2 miles from the parked vehicles and turns into a hiking trail where difficulty increases to moderately difficult.

15 **Upper Rapid Creek**—*Snowbound road. Some off-trail skiing and snowshoeing. All abilities.* The Rapid Creek area used to be the location of a fine system of groomed trails. In 1997, however, the land went up for sale, and the trail system was moved to the Scout Mountain area. The loss of this area will be felt for many years. The rolling hills are perfect for traditional Nordic skiing. Moreover, snow conditions are more reliable here than other locations around Pocatello. In fact, during one particularly dry winter, cross-country ski races could still be held at Rapid Creek, while races in much of the rest of southern Idaho, including Sun Valley, were cancelled.

Not all is lost, however. You can still ski on the snowbound road and on some of the surrounding wheat fields and BLM lands. To get there, drive to the town of Inkom and follow Rapid Creek Road 11 miles from Inkom until reaching a "Y" in the road. The left branch of the "Y" is plowed 100 feet and ends. The right branch turns into a driveway and goes up a hill to a farm house. Park in the plowed portion of the left branch of the "Y".

The skiing or snowshoeing follows the snowbound road beyond the parking area. If not posted, there's also fine skiing on the open wheat fields in the area.

One of the Portneuf Range Yurts: after a hard day of skiing, a great place to relax—and take a nap.

The Spirit of Midnight Creek

JUST OVER THE DIVIDE from the West Fork of Mink Creek is the head of a beautiful little drainage called Midnight Creek. It's an isolated place and not often visited. On some days it can be so cold that the trees crack. Just the slightest of breezes will start a small avalanche of snow falling from heavily laden pines. As it falls, you can hear the thump, thump of snow tumbling down from branch to branch, and one last thump as it hits the ground. If you're alone, you'd swear that it almost sounded like the steps of someone walking nearby.

This was the favorite retreat of William Mullen, one the original pioneers of Pocatello. He would make regular ski trips up the West Fork and into the head of Midnight Creek. In March of 1904, Mullen and four other men started building a cabin along Midnight Creek. Working on it during their spare time, they finally completed it in July.

It didn't look like much. It was a small square-shaped cabin with roughly sawed and notched timbers. It had no door, just an irregular opening in one corner and a set of moose antlers nailed above it. But to William Mullen, the cabin was something special. "It was a favorite haunt for deer and other game," wrote Mullen. But he found there more than the game. It was a place for quiet reflection. He returned to it time after time, particularly in the winter, enjoying the lovely valley and its serenity away from the busy and growing railroad town.

Years later, an aging and frail Mullen, who could no longer make it to the cabin, recalled those delightful days of skiing along Midnight Creek. In his photo album beside an old photo of the cabin he wrote, "And often I'll think of you, empty and black, Moose antlers nailed over your door! Oh! If I should perish my ghost will come back to dwell in you cabin once more."

Mullen passed away years ago. The head of Midnight Creek remains much the same as it was in Mullen's day, quiet and peaceful, a pretty place to visit in the winter. There's something very comfortable and friendly about Midnight Creek, about the snow settled quietly among the pines, the pale green of aspen thickets, the sinuous tracks of animals on their daily forays and the thump, thump, thump of snow falling off the pines. Standing there alone taking it all in, you hope that Mullen got his wish. □

The Spirit of Midnight Creek: William Mullen.

Resources . . .

National Forest Lands in the Pocatello Area
Pocatello District of the Caribou National Forest—Office located in the Federal Building on 4th Ave. in Pocatello. Address: 250 South 4th Ave., Suite 187, Pocatello, Idaho 83201. Phone: (208) 236-7500.

Alpine Ski Area
Pebble Creek Ski Area—Address: PO Box 370, Inkom, Idaho 83245. Phone: (208) 775-4452 or (208) 775-4451 (snow report).

Educational Programs
Idaho State University Outdoor Program—Workshops and educational programs. Sponsors a variety of public educational programs including avalanche safety workshops and houses the Intermountain Regional Outdoor Resource Center. Office located in the Pond Student Union Building on the ISU campus. Address: Box 8128, Pocatello, Idaho 83209. Phone: (208) 236-3912.

Pocatello Parks and Recreation Department—The department offers classes and workshops for children and community members and supervises the maintenance and grooming of the local cross-country ski area. Address: 911 North 7th, Pocatello, Idaho 83201. Phone: (208) 234-6232.

Yurt System
For maps and reservation information on the Portneuf Range Hut System, contact: *Wilderness Rental Center*, Box 8118, Idaho State University, Pocatello, Idaho 83209. Phone: (208) 236-2945.

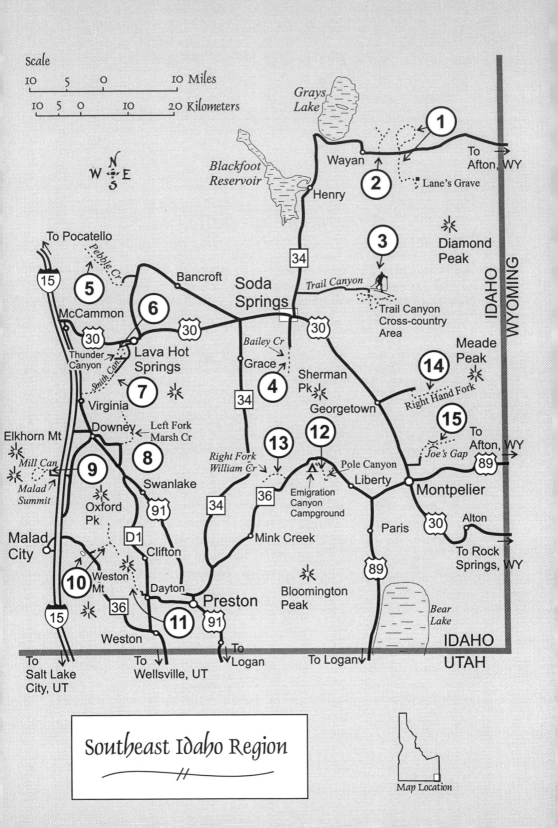

Southeast Idaho Region

CHAPTER 19
SOUTHEAST IDAHO REGION

Area Covered: Southeast Idaho including Wayan, Soda Springs, Lava Hot Springs, Downey, Malad, Preston, Montpelier and nearby towns.

SOUTHEAST IDAHO is an enigma. It is a barren country, void of trees except ragged patches of forests in drainages and on northern hillsides. Ever present, always dominating in the winter landscape are lonely miles and miles of wind crusted snow and sage. Yet there is an allure to this country, an inexplicable elegance which becomes apparent the more you spend time there. And if that time is spent in the winter, when the landscape seems as bleak as ever, you'll find hidden away within Southeast Idaho's sage covered ranges, some of the most incredible touring and backcountry skiing found anywhere.

One of those places is found near Soda Springs. Cross-country skiers along with the Caribou National Forest have created a system of trails in the Trail Creek area, a short drive to the northeast of Soda Springs. The parking lot is shared with snowmobilers, but the cross-country trail system is off-limits to machines, except the groomer. There's a little something for everyone: groomed beginner trails passing beside beaver ponds, intermediate trails through conifer forests and open slopes scattered about for practicing turns.

Thirty eight miles north of Soda Springs, is the Wayan area near the Wyoming line. Some idea of the area's propensity for snow is evidenced by the fact that road maps published in the 1970s mark the road beyond Wayan as "closed in the winter." It's open in winter now, and for traditional style cross-country skiing, the kind of skiing which is done on rolling terrain, it's a splendid area. Unfortunately, there is only one reliably plowed pulloff that is shared with snowmobilers, but because of the sparse population, snowmobile activity is light. The plowed pulloff accesses an easy tour which leads skiers on a part of the Oregon Trail, near the grave of Lane, a pioneer who perished on his way to Oregon.

Southeast Idaho's best access to high snow-country is the Idaho 36 highway as it passes through the Emigration-Strawberry Canyons between Montpelier and Preston. Skiing, snowboarding and snowshoeing in this area are some of the best in the entire region. Snow piles high here. I've seen almost as much snow in Emigration Canyon as along the Teton Pass road. The highway department has gone the extra mile for winter recreationalists and plows at least 10 pullouts along this stretch of highway. Skiers of all abilities, from the beginner to the backcountry devotee, will find something to their liking. Because of its opportunities for off-trail travel, splendid open hillsides and exceptionally good snow conditions, the area is rapidly becoming popular among northern Utah and Southeast Idaho skiers.

In the spring time when Forest Service roads become passable, backcountry skiing becomes even more interesting. Two mountains with appealing spring snow fields for snowboarding and skiing descents are Elkhorn and Oxford Peaks which rise above Interstate 15 just north of Malad. Both can be accessed from the freeway frontage road. South of Soda Springs, there's Sherman Peak which is reached by driving up Eightmile Canyon road. The granddaddy of Southeast Idaho mountains is Mead Peak, the highest point, and it is accessed off of the Georgetown Canyon road east of Georgetown. There's more, of course, beautiful, little tucked away gems among all that . . . yes, all that boring sagebrush countryside.

The Tales . . .

*W*HEN I WAS WORKING on the first version of this book, I made a couple of trips during the fall to potential skiing sites in Southeast Idaho before the snow fell. A good friend of mine, Jeff Smith, came along on one of those trips.

Everyone calls him Barefoot. In fact, to this day, he is known as Barefoot. He hates shoes and only wears them when he has to. Barefoot was and is a good mechanic, and was helping me get my '64 Volkswagen Bug ready for the trip.

I was inside on the front seat while Barefoot was outside. For some reason I had placed my foot against the windshield. I don't remember why or what I was repairing. I needed leverage and since there's not a whole lot of room in the front seat of a Bug, the windshield seemed the best place for my foot. I gave the windshield a push, just a little push, hardly a push at all as I remember it.

All of sudden there was no resistance against my foot and the whole windshield was falling and then crashing against the front hood. Jeff ambled over in his bare feet, inspected it and shook his head. It was shattered and not usable. The day, however, was beautiful, and we took off anyway, driving out of town, without the windshield.

It turned out to be a wonderful trip, cruising the backroads of Southeast Idaho and exploring new places that might make delightful places to ski when winter would come later that year. But what made it more memorable was the lack of a windshield. It was like being transported back in time to the Model T days and a whole new simpler time and world.

We drove slowly, could smell the sage and pines and saw things we'd never seen before. We waved at nearly every car that passed us and everything seemed to be fresh and clear.

The only downside was the bugs, which seemed to be particularly plentiful on that warm fall day. A couple hours into the trip, an assortment of flies and moths were buzzing around inside the car. To Jeff's annoyance, a large number of them tried taking refuge in and around his bare feet and every so often he would briskly rub his feet together and stomp them in a sort of vastly accelerated Western two-step. On the way back, we stopped a couple of times to clean bugs off our sunglasses and spit out those that had collected on our teeth.

I didn't see Barefoot for quite a while, and, it was a longer time after that before he joined me again for another trip. As I remember it, when he showed up at my house for that next trip, he was wearing goggles and tennis shoes. ☐

The Trails . . .

WAYAN AREA

The small town of Wayan (actually it's just a couple of houses) in Southeast Idaho is located 38 miles (61 km) north of Soda Springs on Idaho 34. Just east of Wayan lies a country which, in the winter, is covered by a deep layer of snow. There is only one reliably plowed pulloff which is the starting point for the Lane's Grave Tour.

1

Lane's Grave Tour—*Snowbound roads or off-trail. Moderately easy. Dogs OK. Snowshoeing.* To find the beginning of the tour, start at the Historical Marker in Wayan. Drive 6.4 miles east on Idaho 34 towards Freedom, Wyoming. The pulloff is plowed on the right (south) side of the highway. You have two choices here. One is to follow the snowbound road which starts from the pulloff and leads south. The tour follows roads to the Lane's Grave area. On weekends you may encounter snowmobiles along the roads. The other choice is to cross the highway and ski across the open hilly country to the north. There is no particular route to follow. It's open, rolling country interspersed with aspen groves and plenty of hillsides for practicing **telemarks**. This is probably the best direction if you are snowshoeing.

If you are interested in a tour with some historical significance, the Lane's Grave trip follows the snowbound road leading from the pulloff to the south through an open, sagebrush valley. At 3 miles (5 km) from Idaho 34, another snowbound road leads to the left (east) past a corral and a few scattered, decaying buildings. This road sits on what once was once the Oregon Trail. Unfortunately, no trespassing signs have recently blocked access, but immediately east of the old buildings lies a small fenced-in square area, looking much like a miniature, white painted corral. Within the fence is the grave of Lane, for whom the Oregon Trail emigrants named Lane's Valley and Lane Creek.

There was some controversy surrounding who Lane was, but Peter Harsted, in his authoritative work, *Constructing the Lander Trail*, cleared the matter with this account from Joel Barnett, one of the emigrants accompanying Lane:

> Two or three days after we had layed over, we came to another little valley and camped, and at this camp, Mr. Lane passed away. This cast a great sadness over the camp as he was a fine old man and it was a sad procession that marched up to that grave. We marked it as best we could by putting up a rather flat stone on which we put his name. This was the first grave we had made since leaving home. We named this camp Lane's Valley. [The headstone read: July 18, 1859 J. W. Lane]

Oregon Trail country: Wayan area near Lane's Grave.

2 **Aspen Tour.** *Snowbound road and off-trail. Easy, gradual terrain. Parking may not be available. Dogs OK. Snowshoeing.* One other suggested tour in the Wayan area follows a snowbound road through **rolling terrain** covered with aspens and scattered pines. Unfortunately, this does not have regularly plowed access, so it is one that you may have to save until spring when the snowbanks along the highway have melted back sufficiently for parking. The beginning of this lovely tour is located on the north side of Idaho 34, just slightly less than 4 miles east of Wayan. The route follows the snowbound road to the north and is suitable for beginners.

SODA SPRINGS AREA

3 **Trail Canyon**—*Marked and groomed cross-country ski trails. All abilities. Toilets. Park N' Ski area. Snowboarding on the way to Trail Canyon.* The trails in this area are designed specifically for cross-country skiing. The parking lot, toilets and warming hut at the trailhead are shared with snowmobilers, but the ski trails are off-limits to mechanized vehicles. This is a wonderful area with good snow coverage and a variety of ski terrain. **Beginners** will enjoy the short jaunts out to a beaver pond which is the source of Trail Creek. **Intermediate** skiers

327

will enjoy the loop tour with open hillsides and ridge lines for practicing turns. At this writing, there are five different loop trails varying in lengths from a .5 mile to 5 miles (1 to 8 km). The ski trails are groomed.

To get to Trail Canyon, start at the intersection of US 30 and Idaho 34 in Soda Springs. Drive 3 miles to the north on Idaho 34. Look for Trail Canyon Road, turning off to the right (east). About 5 miles down Trail Canyon Road, you'll see some nice hillsides close to the road which are ideal for short **telemark** and **snowboard** runs. If you're planning to go to the cross-country ski area, keep driving another 3 more miles until the plowed portion of the road ends at a parking area. Park and Ski stickers are required here.

4 **Bailey Creek**—*Snowbound road. Moderately easy. Snowshoeing.* The start of this tour is reached by turning at the intersection of US 30 and Idaho 34 in Soda Springs on Bailey Creek Road. At 4.4 miles from the intersection, the road Y's. Take the right fork and drive through the Bailey Creek Housing Development to its southern edge where you'll find a school bus turnaround area. Park back a distance so that you are out of way of any school buses. The tour follows the snowbound Bailey Creek Road onto Forest Service lands just beyond the plowed portion of the road. The first part of the trip is suitable for **beginners** with intermediate difficulty thereafter.

LAVA HOT SPRINGS AREA

5

Pebble Creek—*Snowbound road. Flat, easy terrain. Dogs OK.* Located 9 miles north of Lava Hot Springs on Old Highway 30. A sign on the west side of the highway indicates Pebble Creek. Drive to the point where Pebble Creek Road is no longer plowed.

The tour follows the snowbound Pebble Creek Road. It is an excellent basic **beginner's** tour with flat terrain for many miles. Note that this is a groomed snowmobile trail, and touring is recommended on weekdays or early in the morning on weekends.

6

Thunder Canyon Cross-country Trails—*Cross-country ski trails. Easy, rolling terrain.* The Lava Hot Springs Nordic Group maintains a system of trails at Lava's golf course, Thunder Canyon. To reach the golf course, drive west on West Main Street and turn left on South 4th West Street which turns into Dempsey Creek Road. Follow Dempsey Creek Road for about 2 miles. Near the Intersection of Dempsey Creek and Merrick Roads, you'll see the Golf Course club house off to the right. Park off the road. The ski trails start from the club house.

The terrain is **rolling** and suited for families or those who want to catch a workout. At the current time, the trails are not groomed, but are usually skied in. Afterwards, treat yourself to a dip in Lava Hot Springs.

7

Smith Canyon—*Snowbound road. Moderately easy. Dogs OK.* The Smith Canyon area gets considerable snowmobile use on weekends, so you may want to plan this one for a week day. It is reached by driving out Dempsey Creek Road beyond the Golf Course where the Thunder Canyon Cross-country trails are located (see description above). From the Dempsey Creek and Merrick Road junction, continue following Dempsey Creek Road for 1.2 miles until reaching Smith Canyon Road, coming in from the right. More houses are being built in the area, and it is likely that the Smith Canyon Road will be plowed all the way to the divide, 3.6 miles from the Dempsey Creek Road.

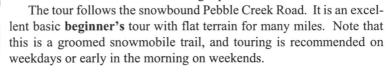

From the divide, you can ski or snowshoe on the snowbound Smith Canyon Road to the southwest. It is a **moderately easy** tour, but be careful to pace yourself since the road heads downhill and at some point you'll need to turn around and climb back up. Ambitious skiers looking for a workout may want take a long **descending** road tour to **Virginia**. This 10-mile tour requires a shuttle vehicle to be left at the Smith Canyon Road, 1.4 miles north of Virginia and the I-15 interchange.

Smith Canyon Road also provides access to snowbound side roads. Two major spur roads, leading to the east and west, are found in the vicinity of a small lake before reaching the top of the pass. Although the snowbound roads are heavily used by snowmobiles, they can be used to reach open, telemarking slopes.

DOWNEY AREA

8

Left Fork of Marsh Creek—*Snowbound road. Moderately easy. Dogs OK. Snowshoeing.* To locate the beginning of this tour, start at the intersection of the Main and Center streets in the town of Downey. Drive east on Center until reaching the airport .7 mile from town. At the airport, the road comes to a "T." Take a right here. Follow this road 4.8 miles from the airport until it takes a sharp bend to the right, leading to a group of farm houses called Grant's Ward. At the bend, a road, Left Fork of Marsh Creek, continues straight. It may be possible to drive up Left Fork Road for a short distance, depending on the snow conditions.

The tour follows the snowbound Left Fork Road. Remaining high above the Marsh Creek drainage for the first couple of miles, the tour passes through wheat fields and open sagebrush country. Two miles (3 km) from the start, Left Fork Road descends into the Left Fork Canyon and continues weaving back and forth as it works its away up the drainage. The canyon, with junipers decorating its sides and maples and birch clustered near the stream, makes for delightful and beautiful skiing. There are a few moderate climbs, but beyond these short grades, beginners and experienced skiers, alike, will enjoy touring in the area. Plan to take a full day for this tour since it involves skiing 2 miles (3 km) through open country before reaching the canyon.

MALAD AREA

9

Malad Pass (Mill Canyon)—*Snowbound road. Easy to moderately difficult. Dogs OK.* Mill Canyon is located on the top of Malad Summit north of Malad just off Interstate 15. Take the old highway to the top of the pass by exiting off Interstate 15 at either the Downey or Devil Creek Reservoir exits.

From the top of the pass, turn west, drive across the bridge over the interstate and follow the road until it is no longer plowed. From the end of the plowed road, ski or snowshoe on the snowbound road to Summit Campground. Depending on where the county stops plowing the road it should be around .5 mile to the campground. The tour to the campground and in the general area is suitable for **beginners**. Beyond this point, however, the skiing difficulty increases.

A **moderately difficult** tour, and a good trip for snowshoers is to make the loop tour from the end of the snowbound road, following the hiking trail to the south into South Canyon. South Canyon is then descended until rejoining the Mill Creek Road near the Caribou National

Forest boundary. Total length of the tour is approximately 9 miles (14 to 15 km). This area also provides backcountry skiing and snowboard access to Elkhorn Mountain, the mountain rising above Mill Creek. Snowmobilers use the area.

10 **Deep Creek-Weston Creek Area**—*Off-trail or snowbound road. Easy to moderately easy. Dogs OK.* The Deep Creek-Weston area on Idaho 36 between Malad and Weston is another one of those unexpected snow zones. The ground in Malad will often be dry, but plenty of snow awaits the skier or snowshoer just a few miles away. The **sportsman's access** at **Deep Creek Reservoir**, 4.4 miles south of the I-15 and Idaho 36 interchange, north of Malad City is a nice place for **easy** ski touring or snowshoeing on the open country around the reservoir. Plus, if you have any ice fisherman in the group, they can fish at the reservoir.

Additionally, for a longer tour, you might try **Third Creek**. It's a snowmobile area, and you'll want to catch it during the week. The developed parking area is located 1.2 miles south of the Sportsman's Access. Turn and head east on 300 North. Follow it to the end of the plowed road. Follow the snowbound road along Third Creek. For backcountry skiers, it provides access to the long South Ridge of **Oxford Peak** which has outstanding **telemark** slopes.

11 **Weston Mountain**—*Snowbound road. Moderately difficult. Dogs OK.* Access to Weston Mountain, a moderately difficult touring area, is located in the town of Dayton, a few miles west of Preston. A road, .3 mile (.5 km) north of the school in Dayton, leads west and is marked with a Forest Service sign indicating Weston Mountain. Drive until this road is no longer plowed.

The tour follows the snowbound road which veers off to the left (west), directly towards the mountains. Often the snow is shallow and the skiing is scratchy on the first part of the trail. It leads up through a narrow rocky canyon and then breaks out of the canyon onto a ridge. The snowbound road eventually turns into a trail that crosses the heads of several creeks and eventually passes to the west side of Weston Mountain approximately 8 miles (13 km) from the start. Snowmobilers use the road.

PRESTON AREA

12 **Strawberry and Emigration Canyon Area**—*Snowbound roads or off-trail. All abilities. Telemarking slopes. Snowboarding. Snowshoeing. Dogs OK.* Idaho 36 between Mink Creek and Liberty passes through

Strawberry and Emigration Canyons. This is a wonderful stretch of highway through a high snow region with many pulloffs to choose from.

One suggested area for some easy touring is the **Emigration Canyon Campground**. Park at the plowed pulloff located on the south side of the highway 6.8 miles east of the LDS Church in Liberty. The tour follows the snowbound road west into the campground about .3 mile from the highway. Although it's not very far, the terrain around the campground is gradual and a fun place for families to tour around. For

a moderately difficult tour, climb the ridge to the southeast of the campground and continue to the southeast, connecting with a trail which leads to a divide between Emigration Canyon and Copenhagen Canyon, 2 miles from the highway. From the divide a **descending tour** can

be made down **Pole Canyon**, coming out close to the plowed parking at the chain-up area 4.4 miles west of Liberty. The total distance of the descending tour into Pole Canyon is 5 miles. If you don't have a shuttle

vehicle, you may just enjoy hanging out in the divide and cutting tellys on the nice slopes in the area.

    Snowmobilers tend to concentrate in an area about 10 miles west of

13 Liberty. At 12 miles from Liberty, a pulloff is plowed on the north side of Idaho 36 near where a power line crosses. Behind the pulloff are some short hills which are used by **snowboarders**. Skiers and snowshoers may also be interested in this area since a trip can be taken up the snowbound road which leads north from the parking area. The snowbound road is moderately easy and follows the **Right Fork of Williams Creek**.

MONTPELIER AREA

14 **Right Hand Fork of Georgetown Canyon**—*Snowbound road. Moderately easy. Snowshoeing.* The Right Hand Fork of Georgetown is reached by driving from the city of Georgetown eastward on Georgetown Canyon Road. Check your odometer at US 30 in Georgetown. Stay on the main Georgetown road and drive 3.3 miles from US 30 in Georgetown. Park here. At this point the Right Hand Fork leads off to the south. A landmark which is helpful in locating the Right Fork is a small concrete dam on Georgetown Creek just after the confluence of the Right Fork and Georgetown Creek.

The tour follows Right Hand Fork Road (initially to the south and then to the east) through an interesting narrow canyon. In its journey along the creek, the snowbound road makes several crossings back and forth over the creek. Early in the tour, you'll find some nice open slopes for practicing **telemarks**.

A large beaver dam blocks the creek 2.5 miles (4 km) from the parking area. Just before the beaver dam, a steep, snowbound jeep trail leads up the ridge on the left (north). From this junction, it is only a .5 mile (.8 km) **moderately difficult** climb to a small saddle on the ridge. The climb, however, is steep, and traversing back and forth is necessary.

From the ridge, you'll have a good view down towards the main Georgetown Canyon and up the Right Hand Fork. Some nice ridge skiing is available at this point, not to mention the great downhill ski run back into Right Hand Fork.

Skiers or snowshoers of **all abilities** should enjoy touring in this area. For an easygoing trip, the tour along the Right Hand Fork is pleasant and enjoyable. For moderately difficult skiing and snowshoeing, you can climb and travel along the ridge. And for the backcountry skier, the Right Hand Fork provides access to Meade Peak, the highest point in Southeast Idaho. Snowmobiles use is light to nonexistent.

15 **Joe's Gap**—*Snowbound road. Easy to the gap, moderately difficult thereafter. Snowshoeing. Dogs OK.* To get to the beginning of the Joe's Gap tour, start in Montpelier at the Oregon Trail Center (at the Junction of US 89 and US 30). Drive 2.2 miles to the north on US 30 and turn right (east) just before a truck stop. Drive back until the road is no longer plowed.

The tour follows the snowbound Joe's Gap Road first through open fields and sagebrush country and then into a canyon. Joe's Gap, a narrow cut through a large, sage-covered hill, is difficult to see until you're almost on top of it. This first section of the tour is suitable for **beginners**.

The snowbound road turns into a trail at the gap, and it is a fun trip through narrow, confining walls of the canyon, but the skiing or snowshoeing becomes more difficult. At this point, the trail turns into a **moderately difficult** tour. At the eastern end of the gap, a broad hidden canyon is entered. Here, the trail climbs moderately through some aspens and a beautiful row of mountain mahogany, forming an archway over the trail.

Resources . . .

National Forest Lands Throughout the Region
Supervisor's Headquarters of the Caribou National Forest—Address: Federal Building, Suite 294, Pocatello, Idaho 83201. Phone: (208) 236-7500.

National Forest Lands in Malad and Weston Mountain Areas
Malad Ranger District—Address: 75 South 140 East, PO Box 142, Malad, Idaho 83252. Phone: (208) 766-4743.

National Forest Lands in the Joe's Gap, Bailey Creek and Strawberry-Emigration Canyon Areas
Montpelier Ranger District—Address: 431 Clay, Montpelier, Idaho 83254. Phone: (208) 847-0375.

National Forest Lands in the Trail Canyon and Wayan Area
Soda Springs Ranger District—Address: 421 West 2nd South, Soda Springs, Idaho 83276. Phone: (208) 547-4356.

ACKNOWLEDGMENTS

Early in this project, I realized that no one person could write a book about skiing and snowshoeing in an area as vast and diverse as the area covered within these pages. I would need help—and lots of it. Fortunately, help was forthcoming. Many people throughout the state of Idaho and neighboring Wyoming and Montana freely gave of their time to help on this project, showing me trails, inviting me along on backcountry trips, sharing stories and providing warm places for me to throw my sleeping bag. This book is the compilation of their wisdom and experiences, and I am eternally indebted to their generosity.

I am particularly indebted to those who assisted in the research for the first version of the book including Dave Arcano who helped me pour through reels of microfilm of old Idaho newspapers and who was always willing to put down what he was doing to join me on a ski trip; Hugh Cooke, the previous director of the McCall Recreation Department, who provided invaluable assistance in the McCall area, and who, on many occasions, offered his home as a stopover place on my frequent forays to North Idaho; Rick Freudenthal who also helped with research in the McCall area and provided updated information for the revised version; Larry Jones who explored southeast Idaho and whose maps were of immense help when we were preparing the second version; Tom Amberson, an Idaho Falls native who passed detailed information on his backyard ski haunts; Bill Wilkerson, an outdoor store owner who helped with the Sandpoint area; and writer and guide, Dave Peterson who assisted with the Moscow area.

A number of individuals were particularly helpful when I was working on the revised edition, and I would like to mention of a few of those. A special thanks is due to my good friend and master gardener Tawna Skinner who for many years has been a guiding force behind the Salmon Nordic Association. Backcountry aficionado, Gene Klein was tremendously generous with ski and snowboard information in the Sandpoint area. He was kind enough to send me a selection of his photographs, a number of which grace the pages of this book.

Dave Hayes took off a Saturday to show me around the outstanding trail system at Fish Creek Meadows area near Grangeville. I first had skied in the area with Jim and Nan Flannigan in the mid 1970s, and I was delighted to see the tremendous progress that has been made since then. Another individual who deserves to be singled out is Mike Beiser who is director of the University of Idaho Outdoor Program. Before I arrived, he had studied the first version of the book and was prepared with updated material and photographs. Mike's support and enthusiasm for the project revitalized me and carried me through the next several weeks of research. In Idaho City, Terry Sexton of the Boise National Forest took time during a busy budgeting week to review the text and make suggestions. Also helping with Idaho City and Boise area trails was Leo Hennessy, who has done a wonderful job commanding Idaho's Park N' Ski program. Leo and trail grooming coordinator, Jack Long, supplied me with photographs which are included in the book.

Mary Austin Crofts, Executive Director of the Blaine County Recreation District, was another person who made time for me in a busy schedule. She provided an overview of the remarkable transformation that Nordic skiing has undergone in the Ketchum-Sun Valley area. A special thanks is due to Tom Downey of Galena Lodge who marked the Galena ski and snowshoe system on the aerial illustration. Speaking of aerial illustrations, I would be remiss not to recognize and thank Mark Sibley. Mark is one of the finest pen-and-ink, landscape artists in the Intermountain West, and his beautiful renditions of aerial photographs have added richly to the book .

The limitations of space prevent me from detailing the contributions of the many other people who were a part of this effort. Though inadequate and formal as it may be, I have listed below all those who have provided information or assisted in some manner on either the first or revised versions of this book. Although some of those listed below have passed away, I hope this book preserves a little of their memory through their stories and winter experiences. I also realize that a number of those who were involved in the original version have relocated, but I have kept their names associated with the regional area on which they originally helped. To one and all, I owe my sincere thanks and heartfelt gratitude.

Sandpoint-Bonners Ferry Region: Marc DeLaVegne, Rob Keene, Russ Keene, Chuck and Berneice Morgen, Bill Straley, Bob Norton, Bryan Rowder and Dave Russell. *Priest Lake Region*: Richard Carlson, Larry Townsend, Chuck Troxal and Debbie Wilkins. *Coeur d'Alene-Moscow Region*: Mark Beattie, Clyde Blake, Ray Brooks, Buzz Durham, Austin Heimers, Evelyn Huender, Jerry Johnson, Steve Kirby, Kim Leatham, Tony Leatham, John Owen, Edith Partridge, Jim Rennie, Ellen Spano and Ken and Ginger Wright. *Lewiston-Grangeville-Lolo Pass Region*: Al Banta, John Barker, Clarence Binninger, Jim and Nan Flannigan, Stu Hoyt, Faith Kenney, John Larson and Wayne Wright. *McCall Region*: Mike Busby, Jerry Dixon, Kathy Eastman, Ron and Jill Frye, Cliff Lee and Art Troutner. *Boise Region*: Dwight Allen, Charley Crist, Lou and Frank Florence, Ed Groomer, Harold Hafterson, Belle Hefner, Laurie Fink, Ken Horwitz, Ed Jagels, Bob Krumm, Charley Lindquist, Mr. and Mrs. Guy McAdams, Tom Naylor, Don Reed, Sue Stacy and Dave Thompson. *Sawtooth Region*: Kirk Bachman, Dave Lee, Joe Leonard and Jack Seagraves. *Sun Valley-Ketchum Region*: George Castle, Brent Demer, Tom Downey, Ken Dickens, Dale Gelsky, Dan Hamilton, Butch Harper, Willi Helming, Andy Hennig, Charley Johnson, Rob Kiesel, Peanut McCoy, Petra Morrison, Leif Odmark, Bob Rosso, Frank Rowland, Louis Stur and Chuck and Judy Webb. *Salmon Region*: Frank Daniels, Grant Havemann and Jennie Smith. *High Desert Mosaic*: Dave Markham, Rob

Burks and Dave Clark. *Yellowstone-Island Park Region*: Tod Cameron, Carl and Kent Swanson, Ron Dent, Bud McCray, Mary McGraw, "Nick" Nichols, Thea Nordling and Robert Wuthrich. *Teton National Park-East Idaho Region*: Stuart Carpenter, Geno Foresyth, Wayne Foltz, Marty Huebner, Susan Marsh, Rod Newcomb, Bert Porter, Bill Radtke, Cyril Slansky and Mark Sibley. *Pocatello and Southeast Regions*: Blaine Gasser; Ray Hunter, Margret McMahon and Al Taylor.

My appreciation and gratitude is extended to hard working staff members of the following National Forests, Ranger Districts and parks who took time to respond to my letters and met with me during research trips: Ashton Ranger District, Boise National Forest, Bridger-Teton National Forest, Caribou National Forest, Clearwater National Forest, Coeur d'Alene District of the Bureau of Land Management, Craters of the Moon National Monument, Farragut State Park, Fields Spring State Park, Grand Teton National Park, Hebgen Ranger District, Idaho City Ranger District, Island Park Ranger District, Ketchum Ranger District, Lower Snake District of the Bureau of Land Management, Lowman Ranger District, Nezperce National Forest, Panhandle National Forest, Palisades Ranger District, Ponderosa State Park, Priest Lake State Park, Round Lake State Park, Sawtooth National Forest, Sawtooth National Recreation Area, Targhee National Forest, Teton Basin Ranger District, Wallowa-Whitman National Forest, Winchester State Park and Yellowstone National Park.

A special thanks to Lloyd Furniss and Susan Duncan who helped with photographic restorations; to Gary Bills and Doug Wood, two very capable pilots who flew me about for aerial photo shots; to Darcie Bush, Carlene Paarmann and Linda Hernadez who helped with typing; and to Patti Dove, Le'Ann McGowan, Linda Stalley and my mother, Phyllis Watters who helped edit the first version of the book—and who suggested the original title. I want to acknowledge the able assistance provided to me by staffs of the Idaho Historical Society, Idaho State Library, the Sierra Club Library, Idaho State University Library, and the Yellowstone Natural History Association.

I am very grateful to the Idaho State University Faculty Research Committee which approved a research grant which enabled me to continue work on the first version of the book. It came just at the right time since my personal resources allocated to the project were running low. Earl Pond, H. Hilbert and Ernie Natzger, my supervisors at Idaho State University, were kind enough to allow me time off to work on the first version, as were Greg Anderson and Dr. Jan Anderson when I was working on the most recent version.

A very special thanks is tendered to Michelle Hiatt who proofread an early version of the manuscript, to Alex Tallant who put all else aside and did a wonderful job of editing and scouring the final typeset copy for mistakes, and to Dori Glennon who gave the book a final proof—and who looks terrific on the cover with the Tetons in the background. Finally, all of this would not be possible without the support, love and editing skills of my wife and backcountry ski companion, Kathy.

SOURCE NOTES

CHAPTER 1: THE LONG SNOWSHOE

13 Restless with the coming of spring: W. A. Goulder, *Reminiscences of a Pioneer* (Boise: Timothy Regan, 1909) p. 203; and Robert Bailey, River of No Return (Lewiston, Idaho: R. G. Bailey Printing Co., 1947), p. 149. Both Goulder and Bailey use the term "snowshoes" to refer to I. C. Smith mode of transportation. It is obvious from Goulder's descriptions of snowshoeing that he is referring to skiing. The usage is further substantiated by E. D. Pierce's description of a "snowshoeing" event in *The Pierce Chronicle*, ed. J. Gary Williams and Ronald W. Stark (Moscow, Idaho: Idaho Research Foundation, 1975).

14 "the winter of 1861-62 ultimately proved to be one of the coldest": Alfreda M. Elsensohn, *Pioneer Days in Idaho County* (Cottonwood, Idaho: The Idaho Corporation of Benedictine Sisters, 1965), I, p. 49.

14 For William Armistead Goulder: This and all other unattributed material about the winter of 1861-62 in the Orofino camp are from Goulder, *Reminiscences*, pp. 218-242.

19 I've found only one written reference: E. Hough, "The Account of Howell's Capture," *Forest and Stream*, May 5, 1894, p. 377.

19 "I used long snowshoes": Elwood Hofer, "Winter in Wonderland: Through The Yellowstone Park on Snowshoes," *Forest and Stream*, April 7, 1887, p. 222.

19 Alta Grete Chadwick in her book: Alta Grete Chadwick, *Tales of Silver City* (Boise, Idaho: Boise Printing Co., nd.), p. 87.

19 In Atlanta, it was the town carpenter: Betty Penson, "Pioneers' Rustic Skis: Magic Feet for Winter," *The Idaho Statesman*, December 13, 1979, p. 1C.

19 "He made many, many skis": Personal interview with A. C. "Nick" Nichols, Ashton, Idaho, March 14, 1977.

19 George Castle, Roy McCoy's nephew: Personal interview with George Castle, Horseshoe Bend, Idaho, February 27, 1977.

20 "The chair had to be turned": Personal interview with Frank Daniels, Salmon, Idaho, April 26, 1976.

20 Laces were employed: Nichols interview.

21 a one to two foot long cylinder of canvas: Personal interview with Jack Seagraves, Twin Falls, Idaho, January 29, 1978.

21 "One shoe stuck perpendicular": *Owyhee Avalanche*, December 23, 1865.

21 "Measuring from the front end": Hofer, p. 222.

22 "the little tuff left on an old broom": Personal interview with Al Taylor, Pocatello, Idaho, January 18, 1978.

22   "I remember Clarence Neihart": Telephone interview with Frank Daniels, January 17, 1978.

22   "heavy wool underwear": E. Hough, "Yellowstone Park Game Exploration," *Forest and Stream,* June 9, 1894, p. 487.

22   "Look out for us": *Idaho World*, December 5, 1879.

24   "To us they were not skis": Chadwick, *Tales of Silver City*, p. 47.

24   "All through the Idaho mountains": Thomas C. Donaldson, *Idaho of Yesterday* (Caldwell, Idaho: Caxton Printers, 1941; reissued, Westport, CT: Greenwood Press, 1970), p. 83.

24   "They had to use them": Personal Interview with Ed Groomer, Emmett, Idaho, February 27, 1977.

24   "We are at the present time snowed in": "Alturas Items," (letter from Atlanta, January 7, 1880), *Idaho World*, January 20, 1880.

25   "I feel sorry for people": *Idaho World*, February 22, 1883.

25   "Before going fifty feet": *Idaho World*, December 23, 1881.

26   "The snow fell so deep": Alonzo Brown, The *Autobiography of Alonzo F. Brown,* np., Los Angeles, 1922 , p. 43.

26   "was the fastest speed": Penson, "Pioneers' Rustic Skis."

27   "She sticks 'em like a California rider": "Items from Banner," January 7, 1882, *Idaho World*, January 13, 1882.

27   Ann Sullivan, a waitress at the boarding house: Pearl Eva Barber, *The Galloping Ghosts of Galena* (Boise: Capitol Lithograph & Printing Co., 1962), pp. 62-64.

27   One group of women in Bellevue: *Owyhee Avalanche*, December 30, 1865.

CHAPTER 2: POACHERS, LAWMAKERS AND THE GLORY DAYS

29   Felix Burgess stood on his skis: This and subsequent quotes concerning the capture of Howell come from E. Hough, "The Account of Howell's Capture," *Forest and Stream*, May 5, 1894, pp. 877-878.

31   Paul Schullery in his book: Paul Schullery, *Yellowstone's Ski Pioneers: Peril and Heroism on the Winter Trail* (Worland, WY: High Plain Publishing Co., 1995), p. 13.

31   "When the snow falls and the fierce winter storms begin": W.E. Strong, *A Trip to the Yellowstone National Park in July, August, and September*, 1875, Richard A. Barlett, ed. (Norman: University of Oklahoma Press, 1968), Vol. 39 of the Western Frontier Library Series, pp. 104-105.

31   Lieutenant Schwatka's expedition in Yellowstone: Aubrey L. Haines, *The Yellowstone Story*, (Yellowstone National Park: Yellowstone Library, 1977), II, pp. 8-11; and Elwood Hofer, "Winter in Wonderland: Through the Yellowstone Park on Snowshoes," *Forest and Stream*, April 14, 1887, p. 246.

32   In the late 1800s, they could sell: Schullery, *Yellowstone's Ski Pioneers*, p. 112.

32   A Swede by the name of Whistling Anderson: Anecdotal material on Whistling Anderson is from Vardis Fisher, ed. *Idaho Lore* (Caldwell, Idaho: Caxton Printers, 1939), pp. 73-74.

36   "travelers are still compelled to foot it": *Idaho World*, February 8, 1881.

37   "When Bill finally received the letter," G. E. Shoup, *History of Lemhi County* (Boise: Idaho State Library, 1969), p. 6. [Originally published in the Salmon Recorder Herald May 8 to October 23, 1940]; and Kirkpatrick, Orion, *History of Leesburg Pioneers* (Salt Lake City: Pyramid Press, 1934). p. 92.

37   "Messrs. J. C. Fox and George Perody arrived here": *Idaho World*, March 19, 1880.

37   George Shearer used skis to travel: Sister M. Alfreda Elsensohn, *Pioneer Days in Idaho County*, (Cottonwood, Idaho: The Idaho Corporation of Benedictine Sisters, 1978), II, pp. 446-447.

38   Thomas Elder has the distance record: Shoup, *History of Lemhi County*, p. 16.

38   "Hailey lost about one-half of her male population": *Wood River Times*, January 4, 1882.

38   Two lovers living in Vienna: *Ketchum Keystone*, February 26, 1887.

CHAPTER 3: THE MAIL CARRIERS . . . HEROES OF THE LONG SNOWSHOE

41   "The Banner mail carrier": *Idaho World*, December 7, 1883.

41   "treasures richer than any mines": W. A. Goulder, *Reminiscences of a Pioneer* (Boise: Timothy Regan, 1909) p. 216.

42   "A crowd left here on Tuesday": *Idaho World*, December 31, 1881.

43   "Charley Magee, the indefatigable mail carrier": *Idaho World*, March 3, 1882.

43   It was also reliance upon horses: *Idaho World*, December 12, 1879.

44   In April, the *Idaho World* carried information on his progress: *Idaho World*, April 9, 1880.

44   One of the more bizarre tales of mail carrying: *Idaho World*, March 28, 1883.

46   In the 1880s, Hailey area newspapers: Dick d'Easum, *Sawtooth Tales* (Caldwell, Idaho: Caxton Printers, 1977), pp. 106-108.

46   In 1870, *The Idaho Statesman* printed news of the death: *The Idaho Tri-weekly Statesman*, December 20, 1870.

47   In March of 1882, 27-year-old Rufus Lester: *Idaho World*, March 28, 1883.

47   Eulogizing the man: *The Idaho Tri-weekly Statesman*, April 4, 1882.

48   Three years after Lester's tragic death: Olive Groefsema, *Elmore County: Its Historical Gleanings*, np., Mountain Home, Idaho, 1949, pp. 311-313.

48   In 1888, Foley Abbott: *Idaho Daily Statesman*, January 15, 1888.

49   In Jack Anderson's pack: Alfreda M. Elsensohn, *Pioneer Days in Idaho County* (Cottonwood, Idaho: The Idaho Corporation of Benedictine Sisters, 1978), I, p. 169.

49   Another unusual story: This and related material on Cowboy Joe are from Adele McGown, *The Far Side of the Mountain, np.*, Stanley, Idaho, 1983), pp. 81-93.

52   In 1904, the mail was carried by Silas Romer: This and subsequent unattributed quotes are from Esther Yarber, *Land of the Yankee Fork* (Denver: Sage Books, 1963), pp. 132-138; and from the author's conversations with Esther Yarber in the summer of 1977.

54   Ole M. Olsen was the youngest skier: Mr. and Mrs. Guy McAdams, correspondence with the author, October 26, 1976.

54   "I was the youngest of the ski troops": O. M. Olsen, "Recalls Toting Mail to Miners," *The Idaho Statesman*, April 9, 1967.

CHAPTER 4: ONE LAST LOOK BACK

55   A. C. "Nick" Nichols was one of those: This and material related to the March, 1936 storm are from a Personal Interview with A. C. "Nick" Nichols, Ashton, Idaho, March 14,1977.

59   "During this time I invented freeze-dried coffee": This and subsequent quotes by Robert Wuthrich are from Personal Interviews with Robert Wuthrich, Island Park, Idaho, February 5, 1977 and March 13, 1977.

61   "In the country around Bone": Personal Interview with Frank Daniels, Salmon, Idaho, April 26, 1976, and Telephone Interview, January 17, 1978.

62   He was tall and lean with huge hands: Author's Observations and Personal Interview with Lum Turner near French Creek on the Salmon River, March 1, 1977.

66   As early as 1911, miners in Dixie: *Idaho County Free Press*, January 5, 1911.

66   Brown, incidently had occasionally used skis: Telephone Interview with Warren Brown, March 1, 1977.

66   "it was more exciting riding it up": Personal Interview with Blaine Gasser, Pocatello, Idaho, November 8, 1976.

67   Hennig explored the untracked mountain wilderness: Author's conversations with Andrew Hennig, Pocatello, Idaho, Fall, 1981.

67   Ski mountaineering historian: Louis W. Dawson, *Wild Snow* (Golden, Colorado: American Alpine Club, 1997), p. 7.

67   The Union Pacific published: *The Sun Valley Ski Book*, by Andy Hennig (New York: Barnes and Co., 1939)

68   "It's old man Keene and his dog": Personal Interview with Russ Keene, Sandpoint, Idaho, March 7, 1977.

70   Russ had been manning a make shift forward hospital: Telephone Interview with Rob Keene, February 11, 1997.

72   he shifted his interest to canoeing: Jane Fritz, "Crossing Open Water," *Sandpoint Magazine*, Summer, 1993, p. 1-4.

73   even though age clouded my last conversation with him: Telephone Interview with Russ Keene, February 11, 1997.

74   "I've been a cross-country skier all my life": Nichols Interview.

INDEX

ABOUT THE AUTHOR

Ron Watters is the author of *The Whitewater River Book, Ski Camping: A Guide to the Delights of Backcountry Skiing* and *Never Turn Back: The Life of Whitewater Pioneer Walt Blackadar*. Since the mid 1970s he has been collecting stories and information on skiing and snowshoeing in Idaho and surrounding areas. This book is a compilation of years of research and is a completely revised edition of the original version which was published in 1978 under the title *Ski Trails and Old-timers Tales*.

Watters has organized a number of long winter backcountry trips, including an east-to-west, 175-mile ski traverse of the Idaho Primitive Area and a north-to-south solo traverse of the River of No Return Wilderness. He is the director of the Idaho State University Outdoor Program.

Photo by Phil Schofield